The New Answers Book 4

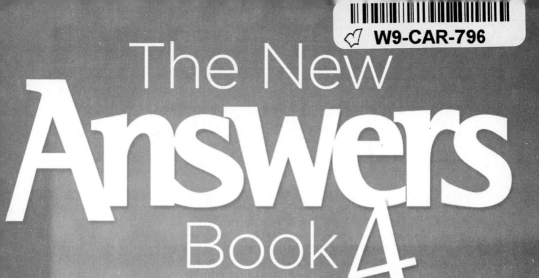

Over 30 Questions on Creation/Evolution and the Bible

Ken Ham General Editor

First printing: August 2013
Second printing: February 2014

ISBN: 9780890517888
Library of Congress Number: 2013947562

Please consider requesting that a copy of this volume be purchased by your local library system.

Printed in the United States of America

Please visit our website for other great titles:
www.masterbooks.net

For information regarding author interviews,
please contact the publicity department at (870) 438-5288.

Master
Books®
A Division of New Leaf Publishing Group
www.masterbooks.net

ACKNOWLEDGMENTS AND SPECIAL THANKS

Our many thanks to the following for the work of reviewing, editing, or illustrating this book.

Dr. Jason Lisle, Dr. John Whitmore, Dr. Ron Samec, Dr. Elizabeth Mitchell, Dr. Tommy Mitchell, Dr. Andrew Snelling, Dr. Danny Faulkner, Dr. Terry Mortenson, Dr. Georgia Purdom, Dr. John Baumgardner, Gary Vaterlaus, Mike Matthews, Bob Hill, Roger Patterson, Troy Lacey, Steve Golden, Jeremy Ham, Buddy Davis, Randall Hedtke, Wayne Strasser, Mike Oard, Scot Chadwick, Erik Lutz, Dan Stelzer, Dan Lietha, Doug Rummager, Laura Strobl, Bodie Hodge, Steve Fazekas, and Diane King.

Contents

Atheistic Devices: Spotting Them . . . but Countering Them, Too?

KEN HAM

Introduction: Atheists Using Churches to Infiltrate and Deceive

Did you know that many Christian leaders are doing exactly what the atheists are encouraging them to do? It's incredible.

You see, there's an "epidemic" that is infecting and destroying many churches around the world. It is the epidemic of Christians (including many church leaders) who are adopting man's religion of evolutionary ideas and adding them to Scripture — thus undermining the authority of the Word of God.

As we see the loss of the foundation of the authority of God's Word in our Western nations, we are also seeing a massive decline in Christian morality in society. Even the great nation of America is on a downward spiral, as we see the absolutes of Christianity being eliminated from the culture (on an almost daily basis).

We spoke to a prominent Christian leader recently. He is the pastor of a large church in a generally conservative denomination (though many of its churches allow for millions of years). He shared with us that within his denomination, he saw the next big theological debate being whether or not Adam and Eve were literal human beings!

Such re-writing of Scripture is sadly coming to this denomination. But is it all that surprising? Once the door was opened when many of its churches (and affiliated seminaries) began to compromise on the foundations of Genesis, as they added millions of years to Genesis, then the slippery slide into unbelief in other areas of Scripture began to escalate — even whether there was a real Adam.

Right into Their Hands

At AiG, we have been saying for years that as churches compromise with millions of years and evolution, eventually they will begin to compromise other parts of Scripture. They will give up on Adam and Eve and original sin — then maybe a literal hell, bodily resurrection, and virgin birth.

Sadly, we are now seeing that happening more and more in the Church. Last year, *Christianity Today* published a cover story about the battle over a literal Adam and Eve. Yes, now even *that* question is beginning to infiltrate theologically conservative churches. We also hear of Christian leaders giving up a belief in a literal hell. And there are those who are beginning to question aspects of the Resurrection and so on.

Yes, what is happening in the Church today is exactly what the atheists want to see happen. The atheists know that if they can get Christians to compromise God's Word in Genesis, eventually there will be a generational decline in the acceptance of the authority of all of God's Word.

The Trojan Horse

Last year, a professed atheist, Dr. Eugenie Scott, mailed a fundraising letter on behalf of her organization called NCSE (National Center for Science Education). This group was set up primarily to oppose biblical creation organizations like AiG.

In this letter, Dr. Scott told blatant untruths about what AiG is doing. But then again, you shouldn't be surprised when atheists don't tell the truth. After all, if they don't believe in an absolute authority, they have no basis for truth — except for how they decide to define it as such! She is obviously greatly concerned about the effect of AiG in society. Well — we can praise the Lord for that!

But in her letter, designed to cause alarm and raise funds for her anti-Christian organization and "motivate the secular troops" to oppose creationist organizations like AiG, Dr. Scott made a statement similar to the one she has made before on her website about how she seeks to recruit religious people to help her atheist group:

> Find common ground with religious communities and ally with them to promote the understanding of evolution.

And back in 2008, Dr. Scott's NCSE website made these statements in an article entitled "How You Can Support Evolution Education."[1]

One section listed these ideas:

- Suggest adult religious education projects focusing on evolution with your religious leaders.
- Encourage your religious leaders to endorse the Clergy Letter Project and to participate in Evolution Weekend.
- Encourage your religious leaders to produce educational resources about evolution and religion, and to take a formal stand in support of evolution education.

The "Evolution Weekend" referred to above was founded (and is still run) by an atheist professor. He now has thousands of clergy who have signed a statement that agrees with the concept of millions of years/evolution and have agreed to conduct an "Evolution Sunday," when they will preach the "truth" of evolution to their congregations.

An Ally of Atheists

Dr. Scott, back in September 2000, in her opening statement at the American Association for the Advancement of Science Conference entitled "The Teaching of Evolution in U.S. Schools: Where Politics, Religion, and Science Converge," said:

> You can't win this by scientific arguments . . . our best allies were members of the mainstream clergy. . . . The clergy went to school board meetings and said, evolution is okay with us . . . they didn't want the kids getting biblical literalism five days a week either, which meant they'd have to straighten them out on the weekends.

In 2005, I wrote about a supporter of AiG who attended a seminar conducted by Dr. Scott on how to teach evolution in public schools. When dealing with the issue of what to do with Christian students, she offered some sad advice. Our supporter reported:

> I attended the "Teaching Evolution" seminar yesterday led by Eugenie Scott. The teachers were advised to suggest to the Bible believers to consult their clergy who would usually assure them that belief in evolution is OK!!

---

1. http://ncse.com/taking-action/29-ways-to-support-science-education.

In her latest fundraising letter, this atheist continues her tactic of trying to influence churchgoers to believe in evolution/millions of years.

Atheists understand that if they can get the Church to compromise with millions of years/evolution, this will undermine the authority of the entire Bible . . . and lead to unbelief about Christianity. The atheists know that getting the Church to compromise today, then coming generations may be won over to atheism. And more of our Church leaders are doing exactly what the atheists (gleefully) want them to do.

Breaking the Yoke

One verse of Scripture I have often used to remind me of the constant battle we are in (and the stand we should be taking) is 2 Corinthians 6:14:

> Do not be unequally yoked together with unbelievers. For what fellowship has righteousness with lawlessness? And what communion has light with darkness?

When Christians compromise with the belief system of millions of years and evolution (in reality, a pagan religion), they are being unequally yoked with unbelievers.

Be Discerning

It seems almost everyone wants something free, right? Now, if you were offered a free curriculum to teach children about Genesis, would you jump at it? After all, we need to be educating young people about the authority of God's Word, correct?

Well, there is now a free curriculum for you to consider. And it's designed to teach children about Genesis. To help you in your decision-making about getting this curriculum, I'll give you some samples of what it teaches.

Now, before you read these samples (and I really urge you to look at the quotes below), consider the biblical example of the Christians at Berea who "searched the Scriptures daily to find out whether these things were so" (Acts 17:11). Okay, now read the following excerpts from this new Genesis curriculum:[2]

> During the sixth day God creates land animals, including man — Day Six began about the time the first land animals appear in the fossil record, about 250 million years ago . . . God created the land dwelling creatures on this day. . . .

---

2. www.oldearth.org/Day6.ppt.

Man is clearly the ruler of earth, even though many animals are larger. God gave man the ability to think, enabling him to rule the earth. . . . Before the creation of Adam, there were other human-like animals, such as Neanderthal and *Australopithecus*. . . . Evolutionists point to them as an evolutionary path from ape to man. . . .

From a Christian perspective, they were not "in the image of God" as Adam was. In other words, they did not have an eternal soul, capable of choosing eternal life with God. . . . Just how "human-like" they were is debatable, and there will always be an argument surrounding their position in God's creation. . . .

Man and animals are given plants to eat. This is often misinterpreted by young-earth creationists. . . . Young-earth creationists claim there was no death before Adam's sin. They claim that only plants could be eaten based on Genesis 1:29-30. . . . First, look back at Genesis 1:28. Man was instructed to subdue the earth (and its animals). . . .

It is clear from the fossil record that there was much death before Adam. . . . Day Six ends with the statement "very good." Young earth proponents say it could not be "very good" if there was death before Adam. . . . Death is a natural process of God's created world, therefore God created death. . . .

So, now would you want this free curriculum to teach your children? Absolutely not!

Twisted Scripture

I hope you will be like the Bereans. AiG supporters would realize that whoever wrote this curriculum accepts fallible man's ideas concerning evolution and millions of years and, as a result, twists and contorts the Scriptures to justify an acceptance of man's pagan religion. In other words, they are mixing the religion of the day with their Christianity just like the Israelites did with Baal in the Old Testament a number of times.

My purpose is *not* to go in-depth and critique these blatant reinterpretations of Scripture. I'm sure you can recognize the problems. But I do want to point out an increasing and related problem I see all over the Church.

Satan is very clever. However, he still uses the same tactic: to work from within the Church to lead generations of people away from the truth of God's Word and the gospel.

Truly we are in a spiritual battle — not just with the world, but also within much of the Church. The attacks on Christianity from the secular world are obvious. But the Church has many wolves in sheep's clothing (as God's Word warns us it would). And as God raises up ministries like Answers in Genesis to battle with the pagan religion of this day (evolution/millions of years) that leads people away from God's Word, Satan is actively recruiting people within the Church to try to combat what we're trying to accomplish.

Truly we are in a spiritual battle — not just with the world, but also within much of the Church. By the way, the compromising web-based curriculum I've mentioned is offered free *in the name of Christianity*. And it has an agenda for parents to teach children in a certain way about the Bible. But this website has a name that is obviously designed to mimic (and even be confused with) Answers in Genesis: it's called Answers in Creation!

Remember our book *Already Gone*? In that publication we presented the detailed research into why two-thirds of our young people are leaving the Church by college age. The major reasons came down to:

- Young people being taught to compromise Genesis with evolution and millions of years; respondents saw this as hypocrisy within the Church.
- Churches and parents not teaching children apologetics — not teaching them how to defend the Christian faith against the secular attacks of our day.

Sadly, free curricula like the new one referred to above, if used by families and churches, will lead to more young people walking away from the Church. At Answers in Genesis, we are so burdened about such sad developments that we stepped out in faith to produce a high-quality Bible curriculum for kindergarten through adult. Titled the *Answers Bible Curriculum*, it is an entirely integrated curriculum for Sunday school so the entire family (no matter the age) can discuss the material when they get home (i.e., children and parents cover the same topics — but at a different level).

Many Attacks on the Bible, Not Just Curriculum

Some days in ministry, it can be exhausting. There seem to be constant daily battles! But I remind myself that Answers in Genesis, a Bible-upholding ministry, is engaged in an ongoing spiritual war; when one battle is over, another front opens. To illustrate, here is a list of just some of the many "battles" that have involved AiG in the last year. It's not a complete list, but it still reminds us of the battles raging around us. Many are quite startling:

- An American Atheist billboard appears near the Lincoln Tunnel entrance at New York City with its message for Christmas: "You KNOW it's a Myth . . . This Season, Celebrate REASON!" The atheists are becoming more active each year, and every Christmas they ramp up their propaganda.

- Rev. Barry Lynn, president of Americans United for Separation of Church and State, and I debate on CNN's *Anderson Cooper 360* TV program over the passing of tourism incentives for our Ark Encounter project.

- The Calvin College biology department issues their "Perspective on Evolution," a statement from a *Christian* college endorsing evolution as the best scientific explanation for life on earth.

- U.S. Congressman Pete Stark of the Bay Area of California introduces a bill to proclaim February 12 as "Darwin Day."

- Bill Nye, "The Science Guy" of PBS-TV fame and well-known atheist, visits the Creation Museum for two minutes to stand in the museum driveway and take photos so he can say he has legitimacy to criticize the Creation Museum.

- Former Eastern Nazarene College physics professor Karl Giberson, and BioLogos founder Francis Collins publish *The Language of Science and Faith*, arguing for theistic evolution and against the origin of sin as taught in Genesis.

- Political activist/blogger Joe Sonka and a friend try to crash "Date Night" at our museum by pretending to be (in their words) a "flamboyantly gay" couple.

- Pastor Rob Bell publishes *Love Wins: A Book About Heaven, Hell, and the Fate of Every Person Who Ever Lived* in which the biblical view of hell is undermined.

- I'm dropped from the "Great Homeschool Conventions" programs in Cincinnati and Philadelphia for revealing the biblically compromised teachings of Peter Enns (who believes Jesus was in error), also a speaker at these conventions.

- NASA astrobiologist Richard Hoover claims life on earth may have come from other planets in the *Journal of Cosmology.*

- The office of the secretary of the Assemblies of God denomination sponsors a conference entitled Faith and Science Conference promoting theistic evolution.

- Tim Keller, well-known author and senior pastor of the Redeemer Presbyterian Church in Manhattan (New York), again endorses evolution as a possible way God created.

- Rev. Barry Lynn of Americans United for Separation of Church and State posts a YouTube video mocking our Ark Encounter project and the Bible's account of Noah.

- *Christianity Today* magazine publishes an article entitled "The Search for the Historical Adam," questioning the historicity of Adam and Eve. The cover features an "ape-man."

- In a *USA Today* article on the recent Miss USA beauty pageant winner, Alyssa Campanella shares how she believes in evolution; the article disparages Answers in Genesis, the Creation Museum, and the Ark Encounter.

- New York attacks the Bible by legalizing "gay marriage."

- A *Washington Post* blog discusses presidential candidate Michele Bachmann as an evolution-doubter and disparages the Creation Museum.

- Chinese scientist Xing Xu claims that *Archaeopteryx* is not a bird, but rather a feathered dinosaur.

- Hank Hanegraaff — the "Bible Answer Man," president of the Christian Research Institute, and host of the *Bible Answer Man* radio program — endorses William Dembski's book *The End of Christianity*, which presents an unbiblical position on the creation and evolution of humans.

- The General Presbytery of the Assemblies of God adopts a revised statement on "The Doctrine of Creation," now allowing for evolution and millions of years.

- Calvin College professor of religion John Schneider is forced to resign after casting doubt on the historical accuracy of Adam and Eve and their fall into sin.

- GOP presidential candidate Texas Governor Rick Perry is questioned about evolution by a child at a political rally and a video of it goes viral.

- Susan Brooks Thistlethwaite, professor of theology at Chicago Theological Seminary, writes an article for the *Washington Post* entitled "The Theological Case for Evolution" that criticizes the Creation Museum.

- A columnist for the United Kingdom Christian website Network Norwich calls Answers in Genesis "a cult."

- BBC TV launches a major new dinosaur series in the United Kingdom that, as expected, promotes evolution and millions of years.

- Prof. Richard Dawkins, Sir David Attenborough, and 28 other prominent UK evolutionists ask the British government to censor the teaching of creation in Britain's publicly funded schools.

- Karl Giberson, former vice president of BioLogos and former physics professor at Eastern Nazarene College, and Randall Stephens, history department chair at Eastern Nazarene College, publish *The Anointed.* Answers in Genesis is singled out at the very outset of the book as a proponent of an "anti-intellectual populism undergirding evangelical 'truth,' and that the movement takes its cues from a handful of enormously influential but only dubiously credentialed authority figures."

- *Science* magazine publishes additional articles supporting the claim that *Australopithecus sediba* was an ancestor of humans.

- Darrel Falk, president of BioLogos and biology professor at Point Loma Nazarene University, responds to my lecture on the "Anti-biblical Teachings of BioLogos" and critiques AiG's stand on Genesis by siding with the atheistic arguments against the Bible.

Did you get tired reading this list? Well, I did — and that's just the *short* list. Many of you likely have lists of attacks of your own. Christians are coming under attack from many directions in today's culture and it is good to spot these attacks so you can counter them.

Equipping the "Troops"

Amidst all this opposition, here is what Answers in Genesis is doing to counter the attacks on the Bible and equip people with effective Bible-defending "weapons":

- Provide incredible new apologetic resources on the AiG websites, with 17 million users a year accessing the sites!

- Write and publish various books [like this one in the *New Answers Book Series*], such as *Already Gone, Already Compromised, The Fall of Satan, How Do We Know the Bible is True?, Demolishing Contradictions, The Tower of Babel, The Lie: Evolution, One Race One Blood, Coming to Grips with Genesis*, and so on.

- *Answers Bible Curriculum* for all ages (seven age levels).

- Produce new faith-defending video sets, including my 12-part *Foundations* series and Dr. David Menton's excellent *Body of Evidence* anatomy series.

- Conduct hundreds of apologetics conferences and other speaking engagements at churches and colleges in the USA and around the world.

- Announce the building of Noah's ark as part of the Ark Encounter project — a reminder that God's Word and its salvation message are true.

- Build a Creation Museum with an observatory, Special Effects Theater, Planetarium, Dinosaur Den, Bug Exhibit, and much more.

- Produce Vacation Bible School (VBS) programs, now used by thousands of churches a year!

Now this kind of list doesn't make me tired at all! It gets me excited! I often tell people that I look on the resources that AiG produces as Christian "patriot missiles," equipping believers in daily spiritual battles that seem to be heating up around the country!

Such resources are needed (and more) to help the Church be discerning to the specific attacks of our age. We need to know what the attacks on the Bible are and how to counter them. This is why this book series is so important — it gives answers in an effort to help ground Christians to have a firm foundation on the authority of the Bible.

CHAPTER 1

Does the Gospel Depend on a Young Earth?

KEN HAM

Can a person believe in an old earth and an old universe (millions or billions of years in age) and be a Christian?

First of all, let's consider three verses that sum up the gospel and salvation. 1 Corinthians 15:17 says, "If Christ is not risen, your faith is futile; you are still in your sins!" Jesus said in John 3:3, "Most assuredly, I say to you, unless one is born again, he cannot see the kingdom of God." Romans 10:9 clearly explains, "If you confess with your mouth the Lord Jesus and believe in your heart that God has raised Him from the dead, you will be saved."

Numerous other passages could be cited, but not one of them states in any way that a person has to believe in a young earth or universe to be saved.

And the list of those who cannot enter God's kingdom, as recorded in passages like Revelation 21:8, certainly does not include "old earthers."

Many great men of God who are now with the Lord have believed in an old earth. Some of these explained away the Bible's clear teaching about a young earth by adopting the classic gap theory. Others accepted a day-age theory or positions such as theistic evolution, the framework hypothesis, and progressive creation.

Scripture plainly teaches that salvation is conditioned upon faith in Christ, with no requirement for what one believes about the age of the earth or universe.

Now when I say this, people sometimes assume then that it does not matter what a Christian believes concerning the supposed millions-of-years age for the earth and universe.

Even though it is not a salvation issue, the belief that earth history spans millions of years has very severe consequences. Let me summarize some of these.

Authority Issue

The belief in millions of years does not come from Scripture, but from the fallible methods that secularists use to date the universe.

To attempt to "fit" millions of years into the Bible, you have to invent a gap of time that almost all Bible scholars agree the text does not allow — at least from a hermeneutical perspective. Or you have to reinterpret the "days" of creation as long periods of time (even though they are obviously ordinary days in the context of Genesis 1). In other words, you have to add a concept (millions of years) from outside Scripture, into God's Word. This approach puts man's fallible ideas in authority over God's Word.

As soon as you surrender the Bible's authority in one area, you "unlock a door" to do the same thing in other areas. Once the door of compromise is open, even if ajar just a little, subsequent generations push the door open wider. Ultimately, this compromise has been a major contributing factor in the loss of biblical authority in our Western world.

The Church should heed the warning of Proverbs 30:6, "Do not add to His words, lest He rebuke you, and you be found a liar."

Contradiction Issue

A Christian's belief in millions of years totally contradicts the clear teaching of Scripture. Here are just three examples:

Thorns. Fossil thorns are found in rock layers that secularists believe to be hundreds of millions of years old, so supposedly they existed millions of years before man. However, the Bible makes it clear that thorns came into existence after the Curse: "Then to Adam He said, 'Because . . . you have eaten from the tree of which I commanded you, saying, "You shall not eat of it": Cursed is the ground for your sake. . . . Both thorns and thistles it shall bring forth for you' " (Genesis 3:17–18).

Disease. The fossil remains of animals, said by evolutionists to be millions of years old, show evidence of diseases (like cancer, brain tumors, and arthritis). Thus, such diseases supposedly existed millions of years before sin. Yet Scripture teaches that after God finished creating everything and placed man at the pinnacle of creation, He described the creation as "very good" (Genesis 1:31). Certainly calling cancer and brain tumors "very good" does not fit with Scripture and the character of God.

Diet. The Bible clearly teaches in Genesis 1:29–30 that Adam and Eve and the animals were all vegetarian before sin entered the world. However, we find fossils with lots of evidence showing that animals were eating each other — supposedly millions of years before man and thus before sin.

Death Issue

Romans 8:22 makes it clear that the whole creation is groaning as a result of the Fall — the entrance of sin. One reason for this groaning is death — the death of living creatures, both animals and man. Death is described as an "enemy" (1 Corinthians 15:26), which will trouble creation until one day it is thrown into the lake of fire.

Romans 5:12 and other passages make it obvious that physical death of man (and really, death in general) entered the once-perfect creation because of man's sin. However, if a person believes that the fossil record arose over millions of years, then death, disease, suffering, carnivorous activity, and thorns existed millions of years before sin.

The first death was in the Garden of Eden when God killed an animal as the first blood sacrifice (Genesis 3:21) — a picture of what was to come in Jesus Christ, the Lamb of God, who would take away the sin of the world. Jesus Christ stepped into history to pay the penalty of sin — to conquer our enemy, death.

By dying on a Cross and being raised from the dead, Jesus conquered death and paid the penalty for sin. Although millions of years of death before sin is not a salvation issue per se, I personally believe that it is really an attack on Jesus' work on the Cross.

Recognizing that Christ's work on the Cross defeated our enemy, death, is crucial to understanding the "good news" of the gospel: "And God will wipe away every tear from their eyes; there shall be no more death, nor sorrow, nor crying. There shall be no more pain, for the former things have passed away" (Revelation 21:4).

Rooted in Genesis

All biblical doctrines, including the gospel itself, are ultimately rooted in the first book of the Bible.

- God specially created everything in heaven and earth (Genesis 1:1).

- God uniquely created man and woman in His image (Genesis 1:26–27).

- Marriage consists of one man and one woman for life (Genesis 2:24).

- The first man and woman brought sin into the world (Genesis 3:1–24).

- From the beginning God promised a Messiah to save us (Genesis 3:15).

- Death and suffering arose because of original sin (Genesis 3:16–19).

- God sets society's standards of right and wrong (Genesis 6:5–6).

- The ultimate purpose of life is to walk with God (Genesis 6:9–10).

- All people belong to one race — the human race (Genesis 11:1–9).

False Claims

The *New York Times* on November 25, 2007, published an article on the modern biblical creation movement. The Creation Museum/Answers in Genesis received a few mentions in the article. However, I wanted to deal with one statement in the article that had the writer done just a little bit of homework, she would have found it not to be true!

The writer, Hanna Rosin, stated concerning the Creation Museum:

> The museum sends the message that belief in a young earth is the only way to salvation. The failure to understand Genesis is literally "undermining the entire word of God," Ken Ham, the founder of Answers in Genesis, says in a video. The collapse of Christianity believed to result from that failure is drawn out in a series of exhibits: school shootings, gay marriage, drugs, porn, and pregnant teens. At the same time, it presents biblical literalism as perfectly defensible science.

Note particularly the statement: "belief in a young earth is the only way to salvation." Even if a Christian believes in an old earth (and even theistic evolution), they would know that such a statement is absolutely false. The Bible makes it clear that, concerning Jesus Christ, "Nor is there salvation in any other, for there is no other name under heaven given among men by which we must be saved" (Acts 4:12). When the Philippian jailer in Acts 16:30 asked, "Sirs, what must I do to be saved?" Paul and Silas (in verse 31) replied, "Believe on the Lord Jesus Christ, and you will be saved, you and your household."

In Ephesians 2:8–9 we are clearly told: "For by grace you have been saved through faith, and that not of yourselves; it is the gift of God, not of works, lest anyone should boast." And Jesus Christ stated: "Jesus said to him, 'I am the way, the truth, and the life. No one comes to the Father except through Me' " (John 14:6).

Creation Museum/Answers in Genesis Teachings

As one walks through the Creation Museum, nowhere does it even suggest that "belief in a young earth is the only way to salvation." In fact, in the theater where the climax of the 7 C's walk-through occurs, people watch a program called *The Last Adam*. This is one of the most powerful presentations of the gospel I have ever seen. This program clearly sets out the way of salvation — and it has nothing to do with believing in a young earth.

As I often tell people in my lectures, Romans 10:9 states: "If you confess with your mouth, 'Jesus is Lord,' and believe in your heart that God raised him from the dead, you will be saved." By confessing "Jesus is Lord," one is confessing that Christ is to be Lord of one's life — which means repenting of sin and acknowledging who Christ is. The Bible DOES NOT state, "That if you confess with your mouth, 'Jesus is Lord,' and believe in your heart that God raised him from the dead — AND BELIEVE IN A YOUNG EARTH — you will be saved"!

Concluding Remarks

So it should be obvious to anyone, even our opponents, that this statement in the *New York Times* is absolutely false. Sadly, I have seen similar statements in other press articles — and it seems no matter what we write in website articles, or how often we answer this outlandish accusation, many in the press continue to disseminate this false accusation, and one has to wonder if it is a deliberate attempt to alienate AiG from the mainstream church!

I believe that one of the reasons writers such as Hanna Rosin make such statements is because AiG is very bold in presenting authoritatively what the Bible clearly states. People sometimes misconstrue such authority in the way Hanna Rosin has. It is also interesting that people who don't agree with us often get very emotional about how authoritatively we present the biblical creation view — they dogmatically insist we can't be so dogmatic in what we present!! It's okay for them to be dogmatic about what they believe, and dogmatic about what we shouldn't believe, but we can't be!

In my lectures, I explain to people that believing in an old earth won't keep someone out of heaven if they are truly "born again" as the Bible defines "born again." Then I'm asked, "Then why does AiG make an issue of the age of the earth — particularly a young age?" The answer is that our emphasis is on the authority of Scripture. The idea of millions of years does NOT come from the Bible; it comes from man's fallible, assumption-based dating methods. If one uses such fallible dating methods to reinterpret Genesis (e.g., the days of creation), then one is "unlocking a door," so to speak, to teach others that they don't have to take the Bible as written (e.g., Genesis is historical narrative) at the beginning — so why should one take it as written elsewhere (e.g., the bodily Resurrection of Christ). If one has to accept what secular scientists say about the age of the earth, evolution, etc., then why not reinterpret the Resurrection of Christ? After all, no secular scientist accepts that a human being can be raised from the dead, so maybe the Resurrection should be reinterpreted to mean just "spiritual resurrection."

The point is, believing in a young earth won't ultimately affect one's salvation, but it sure does affect the beliefs of those that person influences concerning how to approach Scripture. Such compromise in the Church with millions of years and Darwinian evolution, etc., we believe has greatly contributed to the loss of the Christian foundation in the culture.

CHAPTER 2

Do Plants and Leaves Die?

DR. MICHAEL TODHUNTER

Fall in America and throughout much of the Northern Hemisphere is a beautiful time of year. Bright reds, oranges, and yellows rustle in the trees and then blanket the ground as warm weather gives way to winter cold. Many are awed at God's handiwork as the leaves float to the ground like heaven's confetti. But fall may also make us wonder, "Did Adam and Eve ever see such brilliant colors in the Garden of Eden?" Realizing that these plants wither at the end of the growing season may also raise the question, "Did plants die before the Fall of mankind?"

Before we can answer this question, we must consider the definition of *die*. We commonly use the word *die* to describe when plants, animals, or humans no longer function biologically. However, this is not the definition of the word *die* or *death* in the Old Testament. The Hebrew word for *die* (or *death*), *mût* (or *mavet* or *muwth*), is used only in relation to the death of man or animals with the breath of life, not regarding plants.[1] This usage indicates that plants are viewed differently from animals and humans.

Plants, Animals, and Man — All Different

What is the difference between plants and animals or man? For the answer we need to look at the phrase *nephesh chayyah*.[2] *Nephesh chayyah* is used in the

---

1. J. Stambaugh, "Death before Sin?" *Acts & Facts*, 18 (5) (1989); http://www.icr.org/article/295/, and B. Hodge, "Biblically, Could Death Have Existed Before Sin?" *Answers in Genesis* website, March 2, 2010.
2. J.Stambaugh, " 'Life' According to the Bible, and the Scientific Evidence," *Technical Journal*, August 1, 1992; http://www.answersingenesis.org/articles/tj/v6/n2/life.

Bible to describe sea creatures (Genesis 1:20–21), land animals (Genesis 1:24), birds (Genesis 1:30), and man (Genesis 2:7).[3] *Nephesh* is never used to refer to plants. Man specifically is denoted as *nephesh chayyah*, a living soul, after God breathed into him the breath of life. This contrasts with God telling the earth on day 3 to bring forth plants (Genesis 1:11). The science of taxonomy, the study of scientific classification, makes the same distinction between plants and animals.

Since God gave only plants (including their fruits and seeds) as food for man and animals, then Adam, Eve, and all animals and birds were originally vegetarian (Genesis 1:29–30). Plants were to be a resource of the earth that God provided for the benefit of *nephesh chayyah* creatures — both animals and man. Plants did not "die," as in *mût*; they were clearly consumed as food. Scripture describes plants as *withering* (Hebrew *yabesh*), which means "to dry up." This term is more descriptive of a plant or plant part ceasing to function biologically.

A "Very Good" Biological Cycle

When plants wither or shed leaves, various organisms, including bacteria and fungi, play an active part in recycling plant matter and thus in providing food for man and animals. These decay agents do not appear to be *nephesh chayyah* and would also have a life cycle as nutrients are reclaimed through this "very good" biological cycle. As the plant withers, it may produce vibrant colors because, as a leaf ceases to function, the chlorophyll degrades, revealing the colors of previously hidden pigments.

Since decay involves the breakdown of complex sugars and carbohydrates into simpler nutrients, we see evidence for the second law of thermodynamics *before* the Fall of mankind. But in the pre-Fall world, this process would have been a perfect system, which God described as "very good."

What Determines a Leaf's Color?

When trees bud in the spring, their green leaves renew forests and delight our senses. The green color comes from the pigment chlorophyll, which resides in the leaf's cells and captures sunlight for photosynthesis. Other pigments called carotenoids are always present in the cells of leaves as well, but in the summer their yellow or orange colors are generally masked by the abundance of chlorophyll.

In the fall, a kaleidoscope of colors breaks through. With shorter days and colder weather, chlorophyll breaks down, and the yellowish colors become

---

3. Ibid.

visible. Various pigments produce the purple of sumacs, the golden bronze of beeches, and the browns of oaks. Other chemical changes produce the fiery red of the sugar maple. When fall days are warm and sunny, much sugar is produced in the leaves. Cool nights trap it there, and the sugars form a red pigment called anthocyanin.

Leaf colors are most vivid after a warm, dry summer followed by early autumn rains, which prevent leaves from falling early. Prolonged rain in the fall prohibits sugar synthesis in the leaves and thus produces a drabness due to a lack of anthocyanin production.

Still other changes take place. A special layer of cells slowly severs the leaf's tissues that are attached to the twig. The leaf falls, and a tiny scar is all that remains. Soon the leaf decomposes on the forest floor, releasing important nutrients back into the soil to be recycled, perhaps by other trees that will once again delight our eyes with rich and vibrant colors.

A Creation That Groans

It is conceivable that God withdrew some of His sustaining (restraining) power at the Fall to no longer uphold things in a perfect state when He said, "Cursed is the ground" (Genesis 3:17), and the augmented second law of thermodynamics resulted in a creation that groans and suffers (Romans 8:22).[4]

Although plants are not the same as man or animals, God used them to be food and a support system for recycling nutrients and providing oxygen. They also play a role in mankind's choosing life or death. In the Garden were two trees — the Tree of Life and the Tree of the Knowledge of Good and Evil. The fruit of the first was allowed for food, the other forbidden. In their rebellion, Adam and Eve sinned and ate the forbidden fruit, and death entered the world (Romans 5:12).

Furthermore, because of this sin, all of creation, including *nephesh chayyah*, suffers (Romans 8:19–23). We are born into this death as descendants of Adam, but we find our hope in Christ. "For as in Adam all die, even so in Christ shall all be made alive" (1 Corinthians 15:22, KJV). As you look at the "dead" leaves of fall and remember that the nutrients will be reclaimed into new life, recognize that we too can be reclaimed from death through Christ's death and Resurrection.

---

4. Of course, God still upholds all of creation. Furthermore, the second was in effect before and after the Fall, but now we are in a state where things are not upheld in perfect balance so to speak.

CHAPTER 3

Dragons . . . Were They Real?

BODIE HODGE

A Dodo of an Introduction

The dodo was a strange bird, and our understanding of its demise and extinction by 1662 is equally strange. The dodo was a flightless bird that lived on the island of Mauritius in the Indian Ocean. It was easy to catch and provided meat to sailors. There were numerous written accounts, sketches, and descriptions of the bird from the 1500s through the 1600s.

But when the dodo went extinct, no one seemed to notice. And a few years later, scientists began to promote the idea that the dodo was merely a myth. Just look at the evidence:

1. It was a very strange creature.
2. No one could find them.
3. They seemed to exist only in the old descriptions, accounts, and drawings!

Had it not been for specimens popping up in the recesses of museum collections, and finally brought to light, they could have been labeled simply as "myth" for as long as the earth endures! But in the 19th century, at last, there was vindication that the dodo was real and that it had merely gone extinct. Since then, fossils and other portions of specimens have been identified as dodo.

Drawing by Sir Thomas Herbert of a cockatoo, red hen, and dodo in 1634. Courtesy of Wikipedia Commons, http://en.wikipedia.org/wiki/File:Lophopsittacus.mauritianus.jpg.

Parallel to Dragons

So what does this have to do with dragons? Consider the following points:

1. Dragons are very strange creatures.
2. No one can find them.
3. They seem to exist only in the old descriptions, accounts, and drawings!

If we don't know our history, are we doomed to repeat it? Sadly in recent times, secular scientists have relegated dragons to myths also.

But unlike the dodo, which is just a particular type of bird, dragons are a large group of reptilian creatures. Moreover, we have descriptions, drawings, and accounts of dragons. Not just the handful like we have of the dodo, but in *massive numbers* from all over the world! And many of these descriptions and accounts are very similar to creatures known by a different name: dinosaurs. We'll consider this connection below.

Dragons in the Bible

To settle this issue of the reality of dragons, let us turn to the Word of Almighty God who knows all things.

In each case in Table 1, the verses use the word Hebrew *tannin*, or its plural form *tanninim*, which was usually translated as "dragon(s)." In some cases, you might see the translation "serpent" or "monster." There is also the word *tannim* (plural of *tan*, "jackal"), which sounds quite similar to *tannin* in Hebrew. Many previous translators viewed these creatures as dragons, too. But many scholars today suggest these are separate and that *tannim* should be translated as jackals.[1]

---

1. For more information see Steve Golden, Tim Chaffey, and Ken Ham, "*Tannin*: Sea Serpent, Dinosaur, Snake, Dragon, or Jackal?" Answers in Genesis, http://www.answersingenesis.org/articles/aid/v7/n1/tannin-hebrew-mean.

Table 1: Dragons in the Bible[2]

Reference	Verse
Deuteronomy 32:33	Their wine is the poison of **dragons**, and the cruel venom of asps.
Nehemiah 2:13	And I went out by night by the gate of the valley, even before the **dragon** well, and to the dung port, and viewed the walls of Jerusalem, which were broken down, and the gates thereof were consumed with fire.
Job 7:12 (YLT)	A sea-monster am I, or a **dragon**, That thou settest over me a guard?
Psalm 74:13	Thou didst divide the sea by thy strength: thou brakest the heads of the **dragons** in the waters.
Psalm 91:13	Thou shalt tread upon the lion and adder: the young lion and the **dragon** shalt thou trample under feet.
Psalm 148:7	Praise the LORD from the earth, ye **dragons**, and all deeps:
Isaiah 27:1	In that day the LORD with his sore and great and strong sword shall punish leviathan the piercing serpent, even leviathan that crooked serpent; and he shall slay the **dragon** that is in the sea.
Isaiah 51:9	Awake, awake, put on strength, O arm of the LORD; awake, as in the ancient days, in the generations of old. Art thou not it that hath cut Rahab, and wounded the **dragon**?
Jeremiah 51:34	Nebuchadnezzar the king of Babylon hath devoured me, he hath crushed me, he hath made me an empty vessel, he hath swallowed me up like a **dragon**, he hath filled his belly with my delicates, he hath cast me out.
Lamentations 4:3 (GNV)	Even the **dragons** draw out the breasts, and give suck to their young, but the daughter of my people is become cruel like the ostriches in the wilderness.[a]
Ezekiel 29:3	Speak, and say, Thus saith the Lord GOD; Behold, I am against thee, Pharaoh king of Egypt, the great **dragon** that lieth in the midst of his rivers, which hath said, My river is mine own, and I have made it for myself.
Ezekiel 32:2 (GNV)	Son of man, take up a lamentation for Pharaoh King of Egypt, and say unto him, Thou art like a lion of the nations and art as a **dragon** in the sea: thou castedst out thy rivers and troubledst the waters with thy feet, and stampedst in their rivers.
Genesis 1:21 (YLT)	And God prepareth the great monsters [***dragons***], and every living creature that is creeping, which the waters have teemed with, after their kind, and every fowl with wing, after its kind, and God seeth that it is good.[b]

2. All references are taken from the KJV except where noted.

Exodus 7:9, 10, 12	When Pharaoh shall speak unto you, saying, Shew a miracle for you: then thou shalt say unto Aaron, Take thy rod, and cast it before Pharaoh, and it shall become a serpent [***dragon***]. And Moses and Aaron went in unto Pharaoh, and they did so as the LORD commanded: and Aaron cast down his rod before Pharaoh, and before his servants, and it became a serpent [***dragon***]. . . . For they cast down every man his rod, and they became serpents [***dragons***]: but Aaron's rod swallowed up their rods.[c]

a. Some have thought this word for dragons is a copyist mistake in that tannin should be tannim and may represent another animal type (e.g., jackal). But there is no textual support for this. The argument is that reptiles today do not suckle their young. However, we know so little about extinct dragons that we can't say definitely if they suckled or not. Even some mammals were thought to only give birth to live young until we found the platypus and spiny anteaters that lay eggs, so we need to avoid making "blanket statements" about creature types based only on what we know today. We simply do not know all things about extinct creatures, and if Lamentations 4:3 does refer to dragons (or dragons of a specific type), then we would know that some did suckle.

b. Though the word here is not translated as dragon it is still the same word used of dragon elsewhere and could and likely should have been used here as well.

c. The Hebrew word translated "serpent(s)" is tannin (plural tanninim), which is typically translated "dragon." Most translate this as serpent or snake since a staff is similar in shape to a snake (i.e., serpents being a specific form of dragon). Other ancient translations render this as dragon, including the Latin Vulgate (only in v. 12), and the Greek Septuagint.

Consider also the scriptural references to "fiery serpents" or "fiery flying serpents," "leviathan," and "behemoth":

Table 2: Fiery Serpents, Leviathan, and Other Dragon-Like Creatures

Reference	Verse
Numbers 21:6, 8	And the LORD sent **fiery serpents** among the people, and they bit the people; and much people of Israel died. . . . And the LORD said unto Moses, Make thee a **fiery serpent**, and set it upon a pole: and it shall come to pass, that every one that is bitten, when he looketh upon it, shall live.
Deuteronomy 8:15	Who led thee through that great and terrible wilderness, wherein were **fiery serpents**, and scorpions, and drought, where there was no water; who brought thee forth water out of the rock of flint;

Isaiah 14:29	Rejoice not thou, whole Palestina, because the rod of him that smote thee is broken: for out of the serpent's root shall come forth a cockatrice, and his fruit shall be a **fiery flying serpent**.
Isaiah 30:6	The burden of the beasts of the south: into the land of trouble and anguish, from whence come the young and old lion, the viper and **fiery flying serpent**, they will carry their riches upon the shoulders of young asses, and their treasures upon the bunches of camels, to a people that shall not profit them.
Job 41:1	Canst thou draw out **leviathan** with an hook? or his tongue with a cord which thou lettest down?
Psalms 74:14	Thou brakest the heads of **leviathan** in pieces, and gavest him to be meat to the people inhabiting the wilderness.
Psalms 104:26	There go the ships: there is that **leviathan**, whom thou hast made to play therein.
Isaiah 27:1	In that day the LORD with his sore and great and strong sword shall punish **leviathan** the piercing serpent, even **leviathan** that crooked serpent; and he shall slay the dragon that is in the sea.
Job 40:15–24	Behold now behemoth, which I made with thee; he eateth grass as an ox. Lo now, his strength is in his loins, and his force is in the navel of his belly. He moveth his tail like a cedar: the sinews of his stones are wrapped together. His bones are as strong pieces of brass; his bones are like bars of iron. He is the chief of the ways of God: he that made him can make his sword to approach unto him. Surely the mountains bring him forth food, where all the beasts of the field play. He lieth under the shady trees, in the covert of the reed, and fens. The shady trees cover him with their shadow; the willows of the brook compass him about. Behold, he drinketh up a river, and hasteth not: he trusteth that he can draw up Jordan into his mouth. He taketh it with his eyes: his nose pierceth through snares.

These creatures could rightly be lumped among dragons. Even Leviathan is called a dragon in Isaiah 27:1.

Some have argued that the fiery flying serpents (and fiery serpents) were myth, but God clearly reveals them as real creatures, just as other creatures are real in the immediate context like scorpions, lions, vipers, donkeys, camels, and so on.

Some have argued that fiery flying serpents were real but were just venomous snakes that would leap into the air. But that would render a portion of the Scriptures redundant, as the viper, which does that very thing, is mentioned immediately before it in Isaiah 30:6. Even today there is an insect from South America called the bombardier beetle that shoots out two chemicals that essentially ignite and superheat its victim. Leviathan was also a fire breather (Job 41:1–21).

Some have suggested the behemoth as an elephant or a hippo, but neither the elephant nor the hippo eat grass like an ox, nor do they have a tail that moves like a cedar. An elephant has a tail that moves like a weeping willow, and a hippo hardly has a tail! Some have argued that behemoth and leviathan were myth, but why does God speak of real creatures (lion, raven, donkey, wild ox, ostriches, horse, locust, hawk, and eagle) in the same context as the behemoth and leviathan (Job 38–41)?

So some of what we can learn from the Bible is: (1) dragons were real creatures, and (2) the term "dragon" could include land, flying, or sea creatures.

Dragons by Ancient Historians, Literature, and Classic Commentaries

Dragons were viewed as real creatures by virtually all ancient writers who commented on them. While many references could be cited, consider these select accounts:

1. "But according to accounts from Phrygia there are Drakones in Phrygia too, and these grow to a length of sixty feet."[3]
2. "Africa produces elephants, but it is India that produces the largest, as well as the dragon."[4]
3. "Even the Egyptians, whom we laugh at, deified animals solely on the score of some utility which they derived from them; for instance, the ibis, being a tall bird with stiff legs and a long horny beak, destroys a great quantity of snakes: it protects Egypt from plague, by killing and eating the flying serpents that are brought from the Libyan desert by the south west wind, and so preventing them from harming the natives by their bite while alive and their stench when dead."[5]
4. "Among Egyptian birds, the variety of which is countless, the ibis is sacred, harmless, and beloved for the reason that by carrying the eggs of serpents to its nestlings for food it destroys and makes

---

3. Aelian (ca. A.D. 220), *De Natura Animalium.*
4. Pliny (ca. A.D. 70), *Natural History.*
5. Marcus Tullius Cicero (ca. 45 B.C.), *De Natura Deorum,* I, 36.

fewer of those destructive pests. These same birds meet winged armies of snakes which issue from the marches of Arabia, producing deadly poisons, before they leave their own lands."[6]

5. Gilgamesh, hero of an ancient Babylonian epic, killed a huge dragon named Khumbaba in a cedar forest.

6. The epic Anglo-Saxon poem *Beowulf* (ca. A.D. 495–583) tells how the title character of Scandinavia killed a monster named Grendel and its supposed mother, as well as a fiery flying serpent.

7. "The dragon, when it eats fruit, swallows endive-juice; it has been seen in the act."[7]

Ancient historians and writers clearly believed creatures like dragons were real. They describe seeing them first hand — often in the context of other types of animals that still live today. Some historians even describe the fiery flying serpents as real creatures in regions near where Moses and Isaiah were and point out the *winged* nature of these flying serpents. Such things are a great confirmation of the biblical text.

Interestingly, in the Beowulf account, the dragon called Grendel was known to have a heavy claw on its finger, yet had a fairly small arm. (Beowulf was famous for ripping the arm off of this dragon.) Correspondingly, we have a dinosaur with smaller arms (and its remains are found

Baryonyx head and forelimb
(Ballista, Wikimedia Commons)

in Europe) called *baryonyx*, which literally means "heavy claw"! Its arms are actually smaller, too! The common descriptions of Grendel and baryonyx are striking.

Classic commentators often agreed that dragons were real and spoke of them as real, and these are just a small sample of the writings these expositors of Scripture have on the subject:

1. Dr. John Gill wrote, "Of these creatures, both land and sea dragons, see Gill on 'Mic 1:8'; see Gill on 'Mal 1:3'; Pliny says the dragon has no poison in it; yet, as Dalechamp, in his notes on

---

6. Ammianus Marcellius (ca. A.D. 380), *Res Gestae*, 22, 15:25-26a.

7. Aristotle, *Historia Animalium*, http://etext.virginia.edu/etcbin/toccer-new2?id=AriHian. xml&images=images/modeng&data=/texts/english/modeng/parsed&tag=public&part=9& division=div2 (accessed June 14, 2013).

that writer observes, he in many places prescribes remedies against the bite of the dragon; but Heliodorus expressly speaks of some archers, whose arrows were infected with the poison of dragons; and Leo Africanus says, the Atlantic dragons are exceeding poisonous: and yet other writers besides Pliny have asserted that they are free from poison. It seems the dragons of Greece are without, but not those of Africa and Arabia; and to these Moses has respect, as being well known to him."[8]

2. John Calvin stated, "Then he says, he has swallowed me like a dragon. It is a comparison different from the former, but yet very suitable; for dragons are those who devour a whole animal; and this is what the Prophet means. Though these comparisons do not in everything agree, yet as to the main thing they are most appropriate, even to show that God suffered his people to be devoured, as though they had been exposed to the teeth of a lion or a bear, or as though they had been a prey to a dragon. "[9]

Even the artwork for John Calvin's commentary for Genesis (when translated from Latin to English in A.D. 1578) included images of dragons such as the one shown here.

3. Charles Spurgeon, when speaking of London, said, "We are not sure that Nineveh and Babylon were as great as this metropolis, but they certainly might have rivaled it, and yet there is nothing left of it, and the dragon and the owl dwell in what was the very center of commerce and civilization."[10]

4. John Trapp stated, "Anger is a short madness; it is a leprosy breaking out of a burning, and renders a man unfit for civil society; for his unruly passions cause the climate where he lives to be like the torrid zone, too hot for any to live near him. The dog days continue with him all the year long; he rageth, and eateth firebrands, so that every man that will provide for his own safety must flee

8. John Gill, Commentary notes Deuteronomy 32:33.
9. John Calvin, Commentary notes Jeremiah 51:34.
10. C. H. Spurgeon, "A Basket Of Summer Fruit" (sermon, Exeter Hall, London, England, October 28, 1860).

from him, as from a nettling, dangerous and unsociable creature, fit to live alone as dragons and wild beasts, or to be looked on only through a grate, as they; where, if they will do mischief, they may do it to themselves only."[11]

5. Church fathers, on Philip killing a dragon in Hierapolis, stated, "And as Philip was thus speaking, behold, also John entered into the city like one of their fellow-citizens; and moving about in the street, he asked: Who are these men, and why are they punished? And they say to him: It cannot be that thou art of our city, and askest about these men, who have wronged many: for they have shut up our gods, and by their magic have cut off both the serpents and the dragons."[12]

There were numerous dragon slayers in history as well. Not to belabor the point, I've simply made a table of a few:

Table 3: A Few Dragon Slayers and Capturers[13]

	Slayer/Capturer	Approximate Date	Place
1	Martha of Tarascon	A.D. 48–70	Tarasque
2	Apostles Philip and Barnabas	Before A.D. 70	Hierapolis
3	St. George	A.D. 300	North Africa
4	St. Sylvester I	A.D. 300	Italy
5	Sigurd	Before A.D. 400–500?[a]	Northern Europe
6	Beowulf	A.D. 400–500	Denmark, Sweden
7	Tristan	A.D. 700?	British Isles

a. Although the more complete account of Sigurd and the dragon is discussed in the 13th-century document called Volsunga Saga, Sigurd is mentioned in the Beowulf account, so it must have preceded it.

I could continue with hosts of other quotations from the church fathers who often spoke of dragons as real creatures, not questioning their reality. But the point is already made: people believed dragons were real.

---

11. John Trapp, *Complete Commentary*, s.v. Proverbs 22:24, (http://www.studylight.org/com/jtc/view.cgi?bk=19&ch=22 (accessed June 14, 2013).

12. The Acts of Philip, *Of the Journeyings of Philip the Apostle: From the Fifteenth Acts Until the End, and Among Them the Martyrdom*, http://archive.org/stream/apocryphalgospel00edin/apocryphalgospel00edin_djvu.txt (accessed June 14, 2013).

13. Bibliography for this table includes *The Golden Legend*, various texts of the church fathers, *Encyclopædia Britannica, Beowulf, Volsunga Saga*, and several others.

Dragons in Petroglyphs

It would be nearly impossible to have an exhaustive listing of dragons on walls, pottery, textiles, petroglyphs, artwork, maps, books, and so on. Here are a few, and note that some of these dragons are very similar in form to our understanding of dinosaurs.

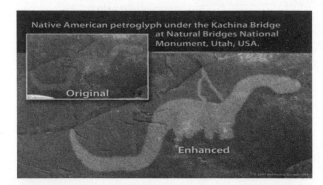

This famous petroglyph by the Anasazi natives looks strikingly like a sauropod dinosaur (i.e., dragon).[14]

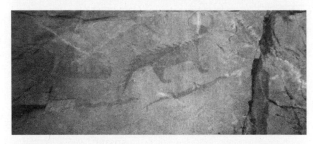

This dragon with back spines is reminiscent to a Kentrosaurus or Amarga but possibly a Lambeosaurus near Lake Superior in Canada.

This flying dragon was made by Native Americans in Utah.

---

14. I. Abrahams, "Feedback: Kachina Bridge Dinosaur Petroglyph," Answers in Genesis, http://www.answersingenesis.org/articles/2011/03/18/feedback-senter-and-cole.

This relief in Angkor, Cambodia, is something akin to Stegosaurus-type of dragon.[15]

Built by the order of King Nebuchadnezzar, the eighth gate of Babylon has aurochs (an extinct type of cattle) and a dragon alternating all the way up the gate. Since this dragon is a reptile (note the scales and tongue), it also has hips that raise the body off the ground; so, by definition it is also a dinosaur.

There are several animals portrayed in this ancient golden diadem from Kazakhstan. The onset of the second portion is a dragon.[16]
(http://www.kazakhembus.com/sites/default/files/documents/Nomads_and_Networks_FS_Images.pdf)

15. K.E. Cole, "Evidence of Dinosaurs at Angkor," Answers in Genesis, http://www.answersingenesis.org/articles/2007/01/15/evidence-dinosaurs-angkor.

16. Diadem (gold, turquoise, carnelian, and coral), Kargaly, Myng-Oshtaky tract, Almaty region. Photo: © The Central State Museum of the Republic of Kazakhstan, Almaty, http://www.kazakhembus.com/sites/default/files/documents/Nomads_and_Networks_FS_Images.pdf.

Dragons in Peru adorn hosts of ancient pottery, rock ark, textiles, and so on. This pottery is from the ancient Moche Culture and is on display at the Museum of the Nation in Lima, Peru.[17]

Dragons on Flags and Banners

It is fairly well known that the Welsh flag endows a dragon. But few realize that this was not the only culture to have a dragon on its flag. These cultures clearly viewed dragons as real.

Even modern flags such as that of Bhutan or Malta also sport dragons referring back to previous accounts. In the case of Malta, it represents St. George killing the dragon in the upper corner.

The flag of Bhutan, though designed in 1947, heralds back to the old tradition of the *druk*, that is, dragons. They also have a national emblem that has two dragons on it.

Many other flags and banners could be added to this list, and diligent searches will turn up numerous ancient flags, banners, and emblems with such things.

The George Cross which is featured on the flag of Malta.

17. Bodie Hodge, "The Dragons of Peru," *Answers*, September 14, 2010, http://www. answersingenesis.org/articles/am/v5/n4/dragons-peru.

Welsh flag

Royal
Bavarian
flag

Imperial China flag

Bhutan flag and national emblem

The famous Bayeux Tapestry that depicts the Norman invasion of England has numerous animals on it. Some are dragons.

Have Dragons Been Relegated to Myths?

It was not until the 20th century that dragons were seen as myths. In 1890, a large flying dragon was killed in Arizona (in the United States), and samples were sent to universities back east. This was recorded in a newspaper under "A Strange Winged Monster Discovered and Killed on the Huachuca Desert," *The Tombstone Epitaph*, on April 26, 1890. No one seemed to entertain the idea they were myths then.

Even the 1902 edition of the *Encyclopædia Britannica,* while trying to explain away the accounts of sea dragons ("sea serpents"), concluded that they might still exist (as their numbers were few by this time):

> It would thus appear that, while, with very few exceptions, all the so-called "sea serpents" can be explained by reference to some well-known animal or other natural object, there is still a residuum sufficient to prevent modern zoologists from denying the possibility that some such creature may after all exist.[18]

Yet only eight years later, it was published that dragons were myth! In 1910, the *Encyclopædia Britannica* states the following:

> Nor were these dragons anything but very real terrors, even in the imaginations of the learned until comparatively modern times. As the waste places were cleared, indeed, they withdrew farther from the haunts of men, and in Europe their last lurking-places were the inaccessible

---

18. William Evans Hoyle, *Encyclopædia Britannica*, 9th ed. s.v. "Sea-Serpent" (New York, NY: The Encyclopædia Britannica Company, 1902), http://www.1902encyclopedia.com/S/SEA/sea-serpent.html.

heights of the Alps, where they lingered till Jacques Balmain set the fashion which has finally relegated them to the realm of myth.[19]

This was only about 100 years ago that the dragon first began being relegated to a mythical status. Apparently, since Jacques Balmain couldn't find one, they were deemed myth. Perhaps the idea that they went extinct was too much to consider.

Though this idea of dragons being myth still defied *Encyclopædia Britannica*'s claim even into the 1920s. They were not too eager to make such bold claims. In 1927, one dictionary consulted still viewed dragons as real but rare:

> A huge serpent or snake (now rare); a fabulous monster variously represented, generally as a huge winged reptile with crested head and terrible claws, and often as spouting fire; in the Bible, a large serpent, a crocodile, a great marine animal, or a jackal.[20]

But it makes sense as more people spread out and settled in more lands, the dragons were pushed to the brink of extinction. Many old accounts of dragons had them living underground, particularly near swamps (e.g., Beowulf). As man develops areas, those habitats are destroyed. But just like the dodo, when you can't find them any longer, they are suddenly considered "myth" instead of being seen as extinct.

Sadly, this also influenced Christians and subsequently modern translations rarely use the word dragon in the Old Testament, due, in my opinion, to these secular influences.

Dragons and Their Relation to "Dinosaurs"

Dragons include land, sea, and water reptiles. Though dragons in old forms of classification also denoted snakes, dinosaurs are more specific.

Dinosaurs are land reptiles that (by definition) have one of two kinds of hip structures that allow the creature to naturally raise itself off the ground.[21] In other words, crocodiles, komodo dragons, alligators, and so on are not seen as dinosaurs since their hip structures have their legs coming out to the side so the belly naturally rests on the ground. But neither would flying

19. Walter Alison Phillips, *Encyclopædia Britannica*, 11th ed. (New York, NY: The Encyclopædia Britannica Company, 1910), 8:467.
20. *The New Century Dictionary* (New York, NY: P.F. Collier & Son Corporation, reprinted in 1948), p. 456.
21. P.S. Taylor, "Dinosaur!," Films for Christ, http://www.christiananswers.net/dinosaurs/dinodef.html.

reptiles like pterodactyls or water reptiles like plesiosaurs be dinosaurs by definition either.

So all dinosaurs are dragons, but not all dragons are dinosaurs. Dinosaurs and other land dragons were made on day 6 (Genesis 1:24–31). Flying dragons and sea dragons were made on day 5 (Genesis 1:20–23).

It is important to realize that the word dinosaur did not exist until the year 1841. Sir Richard Owen invented the term "dinosaur," and it means "terrifying" or "terrible" lizard. Maybe the controversy could have been avoided if they just called dinosaur bones "dragon" bones.

But this means dinosaurs were created and lived the same time as man and went aboard the ark of Noah (Genesis 6:20). Those that did not go aboard died. Many likely rotted and decayed, and others were rapidly buried by sediment from the Flood, making them candidates for fossilization. Hence, we find many of these dragon bones (e.g., dinosaur bones) in rock layers from the Flood. Dinosaurs came off the ark and have been dying out ever since.

One dinosaur resembles a dragon so much that they named it after a dragon from a movie series.
Dracorex Hogswartsia skeleton restoration, The Children's Museum of Indianapolis
(Wikimedia Commons)

Reasons for Extinction?

So why did dragons (e.g., dinosaurs) die out? The simple answer is *sin*. When Adam and Eve sinned (Genesis 3) death came into the world. Living things began to die, and many things began to die out — dragons as well as dodos were no exception.

Some specific reasons for their extinction likely include changing environments (e.g., the ice age that followed the Flood, the destruction of swamp lands by man, and so on), predation by man (cf. Genesis 10:9), diseases, genetic problems, catastrophic events, etc.[22] Keep in mind that most dragon legends end with a dragon getting killed. Like the dodo, man could have been a major factor why dragons no longer survive, as far as we know. The possibility exists that some still live in remote parts of the world or underground and only come out at certain times. This was quite common with old dragon accounts.

22. Ken Ham, gen. ed., *New Answers Book 1* (Green Forest, AR: Master Books, 2006), p. 207–219.

However, it is unlikely that we will find any living ones, in the same way that it is unlikely that we will find passenger pigeons, dodos, and many other things that have been pushed to extinction.

Conclusion: Dragons in Relation to Satan

There is much to be said about dragons, and this short chapter is just a taste. Dragons, including the specific subset of dinosaurs, were real creatures and have simply died out due to sin, just like so many other animals, including the dodo. The land-dwelling, air-breathing dragons survived on the ark of Noah, and they have been dying out ever since (Genesis 6:20, 7:21–22).

Many were surely timid creatures (especially since they are known to have inhabited old ruins), but others were known to terrorize, according to the old accounts of dragons. And when such conflicts arose, a dragon usually ended up dead by someone who could overcome it. Such conquerors were remembered in history with a powerful and strong name.

But such vicious attacks could well be the reason that Satan is metaphorically called a "dragon" in Scripture (e.g., Revelation 12:3); also consider Satan's use of a serpent in Genesis 3:1 to deceive Eve and ultimately get Adam to bring sin and death into the world (Romans 5:12).

Satan's vicious attacks leave many helpless (e.g., 2 Corinthians 2:11; 1 Peter 5:8). But Christ, the "stronger man" in Luke 11:21–22, has conquered Satan (Hebrews 2:14), and has an eternal name above all names (Philippians 2:9). For in Christ, one can have the victory over Satan, the great dragon (1 Corinthians 15:57).

With this in mind, it is good to realize the big picture. Satan *wants* people to accept the idea that dragons were myth as this is simply another attack on the authority of God's Word. Satan wants us to doubt God's Word the same way he attacked Eve using a serpent in the Garden of Eden to doubt His Word (Genesis 3:1–6; 2 Corinthians 2:11). Were dragons a myth, or did they simply die out? It's time to trust God's Word over the fallible ideas of man, who was not there and not in a position of superseding God on the subject (Isaiah 2:22).

Of course dragons were real.

CHAPTER 4

Peppered Moths . . .
Evidence for Evolution?

DR. TOMMY MITCHELL

Stop me if you have heard this tale before. It's about one of the sacred cows of evolution: the peppered moth. The story of this moth has been set forth for decades as *the* prime example of evolution in action. It is a fascinating story about how, due to a combination of environmental changes and selective predation, a moth turned into, well, a moth.

The peppered moth, scientifically known as *Biston betularia*, exists in two primary forms — one light colored with spots and one almost black. As the tale goes, in the mid 1800s, the lighter variety of the moth (*typica*) predominated. During the Industrial Revolution, the lichen on tree trunks died, soot got deposited on trees, and as a result trees got darker. As this change occurred, the population of darker moths (*carbonaria*) increased, presumably due to the camouflage offered by the darker trees. Bird predators could not see the dark moths against the dark bark. As the darker moth population increased, the lighter moth population decreased.[1]

This story has been touted for years as a great example of Darwinian evolution in action. Countless textbooks are lavishly illustrated with photographs of light and dark moths resting on light and dark tree trunks to teach the wonders of evolution. "It is the slam dunk of natural selection, the paradigmatic story

---

1. This darkening of the wings is due to the increased amount of the pigment melanin in the wings of the *carbonaria* variety and is known as "melanism."

that converts high school and college students to Darwin, the thundering left hook to the jaw of creationism."[2]

Much of the "proof" for this evolutionary change came from the work of a man named Dr. Bernard Kettlewell, a medical doctor-turned-entomologist, at Oxford University. Dr. Kettlewell had been intrigued by changes in the relative populations of the moths. In his experiments, he set out to show that the changes were a result of natural selection in response to environmental change and selective predation.

The Work of Kettlewell

First of all, Kettlewell had to show that birds were indeed predators of these moths. Up to that time, many biologists did not consider birds the primary predators of *Biston*. Kettlewell released moths into an aviary and observed the moths being eaten as they rested. This observation settled the issue of bird predation, at least to Kettlewell's satisfaction.[3]

For the next phase of his study, Kettlewell went to a polluted woodland area near Birmingham, England. There the trees had become darkened due to pollution. In the woods, Kettlewell undertook the first of his release-recapture experiments. He released moths, 447 of the *carbonaria* variety and 137 of the *typica* variety. Traps were set to recapture the moths that night, and the numbers of each variety were assessed the next morning. A much higher percentage of darker moths than lighter moths were recovered. Kettlewell recaptured 27.5 percent of the *carbonaria*, but only 13.0 percent of the *typica*. From this data, Kettlewell concluded that "birds act as selective agents"[4] and subsequently felt that this represented evolution by natural selection.

To further examine this, Kettlewell then undertook another release-recapture experiment. This was done in a wooded area near Dorset, England. Here the trees had not been darkened by pollution. As before, both light and dark moths were released and then recaptured and counted. Here 12.5 percent of the *typica* were recaptured but only 6.3 percent of the *carbonaria*. Kettlewell anticipated this result because he hypothesized that birds would more easily prey upon the darker moths than the lighter moths due to the lighter color of the trees.

---

2. Judith Hooper, *Of Moths and Men: An Evolutionary Tale* (New York: W.W. Horton, 2002), p. xvii.
3. H.B.D. Kettlewell, "Selection Experiments on Industrial Melanism in the Lepidoptera," *Heredity* 9 (1955): 323–342.
4. Ibid., p. 342.

Adding credence to Kettlewell's theory, others noted that, as pollution decreased, the population of lighter moths increased in some areas. In the late 1950s, pollution control laws were enacted and air quality improved. In some places, as the lichen returned to the trees, the expected increase in the population of the *typica* variety of moth occurred.[5] Scientists believed this increase further confirmed this living example of evolution.

From this point on, there was no stopping the peppered moth bandwagon. High school and college biology textbooks heralded the peppered moth as the classic example of evolution in action. The peppered moth story has been presented to students for years as a classic case of evolution, the process by which molecules eventually turned into man.

Trouble in Paradise

Scientific claims must be confirmed through repetition, but over the years many attempts to repeat Kettlewell's studies have failed to confirm his results. These contradictory reports showed high populations of *typica* in polluted areas[6] or inordinately high numbers of *carbonaria* in lightly polluted areas.[7] Some studies failed to confirm the observation that the lighter moths increased as the lichen cover of the trees recovered. Nonetheless, the challenges failed to remove the vaunted moth from its lofty perch.

The major challenge to Kettlewell's work came in 1998 when Michael Majerus, a geneticist from Cambridge, published a book entitled *Melanism: Evolution in Action*.[8] Although many of the criticisms of Kettlewell's work had been around for years, Majerus's critique of Kettlewell's methods caused quite a stir in evolutionary circles.

In a review of this book in the journal *Nature*, Dr. Jerry Coyne said this: "My own reaction resembles the dismay attending my discovery, at the age of six, that it was my father and not Santa who brought the presents on Christmas Eve."[9] He further commented; "It is also worth pondering why there has been general and unquestioned acceptance of Kettlewell's work."[10] Things

5. Jonathan Wells, "Second Thoughts about Peppered Moths," The True.Origin Archive, http://trueorigin.org/pepmoth1.asp.
6. R.C. Stewart, "Industrial and Non-industrial Melanism in the Peppered Moth, *Biston betularia* (L.)," *Ecological Entomology* 2 (1977): 231–243.
7. D.R. Lees and E.R. Creed, "Industrial Melanism in *Biston betularia*: The Role of Selective Predation," *Journal of Animal Ecology* 44 (1975): 67–83.
8. M.E.N. Majerus, Melanism: *Evolution in Action* (Oxford: Oxford University Press, 1998).
9. J.A. Coyne, "Not Black and White," *Nature* 396 (1998): 35.
10. Ibid., p. 36.

were starting to look bad for our friend, *Biston betularia*. Then things got worse.

In 2002, a journalist named Judith Hooper published the book *Of Moths and Men: An Evolutionary Tale*. This book detailed the story of the research involving the peppered moth, including an exploration of the lives of the principal people involved. She described the lives and backgrounds of not only Kettlewell but also of E.B. Ford, Kettlewell's mentor at Oxford. The somewhat unflattering portraits of these men were disturbing and, in one sense, made for good reading — if by good reading one likes reveling in the shortcomings of other human beings.

However, it was Hooper's detailed examination of Kettlewell's experimental techniques, which fueled the most controversy. She thoroughly described the method used by Kettlewell in each of his field studies, along with an analysis of the data he collected. Her conclusions were shocking in that she suggests that Kettlewell, after obtaining disappointing data in the early phase of his study, manipulated his collection of data later in the study in order to obtain the desired result. The possibility of outright fraud was even mentioned. The scientific community was aghast. The first and foremost evidence for evolution in action, "the prize horse in our stable,"[11] was apparently in jeopardy.

What's the Problem?

Although there have been many concerns raised about Kettlewell's experimental techniques, the biggest issue seems to revolve around where moths rest during the day. In his study, Kettlewell released moths during the daytime and watched them take resting places on the trunks of trees. He then observed birds preying on the moths. During the night, he collected and counted the moths. He concluded that birds preyed more readily on the more visible moths than on the ones better hidden by their surroundings. The problem with this conclusion is that, over many years of study, it had been determined that *these moths don't rest on tree trunks during the day*! They fly only at night, and they take resting places high in the trees on the underside of branches. In these places they are much better concealed from birds than were the moths in Kettlewell's experiments. According to Howlett and Majerus, ". . . exposed areas of tree trunks are not an important resting site for any form of *B. betularia*."[12]

---

11. Ibid., p. 35.
12. R.J. Howlett and M.E.N. Majerus, "The Understanding of Industrial Melanism in the Peppered Moth (*Biston betularia*) (Lepidoptera: Geometridea)," *Biological Journal of the Linnean Society* 30 (1987): 40.

This is more than an insignificant criticism. Abnormal placement of the moths into a location rendering them much more visible would bring into question the validity of Kettlewell's results. First of all, the distinction between light and dark moths would be much less on the shadowy underside of a branch. Secondly, the unnaturally high concentration of moths in an unusual area might have changed the normal feeding pattern of the birds. In fact, some researchers are not convinced that birds are the primary peppered moth predators in nature — James Carey of the University of California, for example.[13] Also, some researchers (although not Kettlewell himself) have conducted experiments by using dead moths glued to tree trunks,[14] a practice that has been criticized by some observers.

Furthermore, many researchers considered the method by which Kettlewell assessed the degree of moth camouflage to be overly subjective. This bias would call into question the entire body of data. These criticisms bring into question the entire issue of selective bird predation being the driving force behind this so-called splendid example of *natural selection*. Without an observable, defined environmental factor to push the peppered moth to "evolve," the famous moth could not even be a candidate to be used as evidence to support Darwin's theory.

Was Kettlewell Wrong?

So was Kettlewell wrong? One major figure in this discussion has come to Kettlewell's defense, and that person is none other than Majerus, the man whose book fueled much of the recent controversy.

Over the last few years, Majerus has re-examined this question. He has conducted a study that apparently does not suffer from some of the supposed deficiencies of Kettlewell's experimental techniques. He was very careful to ensure that the moth's resting places mimicked those seen in nature, and the moths were released at night.[15] Also, using binoculars, he observed birds eating the moths. He claims that the results of his study validate Kettlewell's work. De Roode concludes, "The peppered moth should be reinstated as a textbook example of evolution in action."[16]

Good scientists must examine and re-examine the methods and techniques used to study our world. The experimental method itself relies on others conducting the same or similar types of investigations to see if previous conclusions

13. J. de Roode, "The Moths of War," *New Scientist* 196 no. 2633 (2007): 49.
14. Wells, "Second Thoughts about Peppered Moths," p. 7.
15. de Roode, "The Moths of War," p. 48.
16. Ibid., p. 49.

are indeed valid. As part of this quest for knowledge, flaws in the methods used by prior investigators are sometimes uncovered. After all, no one makes a perfect plan. Shortcomings in methodology can be corrected and further data collected to ensure proper conclusions are reached. To that end, all those who have questioned Kettlewell's methods should be commended. If there were problems with his methods, and apparently there were, those problems have apparently been corrected in subsequent evaluations.

Further, those who would be too critical of Kettlewell should proceed with some caution. There has been much written in both the pro-evolution and the pro-creation camps that has been very critical of Kettlewell. Some of this seems justified, but much of it does not, particularly the accusation that he falsified his data. There can be no more serious accusation made against a scientist, so it would seem that more proof is needed before that charge be made. After all, others involved in this area have collected data that validates Kettlewell's original conclusions. No one can know another's heart, so some measure of charity needs be given here. Perhaps Kettlewell's shortcomings can best be measured by this quote from a colleague who characterized him as "the best naturalist I have ever met, and almost the worst professional scientist I have ever known."[17]

So Where Are We?

So does all this debate about the validity of Kettlewell's peppered moth data really pose a problem for creationists? The evolutionist claims that the peppered moth story is such a shining example of evolution in action that to question it is to demonstrate unwillingness to accept proven science. Majerus has said, "The peppered moth story is easy to understand because it involves things that we are familiar with: vision and predation and birds and moths and pollution and camouflage and lunch and death. That is why the anti-evolution lobby attacks the peppered moth story. They are frightened that too many will be able to understand."[18]

Exactly what is it that we should be able to understand? To the creationist, it is very, very simple. Over the last 150 years, moths have changed into moths! The creationist has no difficulty with this process. The issue of Kettlewell's shortcomings notwithstanding, the creationist has no problem with the results of his (and other subsequent researchers') work. The concept that a less visible organism would survive better than a more visible one seems obvious in the extreme. What is not to understand here? According to de Roode, "The

17. J.A. Coyne, "Evolution Under Pressure," *Nature* 418 (2002): 19.
18. Ibid., p. 49.

peppered moth was and is a well understood example of evolution by natural selection."[19] The creationist would agree that this population change represents natural selection. However, this change is most certainly *not* molecules-to-man evolution. Natural selection and molecules-to-man evolution are not the same thing, and many are led astray by the misuse of these terms.

Natural selection can easily be seen in nature. Natural selection produces the variations within a kind of organism. Thanks to natural selection, we have the marvelous variety of creatures that we see in our world. However, in this process, fish change into (amazingly) fish, birds change into birds, dogs change into dogs, and moths change into moths. If, during the process of the study of peppered moths, the moths had changed into some other type of creature, a bird perhaps, then we might have something to talk about.

No amount of posturing by the evolutionist can change the fact that these moths are still moths and will continue to be moths. The variation seen is simply the result of sorting and resorting of the genetic material present in the original moths. At no time has there been any new information introduced into the genome of the moth (which is what molecules-to-man evolution would require). There is no evidence of the beginnings of an intermediate form between the present moth and the creature it is destined to evolve into. Moths stay moths, fish stay fish, and people stay people, regardless of the great variety seen within each.

Ultimately, the peppered moth story is more of the same. Although much of the clamor surrounding Kettlewell's work has made for good reading and, in some ways, has made for good science, the results are clear. There is nothing here, in even the smallest way, to provide evidence for the process of molecules-to-man evolution. That is what the creationist is "able to understand."

---

19. de Roode, "The Moths of War," p. 49.

CHAPTER 5

Is Evolutionary Humanism the Most Blood-stained Religion Ever?

BODIE HODGE

Introduction: Man's Authority or God's Authority . . . Two Religions

I f God and His Word are not the authority . . . then by default . . . who is? *Man* is. When people reject God and His Word as the ultimate authority, then man is attempting to elevate his or her thoughts (collectively or individually) to a position of authority *over* God and His Word.

So often, people claim that "Christians are religious and the enlightened unbelievers who reject God are *not* religious." Don't be deceived by such a statement. For these nonbelievers are indeed religious . . . *very* religious, whether they realize it or not. For they have bought into the religion of humanism.

Humanism is the religion that elevates man to be greater than God. Humanism, in a broad sense, encompasses any thought or worldview that rejects God and the 66 books of His Word in part or in whole; hence *all* non-biblical religions have humanistic roots. There are also those that *mix* aspects of humanism with the Bible. Many of these religions (e.g., Mormons, Islam, Judaism, etc.) openly borrow from the Bible, but they also have mixed *human* elements into their religion where they take some of man's ideas to supersede many parts of the Bible, perhaps in subtle ways.[1]

There are many forms of humanism, but secular humanism has become one of the most popular today. Variant forms of secular humanism include atheism, agnosticism, non-theism, Darwinism, and the like. Each shares a belief in an evolutionary worldview with man as the centered authority over God.

Humanism organizations can also receive a tax-exempt status (the same as a Christian church in the United States and the United Kingdom) and they even have religious documents like the *Humanist Manifesto*. Surprisingly, this religion has free rein in state schools, museums, and media under the guise of neutrality, seeking to fool people into thinking it is not a "religion."[2]

Humanism and "Good"

Christians are often confronted with the claim that a humanistic worldview will help society become "better."[3] Even the first *Humanist Manifesto*, of which belief in evolution is a subset, declared: "The goal of humanism is a free and universal society in which people voluntarily and intelligently co-operate for the common good."

But can such a statement be true? For starters, what do the authors mean by "good"? They have no legitimate foundation for such a concept, since one person's "good" can be another's "evil." To have some objective standard (not a relative standard), they must *borrow* from the absolute and true teachings of God in the Bible.

Beyond that, does evolutionary humanism really teach a future of prosperity and a common good? Since death is the "hero" in an evolutionary framework, then it makes one wonder. What has been the result of evolutionary thinking in the past century (20th century)? Perhaps this could be a test of what is to come.

---

1. For example: in Islam, Muhammad's words in the Koran are taken as a higher authority than God's Word (the Bible); in Mormonism, they have changed nearly 4,000 verses of the Bible to conform to Mormon teachings and add the words of Joseph Smith and later prophets as superior to God's Word; in Judaism, they accept a portion of God's Word (the Old Testament) but by human standards, they reject a large portion of God's Word (the New Testament) as well as the ultimate Passover lamb, Jesus Christ.
2. Although the U.S. Supreme Court says that religion is not to be taught in the classroom, this one seems to be allowed.
3. One can always ask the question, by what standard do they mean "better"? God *is* that standard so they refute themselves when they speak of things being better or worse. In their own professed worldview it is merely arbitrary for something to be "better" or "worse."

Let's first look at the death estimates due to aggressive conflicts stemming from leaders with evolutionary worldviews, beginning in the 1900s, to see the hints of what this "next level" looks like:

Table 1: Estimated deaths as a result of an evolutionary worldview

Who/What?	Specific event and estimated dead	Total Estimates
Pre-Hitler Germany/ Hitler and the Nazis	WWI: 8,500,000[a] WWII: 70 million[b] [Holocaust: 17,000,000][c]	95,000,000
Leon Trotsky and Vladimir Lenin	Bolshevik revolution and Russian Civil War: 15,000,000[d]	15,000,000
Joseph Stalin	20,000,000[e]	20,000,000
Mao Zedong	14,000,000–20,000,000[f]	Median estimate: 17,000,000
Korean War	2,500,000?[g]	~2,500,000
Vietnam War (1959– 1975)	4,000,000–5,000,000 Vietnamese, 1,500,000–2,000,000 Lao and Cambodians[h]	Medians of each and excludes French, Australia, and U.S. losses: 6,250,000
Pol Pot (Saloth Sar)	750,000–1,700,000[i]	Median estimate: 1,225,000
Abortion to children[j]	China estimates since 1971–2006: 300,000,000[k] USSR estimates from 1954–1991: 280,000,000[l] US estimates 1928–2007: 26,000,000[m] France estimates 1936–2006: 5,749,731[n] United Kingdom estimates 1958– 2006: 6,090,738[o] Germany estimates 1968–2007: 3,699,624,[p] etc.	621,500,000 and this excludes many other countries
Grand estimate		~778,000,000

a. *The World Book Encyclopedia*, Volume 21, Entry: World War II (Chicago, IL: World Book, Inc.) p. 467; such statistics may have some variance depending on source as much of this is still in dispute.
b. Ranges from 60 to 80 million, so we are using 70 million.
c. Figures ranged from 7 to 26 million.
d. Russian Civil War, http://en.wikipedia.org/wiki/Russian_Civil_War, October 23, 2008.
e. Joseph Stalin, http://www.moreorless.au.com/killers/stalin.html, October 23, 2008.
f. Mao Tse-Tung, http://www.moreorless.au.com/killers/mao.html, October 23, 2008.

g. This one is tough to pin down and several sources have different estimates, so this is a middle-of-the-road estimate from the sources I found.

h. Vietnam War, http://www.vietnamwar.com/, October 23, 2008.

i. Pol Pot, http://en.wikipedia.org/wiki/Pol_Pot, October 23, 2008.

j. This table only lists estimates for abortion deaths in a few countries; so this total figure is likely very conservative, as well as brief stats of other atrocities.

k. Historical abortion statistics, PR China, compiled by Wm. Robert Johnston , last updated June 4 2008, http://www.johnstonsarchive.net/policy/abortion/ab-prchina.html.

l. Historical abortion statistics, USSR, compiled by Wm. Robert Johnston , last updated June 4 2008, http://www.johnstonsarchive.net/policy/abortion/ab-ussr.html.

m. Historical abortion statistics, United States, compiled by Wm. Robert Johnston , last updated June 4 2008, http://www.johnstonsarchive.net/policy/abortion/ab-unitedstates.html.

n. Historical abortion statistics, France, compiled by Wm. Robert Johnston , last updated June 4 2008, http://www.johnstonsarchive.net/policy/abortion/ab-france.html.

o. Historical abortion statistics, United Kingdom, compiled by Wm. Robert Johnston, last updated June 4 2008, http://www.johnstonsarchive.net/policy/abortion/ab-unitedkingdom.html.

p. Historical abortion statistics, FR Germany, compiled by Wm. Robert Johnston , last updated June 4 2008, http://www.johnstonsarchive.net/policy/abortion/ab-frgermany.html.

Charles Darwin's view of molecules-to-man evolution was catapulted into societies around the world in the mid-to-late 1800s. Evolutionary teachings influenced Karl Marx, Leon Trotsky, Adolf Hitler, Pol Pot, Mao Zedong, Joseph Stalin, Vladimir Lenin, and many others. Let's take a closer look at some of these people and events and examine the evolutionary influence and repercussions.

World War 1 and 11, Hitler, Nazis, and the Holocaust

Most historians would point to the assassination of Archduke Francis Ferdinand on June 18, 1914, as the event that triggered World War I (WWI). But tensions were already high considering the state of Europe at the time. Darwinian sentiment was brewing in Germany. Darwin once said:

> At some future period, not very distant as measured by centuries, the civilized races of man will almost certainly exterminate and replace the savage races throughout the world. At the same time the anthropomorphous apes . . . will no doubt be exterminated. The break between man and his nearest allies will then be wider, for it will intervene between man in a more civilized state, as we may hope, even than the Caucasian, and some ape as low as a baboon, instead of as now between the negro or Australian [Aborigine] and the gorilla.[4]

---

4. Charles Darwin, *The Descent of Man* (New York: A.L. Burt, 1874, 2nd ed.), p. 178.

Darwin viewed the "Caucasian" (white-skinned Europeans) as the dominant "race" in his evolutionary worldview. To many evolutionists at the time, mankind had evolved from ape-like creatures that had more hair, dark skin, dark eyes, etc. Therefore, more "evolved" meant less body hair, blond hair, blue eyes, etc. Later, in Hitler's era, Nazi Germany practiced *Lebensborn*, which was a controversial program, the details of which have not been entirely brought to light. Many claim it was a breeding program that tried to evolve the "master race" further — more on this below.

But the German sentiment prior to WWI was very much bent on conquering for the purpose of expanding their territory and their "race." An encyclopedia entry from 1936 states:

> In discussions of the background of the war much has been said of Pan-Germanism, which was the spirit of national consciousness carried to the extreme limit. The Pan-Germans, who included not only militarists, but historians, scientists, educators and statesmen, conceived the German people, no matter where they located, as permanently retaining their nationality. The most ambitious of this group believed that it was their mission of Germans to extend their kultur (culture) over the world, and to accomplish this by conquest if necessary. In this connection the theory was advanced that the German was a superior being, destined to dominate other peoples, most of whom were thought of as decadent.[5]

Germany had been buying into Darwin's model of evolution and saw themselves as the superior "race," destined to dominate the world, and their actions were the consequence of their worldview. This view set the stage for Hitler and the Nazi party and paved the road to WWII.

Hitler and the Nazis

World War II dwarfed World War I in the total number of people who died. Racist evolutionary attitudes exploded in Germany against people groups such as Jews, Poles, and many others. Darwin's teaching on evolution and humanism heavily influenced Adolf Hitler and the Nazis.

Hitler even tried to force the Protestant church in Germany to change fundamental tenants because of his newfound faith.[6] In 1936, while Hitler was in power, an encyclopedia entry on Hitler stated:

---

5. *The American Educator Encyclopedia* (Chicago, IL: The United Educators, Inc., 1936), p. 3914 under entry "World War."
6. *The American Educator Encyclopedia*, p. 1702 under entry "Hitler."

. . . a Hitler attempt to modify the Protestant faith failed.[7]

His actions clearly show that he did not hold to the basic fundamentals taught in the 66 books of the Bible. Though some of his writings suggest he did believe in some form of God early on (due to his upbringing within Catholicism), his religious views moved toward atheistic humanism with his acceptance of evolution. Many atheists today try to disavow him, but actions speak louder than words.

The Alpha History site (dedicated to much to the history of Nazi Germany by providing documents, transcribed speeches, and so on) says:

> Contrary to popular opinion, Hitler himself was not an atheist. . . . Hitler drifted away from the church after leaving home, and his religious views in adulthood are in dispute.[8]

So this history site is not sure what his beliefs were, but they seem to be certain that he was not an atheist! If they are not sure what beliefs he held, how can they be certain he was not an atheist?[9] The fact is that many people who walk away from church become atheists (i.e., they were never believers in the first place as 1 John 2:19 indicates). And Hitler's actions were diametrically opposed to Christianity . . . but not atheism, where there is no God who sets what is right and wrong.[10]

Regardless, this refutes notions that Hitler was a Christian as some have falsely claimed. Hitler's disbelief started early. He said:

> The present system of teaching in schools permits the following absurdity: at 10 a.m. the pupils attend a lesson in the catechism, at which the creation of the world is presented to them in accordance with the teachings of the Bible; and at 11 a.m. they attend a lesson in natural science, at which they are taught the theory of evolution. Yet the two doctrines are in complete contradiction. As a child, I suffered from this contradiction, and ran my head against a wall . . . Is there a single religion that can exist without a dogma? No, for in that case it would belong to the order of science . . . But there have been human

---

7. *The American Educator Encyclopedia*, p. 1494 under entry "Germany."
8. "Religion in Nazi Germany," http://alphahistory.com/nazigermany/religion-in-nazi-germany/, April 3, 2013.
9. Romans 1 makes it clear that all people believe in God, they just suppress that knowledge, and this is also the case with any professed atheist.
10. For an extensive treatise on Hitler's (and the Nazi's) religious viewpoints, see J. Bergman, *Hitler and the Nazi Darwinian Worldview* (Kitchener, Ontario, Canada: Joshua Press Inc., 2012).

beings, in the baboon category, for at least three hundred thousand years. There is less distance between the man-ape and the ordinary modern man than there is between the ordinary modern man and a man like Schopenhauer. . . . It is impossible to suppose nowadays that organic life exists only on our planet.[11]

Consider this quote in his unpublished second book:

The types of creatures on the earth are countless, and on an individual level their self-preservation instinct as well as the longing for procreation is always unlimited; however, the space in which this entire life process plays itself out is limited. It is the surface area of a precisely measured sphere on which billions and billions of individual beings struggle for life and succession. In the limitation of this living space lies the compulsion for the struggle for survival, and the struggle for survival, in turn contains the precondition for evolution.[12]

Hitler continues:

The history of the world in the ages when humans did not yet exist was initially a representation of geological occurrences. The clash of natural forces with each other, the formation of a habitable surface on this planet, the separation of water and land, the formation of the mountains, plains, and the seas. That [was] is the history of the world during this time. Later, with the emergence of organic life, human interest focuses on the appearance and disappearance of its thousandfold forms. Man himself finally becomes visible very late, and from that point on he begins to understand the term "world history" as referring to the history of his own development — in other words, the representation of his own evolution. This development is characterized by the never-ending battle of humans against animals and also against humans themselves.[13]

Hitler fully believed Darwin as well as Darwin's precursors — such as Charles Lyell's geological ages and millions of years of history. In his statements here, there is no reference to God. Instead, he unreservedly flew the banner of

---

11. Adolf Hitler, translated by Norman Cameron and R.H. Stevens, *Hitler's Secret Conversations*, 1941–1944 (The New American Library of World Literature, Inc., 1961).
12. *Hitler's Second Book*, Adolf Hitler, edited by Gerald L. Weinberg, translated by Krista Smith (New York: Enigma Books, 2003), p. 8.
13. *Hitler's Second Book*, p. 9.

naturalism and evolution and only mentioned God in a rare instance to win Christians to his side, just as agnostic Charles Darwin did in his book *On the Origin of Species.*[14]

One part of the Nazi party political platform's 25 points in 1920 says:

> We demand freedom of religion for all religious denominations within the state so long as they do not endanger its existence or oppose the moral senses of the Germanic race. The Party as such advocates the standpoint of a positive Christianity without binding itself confessionally to any one denomination.[15]

Clearly this "positive Christianity" was an appeal to some of Christianity's morality, but not the faith itself. Many atheists today still appeal to a "positive Christian" approach, wanting the morality of Christianity (in many respects), but not Christianity.

Christianity was under heavy attack by Hitler and the Nazis as documented from original sources prior to the end of WWII by Bruce Walker in *The Swastika against the Cross.*[16] The book clearly reveals the anti-Christian sentiment by Hitler and the Nazis and their persecution of Christianity and their attempt to make Christianity change and be subject to the Nazi state and beliefs.

In 1939–1941, the Bible was rewritten for the German people at Hitler's command, eliminating all references to Jews, and made Christ out to be pro-Aryan! The Ten Commandments were replaced with these twelve:[17]

1. Honor your Fuhrer and master.
2. Keep the blood pure and your honor holy.
3. Honor God and believe in him wholeheartedly.
4. Seek out the peace of God.
5. Avoid all hypocrisy.
6. Holy is your health and life.

---

14. In the first edition of *Origin of Species*, God is not mentioned; in the sixth edition, "God" was added several times to draw Christians into this false religion. See R. Hedtke, *Secrets of the Sixth Edition* (Green Forest, AR: Master Books, 2010).
15. Nazi Party 25 Points (1920), http://alphahistory.com/nazigermany/nazi-party-25-points-1920/.
16. B. Walker, *The Swastika against the Cross* (Denver, CO: Outskirts Press, Inc., 2008).
17. "Hitler Rewrote the Bible and Added Two Commandments," Pravda News Site, 8/10/2006; http://english.pravda.ru/world/europe/10-08-2006/83892-hitler-0/; "Jewish References Erased in Newly Found Nazi Bible," Daily Mail Online, August 7, 2006; http://www.dailymail.co.uk/news/article-399470/Jewish-references-erased-newly-Nazi-Bible.html.

7. Holy is your well-being and honor.
8. Holy is your truth and fidelity.
9. Honor your father and mother — your children are your aid and your example.
10. Maintain and multiply the heritage of your forefathers.
11. Be ready to help and forgive.
12. Joyously serve the people with work and sacrifice.

Hitler had *replaced* Christ in Nazi thought; and children were even taught to pray to Hitler instead of God![18] Hitler and the Nazis were not Christian, but instead were humanistic in their outlook, and any semblance of Christianity was cultic. The Nazis determined that their philosophy was the best way to bring about the common good of all humanity.

Interestingly, it was Christians alone in Germany who were unconquered by the Nazis, and they suffered heavily for it. Walker summarizes in his book:

> You would expect to find Christians and Nazis mortal enemies. This is, of course, exactly what happened historically. Christians, alone, proved unconquerable by the Nazis. It can be said that Christians did not succeed in stopping Hitler, but it cannot be said that they did not try, often at great loss and nearly always as true martyrs (people who could have chosen to live, but who chose to die for the sake of goodness.)[19]

Hitler and the Nazis' evolutionary views certainly helped lead Germany into WWII because they viewed the "Caucasian" as more evolved (and, more specifically, the Aryan peoples of the Caucasians), which to them justified their adoption of the idea that lesser "races" should be murdered in the struggle for survival. Among the first to be targeted were Jews, then Poles, Slavs, and then many others — including Christians, regardless of their heritage.

Trotsky, Lenin

Trotsky and Lenin were both notorious leaders of the USSR — and specifically the Russian revolution. Lenin, taking power in 1917, became a ruthless leader and selected Trotsky as his heir. Lenin and Trotsky held to Marxism, which was built, in part, on Darwinism and evolution applied to a social scheme.

18. Walker, p. 20–22.
19. Walker, p. 88.

Karl Marx regarded Darwin's book as an "epoch-making book." With regards to Darwin's research on natural origins, Marx claimed, "The latter method is the only materialistic and, therefore, the only scientific one."[20]

Few realize or admit that Marxism, the primary idea underlying communism, is built on Darwinism and materialism (i.e., no God). In 1883, Freidrich Engels, Marx's longtime friend and collaborator, stated at Marx's funeral service, that "Just as Darwin discovered the law of evolution in organic nature, so Marx discovered the law of evolution in human history."[21] Both Darwin and Marx built their ideologies on naturalism and materialism (tenants of evolutionary humanism). Trotsky once said of Darwin:

> Darwin stood for me like a mighty doorkeeper at the entrance to the temple of the universe. I was intoxicated with his minute, precise, conscientious and at the same time powerful, thought. I was the more astonished when I read . . . that he had preserved his belief in God. I absolutely declined to understand how a theory of the origin of species by way of natural selection and sexual selection and a belief in God could find room in one and the same head.[22]

Trotsky's high regard for evolution and Darwin were the foundation of his belief system. Like many, Trotsky probably did not realize that the precious few instances of the name "God" did not appear in the first edition of *Origin of Species*. These references were added later, and many suspect that this was done to influence church members to adopt Darwinism. Regardless, Trotsky may not have read much of Darwin's second book, *Descent of Man*, in which Darwin claims that man invented God:

> The same high mental faculties which first led man to believe in unseen spiritual agencies, then in fetishism, polytheism, and ultimately in monotheism, would infallibly lead him, as long as his reasoning powers remained poorly developed, to various strange superstitions and customs.[23]

20. *Great Books of the Western World*, Volume 50, *Capital*, Karl Marx (Chicago, IL: William Benton Publishers, 1952), footnotes on p. 166 and p. 181.
21. Gertrude Himmelfarb, *Darwin and the Darwinian Revolution* (London: Chatto & Windus, 1959), p. 348.
22. Max Eastman, *Trotsky: A Portrait of His Youth* (New York, 1925), p. 117–118.
23. Charles Darwin, *The Descent of Man and Selection in Relation to Sex*, Chapter III, "Comparison of the Mental Powers of Man and the Lower Animals," 1871. As printed in *Great Books of the Western World*, Volume 49, Robert Hutchins, ed. (Chicago, IL: William Benton Publishers, 1952), p. 303.

Vladimir Lenin picked up on Darwinism and Marxism and ruled very harshly as an evolutionist. His variant of Marxism has become known as Leninism. Regardless, the evolutionist roots of Marx, Trotsky, and Lenin were the foundation that communism has stood on — and continues to stand on.

Stalin, Mao, and Pol Pot, to Name a Few

Perhaps the most ruthless communist leaders were Joseph Stalin, Mao Zedong, and Pol Pot. Each of these were social Darwinists, ruling three different countries — the Soviet Union, China, and Cambodia, respectively. Their reigns of terror demonstrated the end result of reducing the value of human life to that of mere animals, a Darwinistic teaching.[24] Though I could expand on each of these, you should be getting the point by now. So let's move to another key, but deadly, point in evolutionary thought.

Abortion — the War on Babies

The war on children has been one of the quietest, and yet bloodiest, in the past hundred years. In an evolutionary mindset, the unborn have been treated as though they are going through an "animal phase" and can simply be discarded.

Early evolutionist Ernst Haeckel first popularized the concept that babies in the womb are actually undergoing animal developmental stages, such as a fish stage and so on. This idea has come to be known as *ontogeny recapitulates phylogeny*. Haeckel even faked drawings of various animals' embryos and had them drawn next to human embryos looking virtually identical.

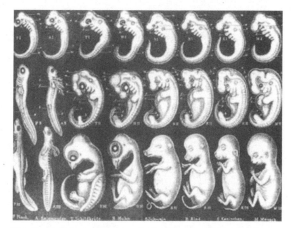

Haeckel's faked embryos: A detailed analysis of this subject will be done in chapter 26

---

24. R. Hall, "Darwin's Impact — The Bloodstained Legacy of Evolution," *Creation* Magazine 27(2) (March 2005): 46–47, http://www.answersingenesis.org/articles/cm/v27/n2/darwin.

These drawings have been shown to be completely false.[25] Haeckel himself partially confessed as much.[26] However, this discredited idea has been used repeatedly for a hundred years! Textbooks today still use this concept (though not Haeckel's drawings), and museums around the world still teach it.

Through this deception, many women have been convinced that the babies they are carrying in their wombs are simply going through an animal phase and can be aborted. Author and general editor of this volume, Ken Ham, states:

> In fact, some abortion clinics in America have taken women aside to explain to them that what is being aborted is just an embryo in the fish stage of evolution, and that the embryo must not be thought of as human. These women are being fed outright lies.[27]

Evolutionary views have decreased the value of human life. Throughout the world, the casualties of the war on children is staggering. Though deaths of children and the unborn did exist prior to the "evolution revolution," they have increased exponentially after the promotion of Darwinian teachings.

Conclusion

Is evolution the cause of wars and deaths? Absolutely not — both existed long before Darwin was born. Sin is the ultimate cause.[28] But an evolutionary worldview has done nothing but add fuel to the fire.

In spite of the wars and atrocities caused by those who subscribed to an evolutionary worldview in recent times, there is still hope. We can end the seemingly endless atrocities against the unborn and those deemed less worthy of living, including the old and impaired.

25. Michael Richardson et al, *Anatomy and Embryology*, 196(2) (1997): 91–106.
26. Haeckel said, "A small portion of my embryo-pictures (possibly 6 or 8 in a hundred) are really (in Dr Brass's [one of his critics] sense of the word) "falsified" — all those, namely, in which the disclosed material for inspection is so incomplete or insufficient that one is compelled in a restoration of a connected development series to fill up the gaps through hypotheses, and to reconstruct the missing members through comparative syntheses. What difficulties this task encounters, and how easily the draughts — man may blunder in it, the embryologist alone can judge." "The Truth about Haeckel's Confession," *The Bible Investigator and Inquirer*, M.L. Hutchinson, Melbourne (March 11, 1911): p. 22–24.
27. Ken Ham, *The Lie: Evolution*, chapter 8, "The Evils of Evolution (Green Forest, AR: Master Books, 1987), p. 105.
28. Ken Ham, gen. ed., *The New Answers Book 1* (Green Forest, AR: Master Books, 2006), chapter 26, "Why Does God's Creation Include Death and Suffering? p.325–338; http://www.answersingenesis.org/articles/nab/why-does-creation-include-suffering.

In Egypt, Israelite boys were slaughtered by being thrown into the Nile at the command of Pharaoh (Exodus 1:20). And yet, by the providence of God, Moses survived and led the Israelites to safety, and the Lord later judged the Egyptians.

In Judea, under the Roman Empire, subordinate King Herod the Great commanded the slaughter of all the boys under the age of two in and around Bethlehem. And yet, by the providence of God, Jesus, the Son of God, survived and later laid down His life to bring salvation to mankind as the Prince of Peace. Herod's name, however, went down in history as an evil tyrant and murderer.

In this day and age, governments readily promote and fund the killing of children, both boys and girls, and sometimes command it, through abortion. By providence, however . . . you survived. While we can't change the past, we can learn from it. If we are to stop this continuing bloodshed, we must get back to the Bible and realize the bankrupt religion of evolutionary humanism has led only to death — by the millions. We need to point those who think humanity is the answer to the Savior who took the sins of humanity on Himself to offer them salvation.

CHAPTER 6

Was Charles Darwin
a Christian?

DR. TOMMY MITCHELL

Much has been written about the religious views of Charles Darwin. What exactly did he believe, and when? Did he "reject" Christianity? Was he out to "destroy" Christianity, as some in the Church have come to believe?

While it is true that Darwin's ideas have caused great harm to the Church and have led many people to openly question the authority of the Bible, what did the man himself actually believe? Did he ever become a Christian?

Beginnings

Charles Darwin was born in 1809. He was part of a well-to-do family in England.

His grandfather, Erasmus, was a prominent physician, poet, and somewhat of an activist. He could best be described as a "progressive" or "free" thinker. Dr. Erasmus had a naturalistic view of origins and even promoted basic evolutionary ideas. His religious stand was as a deist, and he rejected the idea that the Bible was supernaturally inspired.

Charles never met his grandfather, who died before Charles was born. He did, however, become familiar with his grandfather's beliefs and ideas through reading his writings.

Charles's father, Robert, was also a physician. Beyond that, Robert was also a very successful investor, which provided the Darwin family with a very comfortable life.

As is often the case, the rejection of the authority of God's Word by one generation led to complete rejection of God in the next. Robert Darwin was an atheist.

In spite of Robert's lack of belief, Charles was christened in the Church of England (Anglican). This was obviously not due to any conviction that Robert had about the doctrine of the Anglican Church. It was most probably done to keep up appearances within the social order of the day.

There was, however, the influence of the mother. Susannah Darwin, Charles' mother, was a Unitarian. She took Charles to chapel for worship services. After her sudden death, Darwin's sisters took him to services at the Anglican Church.

For a year, Charles attended a Unitarian day school and later attended Shrewsbury Grammar School.

One writer has stated that Darwin "was thoroughly orthodox" during this time in his life. However, given the varied influences during his upbringing, it is difficult if not impossible, to imagine that Darwin's thinking was in any way "orthodox."

Higher Education

As was expected, Charles was to go to college to train to be a physician, like his father and grandfather. So he was soon off to Edinburgh to study medicine. That did not last long.

Darwin hated dealing with corpses, and he disliked dissection, both of which were necessary to become a doctor. To further hasten his retreat from medicine, he had developed a great interest in natural history and zoology. These pursuits began to occupy more and more of his time. His great interest in geology also took shape during these years.

It soon became clear that medicine would not be his life's work. In his autobiography Darwin wrote about this time in his life, stating, "He [Darwin's father] was very properly vehement against my turning an idle sporting man, which then seemed my probable destination."[1]

Further, Darwin wrote, "To my deep mortification my father once said to me, 'You care for nothing but shooting, dogs, and rat-catching, and you will be a disgrace to yourself and all your family.' "[2]

So at the advice of his father, it was decided that Charles would become a country clergyman. After all, this was a position with a steady income, some

---

1. Nora Barlow, ed., The Autobiography of Charles Darwin, 1809–1882 (New York: W.W. Norton, 1958), p. 49.
2. Ibid., p. 27.

social stature, and plenty of time to collect beetles and follow his natural history pursuits. The only thing lacking here was a genuine, heartfelt calling to the ministry.

In Darwin's own words:

> I asked for some time to consider, as from what little I had heard and thought on the subject I had scruples about declaring my belief in all the dogmas of the Church of England; though otherwise I liked the thought of being a country clergyman . . . and as I did not then in the least doubt the strict and literal truth of every word of the Bible, I soon persuaded myself that our Creed must be fully accepted. It never struck me how illogical it was to say that I believed in what I could not understand and what is in fact unintelligible.[3]

So he was off to Cambridge for his "theological" training. Unfortunately for Darwin, Cambridge was not the place to convict him of the authority of the Bible. At this time, theology training at Cambridge consisted mostly of coursework in the classics and philosophy along with a heavy emphasis on the works of William Paley — works that presented a rationalistic view of Christianity. Paley is best remembered for his arguments in favor of one of the primary theological positions of the day, natural theology. Basically, Paley held that one can know God, the Designer, by close examination of His creation, that is, nature. More simply, if it looks designed, there must be a designer. Early on, Darwin was fascinated by this argument. However, he rejected it later.

Even though Paley's theology also presented a biblical argument, this was largely ignored. During this period, the authority and historicity of the Bible had been called into question. Through the study of nature one could come to sufficiently understand God, it was believed. But the Bible was not held to be the ultimate authority. In fact, the Bible itself was being called into question, particularly regarding the actual nature of the Noahic Flood and the age of the earth. It was at this time that the idea of the earth being millions of years old was taking hold, not only in secular "scientific" circles but also in the Church itself.

Even though Darwin was at Cambridge for a degree in theology, his interest in natural science only strengthened. He attended lectures on botany, and his interest in geology grew. Most of the academics that taught Darwin in these areas were either openly critical of or outright denied the authority of the Bible.

---

3. Ibid., p. 49.

Again, the foundation of a system of belief was being laid that Darwin built upon in later life.

Though Darwin did get his degree in theology, he still had no heartfelt call to ministry. As reported by two of Darwin's biographers, Desmond and Moore,

> Darwin had asked Herbert whether he really felt "inwardly moved by the Holy Spirit" to enter the Church. When the Bishop put the question to him in the ordination service, what would he reply? "No," answered Herbert; he could not say he felt moved. Darwin chimed in, "Neither can I, and therefore I cannot take orders."[4]

So much for a genuine call to ministry. While some in the Church today point to Darwin's preparation for Christian ministry as evidence that he had some Christian beliefs, this is clearly not the case.

The *Beagle*

After leaving Cambridge, Darwin was presented an opportunity to participate in a South American survey expedition aboard the HMS *Beagle*. He was to join the ship's company as a naturalist and gentleman companion to the ship's captain, Robert FitzRoy.

During the voyage, Darwin was actually more interested in the geology of the lands he visited than the zoology of these new places. In fact, over half of the notes he made were geologic in nature. As he observed the geology, he became convinced that the strata were laid down over millions of years. Much of this was because he admired the works of a man named Charles Lyell. Lyell was the author of the book *Principles of Geology*.[5] As he studied Lyell's work, Darwin became convinced the uniformitarian view of geology was correct. Simply put, he came to believe that "the present is the key to the past." In other words, denying that events such as the catastrophic global Flood had a major role in shaping the earth, he believed that the ordinary geological processes we see today have always proceeded at the same rate so that the geological formations we see today required millions of years to form.

Here was a situation where a man who had already come to doubt the authority of the Bible was becoming more captivated with the secular thinking of his day. So the Bible was wrong, he decided, and the millions of years were true.

---

4. Adrian Desmond and James Moore, *Darwin* (New York: Warner Books, 1991), p. 66.
5. Incredibly, it was Capt. FitzRoy, an evangelical, who presented Darwin with Volume 1 of Lyell's book before the voyage began.

However, at that point, he had not rejected the Bible as completely untrue, rather "whilst on board the *Beagle* I was quite orthodox," he wrote, "and I remember being heartily laughed at by several of the officers (though themselves orthodox) for quoting the Bible as an unanswerable authority on some point of morality. I supposed it was the novelty of the argument that amused them."[6]

So here Darwin was using the Bible as a basis for morality although it was without any real confidence in its authority, because he then wrote, "But I had gradually come, by this time, to see that the Old Testament from its manifestly false history of the world . . . was no more to be trusted than the sacred books of the Hindoos, or the beliefs of any barbarian."[7] Later in life, he would come to understand the inconsistency in accepting biblical morality while denying its history. Unfortunately, his solution was to reject the Bible completely.

After the *Beagle*

The voyage of the *Beagle* ended October 2, 1836. Darwin soon began the process of studying the specimens he collected and pondering the observations he had made.

He was also considering spiritual things. In his autobiography, Darwin wrote, "During these two years [October 1836 to January 1839], I was led to think much about religion."[8] Unfortunately, this consideration did not lead in any way to a genuine understanding of Christianity or his need for salvation. This is obvious in his relationship to his new wife.

In January 1839, he married his first cousin, Emma. She was a very religious woman who was understandably concerned about the spiritual state of her husband. Although some have suggested that Darwin was at least a nominal Christian at that point, his own writings put that idea to rest with statements like "before I was engaged to be married, my father advised me to conceal carefully my doubts . . . some women suffered miserably by doubting about the salvation of their husbands."[9] If Darwin were saved, why would this even be an issue?

Death and Suffering

One of the most important issues in Darwin's life was his struggle with death and suffering. Perhaps it was this issue that tipped the scales for Darwin more than any other. It was a theme that he considered all his life. All around

---

6. Barlow, *The Autobiography of Charles Darwin, 1809–1882*, p. 71.
7. Ibid., p. 71.
8. Ibid., p. 71.
9. Ibid., p. 79.

him he saw death, disease, and struggle. And with all he saw, he doubted more and more that a caring God could exist. This is evident when Darwin said, "I cannot persuade myself that a beneficent and omnipotent God would have designedly created the *Ichneumonidae* with the express intention of their feeding within the living bodies of Caterpillars, or that a cat should play with mice."[10]

He further concluded, "This very old argument from the existence of suffering against the existence of an intelligent first cause seems to me a strong one; whereas, as just remarked, the presence of much suffering agrees well with the view that all organic beings have been developed through variation and natural selection."[11]

So if there is death and suffering, there cannot be a God that cares, he reasoned. Why would God create creatures to prey upon and kill each other? This was particularly brought home to him at the death of his daughter, Annie. She died at age ten after a brief illness. At the time, Darwin wrote, "Poor dear Annie . . . was taken with a vomiting attack, which at first thought of the smallest importance; but it rapidly assumed the form of a low and dreadful fever, which carried her off in 10 days. Thank God, she hardly suffered at all. . . . She was my favourite child. . . . Poor dear little soul."[12]

One can only imagine the grief he felt at the loss of his child. One of Darwin's major biographies states, "Annie's cruel death destroyed Charles's tatters of beliefs in a moral, just universe. Later he would say that this period chimed the final death-knell for his Christianity, St. Charles now took his stand as an unbeliever."[13]

While there is no case to be made that Darwin was in any way a Christian at that time, it is easy to understand how such an event could cause a "spiritual" person to give up his "spirituality."

Life and Faith

For much of his life, Darwin did consider issues of spirituality. Perhaps this was a result of his understanding of the logical outcome of the ideas he proposed. He did seem, at least at times, to struggle to reconcile the inconsistencies: "My theology is a simple muddle; I cannot look at the universe as the result of blind chance, yet I can see no evidence of beneficent design, or indeed of design of any kind, in the details."[14]

---

10. Francis Darwin, ed., *The Life and Letters of Charles Darwin*, Vol. II (New York: Appleton, 1897), p. 105.
11. Barlow, *The Autobiography of Charles Darwin, 1809–1882*, p. 75.
12. Darwin, *The Life and Letters of Charles Darwin*, Vol. I, p. 348.
13. Desmond and Moore, *Darwin*, p. 387.
14. Barlow, *The Autobiography of Charles Darwin, 1809–1882*, p. 130.

Further, he wrote, "When thus reflecting I feel compelled to look to a First Cause having an intelligent mind in some degree analogous to that of man; and I deserve to be called a Theist."

While he postulated ideas that would be a basis for an understanding of the world governed by natural processes alone, he acknowledged, for a time at least, a First Cause. This First Cause was needed to help explain the origin of life, but this "god" was detached and did not interact with man or man's affairs. This acknowledgement of even an impersonal "god" did not last.

Eventually, Darwin concluded, "The mystery of the beginning of all things is insoluble by us; and I for one must be content to remain an Agnostic."[15]

As he came to more completely realize the logical outcome of his materialist worldview, he apparently understood that his defense of the Bible while on board the *Beagle* was without basis. Those many years later he wrote, "A man who has no assured and ever present belief in the existence of a personal God or of a future existence with retribution and reward, can have for the rule of his life, as far as I can see, only to follow those impulses and instincts which are the strongest or which seem to him the best ones."[16]

As his life continued, whatever vestiges of genuine spirituality that may have existed gradually faded and died. That he never understood or accepted the basis tenets of Christianity was well described when he wrote, "I can indeed hardly see how anyone ought to wish Christianity to be true; for if so the plain language of the text seems to show that the men who do not believe, and this would include my Father, Brother and almost all my best friends, would be everlastingly punished. And this is a damnable doctrine."[17]

If Darwin ever even remotely considered that Christianity might be true, that idea was now dead. "I was very unwilling to give up my belief. . . . But I found it more and more difficult, with free scope given to my imagination, to invent evidence which would suffice to convince me. Thus disbelief crept over me at a very slow rate, but was at last complete."[18]

Did Darwin Become a Christian on His Deathbed?

One of the most popular misconceptions about Darwin is that he came to Christ on his deathbed. While it would be wonderful if it were true, unfortunately this is nothing but an urban legend.

---

15. Ibid., p. 78.
16. Ibid., p. 78.
17. Ibid., p. 72.
18. Ibid., p. 72.

Reports of Darwin having some sort of conversion experience began within weeks of his death. These began in England but before long at least one was reported from as far away as Canada. The most famous of them all came from a woman known as Lady Hope.

Lady Hope was born Elizabeth Reid Cotton and was the daughter of General Sir Arthur Cotton. She and her father were active evangelists in Kent, near the home of Charles Darwin. In 1877, she married Admiral Sir James Hope and thus became Lady Hope.

While attending a conference in Massachusetts in 1915, Lady Hope told of a visit that she had with Darwin some months before his death. According to her, Darwin had been bedridden for some months before he died. The report was that at the time of the visit she found Darwin sitting in bed. When she asked what he was reading, he was reported to say, "Hebrews . . . the Royal Book!" Additionally, Darwin supposedly commented, "I was a young man with unformed ideas."

Lady Hope further claimed that before her departure she was asked by Darwin to return and speak to his servants in his summerhouse. When asked about the subject on which she should speak, Darwin was said to have replied, "Christ Jesus!"

While it would be wonderful to report that this account of Darwin's conversion was true, there are just too many inconsistencies in the account. First, if Lady Hope did indeed visit Darwin, it would have been at least six months before his death. At this time Darwin was not bedridden, nor was he bedridden for an extended period of time before he died.

Second, this supposed conversion was never mentioned in any of Darwin's correspondence. Given that Darwin wrote extensively (totaling over 14,000 notes and letters), it is curious to suggest that if he did have a genuine conversion experience it was not mentioned at all in any of his writings.

Third, and most importantly, his family denied each and every report that Charles Darwin came to Christ. Certainly, a genuine conversion would be something to be celebrated and joyously shared with family and friends, especially for his wife. In 1915, Darwin's son Francis wrote, "He [Darwin] could not have become openly and enthusiastically Christian without the knowledge of his family, and no such change occurred."[19]

Also, if the story were credible, why did Lady Hope wait 33 years before relating it?

19. James Moore, *The Darwin Legend* (Grand Rapids: Baker Books, 1994), p. 144.

A close examination of this tale is fascinating because of what it does not claim. The actual report of Lady Hope's story does not say that Darwin actually renounced evolution; it merely says that Darwin speculated over the outcome of his ideas. Also, it was obviously not a deathbed meeting. It took place several months before Darwin died. Most telling is that Lady Hope never described Darwin actually professing faith in Christ. She simply reported that Darwin was reading the Bible. Even if true, this is a far cry from a saving knowledge of Jesus Christ.

So no matter how earnestly this tale is repeated in churches around the world, there is no truth to the "deathbed conversion" account.

In Conclusion

As much as we might wish it to be true, there is no evidence in the life of Charles Darwin that he was a Christian. Certainly, he struggled with spiritual issues, but that is not the same thing at all.

Many have tried to paint a picture that Darwin was a Christian, but because of circumstance or issues in his life walked away from the faith. Darwin's words themselves cause us to reject that position out of hand: "Although I did not think much about the existence of a personal God until a considerably later period of my life."[20]

There is no more personal God than Jesus Christ. If this was not a consideration for Darwin earlier in his life, then how could one even consider him to be a Christian during those years?

In a letter to F.A. McDermott dated November 24, 1880, Darwin wrote, "I am sorry to have to inform you that I do not believe in the Bible as divine revelation, & therefore not in Jesus Christ as the son of God."[21]

Charles Darwin rejected the Bible. Thus he had no basis to truly understand the world around him. He did not truly understand the geology of the world. Rejecting biblical creation, he could not answer the question of how life itself started. He never could reconcile the issue of a loving God amidst the death and suffering in the world.

Ultimately, he never acknowledged sin. He did not understand that the world is broken because of sin. Most importantly, he did not recognize that he was a sinner in need of a Savior.

Was Charles Darwin a Christian? The answer is no. More than anything else about his life, this is the tragedy. A soul lost for eternity, separated from God.

20. Barlow, *The Autobiography of Charles Darwin, 1809–1882*, p. 73.
21. Darwin Correspondence Project, letter 12851; www.darwinproject.ac.uk/entry-12851.

CHAPTER 7

Cavemen . . . Really?

DR. DAVID MENTON, DR. GEORGIA PURDOM, AND JOHN UPCHURCH

As far as stereotypes go, cavemen make easy targets — especially when transplanted into the 21st century. Their brutish way of dealing with contemporary situations earns a laugh on commercials and TV shows. They just don't understand us modern humans, and their misunderstanding strikes humor gold.

But when we cut away the laugh track and the bumbling ways, we're left with something of an enigmatic figure — a being without a settled place in our understanding of history. Perhaps, in fact, it's our discomfort with not knowing what to do with cavemen that makes us laugh. So just who were they?

Would the Real "Caveman" Please Stand Up?

Before we go spelunking, we need to limit our scope somewhat. At its most basic, the term *caveman* simply means "a person who dwells in a cave," which isn't unheard of even today. But that's rarely what we mean when we use the word. Instead, we're usually talking about a group of ancient cave hoppers who left behind animal artwork, rough-hewn weapons, and bones — at least, that's the common assumption. While the collective opinion of history and science has moved beyond considering these early humans as animal-like brutes, the term still carries with it the baggage of a being somewhat lesser than modern *Homo sapiens* (us today). And that's unfortunate — as we'll see.

Those early humans commonly classified as "cavemen" break down into several groups, scattered throughout Europe, the Middle East, Africa, and Asia. Calling these groups "cavemen" may, in fact, be somewhat misleading. Many of them simply found temporary shelter or buried their dead in caves, which tend to preserve remains and artifacts more often than houses in the open. (They probably preferred living in caves about as much as we do.)

Nevertheless, the term caveman is often used as a catch-all for peoples who lived in an earlier era in human history — the Ice Age. We'll focus on five of these groups: Neanderthals, early *Homo sapiens* (Cro-Magnon man), *Homo erectus*, Denisovans, and *Homo floresiensis*.[1] The first three have long been stalwarts of the caveman discussion, but the latter two have only recently been uncovered — the Denisovans in Siberia and *Homo floresiensis* (sometimes called hobbits) in Indonesia.[2]

Neanderthals

Neanderthals may be the most well-known of the five groups — with hundreds of individuals to study. After they served time as a separate "hominid" (human-like) species according to evolutionary scientists, DNA testing in particular has significantly trimmed their distance from *Homo sapiens*.[3] This shouldn't surprise us, considering the overwhelming evidence of their humanity.

In dozens of caves and rock shelters, for instance, we find evidence of bodies that have been carefully buried with all the care you might expect from a modern funeral.

---

1. The term *species* is a modern convention established by the creationist Carolus Linneaus. It traditionally refers to separate populations that are similar but can no longer produce viable offspring. But this is not the case of any humans. We need some sort of term to describe different peoples, such as Europeans or Parisians. But in this instance, some names are unfortunately scientific terms that imply "species," and there are no easily recognizable alternative names. So *Homo erectus* and early *Homo sapiens* are used in this article to describe our ancestors at certain times and places, but this is not a reference to their being different species.

2. There are some who try to take apes and lump them as humans. One needs to be discerning about such instances. Take for example *A. sediba*, which is *not* human. First let us consider just a few of the non-trivial differences between *Australopithecus sediba* and humans. *Australopithecus sediba* has a brain measuring between one-third and one-fourth the size of that of a typical human of comparable size (but well within the range of apes). A comparison of the skull of *Australopithecus sediba* with that of humans reveals that the lower face of *Australopithecus sediba* is sloped like that of apes. And, like apes, the forehead of *Australopithecus sediba* is flat, making the orbits of the eyes barely visible when viewed from the side. The mandible of *Australopithecus sediba* bears no close resemblance to that of man (or even a chimpanzee) but rather is more similar to that of a gorilla. The postcranial skeleton of *Australopithecus sediba* is also very ape-like. It has a small body with ape-like large-jointed upper and lower limbs. The arms and hands of *Australopithecus sediba* extend down to the knees, typical of long-armed knuckle walkers. In short, this is an ape, not a human, and not a caveman at all!

3. http://www.scientificamerican.com/article.cfm?id=ourneandertal-brethren.

Neanderthal remains have also been unearthed with mammoths and other big game bearing bone marks and other indicators that these animals were hunted and butchered in complex community activities. And everywhere Neanderthals are found (not always in caves), they have complex axes and other stone tools.

In fact, the title of "mere caveman" may be in jeopardy, as researchers recently unearthed a complex dwelling made from mammoth bones, which wasn't in a cave at all.[4] With all the similarities, however, Neanderthals weren't exactly like us — their physical characteristics (such as larger brows in adults and wide nasal cavities) would certainly make them stand out today.

Cro-Magnon Man

On the other hand, early *Homo sapiens* (often called Cro-Magnon man) would fit right in nowadays, though perhaps more likely on a North American football team than in an office building. The robust build, larger brain on average (1600cc vs. 1350cc), and DNA differentiate the European Cro-Magnon from modern humans.[5] However, they show a clear affinity with us.

Everything you might expect to find from the settlements of any non-industrialized people is found with Cro-Magnons. For instance, the Dzudzuana Cave in the country of Georgia contained wild flax fibers that suggest these early travelers sewed garments or wove baskets,[6] and the Lascaux caves in France long hid colorful cave paintings that may relate to phases of the moon.[7] Site after site reveals thousands of small, beautifully made javelins, arrows, and ornate artifacts, often with carvings and designs on them, such as the ivory pendant made from mammoth tusk that was found with the so-called "red lady" (actually a male) in south Wales.[8]

And the recent discovery of a buried dog's skull in Předmostí (Czech Republic) suggests that Cro-Magnon man enjoyed the company of "man's best friend."[9]

In light of these finds, the idea that these particular post-Babel humans were some mysterious "other" loses its punch.

---

4. http://www.physorg.com/news/2011-12-neanderthal-home-mammoth-bones-ukraine.html

5. David Caramelli et al., "A 28,000 Years Old Cro-Magnon mtDNA Sequence Differs from All Potentially Contaminating Modern Sequences," *PLoS One* 3 (2008): e2700.

6. Eliso Kvavadze et al., "30,000-Year-Old Wild Flax Fibers," *Science* 325 (2009): p. 1359.

7. http://news.bbc.co.uk/2/hi/science/nature/975360.stm.

8. http://www.britarch.ac.uk/ba/ba61/feat3.shtml.

9. Mietje Germonpré et al., "Palaeolithic Dog Skulls at the Gravettian Předmostí Site, the Czech Republic," *Journal of Archaeological Science* 39 (2012): p. 184–202.

Homo Erectus

That brings us to *Homo erectus*, a group that long held the title as most enigmatic and disputed of all early humans. As the name *erectus* implies, we're meant to be amazed at their upright, two-legged gait that allowed them to tromp across Africa, Europe, and Asia. However, the *Homo appellation* (that is, human) came later. When these ancient humans were first uncovered in Java (Indonesia), their bones were trumpeted as *Pithecanthropus erectus*, which essentially means "upright ape-man." That was certainly a misnomer.

What's truly incredible is how widespread these early humans were. They may have built fires in the Middle East (as indicated by charred bones and plant remains),[10] and they hunted across Asia and Europe, where we find many butcher sites and the stone tools they used. They must have built seafaring vessels of some sort to reach the Indonesian islands against the currents. In fact, we find their fossils before any other human remains. So we can safely say that their "primitive" ways got them pretty far. Not bad for a carless society.

Homo Floresiensis and Denisovans

Two new finds suggest that we may only be scratching the surface of the variety apparent in post-Babel humans. Recently, an unusually large tooth and a finger bone found in Denisova Cave in Altai Krai, Russia, point to a mysterious new group of wayfarers. The Denisovans, as they're being called, occupied the region around the same time as Neanderthals.

But DNA testing of the finger and two other bones indicates that this new group differed from Neanderthals.[11] Beyond that, we have only a handful of artifacts to understand these mysterious people, such as a stone bracelet that was ground and polished.

But the impact of the Denisovans has been relatively minor compared to the huge debate surrounding a group of tiny human skeletons. So far, nine members of this group have been found on the Indonesian island of Flores, giving us the tentative name *Homo floresiensis*. However, you may have heard them referred to as "hobbits," which fits their three-foot (1 m) height.

Since the discovery of the first non- fossilized skeleton in 2003, dueling scientific papers have raised, lowered, and stretched the status of these so-called hobbits — all without a single strand of DNA (which has so far eluded

10. http://www.answersingenesis.org/articles/am/v6/n1/camp-after-babel.
11. Pontus Skoglunda and Mattias Jakobssona, "Archaic Human Ancestry in East Asia," *PNAS* 108 (2011): p. 18301–18306.

scientists). Because access to the remains is so limited, the intrigue — and rancor — may continue for years.

Despite the debate, what's found in the dirt on Flores reveals much about the inhabitants. Numerous charred bones of the dwarf elephant Stegodon — many of them juvenile — paint the picture of a group of opportunistic hunters who roasted up the small elephant that once lived on the island — perhaps leading to its extinction.

To do so, they employed a number of advanced stone tools, quite capable of slicing and dicing tough animal skin. And while we find no evidence of their boats, these people are most similar to *Homo erectus* found on Java. Since they lived on the island of Flores, this suggests they must have built boats that could fight against strong ocean currents to get there.

The Makings of a Human

Variation among post-Babel humans has led to a great debate among evolutionists, who wonder where they fit on the roadway to being "truly human." But that way of thinking misses the fundamental truth. When God created humans, He didn't define our humanness in terms of physical characteristics. We aren't human because we have two arms or legs or skulls of a certain shape or size. Our Creator, who is spirit, made us in His spiritual image.

Genesis reveals aspects of what this implies. Our early ancestors made musical instruments and tools, farmed, built cities, and otherwise represented God as stewards of His creation (Genesis 4). With that as our standard, we can cut through the confusion and bias. All those we call "cavemen" (probably a misnomer) show the same characteristics as the first humans in the Bible.

Neanderthals buried their dead and may have worn jewelry.[12] *Homo erectus* seems to have divvied up jobs to prepare food and sailed the high seas. Even with little to go on, we can be fairly certain the Denisovans wore jewelry, and the much-maligned "hobbits" left tools useful for dicing up lunch. All uniquely human traits — traits that show creatures made in the image of God.

In other words, we can be sure that they all descended from Adam through Noah's family. These certainly aren't unique species, in the sense of being something "less than modern humans" — they're just more evidence of beautiful variations in the appearance of individuals in our one unique race. Our relatives may have looked different, but they weren't bumbling brutes. They had

---

12. http://www.answersingenesis.org/articles/aid/v2/n1/worthy-ancestors-2.

the very human and God-given ability to discover creative solutions in a dangerous, sin-cursed world. And they were all rebels from God, in need of His grace.

Finding a Home for Cavemen

New DNA technology has allowed scientists to peer into the past by mapping the DNA of so-called cavemen. And they have found some noticeable differences. So, what do those differences really mean — are those early people somehow less "human" than we are?

Before we can answer that question, we first need to understand two related issues. What can DNA tell us about the differences among people? And how does the biblical account of human origins shed light on these differences?

Cavemen Genetics

The ability to map DNA is an amazing feat, considering the DNA is thousands of years old! Many ancient human remains are found in equatorial regions where heat and humidity have destroyed the DNA. However, remains of the Neanderthals and another group of humans discovered in a cave in southern Siberia, the Denisovans, have been found in cold, dry, protected areas that better preserved the DNA.

When the first draft of Neanderthal DNA was published, the researchers concluded that it is 99.7 percent identical to modern human DNA. They also found that approximately 1 to 4 percent of DNA specific to Neanderthals can also be found in modern Eurasians. This led them to conclude that a very small number of Neanderthals mixed with early modern humans and produced children. Neanderthals had a wide geographic distribution in Eurasia, from Spain to southern Siberia, and from Germany to the Middle East, so it is not surprising that more of their DNA is found in modern Eurasians as opposed to other populations, such as Africans.[13]

To date, approximately 80 genes have been shown to differ between Neanderthals and modern humans.[14] These genes produce proteins that govern a wide range of functions such as metabolism (how we burn food), the growth of the skull, and skin shade. Further study of these genes may help us understand how Neanderthals were different and perhaps why they died out.

13. Richard E. Green et al., "A Draft Sequence of the Neandertal Genome," *Science* 328 (2010): p. 710–722.
14. Carles Lalueza-Fox and M. Thomas P. Gilbert, "Paleogenomics of Archaic Hominins," *Current Biology* 21 (2011): R1002– R1009.

For instance, one gene produces a protein involved in skin and hair color. Rare variants of this gene among modern humans lead to pale skin and red hair. The Neanderthal gene has a variation so far unknown in humans today. It is likely that this variant led to pale skin and red hair in Neanderthals.[15] If this is so, Neanderthals would have been able to absorb more sunlight than if they had darker skin. This would have been useful in producing enough vitamin D to live healthy lives in the northern regions.

Denisovan DNA is also similar to DNA in modern humans. Approximately 4 to 6 percent of DNA that is specific to Denisovans can also be found in modern Melanesians (those who live in the islands northeast of Australia).[16] As with the Neanderthals, this indicates that very few Denisovans mixed with and produced offspring with early modern humans — at least with those in Southeast Asia.[17]

Both Neanderthals and Denisovans do have small-scale differences with modern humans. Before the first draft of Neanderthal DNA, they were sometimes considered to be different human species or subspecies. But this is an arbitrary, man-made designation since two modern chimps of the same species will have more DNA variation than Neanderthals or Denisovans have to modern humans. In light of the genetic evidence, Neanderthals and Denisovans are fully human and should be classified as *Homo sapiens.*

Are the DNA Sequences Accurate?

Many difficulties must be overcome to accurately sequence ancient DNA. Sequencing DNA involves determining the correct order of the individual components (bases) that comprise the DNA. Contamination and degradation are two of the biggest obstacles.[18] Contamination comes both from bacteria found in the fossil (which can sometimes account for more than 90 percent of the DNA found!) and from bacteria transferred through handling by modern humans. Degradation occurs when the DNA is "chopped up" and certain DNA components are modified by chemical reactions. Fortunately, scientists have developed techniques that greatly limit the danger of contamination and degradation altering the actual human DNA sequence, so their impact is usually negligible.

---

15. Carles Lalueza-Fox, et al., "A Melanocortin 1 Receptor Allele Suggests Varying Pigmentation among Neanderthals," *Science* 318 (2007): p. 1453–1455.
16. David Reich et al., "Genetic History of an Archaic Hominin Group from Denisova Cave in Siberia," *Nature* 468 (2010): p. 1053–1060.
17. David Reich, et al., "Denisova Admixture and the First Modern Human Dispersals into Southeast Asia and Oceania," *The American Journal of Human Genetics* 89 (2011): p. 1–13.
18. Dan Criswell, "Neandertal DNA and Modern Humans," *Creation Research Society Quarterly* 45 (2009): p. 246–254.

Another issue involves the limited number of ancient individuals with viable DNA. For example, there are only two known fossil remains for Denisovans from a single cave. At the most, they represent two individuals. Compare that to the thousands of modern humans whose DNA has been sequenced. A small sampling of an ancient population may not truly reflect the full range of variety in that particular group.

The Neanderthal samples, in contrast, come from over a dozen different individuals at sites on different continents, so they are much more likely to represent the population as a whole. It is also important to acknowledge the many evolutionary assumptions that are made when comparing the DNA sequence of ancient individuals to modern humans.[19] For example, a common human-chimp ancestor was assumed. One paper stated, "To estimate the DNA sequence divergence . . . between the genomes of Neanderthals and the reference human genome sequence . . . [we used] an inferred genome sequence of the common ancestor of humans and chimpanzees as a reference to avoid potential biases."[20] Apparently the authors of the paper don't consider assumed human-chimp ancestry as a bias, but it is! Creation scientists are actively studying methods to avoid these biases so that more valid comparisons can be made.

A Biblical Perspective

Researchers studying genetics have clearly established that Neanderthals and Denisovans were fully human. Any physical differences should be viewed as nothing more than variations that can occur within the human race descended from Adam and Eve. For a time, these descendants all lived together at the Tower of Babel. Following the post-Babel migration and late into the Ice Age, differing human populations began to appear in the fossil record, such as Neanderthals and Denisovans.

The next questions for creationists are how and why these differences appeared.[21] How is much easier to answer than why! One possibility is that

---

19. As creation scientists have shown, bias can affect the reported similarities and differences in the DNA sequences between organisms. See Jeffrey P. Tompkins, "Genome-wide DNA alignment similarity (identity) for 40,000 chimpanzee DNA sequences queried against the human genome is 86–89%," *Answers Research Journal* 4 (2011): p. 233–241.
20. Richard E. Green et al., "A Draft Sequence of the Neandertal Genome," *Science* 328 (2010): p. 710–722.
21. Robert W. Carter, "The Neandertal Mitochondrial Genome Does Not Support Evolution," *Journal of Creation* 23 (2009): p. 40–43; Kurt P. Wise, "The Flores Skeleton and Human Baraminology," *Occasional Papers of the BSG* 6 (2005): p. 1–13; Robert W. Carter, "Neandertal Genome Like Ours," June 1, 2010, http://creation.com/neandertal-genome-like-ours.

environmental pressures, such as the Ice Age, "selected" for or against traits within the range of human genetic diversity. (In other words, those that had a particular combination of characteristics survived in that environment, and others did not.) This may have led to the specific set of features found in Neanderthal people. Many animals, following the Flood and during the Ice Age, experienced an explosion of variations that allowed them to live and function well in new environments. This could also have been true for humans.

Other possibilities include genetic effects seen mainly in small populations. Small populations would have been typical for a period of time following the breakup of the human population at Babel, as people were separated based on language. The groups that left Babel would have begun with only a few reproducing individuals and not interbred initially with other groups.

A phenomenon known as genetic drift can cause certain genetic variations to become "fixed." If the population is small, everyone with certain variations can die, without passing them down, and the survivors pass down just one variation to future generations. If no people are moving in or out of the population, characteristics like the pronounced brow ridge or the robust body form in Neanderthals can become dominant.

Another possible impact of the Babel breakup is the founder effect. The founders of each group leaving Babel might simply have differed from one another. Certain traits in one group might have been unknown among the founders of any other group. Those traits would then be unique to each group. Rather than being fixed by genetic drift, the Neanderthals' pronounced brow ridge or robust body form may have been found among the founders of only one group after they left Babel. Those people may have migrated intentionally to places where they were most comfortable (similar to human behavior today).

As time passed, the different groups would have migrated, as humans have always done. People who had the traits of modern humans possibly interbred, at times, with the other groups, such as Neanderthals and Denisovans. Yet there seems to have been a sudden loss, or a dilution, of the characteristics possessed by those other groups. The genetic makeup of modern humans became dominant.

Inbreeding can have disastrous effects on small populations by amplifying defective genes. Maybe this is why Neanderthals and Denisovans eventually became extinct. We don't know. Why this happened is still a mystery.

Conclusion

Caves have never gone out of fashion as a place to seek refuge. For instance, hermits lived in caves throughout the Middle Ages, and until recent times a clan of people were living in caves on the Mediterranean island of Malta. Even the Bible records a number of cave refugees, such as Elijah (1 Kings 19), David (1 Samuel 22:1), and Obadiah (1 Kings 18:3–4). After fleeing the destruction of Sodom and Gomorrah, Lot and his daughters found shelter in a cave (Genesis 19:30).

It seems cavemen are simply that — people who lived in caves and they have little, if anything, to do with evolution. What is not a mystery is that so-called cavemen, including Neanderthals and Denisovans, were fully human. They were among the descendants of the people scattered at the Tower of Babel — made in God's image to bring Him glory.

CHAPTER 8

Should There Really Be a Battle between Science and the Bible?

ROGER PATTERSON

There is much debate in our culture about the nature of science and religion and the interaction of the two. Some will argue that the two areas give us understanding in distinct ways that do not overlap.[1] Others suggest that science should drive our understanding of religion. Still others argue that religion should drive our scientific understanding. There are truly deep divisions in many senses as people claim different sources of authority on these issues.

But there are many contrasting ideas that are presented in the popular discussions of this topic that need to be carefully considered. Words have meanings, and we need to make sure that we are using our own words in a manner that is clear and does not hide or change the meaning of certain terms and concepts. We all recognize when a politician talks out of both sides of his mouth, but it can be a little harder to spot when we see religious leaders and scientists

---

1. The idea of "non-overlapping magisteria" was promoted by the late Dr. Stephen Jay Gould and proposes that science cannot answer the questions of religion, and vice versa. This forces a false dichotomy between secular and sacred, a concept that is foreign to the Bible. Christians are called to take every thought captive to the obedience of Christ (2 Corinthians 10:5), not to compartmentalize their thinking and actions into secular and sacred.

talking in the same manner.[2] While we can learn from those who have studied various ideas, we need to be careful not to accept those ideas just because some scientist, religious leader, or news analyst says something is so.

Everyone has a point he or she is trying to make! Many people will try to tell you that they do not have such biases, but it is impossible to be neutral: our thinking always begins from a specific starting point. All of the arguments that we make are based in our worldview, and our worldview is based on specific assumptions we believe to be true. The goal of this chapter is to explore some of those underlying assumptions and their implications for the arguments that are often used in the broad creation-evolution debate.

Where Did Science Come From?

What we understand today as the modern scientific method and the technologies and theories it produces has its foundations in beliefs about the nature of the universe and the God who created the universe. The scientific method is grounded in the ideas of repeatability, falsifiability, and testability. Each of these ideas assumes that there is a uniformity to the world that we live in. (This will be discussed in more detail below.) But on what grounds can we assume that the world should operate in a uniform way? Only on the grounds that God has created the universe to function according to specific laws.

Modern science blossomed in the fertile soils of Western culture where God was known as the Creator and Lawgiver of the universe. While some mathematical and technological concepts were known in the millennia prior to this time, rigorous experimentation and careful correlation of cause and effect became the focus of the discipline known then as natural philosophy. During the Middle Ages, there was much advancement in the study of nature, though it is often denigrated as a time of little advancement in the development of new ideas. These advances primarily came in the monasteries and universities that were funded and directed by the Roman Catholic Church. Surely, much of this thinking was misguided and has been corrected, but it was the notion of a Creator God who arranged an orderly universe that directed and encouraged the study of natural philosophy. It would be anachronistic to refer to these studies

---

2. The logical fallacy of equivocation occurs when a word is used to express an idea, but the meaning of the word changes within the argument. Similarly, the logical fallacy of special pleading is using or defining words in a way that is beneficial to the argument and not necessarily agreed upon by others. Both of these tactics are used by those arguing over the roles of religion and science. As Christians and ambassadors for Christ, we must be careful to avoid these invalid forms of argumentation because they reflect poorly on our King.

as scientific, but the foundation of scientific thinking was laid in these early centuries in the West.

And this perspective is not simply biblical creationist propaganda used to prop up a particular point of view. Dr. James Hannam, historian and physicist, writes in the conclusion to his *The Genesis of Science*:

> The starting point for all natural philosophy in the Middle Ages was that nature had been created by God. This made it a legitimate area of study because through nature man could learn about its creator. Medieval scholars thought that nature followed the rules that God had ordained for it. Because God was consistent and not capricious, these natural laws were constant and worth scrutinizing. However, these scholars rejected Aristotle's contention that the laws of nature were bound by necessity. God was not constrained by what Aristotle thought. The only way to find out which laws God had decided on was by the use of experience and observation. The motivations and justifications of medieval natural philosophers were carried over almost unchanged by the pioneers of modern science.[3]

Demonstrating that he is not interested in propping up the Bible or the existence of the Creator as truth, Hannam goes on to quote Sir Isaac Newton's insistence on God's existence to corroborate the diversity of life on earth, but states that Darwin later proved Newton wrong in this area.

"But wait, what about the Chinese in the East! They invented gunpowder!" you might protest. Developing gunpowder is one thing, but deciphering the underlying mechanics that explains how the gunpowder formed and why it explodes, even predicting how it will react with other chemicals, is an entirely different type of thinking. While a defense of this perspective is beyond the scope of this chapter, several authors have discussed this theme at length and proposed very plausible explanations for why scientific thinking and methodology did not develop in stable and flourishing cultures like China, India, and Egypt despite the talents and resources available to them.[4] Scientific thinking

---

3. James Hannam, *The Genesis of Science: How the Christian Middle Ages Launched the Scientific Revolution* (Washington, DC: Regnery Publishing Inc., 2011), p. 348–349.

4. For a condensed version of these theories, see Eric V. Snow, "Christianity: A Cause of Modern Science?" Institute for Creation Research, http://www.icr.org/article/427/290. For more thorough treatments of these ideas, several books have been written, though the authors are not all approaching the topic from a Christian or biblical presupposition: Nancy R. Pearcey and Charles B. Thaxton, *The Soul of Science: Christian Faith and Natural Philosophy* (Wheaton, IL: Crossway, 1994); Stanley L. Jaki, *Science and Creation*

cannot thrive in cultures where superstitions about capricious gods acting on whims influence daily events. It is only the biblical view of the nature of God and His creation that allows for the expectation of reliably discovering the underlying truths of the operation of the universe created by God. And it is only the biblical worldview that calls for a study of the creation to better understand the Creator and to properly rule the creation (Genesis 1:28) to find cures for disease, produce technology, increase food production, etc., for the good of mankind.

With that foundation, let us turn to some of the common contrasting ideas that are used to frame the discussion and examine them one at a time.

Science vs. Science

It is the very nature of language that the meanings of words change. If I had told you in 1947 that I found my missing mouse in my briefcase, you would have had a different reaction than you would today. The same is true for the word *science*. In its simplest form, science means knowledge. Examining the 1828 definition of science from Noah Webster:

> In *a general sense*, knowledge, or certain knowledge; the comprehension or understanding of truth or facts by the mind. The *science* of God must be perfect.[5]

In a general sense, science means knowledge. Interestingly, the first definition in the modern Merriam-Webster Collegiate Dictionary (2003) is not that much different:

> the state of knowing : knowledge as distinguished from ignorance or misunderstanding[6]

In another sense, science is the systematic study of a subject and the knowledge that is generated by that study. In the past, theology was known as the queen of the sciences (as was mathematics) and the supernatural origins of the universe and the creatures[7] on the planet were assumed to be true because they are revealed in Scripture. Today, many have hijacked science, insisting that it

---

(Edinburgh, Scotland: Scottish Academic Press, 1986); James Hannam, *The Genesis of Science: How the Christian Middle Ages Launched the Scientific Revolution* (Washington, DC: Regnery Publishing Inc., 2011).

5. *American Dictionary of the English Language*, 9th ed., s.v. "Science."
6. *Merriam-Webster's Collegiate Dictionary*, 11th ed., s.v. "Science."
7. Even the term *creature* naturally implies that there was a Creator who made it.

can only be done within an atheistic frame of reference (or worldview), thus completely removing God from our thinking about the physical world.

It is possible to categorize science into many different categories. Classically, the pure sciences were distinguished from the applied sciences. For an example, as we studied the pure science of how x-rays interact with matter, we were able to apply that knowledge to taking pictures of the bones inside the body. Christians understand this x-ray phenomenon as an extension of the natural laws God has programmed into the universe and employ this knowledge to exercise dominion over the earth (Genesis 1:26–28) and to reverse some of the effects of the Curse (Genesis 3) that our sin brought into the world. They do this by finding cures for disease or developing new technology. Those who hold a naturalistic worldview believe that this phenomenon is just the product of some random events culminating in some beams of radiation that can shoot through some matter and not others. All of this involves testing, observing, and repeating experiments in the present to apply that knowledge in the present.

Another important distinction to make is between operational science and historical science. Operational science employs the pure and applied methods of scientific inquiry to figure out how physical things operate or function to find cures for disease, develop new technology, or otherwise improve our standard of living. In this kind of science, researchers use observable, repeatable experiments to test hypotheses and develop our understanding of the world. Most of chemistry, physics, astronomy, biology, engineering, and medical research are in the realm of operational or experimental science. These types of things can be observed and tested by different individuals with repeatability and can be falsified if contrary evidence comes to light.

Historical science deals with questions of history and origins, such as how the Grand Canyon formed or how living creatures came into existence. Paleontology, archeology, cosmogony, much of geology, and forensics (criminal investigation) fall in the realm of historical or origin science. It looks at evidence in the present to try to figure out what happened in the unobservable, unrepeatable past to produce the evidence that we see, though there is no opportunity to repeat the initial conditions and observe their outcome. There is much conjecture involved in historical science because scientists have to make assumptions about the past. Those assumptions may or may not be correct and, in many cases, may not even be verifiable. So we must take care to understand the limits of this approach. To be clear, both creationists and evolutionists engage in historical science, but biblical creationists look to the authority of the Bible to inform their understanding of the past because it contains the eyewitness testimony of the Creator about key events in the past that explain the world we live it. But in a naturalistic (atheistic), evolutionary viewpoint, there is no eyewitness of the imagined events of millions of years ago and thus no objective standards to judge the validity of the evolutionary stories. The past cause or sequence of events that produced what we see in the present must be inferred by assuming that present processes have always operated in the same way or at the same rate as we observe today.

While operational science surely involves some levels of inference, when we move into the category of historical science, the level of inference increases greatly. Biological, geological, and cosmological evolution are all based on chains of assumptions and inferences that cannot be observed, tested, or repeated. An inference based on an inference based on an inference leaves a very weak chain.

One example of this chain of assumptions comes in the materialistic view of the age of the earth. First, the assumptions of radiometric dating must be accepted. Then, rather than dating rocks that are from earth, meteorites that are found on the earth are dated. This assumes that these meteorites formed at the same time as the earth, so they will be the same age as the earth. This then assumes that the earth formed from a cloud of dust that encircled the young, forming sun, a process known as the nebular hypothesis, and the particles collected into the earth with fragments left floating in space and later falling to earth as meteorites. The nebular hypothesis assumes that the big bang is true. This is a long chain of assumptions with no directly observed evidence. From a biblical perspective, none of this is consistent with the creation account of Genesis, the eyewitness testimony to the events of creation.

Many people try to discredit biblical creationists and say they can't be real scientists if they don't believe in evolution. However, this is a silly argument. Many will say that it is hypocritical for a biblical creationist to talk on a cell phone and take antibiotics, yet reject the "truths" of the big bang and biological evolution. But what does the big bang have to do with designing a cell phone? And what does the acceptance of a fish changing into a frog over millions of years have to do with testing bacteria in a petri dish to see what chemicals kill the bacteria? To make such claims is to confuse categories of science and appeals to the emotions by getting people to fear that technology cannot advance if people look at the world through the lens of Scripture. Knowing that many of the founders of scientific disciplines were Bible-believing scientists should give those using these scare tactics pause, but they continue to make such claims in the face of many biblical creationists carrying out scientific research and advancing our understanding of the world that God has created.

Uniformity vs. Uniformitarianism

As mentioned earlier, because God has created the universe, it follows that certain natural laws were put into place by Him. He has chosen the laws that determine how the planets orbit the sun, how water molecules form and stick to one another, how electricity travels through wires, and every other conceivable interaction of matter and energy in the universe . . . not to mention the spiritual elements of the universe. God has created a universe that operates in uniform ways, and as we study the creation we are uncovering the ways that He has ordered the universe to function or operate. Isaac Newton did not invent the laws of gravity; he simply described the way God had ordained for the universe to function. He was able to do this because God had created an orderly universe in the first place.

We see the principle of uniformity present in the early chapters of Genesis where God created the various kinds of plants and animals to reproduce after their kind. More explicitly, Genesis 8:22 communicates God's intention to uphold the earth in a way that is consistent. Connecting this to passages like Hebrews 1:3 and Colossians 1:17 provides a solid foundation for understanding why the universe is the way it is.[8]

Someone who rejects the Bible can believe that there is uniformity in the universe, but he has no reason to believe that the universe should be a place of order. He is making an arbitrary assumption about the universe with no reasoning to support that assumption. Extending that assumption, many believe in the doctrine of uniformitarianism. This doctrine is often summarized in the phrase "the present is the key to the past." As an example, the doctrine of uniformitarianism is often applied to the layers of rocks we find under our feet. We can observe the rate at which layers are forming today. If we assume that the rates we see today are the same as they were in the past, we can just look backward and see how long it took for all of the layers to form, right?

Well, the Bible makes clear that there was a global Flood that covered the entire surface of the earth about 4,350 years ago. If that is true, then that would have a major effect on the surface of the earth — the present would be dramatically different from the past. While the laws of nature were in effect during the Flood — uniformity of nature — the rates of the layers being deposited would have been dramatically different because the magnitude and duration of that

---

8. For a more thorough treatment of the assumptions of uniformitarianism and the illogical nature of a naturalistic, atheistic worldview, see Jason Lisle, *The Ultimate Proof of Creation* (Green Forest, Arkansas: Master Books, 2009).

catastrophic Flood far exceeded the scale of any floods, earthquakes, hurricanes, and tsunamis we observe today. The present is not the key to understanding the past. Rather, the Bible is the key to understanding both the past and the present because it gives us the key events in history to understand both!

Faith vs. Fact

Many people have bought into the myth of neutrality — the idea that people can examine ideas in a truly neutral manner. Everyone has a bias, and everyone starts their reasoning from their foundational worldview. Many people claim that those who have a naturalistic, atheistic scientific worldview, what is also called philosophical naturalism, are neutral and approach their study of the world (its operation and its history and origin) in a totally objective way. But stop and think about that . . . if you believe that there can be no supernatural influences in the world, you are biased against the supernatural.

The question becomes, which bias is the best bias to be biased by? Put another way, which worldview provides the true foundation for examining the world we live in? Every person takes these starting assumptions on faith. Faith is inescapable when we examine the world around us, regardless of whether we are Christian, Muslim, Jewish, agnostic, atheist, or whatever.

If we start from a biblical definition, faith is believing things that we have not seen or, by extension, experienced (Hebrews 11:1). "By faith we understand that the worlds were framed by the word of God, so that the things which are seen were not made of things which are visible" (Hebrews 11:3). Christians trust that God created the universe out of nothing because He has told us that He did, not because we have seen or experienced the origin of the universe. This is taken on faith in light of the truths of Scripture, which is the absolutely truthful eyewitness history from the eternal Creator. A Christian's faith does not stand isolated from evidence but is affirmed by examining evidence in light of the truths of the Bible.

On the contrary, those who believe that the big bang was the origination of the universe do so with a faith that rests on many assumptions rather than the infallible Word of God. They take on faith that which they have not seen. Despite the claim that we can "see" the beginning of the universe in the cosmic microwave background radiation and other features of the universe, that belief is based on assumptions about those observations and should rightly be called positions of faith — a faith based in naturalism rather than the testimony of our Creator God.

Likewise, the formation of the solar system by the nebular hypothesis is taken on faith. The supposed steps in the process have never been observed, but only inferred. Moving forward, the chance origin of life from non-living matter is another point that the naturalistic scientist can only hold to by faith. "It must have happened," they say, "since we are here." Within that context, the origin of the information coded in the DNA of every living organism must be taken on faith since there is no known natural mechanism that can explain its origin. Continuing on in the chain of assumptions, the evolution of one kind of organism into another different kind of organism (e.g., a reptile into a bird or mammal) must be taken on faith since it has never been observed, but is only inferred from interpreting the fossils and comparisons of biochemical molecules.

It takes a lot of faith[9] to believe in the naturalistic origins of the universe, our planet, and all of the life on it.

In many contexts, the big bang, geologic evolution, and biological evolution are referred to as scientific facts, though these are only "facts" in some redefinition of the word (special pleading). In *Science, Evolution, and Creationism*, produced in 2008 by the National Academy of Sciences Institute of Medicine, there is a page dedicated to the question of whether evolution is a theory or a fact. In the conclusion to that discussion, they state:

> In science, a "fact" typically refers to an observation, measurement, or other form of evidence that can be expected to occur the same way under similar circumstances. However, scientists also use the term "fact" to refer to a scientific explanation that has been tested so many times that there is no longer a compelling reason to keep testing it or looking for additional examples. In that respect, the past and continuing occurrence of evolution is a scientific fact. Because the evidence supporting it is so strong, scientists no longer question whether biological evolution has occurred and is continuing to occur. Instead, they investigate the mechanisms of evolution, how rapidly evolution can take place, and related questions.[10]

So, in the minds of those who believe evolution is a fact, it is a fact. Within that paragraph, we also see the subtle assertion that "scientists" no longer even question evolution. So if you question evolution, you must not be a scientist.

9. Dr. David Menton has suggested that a better term would be *credulity*, since there is no foundation for the naturalistic worldview apart from the opinions of man. The biblical position is one of faith because it is founded in the truth revealed in Scripture. However, credulity is not a word most would understand and should be reserved for the right context.

10. Francisco J. Ayala et al., *Science, Evolution, and Creationism* (Washington, DC: National Academies Press, 2008), p. 11.

This is known as the "no true Scotsman" fallacy and is simply an approach used to defame those who question or reject evolution. In fact, I have many colleagues who have earned PhDs in various scientific fields who reject evolution, so that assertion is patently false.

If you ever hear someone say, "Science says such and such," a flag should go up in your mind. Used in an argument, this is called the reification fallacy; giving personal qualities to an abstract idea. Science can't say anything, but the scientists can. Related to this idea is the use of the term "data." When you read that "the data all points to conclusion X," you should again take pause. Rather than the data (the actual observations from experimentation or measurements of a geological formation or of light from a star or galaxy) these are likely interpretations of the data. The data from the observations are facts and are the same for everyone (creationist or evolutionist), but data may not include all the relevant observations that could be made and also must always be interpreted to arrive at conclusions. In order to interpret the data, we will always apply our worldview to present an explanation that makes sense of the data. Neither science nor the data can ever truly tell us anything. Facts are always interpreted in light of faith (our unprovable worldview assumptions).

Science vs. Religion

To be very clear, there is no conflict between evolution and religion — the conflict arises between evolution and biblical Christianity. In fact, many people have made evolution a fundamental tenet of their religion. For example, Hinduism, Buddhism, animistic religions of all sorts, liberal theology, and other expressions of Christianity that do not hold to Scripture as the supremely authoritative, inerrant Word of God are perfectly compatible with evolution and millions of years. Those who call themselves humanists and look to the Humanist Manifesto III as a document with guiding principles also embrace naturalism and unguided evolutionary processes. In that document we find the following statements about how humanists understand the world we live in and how life evolved:

> Knowledge of the world is derived by observation, experimentation, and rational analysis. Humanists find that science is the best method for determining this knowledge as well as for solving problems and developing beneficial technologies. We also recognize the value of new departures in thought, the arts, and inner experience — each subject to analysis by critical intelligence.

Humans are an integral part of nature, the result of unguided evolutionary change. Humanists recognize nature as self-existing. We accept our life as all and enough, distinguishing things as they are from things as we might wish or imagine them to be. We welcome the challenges of the future, and are drawn to and undaunted by the yet to be known.[11]

The modern Merriam-Webster's dictionary defines religion in several forms, including:

a cause, principle, or system of beliefs held to with ardor and faith[12]

While the humanist might argue that they do not hold to these views on faith, they have no other foundation upon which to build their case. How do they know that knowledge can only come through "observation, experimentation, and rational analysis"? What experiment can be done to show that this is true? If they say they know that by rationally analyzing what they have observed, they have worked themselves into a vicious circle of thought that must be accepted by faith — the very thing they try to denounce.

In many cases, the people who are making this comparison are seeking to exclude the teaching of biblical creation from the public school classroom and other settings, believing religious views should be censored from the science classroom. However, they fail to recognize that evolution is a religious tenet of the religion of humanism and that they are forcing their own religious views into the classrooms and publicly funded museums that exclude a biblical view of the world we live in. Rather than excluding religion from the classroom, Christianity has been replaced by the religious teachings of secular humanism (which is really the religion of atheism).

The issue is not science vs. religion, but one religious view set against another. The Bible offers us an authoritative source of truth from which to begin our study of the universe. It is the only rational faith that can even explain the existence of scientific thought in the first place.[13]

Conclusion

Regardless of which of the ways the conflict is presented, Christians must always look to the Bible as the supreme source of truth and authority in every

11. American Humanist Association, "Humanist Manifesto III," http://www.americanhumanist.org/Humanism/Humanist_Manifesto_III.
12. *Merriam-Webster's Collegiate Dictionary*, 11th ed., s.v. "Religion."
13. Jason Lisle, "Evolution: The Anti-science," Answers in Genesis, http://www.answersingenesis.org/articles/aid/v3/n1/evolution-anti-science.

area. We must also call those who do not believe to look to the Creator as the truth and help them to see that we can only ultimately make sense of the world around us by starting with the truths God has revealed in the Bible.

While some people try to suggest that the facts of nature speak for themselves, a rock does not tell you how old it is — the age of the rock is an interpretation. You must make several assumptions in order to arrive at the supposed 4.5-billion-year age of the earth, including the assumptions of uniformitarianism. These assumptions are in direct conflict with the clear teaching of Scripture and deny a global Flood and the special creation of the universe only about 6,000 years ago.

Unlike rocks and fossils, the Bible does offer clear propositions and descriptions of the past. We must read the Bible much differently than we read the "book" of nature. We can only understand what nature reveals when we understand that the world we are living in has been cursed by God as a result of man's sin. We must also take into account the effects of other events like the Flood and the Tower of Babel. Ignoring these truths will naturally lead to faulty conclusions about the history of the earth and all the life on it.

Scientific thinking was born in the cradle of Christian Europe because the men who believed in the true Creator God believed they could understand the world He had created. They believed they could understand the creation because they knew God was a God of order. They believed He was a God of order because that is what the Bible clearly reveals. We must surely acknowledge that we would not have the scientific understanding that we have today apart from what God has revealed to us in the Bible. We would be fools to set aside the Bible as we continue to pursue a deeper understanding of what we see as we peer through our microscopes and telescopes or look with unaided eyes to examine God's creation.

But that is exactly what many scientists are trying to do. Having stood on the shoulders of men who trusted in God's revelation, they have denied the need for God to continue their study. It would be just as foolish for a man who has flown to the moon on a rocket to deny the rocket that took him there, claiming that he can return to earth on his own without the rocket. Sadly, he will perish there on the moon without acknowledging his need for the rocket for his safe return to earth.

Likewise, those who deny the God of the Bible as the foundation for understanding the world we live in do so at their own peril. God has created the universe, this world that we live in, and each one of us. Through the first man God created, Adam, all have become sinners. Each of us has chosen to rebel against

God and His authority as our Creator. Unless we trust what God has said about our condition in the world (that we are sinners), His just judgment against our rebellion lies on our heads and we will never know His wonderful love, mercy, and grace. Just as Scripture calls us to acknowledge God as the Creator, it also calls us to look to Jesus Christ as the only remedy for avoiding God's wrath against our sin. Each person must acknowledge those truths and look to Christ in repentant faith for the forgiveness of their sins.

As we continue to pursue scientific understanding about the universe we live in, let us do so by building on the firm foundation of what God has revealed to us in His Word. The God who has revealed Himself to us in the Bible makes science possible. Let God be true and every man a liar.

CHAPTER 9

What Did the Reformers Believe about the Age of the Earth?

DR. JOEL R. BEEKE

All Christians believe that God the Father Almighty is the Maker of heaven and earth. This belief is like a great river that runs through Christian history. It distinguishes Christianity from other forms of spirituality. Yet within this river there have been two streams of thought about how to understand Genesis: the allegorical reading and the literal reading.[1]

The Reformation of the 16th and 17th centuries marked a return to the literal reading of Scripture. The Reformers taught that God revealed in Genesis that He created all things in six ordinary days about six thousand years ago.

In this chapter, I will sketch out these two streams of thought, describe the teachings of the Reformers, and show how these teachings crystallized in their confessions of faith.

Two Views of Genesis 1 in Christian History

There have been many Christians through history who believed in a literal interpretation of Genesis 1. Basil of Caesarea (A.D. 329–379) wrote that in the context of "morning" and "evening" a "day" in Genesis 1 referred to a day of "twenty-four hours."[2] Ambrose (c. A.D. 339–397) wrote in his commentary on

---

1. I thank David Clayton and Paul Smalley for their research assistance on this article.
2. Basil, *Hexaemeron*, Homily 2.8, http://www.newadvent.org/fathers/32012.htm (accessed May 23, 2013).

Genesis, "The length of one day is twenty-four hours in extent."[3] The English historian and theologian Bede (c. A.D. 672–735) commented on Genesis 1:5 that the first day was "without a doubt a day of twenty-four hours."[4]

On the other hand, other Christians read Genesis 1 as an allegory or symbolic story. Origen (c. A.D. 185–254) rejected a literal interpretation of Genesis 1.[5] The great theologian Augustine (A.D. 354–430) believed that the six days were not periods of time but the way God taught the angels about creation.[6] Why did they believe this? First, they were influenced by an ancient book of Jewish wisdom that is not part of the Bible, misunderstanding it to say that God created all things in an instant.[7] Second, they wanted to reconcile Christianity with Greek philosophy much as the Jewish writer Philo of Alexandria (20 B.C.– A.D. 50) had tried to do, while not rejecting the major biblical doctrine that one God created all things.

The allegorical approach to the Bible prevailed in the Middle Ages, but some major theologians still favored a literal reading of Genesis 1. Peter Lombard (c. A.D. 1096–1164) acknowledged both ways Christians had understood the days of Genesis 1, but took the view that he believed fit Genesis better, namely, that God created everything out of nothing and shaped it into its perfected form over the period of "six days."[8] Lombard taught that the days of Genesis 1, defined by mornings and evenings, should be understood as "the space of twenty four hours."[9] Bonaventure (A.D. 1221–1274) argued that God created "in the space of six days" — a phrase that will appear later in Reformed writings.[10]

---

3. Ambrose, *Hexameron, Paradise, and Cain and Abel*, trans. John J. Savage, *The Fathers of the Church: A New Translation* (New York: Fathers of the Church, 1961), vol. 42 [1.37].

4. Bede, *On Genesis*, trans. Calvin B. Kendall (Liverpool: Liverpool University Press, 2008), p. 75.

5. Robert Letham, "In the Space of Six Days," *Westminster Theological Journal* 61 (1999): p. 150–51.

6. Ibid., p. 156.

7. The reference is Sirach or Ecclesiasticus 18:1, "The One who lives forever created all things together." The Latin Vulgate had *simul* or "at the same time" for "together," but the Greek reads *koine* or "in common."

8. Peter Lombard, *The Four Books of Sentences*, trans. Alexis Bugnolo, book 2, distinction 12, ch. 2, http://www.franciscan-archive.org/lombardus/opera/ls2-12.html (accessed May 29, 2013).

9. Ibid., distinction 13, ch. 4, http://www.franciscan-archive.org/lombardus/opera/ls2-13.html (accessed May 28, 2013). The word "space" translates Lombard's Latin term *spatium*, the same word later used by Calvin and the Westminster divines.

10. The Latin phrase *sex dierum spatium* appears in Bonaventure's *Commentaries on the Four Books of Sentences*, trans. Alexis Bugnolo, book 2, commentary on distinction 12, art. 1, question 2, http://www.franciscan-archive.org/bonaventura/opera/bon02295.html (accessed May 28, 2013). Bonaventure made the same argument that Calvin would that God created over a span of time "to communicate to the creature what it was able to receive."

Though they interpreted Genesis 1 in different ways, virtually all these Christians still believed that the world was only several thousand years old, in contrast to the Greek philosophical view of an eternal or nearly eternal world. They did not see creation as a process spanning long eras, but a relatively short event, whether God completed it in an instant, or in six ordinary days.[11]

The Reformation and the Interpretation of Genesis

When God brought the Reformation to the church in the 16th century, one great effect was the return to the literal sense of the Bible. For centuries the church had muddied the waters of biblical interpretation by giving each text four meanings as if the Bible consisted entirely of spiritual parables. William Tyndale (c. A.D. 1494–1536) asserted, "The Scripture hath but one sense, which is the literal sense."[12] He did not deny that the Bible uses parables and figures of speech, just as we speak and write today. But we discover the meaning of Scripture by reading it carefully in context.[13] We do not turn history into allegory.

As a result of this approach to the Bible, the Reformers embraced a literal view of Genesis. Martin Luther (A.D. 1483–1546) wrote, "We know from Moses that the world was not in existence before 6,000 years ago."[14] He relied on biblical records to compute the age of the earth, estimating that in 1540 the world was 5,500 years old.[15] He acknowledged that some people followed Aristotle's view that the world had always existed, or Augustine's view that Genesis 1 was an allegory. But Luther believed that Moses wrote Genesis in a plain sense. He said,

> Therefore, as the proverb has it, he calls "a spade a spade," i.e., he employs the terms "day" and "evening" without allegory, just as we customarily do. . . . Moses spoke in the literal sense, not allegorically or figuratively, i.e., that the world, with all its creatures, was created within six days, as the words read. If we do not comprehend the reason

---

11. For an overview of the views of writers through the Christian era on the origins of man, see William Vandoodewaard, *The Quest for the Historical Adam* (Grand Rapids, MI: Reformation Heritage Books, forthcoming).

12. William Tyndale, *Obedience of a Christian Man*, in *Doctrinal Treatises and Introductions to Different Portions of the Holy Scriptures*, ed. Henry Walter (Cambridge: Cambridge University Press, 1848), 304.

13. Ibid., p. 305.

14. Martin Luther, *Lectures on Genesis*, in *Luther's Works*, ed. Jaroslav Pelikan (St. Louis, MO: Concordia, 1958), 1:ix, 3.

15. Martin Brecht, *Martin Luther: The Preservation of the Church, 1532–1546* (Minneapolis, MN: Augsburg Fortress, 1993), p. 138.

for this, let us remain pupils and leave the job of teacher to the Holy Spirit.[16]

Luther's advice is sound. When the Bible speaks of God creating Adam on the sixth day, teaching Adam His command about the trees, and bringing the animals to him, these are not just spiritual parables or eternal principles but "all these facts refer to time and physical life."[17] Genesis presents itself to us not as a poem or allegory, but as an account of real history. We should accept it as such, even if we cannot answer every question one might raise about the origins of the universe. The words of the Bible are infallibly given by the Holy Spirit (2 Tim. 3:16; 2 Peter 1:21). God is the teacher, and we must be His students.

Luther understood that the world would regard Genesis as a "foolish fairy tale."[18] When he commented on the creation of Adam in Genesis 2, he said, "If Aristotle heard this, he would burst into laughter and conclude that although this is not an unlovely yarn, it is nevertheless a most absurd one."[19] But Luther said that in reality Genesis is not foolishness but wisdom, for science can only investigate what things are made of, but God's Word can reveal how they were made and for what purpose.[20]

Calvin on the Time of Creation

Though God worked through many Reformers alongside and after Luther, none is so well known as John Calvin (A.D. 1509–1564). Like Luther, he read Genesis as "the history of creation." He believed that "the duration of the world . . . has not yet attained six thousand years."[21] He also rejected Augustine's belief that creation was completed in a moment, [22] writing, "Moses relates that God's work was completed not in a moment but in six days."[23]

The Reformers were not naïve; they too faced atheistic skeptics. We should not think that only in this modern age have people tried to explain the origin of the universe and biological life without giving glory to the Creator. Calvin knew

16. Luther, *Lectures on Genesis*, in *Works*, 1:5. See also John A. Maxfield, *Luther's Lectures on Genesis and the Formation of Evangelical Identity* (Kirksville, MO: Truman State University Press, 2008), p. 41.
17. Ibid., 1:122.
18. Ibid., 1:128.
19. Ibid., 1:84.
20. Ibid., 1:124. He used the terminology of efficient and final causes.
21. John Calvin, *Institutes of the Christian Religion*, trans. Ford Lewis Battles, ed. John T. McNeill (Philadelphia, PA: Westminster Press, 1960), 1.14.1.
22. Susan E. Schreiner, "Creation and Providence," in *The Calvin Handbook*, ed. Herman J. Selderhuis (Grand Rapids, MI: Eerdmans, 2009), p. 270.
23. Calvin, *Institutes of the Christian Religion*, 1.14.2.

that the Bible's teaching of the relatively young age of the earth would provoke some to laugh and sneer, but realized that profane men will mock at almost every major teaching of Christianity.[24] He was aware that some people taught that "the world came together by chance" as "tiny objects tumbling around" formed the stars, the earth, living creatures, and human beings. Calvin believed that the excellence and artistry of the smallest parts of the human body showed such theories of random creation to be ridiculous.[25] God revealed that He created the world in six days about six thousand years ago to protect the Church from pagan fables about our origins, to glorify Himself as the only Creator and Lord, and to call us to submit our minds to God's will and Word.[26]

Calvin regarded the early chapters of Genesis as "the history of the creation of the world," and delighted in them because creation is "the splendid mirror of God's glory."[27] To be sure, the Bible does not reveal all the facts that can be discovered by astronomy — though Calvin said that astronomy is "pleasant" and "useful" for Christians.[28] Scripture records creation in words that ordinary people can understand, not technical scientific language.[29] Still, the Bible is true, and Genesis is real history. Foolish men may ridicule God's ways, but the humble know better: "Since his will is the rule of all wisdom, we ought to be contented with that alone."[30]

If someone objects that Moses was not alive at creation and so could only write fables about it, Calvin replied that Moses was not writing thoughts he invented or discovered himself, but "is the instrument of the Holy Spirit." That same Spirit enabled Moses to foretell events that would happen long after his death, such as the calling of the Gentiles to Christ. Furthermore, the Spirit helped Moses to make use of traditions handed down from Adam, Abraham, and others.[31]

---

24. Calvin, *Institutes of the Christian Religion*, 3.21.4.
25. John Calvin, *Sermons on Genesis: Chapters 1:1–11:4*, trans. Rob Roy McGregor (Edinburgh: Banner of Truth, 2009), p. 9, 11–12. See also his commentaries on Exod. 2:4 and Ps. 104:24. Calvin attributed such views to a form of atheism that he associated with the teachings of Epicurus (341–270 B.C.), an ancient Greek philosopher. See Nicolaas H. Gootjes, "Calvin on Epicurus and the Epicureans," in *Calvin Theological Journal* 40 (2006): p. 33–48.
26. Calvin, *Institutes of the Christian Religion*, 1.14.1–2.
27. John Calvin, *Commentaries on the First Book of Moses called Genesis*, trans. John King (Edinburgh: Calvin Translation Society, 1847), 1:xlviii; cf. 1:57.
28. Ibid., 1:79.
29. Ibid., 1:86–87.
30. Ibid., 1:61.
31. Ibid., 1:58.

Someone else might object that it makes no sense that God created light on the first day before God created the sun on the fourth day. Here too, Calvin helps us by saying that God has an important lesson for us in this: "The Lord, by the very order of creation, bears witness that he holds in his hand the light, which he is able to impart to us without the sun and moon."[32] Thus the order of the creation week reveals that God can meet all our needs even without the natural means He ordinarily uses.

Calvin was aware that some people said that the six days of Genesis 1 were a metaphor. But he believed this did not do justice to the text of Scripture. He wrote, "For it is too violent a cavil [objection] to contend that Moses distributes the work which God perfected at once into six days, for the mere purpose of conveying instruction. Let us rather conclude that God himself took the space of six days, for the purpose of accommodating his works to the capacity of men." He went on to explain that God "distributed the creation of the world into successive portions, that he might fix our attention, and compel us, as if he had laid his hand upon us, to pause and reflect."[33] Joseph Pipa writes, "Calvin's commitment to six days and the order of the days stands in bold contrast to modern theories such as the framework hypothesis and the analogical view of Genesis 1. He emphatically insists on the order of the six days as both advantageous to man and instructive about the character of God."[34]

Lutheran and Early Reformed Confessions on Creation

The Reformation was a time of tremendous rediscoveries of biblical truth. To show their faithfulness to the Scriptures and pass these truths on to future generations, evangelicals published their beliefs in confessions and catechisms.

The doctrine of creation was not a major point of disagreement between the Roman Catholic Church and the evangelical churches of the Reformation. Therefore, it did not receive much attention in the Lutheran confessions, except to affirm briefly that one God created all things.[35] The major Reformed confessions of the 16th century offered more developed statements about the creation

32. Ibid., 1:76.
33. Ibid., 1:78. See also *Sermons on Genesis*, p. 19.
34. Joseph A. Pipa Jr., "Creation and Providence," in *A Theological Guide to Calvin's Institutes*, ed. David W. Hall and Peter A. Lillback (Phillipsburg, NJ: P&R Publishing, 2008), p. 129.
35. Augsburg Confession, art. 1, and Small Catechism, part 2, art. 1, in *The Book of Concord: The Confessions of the Evangelical Lutheran Church*, trans. and ed. Theodore G. Tappert (Philadelphia, PA: Fortress Press, 1959), p. 28, 344.

of the world, angels, and mankind, but did not address the time of creation.[36] The Belgic Confession (article 14) does say that "God created man out of the dust of the earth."[37] Thus it confessed a literal understanding of Genesis 2:7, which logically contradicts the modern notion that man evolved by a natural process from other forms of life over millions of years.

Girolamo Zanchi (A.D. 1516–1590) was a professor of Old Testament and theology who taught at Strassburg and Heidelberg. A few years before he died, Zanchi published a detailed confession of faith, which said that God created the world "in the space of six days."[38] He also published a massive book titled *Concerning the Works of God in Creation during the Space of Six Days*, where he argued that Genesis 1 clearly says God created the world in six literal days.[39]

James Ussher (A.D. 1581–1656), bishop of Armagh, is now best known for his biblical history of the world, where he famously calculated the date of creation at 4004 B.C. In 1615, he led a gathering of church leaders in Dublin to adopt the Irish Articles, which say, "In the beginning of time, when no creature had any being, God by his Word alone, *in the space of six days*, created all things."[40] These words come directly from Ussher's *Principles of Christian Religion*, which he wrote around 1603.[41] Ussher was invited to participate in the Westminster Assembly, and though he declined, his writings still influenced the documents written there.

The Westminster Standards on Creation

Meeting from 1643 to 1649, British Reformed theologians wrote the Westminster Confession of Faith (WCF), Shorter Catechism (WSC), and Larger Catechism (WLC). The Westminster Standards continue to serve as

---

36. Belgic Confession, art. 12, Heidelberg Catechism, Q. 6, and Second Helvetic Confession, art. 7, in *Reformed Confessions Harmonized*, ed. Joel R. Beeke and Sinclair B. Ferguson (Grand Rapids, MI: Baker, 1999), p. 36–38.
37. Belgic Confession, art. 14., in *Doctrinal Standards, Liturgy, and Church Order*, ed. Joel R. Beeke (Grand Rapids, MI: Reformation Heritage Books, 2003), p. 11.
38. H. Zanchius, *Confession of Christian Religion* (London: Iohn Legat, 1599), p. 21 [5.1]. The Latin reads *intra spacium sex dierum* (H. Zanchii, *De Religione Christiana Fides* (Neostadii Palatinorvm: Matthaus Harnisch, [1588]), 17–18 [5.1]).
39. Hieron. Zanchii, *De Operibus Dei intra Spacium Sex Dierum Creatis* (1591). See Vandoodewaard, *The Quest for the Historical Adam*, for discussion.
40. Irish Articles, art. 4, sec. 18, in *Documents of the English Reformation*, ed. Gerald Bray (Minneapolis, MN: Fortress Press, 1994), p. 440, emphasis added.
41. *The Whole Works of the Most Rev. James Ussher* (Dublin: Hodges, Smith, and Col, 1864), 11:179, 183.

the confessional declarations of Presbyterian churches around the world. The Larger Catechism (Q. 17) taught a literal view of Genesis 1–2 by stating, "After God had made all other creatures, He created man male and female; formed the body of the man out of the dust of the ground, and the woman of the rib of the man."[42] The confession and both catechisms state that God created the universe in "the space of six days."[43] This same language also carried over into the confessions of the Congregationalists and Particular Baptists when they adapted the Westminster Confession for use in their own churches.[44]

What do the Westminster Standards and their daughter confessions mean by creation in "the space of six days"? Why did they not simply say, "in six days"? First, by using the word "space" they made it clear they were talking about a definite span of time, not just a metaphor with six parts. Other books from the 17th century used the words "the space of six days" to refer to the duration of six ordinary days.[45] Thus one book printed in 1693 talks about how a king conquered an entire region "in the space of six days."[46]

Second, in taking up the language of "the space of six days," the Westminster Assembly declared that it stood with previous theologians in affirming a literal six-day creation. The expression has its roots in at least four previous theologians whom the Westminster divines knew. As we have seen, the words "in the space of six days" appear in the writings of Bonaventure, Calvin, Zanchi, and Ussher.[47] Zanchi's *Confessions* may have influenced the Westminster divines, for it was a prime example of early Reformed orthodox confessions from which

---

42. WLC, Q. 17, in *Reformed Confessions Harmonized*, p. 39.
43. WCF 4.1, WSC Q. 9, and WLC Q. 15, in *Reformed Confessions Harmonized*, 37. The Latin phrase is *sex dierum spatium* (Philip Schaff, *Creeds of Christendom* [New York: Harper, 1877], 3:611).
44. A comparison of the WCF to the Savoy Declaration (1658) and the Second London Baptist Confession (1677/1689) may be found at http://www.proginosko.com/docs/wcf_sdfo_lbcf.html (accessed May 24, 2013).
45. *Journals of the House of Lords* (1642), 5:535; Nathan Bailey, "Founday," in *An Universal Etymological English Dictionary* (London: for R. Ware et al, 1675); *The Laws and Acts Made in the First Parliament of Our Most High and Dread Soveraign James VII*, ed. George, Viscount of Tarbet (Edinburgh: Andrew Anderson, 1685), p. 141; Pierre Danet, "Judaei," in *A Complete Dictionary of the Greek and Roman Antiquities* (London: for John Nicholson et al., 1700).
46. *The History of Polybius the Megapolitan*, 2nd ed. (London: Samuel Briscoe, 1693), 2:128.
47. Bonaventure, *Commentaries on the Four Books of Sentences*, book 2, distinction 12, art. 1, question 2; Calvin, *Commentaries on Genesis*, 1:78; Zanchius, *Confession of Christian Religion*, 21 [5.1]; *De Operibus Dei intra Spacium Sex Dierum Creatis*; Ussher, *Works*, 11:183.

to draw.[48] Certainly the Irish Articles of Ussher influenced the Westminster Confession.[49]

Research into the writings of several members of the Westminster Assembly has confirmed that they believed in a relatively young earth and a literal six-day creation.[50] In 1674, Thomas Vincent wrote the following in his explanation of the Westminster Shorter Catechism: "In what time did God create all things? God created all things in the space of six days. He could have created all things together in a moment, but he took six days' time to work in."[51] Thus, we have good reason to conclude that the Westminster Confession, Larger Catechism, and Shorter Catechism teach us to regard Genesis 1 as a real week of time in history.

Some godly men who love the Westminster Confession disagree with me, arguing that "the space of six days" is ambiguous and it was only meant to exclude the idea of creation in an instant.[52] But the Westminster Standards do more than reject instantaneous creation. They also affirm creation over a specified period of time: "the space of six days."

Conclusion

Though all Christians believe that God created the world, through the history of the Church a literal reading of Genesis has competed with an allegorical reading. In the Reformation, Luther and Calvin embraced the literal reading of Genesis, with the result that they believed in a six-day creation some six thousand years ago. We also find evidence of the literal view in the Belgic Confession, the *Confession of Faith* by Zanchi, the Irish Articles, and the Westminster Confession of Faith.

---

48. Richard Muller, *Post-Reformation Reformed Dogmatics, Volume Two, Holy Scripture: The Cognitive Foundation of Theology*, 2nd ed. (Grand Rapids, MI: Baker Academic, 2003), p. 85.
49. Benjamin B. Warfield, *The Westminster Assembly and Its Work* (New York: Oxford University Press, 1931), p. 127, 148, 169–74.
50. David W. Hall, "What Was the View of the Westminster Assembly Divines on Creation Days?" in *Did God Create in Six Days?* ed. Joseph A. Pipa, Jr., and David W. Hall (Taylors, SC: Southern Presbyterian Press, 1999), p. 41–52.
51. Thomas Vincent, *An Explicatory Catechism: Or, An Explanation of the Assembly's Shorter Catechism* (New Haven, CT: Walter, Austin, and Co., 1810), p. 42, on WSC Q. 9.
52. "Westminster Theological Seminary and the Days of Creation," Westminster Theological Seminary, http://www.wts.edu/about/beliefs/statements/creation.html (accessed May 28, 2013); R. Scott Clark, *Recovering the Reformed Confession* (Phillipsburg, NJ: P&R Publishing, 2008), p. 49. A critique of some of Hall's conclusions may be found in William S. Barker, *Word to the World* (Ross-shire, UK: Christian Focus Publications, 2005), p. 259–270. This article also appeared in *Westminster Theological Journal* 62 (2000): p. 113–120. I note, however, that Barker does not offer examples of Westminster divines who rejected creation in six literal days.

But in this modern era, an increasing number of evangelical and Reformed Christians are turning back to the old error of embracing a symbolic view of Genesis, albeit often in new forms. I believe that we face a double danger here. First, we are in danger of losing our confidence that words can clearly communicate truth. There seems to be a hermeneutical issue at stake here, namely, the perspicuity of Scripture. It is fascinating that, generally speaking, the same Reformed scholars who argue for some kind of allegorical interpretation of the plain and literal words of Genesis 1 tend to reinterpret the plain and literal words of the Westminster Confession when it states that creation took place "in the space of six days." If plain words can take on allegorical or alternative meanings so easily so that they do not mean what they plainly state, how do we know what anything means? The resulting uncertainty that such interpretations convey leads into the second danger, that of doctrinal minimalism. If we cut back the meaning of our confessions by saying their statements merely stand against some specific error, then we lose the richness of what the confessions positively affirm. Similarly, if we reduce Genesis 1 to the bare truth that "God created everything," then we lose the richness of what God reveals in the whole chapter.

An uncertain and minimalist approach to the doctrine of creation opens the door for serious errors to enter the church, such as the evolution of man from animals or the denial that Adam and Eve were real, historical people. Happily, a robust doctrine of creation provides a strong foundation for our faith.

CHAPTER 10

What Are Some of the Best Evidences in Science of a Young Creation?

DR. ANDREW A. SNELLING, DR. DAVID MENTON,
DR. DANNY R. FAULKNER, AND DR. GEORGIA PURDOM

The earth is only a few thousand years old. That's a fact, plainly revealed in God's Word. So we should expect to find plenty of evidence for its youth. And that's what we find — in the earth's geology, biology, paleontology, and even astronomy.

Literally hundreds of dating methods could be used to attempt an estimate of the earth's age, and the vast majority of them point to a much younger earth than the 4.5 billion years claimed by secularists. The following series of articles presents what Answers in Genesis researchers picked as the ten best scientific evidences that contradict billions of years and confirm a relatively young earth and universe.

Despite this wealth of evidence, it is important to understand that, from the perspective of observational science, no one can prove absolutely how young (or old) the universe is. Only one dating method is absolutely reliable — a witness who doesn't lie, who has all evidence, and who can reveal to us when the universe began!

And we do have such a witness — the God of the Bible! He has given us a specific history, beginning with the six days of creation and followed by detailed genealogies that allow us to determine when the universe began. Based on this history, the beginning was only about six thousand years ago (about four thousand years from creation to Christ).

In the rush to examine all these amazing scientific "evidences," it's easy to lose sight of the big picture. Such a mountain of scientific evidence, accumulated by researchers, seems to obviously contradict the supposed billions of years, so why don't more people rush to accept the truth of a young earth based on the Bible?

The problem is, as we consider the topic of origins, all so-called "evidences" must be interpreted. Facts don't speak for themselves. Interpreting the facts of the present becomes especially difficult when reconstructing the historical events that produced those present-day facts, because no humans have always been present to observe all the evidence and to record how all the evidence was produced.

Forensic scientists must make multiple assumptions about things they cannot observe. How was the original setting different? Were different processes in play? Was the scene later contaminated? Just one wrong assumption or one tiny piece of missing evidence could totally change how they reconstruct the past events that led to the present-day evidence.

When discussing the age of the earth, Christians must be ready to explain the importance of starting points. The Bible is the right starting point.

That's why, when discussing the age of the earth, Christians must be ready to explain the importance of starting points and assumptions. Reaching the correct conclusions requires the right starting point.

The Bible is that starting point. This is the revealed Word of the almighty, faithful, and true Creator, who was present to observe all events of earth history and who gave mankind an infallible record of key events in the past.

The Bible, God's revelation to us, gives us the foundation that enables us to begin to build the right worldview to correctly understand how the present and past are connected. All other documents written by man are fallible, unlike the "God-breathed" infallible Word (2 Timothy 3:16). The Bible clearly and unmistakably describes the creation of the universe, the solar system, and the earth around six thousand years ago. We know that it's true based on the authority of God's own character. "Because He could swear by no one greater, He swore by Himself" (Hebrews 6:13).

In one sense, God's testimony is all we need; but God Himself tells us to give reasons for what we believe (1 Peter 3:15). So it is also important to conduct scientific research (that is part of taking dominion of the earth, as Adam was told to do in Genesis 1:28). With this research we can challenge those who reject God's clear Word and defend the biblical worldview.

Indeed, God's testimony must have such a central role in our thinking that it seems demeaning even to call it the "best" evidence of a young earth. It is, in truth, the only foundation upon which all other evidences can be correctly understood!

Following are the ten best evidences from science that confirm a young earth.

#1 Very Little Sediment on the Seafloor

If sediments have been accumulating on the seafloor for three billion years, the seafloor should be choked with sediments many miles deep.

Every year, water and wind erode about 20 billion tons of dirt and rock debris from the continents and deposit them on the seafloor[1] (figure 1). Most of this material accumulates as loose sediments near the continents. Yet the average thickness of all these sediments globally over the whole seafloor is not even 1,300 feet (400 m).[2]

Some sediments appear to be removed as tectonic plates slide slowly (an inch or two per year) beneath continents. An estimated 1 billion tons of sediments are removed this way each year.[3] The net gain is thus 19 billion tons per year. At this rate, 1,300 feet of sediment would accumulate in less than 12 million years, not billions of years.

This evidence makes sense within the context of the Genesis Flood cataclysm, not the idea of slow and gradual geologic evolution. In the latter stages of the year-long global Flood, water swiftly drained off the emerging land, dumping its sediment-chocked loads offshore. Thus most seafloor sediments accumulated rapidly about 4,350 years ago.[4]

Rescuing Devices

Those who advocate an old earth insist that the seafloor sediments must have accumulated at a much slower rate in the past. But this rescuing device doesn't "stack up"! Like the sediment layers on the continents, the sediments on the continental shelves and margins (the majority of the seafloor sediments)

---

1. John D. Milliman and James P. N. Syvitski, "Geomorphic/Tectonic Control of Sediment Discharge to the Ocean: The Importance of Small Mountainous Rivers," *The Journal of Geology* 100 (1992): p. 525–544.
2. William W. Hay, James L. Sloan II, and Christopher N. Wold, "Mass/Age Distribution and Composition of Sediments on the Ocean Floor and the Global Rate of Sediment Subduction," *Journal of Geophysical Research* 93, no. B12 (1998): p. 14,933–14,940.
3. Ibid.
4. For a fuller treatment and further information see John D. Morris, *The Young Earth* (Green Forest, AR: Master Books, 2000), p. 88–90; Andrew A. Snelling, *Earth's Catastrophic Past: Geology, Creation and the Flood* (Dallas, TX: Institute for Creation Research, 2009), p. 881–884.

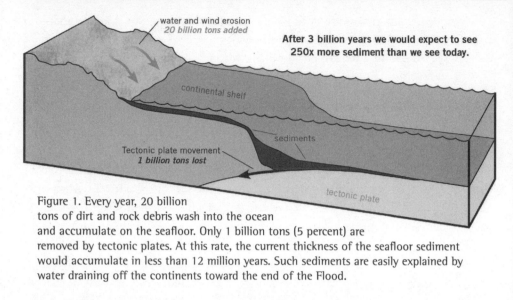

Figure 1. Every year, 20 billion tons of dirt and rock debris wash into the ocean and accumulate on the seafloor. Only 1 billion tons (5 percent) are removed by tectonic plates. At this rate, the current thickness of the seafloor sediment would accumulate in less than 12 million years. Such sediments are easily explained by water draining off the continents toward the end of the Flood.

have features that unequivocally indicate they were deposited much faster than today's rates. For example, the layering and patterns of various grain sizes in these sediments are the same as those produced by undersea landslides, when dense debris-laden currents (called turbidity currents) flow rapidly across the continental shelves and the sediments then settle in thick layers over vast areas. An additional problem for the old-earth view is that no evidence exists of much sediment being subducted and mixed into the mantle.

#2 Bent Rock Layers

In many mountainous areas, rock layers thousands of feet thick have been bent and folded without fracturing. How can that happen if they were laid down separately over hundreds of millions of years and already hardened?

Hardened rock layers are brittle. Try bending a slab of concrete sometime to see what happens! But if concrete is still wet, it can easily be shaped and molded before the cement sets. The same principle applies to sedimentary rock layers. They can be bent and folded soon after the sediment is deposited, before the natural cements have a chance to bind the particles together into hard, brittle rocks.[5]

The region around Grand Canyon is a great example showing how most of the earth's fossil-bearing layers were laid down quickly and many were folded

5. R.E. Goodman, *Introduction to Rock Mechanics* (New York: John Wiley and Sons, 1980); Sam Boggs Jr., *Principles of Sedimentology and Stratigraphy* (Upper Saddle River, NJ: Prentice-Hall, 1995), p. 127–131.

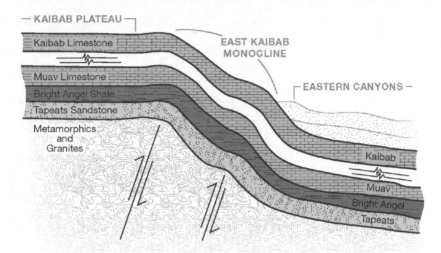

Figure 2. The Grand Canyon now cuts through many rock layers. Previously, all these layers were raised to their current elevation (a raised, flat region known as the Kaibab Plateau). Somehow this whole sequence was bent and folded without fracturing. That's impossible if the first layer, the Tapeats Sandstone, was deposited over North America 460 million years before being folded. But all the layers would still be relatively soft and pliable if it all happened during the recent, global Flood.

while still wet. Exposed in the canyon's walls are about 4,500 feet (1,370 m) of fossil-bearing layers, conventionally labeled Cambrian to Permian.[6] They were supposedly deposited over a period lasting from 520 to 250 million years ago. Then, amazingly, this whole sequence of layers rose over a mile, around 60 million years ago. The plateau through which Grand Canyon runs is now 7,000–8,000 feet (2,150–3,450 m) above sea level.

Think about it. The time between the first deposits at Grand Canyon (520 million years ago) and their bending (60 million years ago) was 460 million years!

Look at the photos on the following page of some of these layers at the edge of the plateau, just east of the Grand Canyon. The whole sequence of these hardened sedimentary rock layers has been bent and folded, but without fracturing (figure 2).[7] At the bottom of this sequence is the Tapeats Sandstone, which is 100–325 feet (30–100 meters) thick. It is bent and folded 90° (photo 1). The Muav Limestone above it has similarly been bent (photo 2).

6. Stanley S. Beus and Michael Morales, eds., *Grand Canyon Geology*, 2nd edition (New York: Oxford University Press, 2003).
7. Andrew A. Snelling, "Rock Layers Folded, Not Fractured," *Answers* 4, no. 2 (April–June 2009): p. 80–83.

Photo 1. The whole sequence of sedimentary layers through which Grand Canyon cuts has been bent and folded without fracturing. This includes the Tapeats Sandstone, located at the bottom of the sequence. (A 90° fold in the eastern Grand Canyon is pictured here.)
(Photo courtesy of Andrew Snelling)

Photo 2. All the layers through which Grand Canyon cuts — including the Muav Limestone shown here — have been bent without fracturing.
(Photo courtesy of Andrew Snelling)

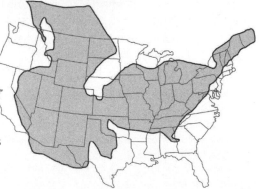

Figure 3. This phenomenon was not regional. The Tapeats Sandstone spans the continent, and other layers span much of the globe.

However, it supposedly took 270 million years to deposit these particular layers. Surely in that time the Tapeats Sandstone at the bottom would have dried out and the sand grains cemented together, especially with 4,000 feet (1,220 m) of rock layers piled on top of it and pressing down on it. The only viable scientific explanation is that the whole sequence was deposited very quickly — the creation model indicates that it took less than a year, during the global Flood cataclysm. So the 520 million years never happened, and the earth is young.

Rescuing Devices

What solution do old-earth advocates suggest? Heat and pressure can make hard rock layers pliable, so they claim this must be what happened in the eastern Grand Canyon, as the sequence of many layers above pressed down and heated up these rocks. Just one problem. The heat and pressure would have transformed these layers into quartzite, marble, and other metamorphic rocks. Yet Tapeats Sandstone is still sandstone, a sedimentary rock!

But this quandary is even worse for those who deny God's recent creation and the Flood. The Tapeats Sandstone and its equivalents can be traced right across North America (figure 3),[8] and beyond to right across northern Africa to southern Israel.[9] Indeed, the whole Grand Canyon sedimentary sequence is an integral part of six megasequences that cover North America.[10] Only a global Flood cataclysm could carry the sediments to deposit thick layers across several continents one after the other in rapid succession in one event.[11]

#3 Soft Tissue in Fossils

Ask the average layperson how he or she knows that the earth is millions or billions of years old, and that person will probably mention the dinosaurs, which nearly everybody "knows" died off 65 million years ago. A recent discovery by Dr. Mary Schweitzer, however, has given reason for all but committed evolutionists to question this assumption.

Bone slices from the fossilized thigh bone (femur) of a *Tyrannosaurus rex* found in the Hell Creek Formation of Montana were studied under the

8. F. Alan Lindberg, *Correlation of Stratigraphic Units of North America (COSUNA)*, Correlation Charts Series (Tulsa, OK: American Association of Petroleum Geologists, 1986).

9. Andrew A. Snelling, "The Geology of Israel within the Biblical Creation-Flood Framework of History: 2. The Flood Rocks," *Answers Research Journal* 3 (2010): p. 267–309.

10. L.L. Sloss, "Sequences in the Cratonic Interior of North America," *Geological Society of America Bulletin* 74 (1963): p. 93–114.

11. For a fuller treatment and further information see Morris, *The Young Earth*, p. 106–109; Snelling, *Earth's Catastrophic Past: Geology, Creation and the Flood*, p. 528–530, 597–605.

microscope by Schweitzer. To her amazement, the bone showed what appeared to be blood vessels of the type seen in bone and marrow, and these contained what appeared to be red blood cells with nuclei, typical of reptiles and birds (but not mammals). The vessels even appeared to be lined with specialized endothelial cells found in all blood vessels.

Amazingly, the bone marrow contained what appeared to be flexible tissue. Initially, some skeptical scientists suggested that bacterial biofilms (dead bacteria aggregated in a slime) formed what only appear to be blood vessels and bone cells. Recently, Schweitzer and co-workers found biochemical evidence for intact fragments of the protein collagen, which is the building block of connective tissue. This is important because collagen is a highly distinctive protein not made by bacteria.[12]

Some evolutionists have strongly criticized Schweitzer's conclusions because they are understandably reluctant to concede the existence of blood vessels, cells with nuclei, tissue elasticity, and intact protein fragments in a dinosaur bone dated at 68 million years old. Other evolutionists, who find Schweitzer's evidence too compelling to ignore, simply conclude that there is some previously unrecognized form of fossilization that preserves cells and protein fragments over tens of millions of years.[13] Needless to say, no evolutionist has publically considered the possibility that dinosaur fossils are not millions of years old.

An obvious question arises from Schweitzer's work: is it even remotely plausible that blood vessels, cells, and protein fragments can exist largely intact over 68 million years? While many consider such long-term preservation of tissue and cells to be very unlikely, the problem is that no human or animal remains are known with certainty to be 68 million years old (figure 4). But if creationists are right, most dinosaurs were buried in the Flood 3,000 to 4,000 years ago. So would we expect the preservation of vessels, cells, and complex molecules of the type that Schweitzer reports for biological tissues historically known to be 3,000 to 4,000 years old?

The answer is yes. Many studies of Egyptian mummies and other humans of this old age (confirmed by historical evidence) show all the sorts of detail Schweitzer reported in her *T. rex*. In addition to Egyptian mummies, the Tyrolean iceman, found in the Alps in 1991 and believed to be about 5,000 years old according to long-age dating, shows such incredible preservation of DNA and other microscopic detail.

12. See Schweitzer's review article, "Blood from Stone," *Scientific American* (December 2010): p. 62–69.
13. Marcus Ross, "Those Not-So-Dry Bones," *Answers* (Jan–Mar 2010): p. 43–45.

We conclude that the preservation of vessels, cells, and complex molecules in dinosaurs is entirely consistent with a young-earth creationist perspective but is highly implausible with the evolutionist's perspective about dinosaurs that died off millions of years ago.

#4 Faint Sun Paradox

Figure 4. A little skin: a largely intact dinosaur mummy, named Dakota, was found in the Hell Creek Formation of the western United States in 2007. Some soft tissue from the long-necked hadrosaur was quickly preserved as fossil, such as the scales from its forearm shown here.

Evidence now supports astronomers' belief that the sun's power comes from the fusion of hydrogen into helium deep in the sun's core, but there is a huge problem. As the hydrogen fuses, it should change the composition of the sun's core, gradually increasing the sun's temperature. If true, this means that the earth was colder in the past. In fact, the earth would have been below freezing 3.5 billion years ago, when life supposedly evolved.

The rate of nuclear fusion depends upon the temperature. As the sun's core temperatures increase, the sun's energy output should also increase, causing the sun to brighten over time. Calculations show that the sun would brighten by 25 percent after 3.5 billion years. This means that an early sun would have been fainter, warming the earth 31°F (17°C) less than it does today. That's below freezing!

But evolutionists acknowledge that there is no evidence of this in the geologic record. They even call this problem the faint young sun paradox. While this isn't a problem over many thousands of years, it is a problem if the world is billions of years old.

Rescuing Devices

Over the years, scientists have proposed several mechanisms to explain away this problem. These suggestions require changes in the earth's atmosphere. For instance, more greenhouse gases early in earth's history would retain more heat, but this means that the greenhouse gases had to decrease gradually to compensate for the brightening sun.

None of these proposals can be proved, for there is no evidence. Furthermore, it is difficult to believe that a mechanism totally unrelated to the sun's brightness could compensate for the sun's changing emission so precisely for billions of years.

#5 Rapidly Decaying Magnetic Field

The earth is surrounded by a magnetic field that protects living things from solar radiation. Without it, life could not exist. That's why scientists were surprised to discover that the field is quickly wearing down. At the current rate, the field and thus the earth could be no older than 20,000 years old.

Several measurements confirm this decay. Since measuring began in 1845, the total energy stored in the earth's magnetic field has been decaying at a rate of 5 percent per century.[14] Archaeological measurements show that the field was 40 percent stronger in A.D. 1000.[15] Recent records of the International Geomagnetic Reference Field, the most accurate ever taken, show a net energy loss of 1.4 percent in just three decades (1970–2000).[16] This means that the field's energy has halved every 1,465 years or so.

Creationists have proposed that the earth's magnetic field is caused by a freely decaying electric current in the earth's core. This means that the electric current naturally loses energy, or "decays," as it flows through the metallic core. Though it differs from the most commonly accepted conventional model, it is consistent with our knowledge of what makes up the earth's core.[17] Furthermore, based on what we know about the conductive properties of liquid iron, this freely decaying current would have started when the earth's outer core was formed. However, if the core were more than 20,000 years old, then the starting energy would have made the earth too hot to be covered by water, as Genesis 1:2 reveals.

Reliable, accurate, published geological field data have emphatically confirmed the young-earth model: a freely decaying electric current in the outer core is generating the magnetic field.[18] Although this field reversed direction several

14. A.L. McDonald and R.H. Gunst, "An Analysis of the Earth's Magnetic Field from 1835 to 1965," *ESSA Technical Report*, IER 46-IES 1 (Washington, DC: U.S. Government Printing Office, 1967).

15. R.T. Merrill and M.W. McElhinney, *The Earth's Magnetic Field* (London: Academic Press, 1983), p. 101–106.

16. These measurements were gathered by the International Geomagnetic Reference Field. See D. Russell Humphreys, "The Earth's Magnetic Field Is Still Losing Energy," *Creation Research Society Quarterly* 39, no. 1 (2002): p. 1–11.

17. Thomas G. Barnes, "Decay of the Earth's Magnetic Field and the Geochronological Implications," *Creation Research Society Quarterly* 8, no. 1 (1971): p. 24–29; Thomas G. Barnes, *Origin and Destiny of the Earth's Magnetic Field, Technical Monograph no. 4*, 2nd edition (Santee, CA: Institute for Creation Research, 1983).

18. D. Russell Humphreys, "Reversals of the Earth's Magnetic Field During the Genesis Flood," in *Proceedings of the First International Conference on Creationism*, vol. 2, R.E. Walsh, C.L. Brooks, and R.S. Crowell, eds. (Pittsburgh, PA: Creation Science Fellowship, 1986), p. 113–126.

Figure 5. Creationists have proposed that the earth's magnetic field is caused by a freely decaying electric current in the earth's core. (Old-earth scientists are forced to adopt a theoretical, self-sustaining process known as the dynamo model, which contradicts some basic laws of physics.) Reliable, accurate, published geological field data have emphatically confirmed this young-earth model.

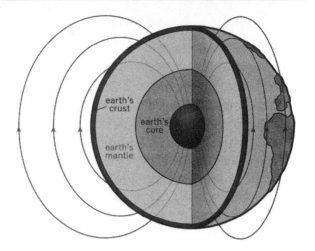

times during the Flood cataclysm when the outer core was stirred (figure 5), the field has rapidly and continuously lost total energy ever since creation (figure 6). It all points to an earth and magnetic field only about 6,000 years old.[19]

Rescuing Devices

Old-earth advocates maintain the earth is over 4.5 billion years old, so they believe the magnetic field must be self-sustaining. They propose a complex, theoretical process known as the dynamo model, but such a model contradicts some basic laws of physics. Furthermore, their model fails to explain the modern, measured electric current in the seafloor.[20] Nor can it explain the past field reversals, computer simulations notwithstanding.[21]

To salvage their old earth and dynamo, some have suggested the magnetic field decay is linear rather than exponential, in spite of the historic measurements and decades of experiments confirming the exponential decay. Others have suggested that the strength of some components increases to make up for other components that are decaying. That claim results from confusion about the difference between magnetic field intensity and its energy, and has been refuted categorically by creation physicists.[22]

19. For a fuller treatment and further information see Morris, *The Young Earth*, p. 74–85; Snelling, *Earth's Catastrophic Past: Geology, Creation and the Flood*, p. 873–877.
20. L.J. Lanzerotti et al., "Measurements of the Large-Scale Direct-Current Earth Potential and Possible Implications for the Geomagnetic Dynamo," *Science* 229, no. 4708 (1985): p. 47–49.
21. D. Russell Humphreys, "Can Evolutionists Now Explain the Earth's Magnetic Field?" *Creation Research Society Quarterly* 33, no. 3 (1996): p. 184–185.
22. D. Russell Humphreys, "Physical Mechanism for Reversal of the Earth's Magnetic Field During the Flood," in *Proceedings of the Second International Conference on Creationism*, vol. 2, p. 129–142.

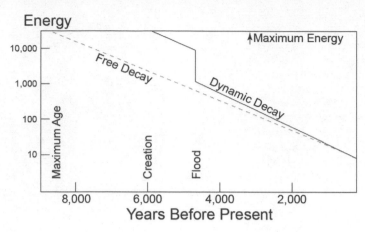

Figure 6: The earth's magnetic field has rapidly and continuously lost total energy since its origin, no matter which model has been adopted to explain its magnetism. According to creationists' dynamic decay model, the earth's magnetic field lost more energy during the Flood, when the outer core was stirred and the field reversed direction several times.

#6 Helium in Radioactive Rocks

During the radioactive decay of uranium and thorium contained in rocks, lots of helium is produced. Because helium is the second lightest element and a noble gas — meaning it does not combine with other atoms — it readily diffuses (leaks) out and eventually escapes into the atmosphere. Helium diffuses so rapidly that all the helium should have leaked out in less than 100,000 years. So why are these rocks still full of helium atoms?

While drilling deep Precambrian (pre-Flood) granitic rocks in New Mexico, geologists extracted samples of zircon (zirconium silicate) crystals from different depths. The crystals contained not only uranium but also large amounts of helium.[23] The hotter the rocks, the faster the helium should escape, so researchers were surprised to find that the deepest, and therefore hottest, zircons (at 387°F or 197°C) contained far more helium than expected. Up to 58 percent of the helium that the uranium could have ever generated was still present in the crystals.

---

23. R.V. Gentry, G.L. Glish, and E.H. McBay, "Differential Helium Retention in Zircons: Implications for Nuclear Waste Containment," *Geophysical Research Letters* 9, no. 10 (1982): p. 1129–1130.

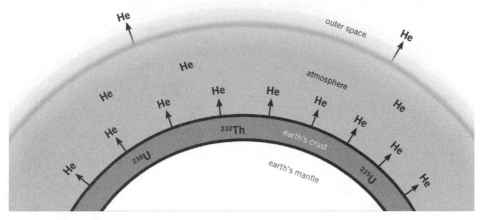

Figure 7. Radioactive elements in rocks produce a lot of helium as they decay; and this gas quickly slips away into the atmosphere, especially when the rocks are hot. Yet radioactive rocks in the earth's crust contain a lot of helium. The only possible explanation: the helium hasn't had time to escape!

The helium leakage rate has been determined in several experiments.[24] All measurements are in agreement. Helium diffuses so rapidly that all the helium in these zircon crystals should have leaked out in less than 100,000 years. The fact that so much helium is still there means they cannot be 1.5 billion years old, as uranium-lead dating suggests. Indeed, using the measured rate of helium diffusion, these pre-Flood rocks have an average "diffusion age" of only 6,000 (± 2,000) years.[25]

These experimentally determined and repeatable results, based on the well-understood physical process of diffusion, thus emphatically demonstrate that these zircons are only a few thousand years old. The supposed 1.5-billion-year

24. S.W. Reiners, K.A. Farley, and H.J. Hicks, "He Diffusion and (U-Th)/He Thermochronometry of Zircon: Initial Results from Fish Canyon Tuff and Gold Butte, Nevada," *Tectonophysics* 349, no. 1–4 (2002): p. 297–308; D. Russell Humphreys et al., "Helium Diffusion Rates Support Accelerated Nuclear Decay," in *Proceedings of the Fifth International Conference on Creationism*, R.L. Ivey Jr., ed. (Pittsburgh, PA: Creation Science Fellowship, 2003), p. 175–196; D. Russell Humphreys, "Young Helium Diffusion Age of Zircons Supports Accelerated Nuclear Decay," in *Radioisotopes and the Age of the Earth: Results of a Young-Earth Creationist Research Initiative*, L. Vardiman, A.A. Snelling, and E.F. Chaffin, eds. (El Cajon, CA: Institute for Creation Research, and Chino Valley, AZ: Creation Research Society, 2005), p. 25–100.
25. Humphreys et al., "Helium Diffusion Rates Support Accelerated Nuclear Decay"; Humphreys, "Young Helium Diffusion Age of Zircons Supports Accelerated Nuclear Decay."

age is based on the unverifiable assumptions of radioisotope dating that are radically wrong.[26]

Another evidence of a young earth is the low amount of helium in the atmosphere. The leakage rate of helium gas into the atmosphere has been measured.[27] Even though some helium escapes into outer space, the amount still present is not nearly enough if the earth is over 4.5 billion years old (figure 7).[28] In fact, if we assume no helium was in the original atmosphere, all the helium would have accumulated in only 1.8 million years even from an evolutionary standpoint.[29] But when the catastrophic Flood upheaval is factored in, which rapidly released huge amounts of helium into the atmosphere, it could have accumulated in only 6,000 years.[30]

Rescuing Devices

So glaring and devastating is the surprisingly large amount of helium that old-earth advocates have attempted to discredit this evidence.

One critic suggested the helium didn't all come from uranium decay in the zircon crystals but a lot diffused into them from the surrounding minerals. But this proposal ignores measurements showing that less helium gas is in the surrounding minerals. Due to the well-established diffusion law of physics, gases always diffuse from areas of higher concentration to surrounding areas of lower concentration.[31]

Another critic suggested the edges of the zircon crystals must have stopped the helium from leaking out, effectively "bottling" the helium within the zircons. However, this postulation has also been easily refuted because the zircon crystals are wedged between flat mica sheets, not wrapped

26. Andrew A. Snelling, "Radiometric Dating: Back to Basics," *Answers* 4, no. 3 (July–Sept. 2009): p. 72–75; Andrew A. Snelling, "Radiometric Dating: Problems With the Assumptions," *Answers* 4, no. 4 (Oct.–Dec. 2009): p. 70–73.

27. G.E. Hutchinson, "Marginalia," *American Scientist* 35 (1947): p. 118; Melvin A. Cook, "Where Is the Earth's Radiogenic Helium?" *Nature* 179, no. 4557 (1957): p. 213.

28. J.C.G. Walker, Evolution of the Atmosphere (London: Macmillan, 1977); J.W. Chamberlain and D.M. Hunten, *Theory of Planetary Atmospheres*, 2nd edition (London: Academic Press, 1987).

29. Larry Vardiman, *The Age of the Earth's Atmosphere: A Study of the Helium Flux Through the Atmosphere* (El Cajon, CA: Institute for Creation Research, 1990).

30. For a fuller treatment and further information see Morris, *The Young Earth*, p. 83–85; DeYoung, *Thousands . . . Not Billions*, p. 65–78; Snelling, *Earth's Catastrophic Past: Geology, Creation and the Flood*, p. 887–890.

31. D. Russell Humphreys et al., "Helium Diffusion Age of 6,000 Years Supports Accelerated Nuclear Decay," *Creation Research Society Quarterly* 41, no. 1 (2004): p. 1–16.

in them, so that helium could easily flow between the sheets unrestricted.[32] All other critics have been answered.[33] Thus all available evidence confirms that the true age of these zircons and their host granitic rock is only 6,000 (± 2,000) years.

#7 Carbon-14 in Fossils, Coal, and Diamonds

Carbon-14 (or radiocarbon) is a radioactive form of carbon that scientists use to date fossils. But it decays so quickly — with a half-life of only 5,730 years — that none is expected to remain in fossils after only a few hundred thousand years. Yet carbon-14 has been detected in "ancient" fossils — supposedly up to hundreds of millions of years old — ever since the earliest days of radiocarbon dating.[34]

Even if every atom in the whole earth were carbon-14, they would decay so quickly that no carbon-14 would be left on earth after only 1 million years. Contrary to expectations, between 1984 and 1998 alone, the scientific literature reported carbon-14 in 70 samples that came from fossils, coal, oil, natural gas, and marble representing the fossil-bearing portion of the geo-

Figure 8. A sea creature, called an ammonite, was discovered near Redding, California, accompanied by fossilized wood. Both fossils are claimed by strata dating to be 112–120 million years old but yielded radiocarbon ages of only thousands of years.

logic record, supposedly spanning more than 500 million years. All contained radiocarbon.[35] Further, analyses of fossilized wood and coal samples, supposedly spanning 32–350 million years in age, yielded ages between 20,000 and 50,000

32. Humphreys, "Young Helium Diffusion Age of Zircons Supports Accelerated Nuclear Decay."

33. D. Russell Humphreys, "Critics of Helium Evidence for a Young World Now Seem Silent," *Journal of Creation* 24, no. 1 (2010): p. 14–16; D. Russell Humphreys, "Critics of Helium Evidence for a Young World Now Seem Silent?" *Journal of Creation* 24, no. 3 (2010): p. 35–39.

34. Robert L. Whitelaw, "Time, Life, and History in the Light of 15,000 Radiocarbon Dates," *Creation Research Society Quarterly* 7, no. 1 (1970): p. 56–71.

35. Paul Giem, "Carbon-14 Content of Fossil Carbon," *Origins* 51 (2001): p. 6–30.

years using carbon-14 dating.[36] The fossilized sea creature and wood in figure 8 both yield radiocarbon ages of only thousands of years. Diamonds supposedly 1 to 3 billion years old similarly yielded carbon-14 ages of only 55,000 years.[37]

Even that is too old when you realize that these ages assume that the earth's magnetic field has always been constant. But it was stronger in the past, protecting the atmosphere from solar radiation and reducing the radiocarbon production. As a result, past creatures had much less radiocarbon in their bodies, and their deaths occurred much more recently than reported!

So the radiocarbon ages of all fossils and coal should be reduced to less than 5,000 years, matching the timing of their burial during the Flood. The age of diamonds should be reduced to the approximate time of biblical creation — about 6,000 years ago.[38]

Rescuing Devices

Old-earth advocates repeat the same two hackneyed defenses, even though they were resoundingly demolished years ago. The first cry is, "It's all contamination." Yet for 30 years, AMS radiocarbon laboratories have subjected all samples, before they carbon-14 date them, to repeated brutal treatments with strong acids and bleaches to rid them of all contamination.[39] And when the instruments are tested with blank samples, they yield zero radiocarbon, so there can't be any contamination or instrument problems.

The second cry is, "New radiocarbon was formed directly in the fossils when nearby decaying uranium bombarded traces of nitrogen in the buried fossils." Carbon-14 does form from such transformation of nitrogen, but actual calculations demonstrate conclusively this process does not produce the

36. John R. Baumgardner et al., "Measurable ¹⁴C in Fossilized Organic Materials: Confirming the Young Earth Creation-Flood Model," in *Proceedings of the Fifth International Conference on Creationism*, R.L. Ivey, Jr., ed. (Pittsburgh, PA: Creation Science Fellowship, 2003), p. 127–142.
37. John R. Baumgardner, "¹⁴C Evidence for a Recent Global Flood and a Young Earth," in *Radioisotopes and the Age of the Earth: Results of a Young-Earth Creationist Research Initiative*, p. 587–630.
38. For a fuller treatment and further information see Don B. DeYoung, *Thousands . . . Not Billions*, p. 45–62; Snelling, *Earth's Catastrophic Past: Geology, Creation and the Flood*, p. 855–864; Andrew A. Snelling, "Carbon-14 Dating — Understanding the Basics," *Answers* 5, no. 4 (Oct.–Dec. 2010): p. 72–75; Andrew A. Snelling, "Carbon-14 in Fossils and Diamonds — an Evolution Dilemma" *Answers* 6, no. 1 (Jan.–Mar. 2011): p. 72–75; Andrew A. Snelling, "50,000-Year-Old Fossils — A Creationist Puzzle," *Answers* 6, no. 2 (April–June 2011): p. 70–73.
39. Andrew A. Snelling, "Radiocarbon Ages for Fossil Ammonites and Wood in Cretaceous Strata near Redding, California," *Answers Research Journal* 1 (2008): p. 123–144.

levels of radiocarbon that world-class laboratories have found in fossils, coal, and diamonds.[40]

#8 Short-Lived Comets

A comet spends most of its time far from the sun in the deep freeze of space. But, once each orbit, a comet comes very close to the sun, allowing the sun's heat to evaporate much of the comet's ice and dislodge dust to form a beautiful tail. Comets have little mass, so each close pass to the sun greatly reduces a comet's size, and eventually comets fade away. They can't survive billions of years.

Two other mechanisms can destroy comets — ejections from the solar system and collisions with planets. Ejections happen as comets pass too close to the large planets, particularly Jupiter, and the planets' gravity kicks them out of the solar system. While ejections have been observed many times, the first observed collision was in 1994, when Comet Shoemaker-Levi IX slammed into Jupiter.

Given the loss rates, it's easy to compute a maximum age of comets. That maximum age is only a few million years. Obviously, their prevalence makes sense if the entire solar system was created just a few thousand years ago, but not if it arose billions of years ago.

Rescuing Devices

Evolutionary astronomers have answered this problem by claiming that comets must come from two sources. They propose that a Kuiper belt beyond the orbit of Neptune hosts short-period comets (comets with orbits under 200 years), and a much larger, distant Oort cloud hosts long-period comets (comets with orbits over 200 years).

Yet there is no evidence for the supposed Oort cloud, and there likely never will be. In the past 20 years, astronomers have found thousands of asteroids orbiting beyond Neptune, and they are assumed to be the Kuiper belt. However, the large size of these asteroids (Pluto is one of the larger ones) and the difference in composition between these asteroids and comets argue against this conclusion.

#9 Very Little Salt in the Sea

If the world's oceans have been around for three billion years as evolutionists believe, they should be filled with vastly more salt than the oceans contain today.

---

40. Baumgardner, "¹⁴C Evidence for a Recent Global Flood and a Young Earth," p. 614–616.

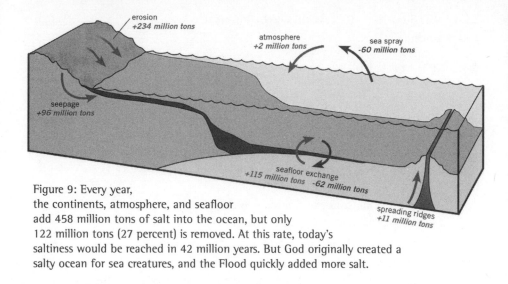

Figure 9: Every year,
the continents, atmosphere, and seafloor
add 458 million tons of salt into the ocean, but only
122 million tons (27 percent) is removed. At this rate, today's
saltiness would be reached in 42 million years. But God originally created a
salty ocean for sea creatures, and the Flood quickly added more salt.

Every year rivers, glaciers, underground seepage, and atmospheric and volcanic dust dump large amounts of salts into the oceans (figure 9). Consider the influx of the predominant salt, sodium chloride (common table salt). Some 458 million tons of sodium mixes into ocean water each year,[41] but only 122 million tons (27 percent) is removed by other natural processes.[42]

If seawater originally contained no sodium (salt) and the sodium accumulated at today's rates, then today's ocean saltiness would be reached in only 42 million years[43] — only about 1/70 the three billion years evolutionists propose. But those assumptions fail to take into account the likelihood that God created a saltwater ocean for all the sea creatures He made on day 5. Also, the year-long global Flood cataclysm must have dumped an unprecedented amount of salt into the ocean through erosion, sedimentation, and volcanism. So today's ocean saltiness makes much better sense within the biblical time scale of about six thousand years.[44]

41. M. Meybeck, "Concentrations des eaux fluvials en majeurs et apports en solution aux oceans," *Revue de Géologie Dynamique et de Géographie Physique* 21, no. 3 (1979): p. 215.
42. F.L. Sayles and P.C. Mangelsdorf, "Cation-Exchange Characteristics of Amazon with Suspended Sediment and Its Reaction with Seawater," *Geochimica et Cosmochimica Acta* 43 (1979): p. 767–779.
43. Steven A. Austin and D. Russell Humphreys, "The Sea's Missing Salt: A Dilemma for Evolutionists," in *Proceedings of the Second International Conference on Creationism*, p. 17–33.
44. For a fuller treatment and further information see Morris, *The Young Earth*, p. 85–87; Snelling, *Earth's Catastrophic Past: Geology, Creation and the Flood*, p. 879–881.

Rescuing Devices

Those who believe in a three-billion-year-old ocean say that past sodium inputs had to be less and outputs greater. However, even the most generous estimates can only stretch the accumulation time frame to 62 million years.[45] Long-agers also argue that huge amounts of sodium are removed during the formation of basalts at mid-ocean ridges,[46] but this ignores the fact that the sodium returns to the ocean as seafloor basalts move away from the ridges.[47]

#10 DNA in "Ancient" Bacteria

In 2000, scientists claimed to have "resurrected" bacteria, named Lazarus bacteria, discovered in a salt crystal conventionally dated at 250 million years old. They were shocked that the bacteria's DNA was very similar to modern bacterial DNA. If the modern bacteria were the result of 250 million years of evolution, its DNA should be very different from the Lazarus bacteria (based on known mutation rates). In addition, the scientists were surprised to find that the DNA was still intact after the supposed 250 million years. DNA normally breaks down quickly, even in ideal conditions. Even evolutionists agree that DNA in bacterial spores (a dormant state) should not last more than a million years. Their quandary is quite substantial.

However, the discovery of Lazarus bacteria is not shocking or surprising when we base our expectations on the Bible accounts. For instance, Noah's Flood likely deposited the salt beds that were home to the bacteria. If the Lazarus bacteria are only about 4,350 years old (the approximate number of years that have passed since the worldwide flood), their DNA is more likely to be intact and similar to modern bacteria.

Rescuing Devices

Some scientists have dismissed the finding and believe the Lazarus bacteria are contamination from modern bacteria. But the scientists who discovered the bacteria defend the rigorous procedures used to avoid contamination. They claim the old age is valid if the bacteria had longer generation times, different mutation rates, and/or similar selection pressures compared to modern bacteria. Of course these "rescuing devices" are only conjectures to make the data fit their worldview.

---

45. Austin and Humphries, "The Sea's Missing Salt: A Dilemma for Evolutionists."
46. Glenn R. Morton, pers. comm., Salt in the sea, http://www.asa3.org/archive/evolution/199606/0051.html.
47. Calculations based on many other seawater elements give much younger ages for the ocean, too. See Stuart A. Nevins (Steven A. Austin), "Evolution: The Oceans Say No!" *Impact* no. 8. (Santee, CA: Institute for Creation Research, 1973).

CHAPTER 11

Have People Always Been Brilliant or Were They Originally Dumb Brutes?

DON LANDIS[1]

Many Christians today have unanswered questions about the authority of the Bible due to their acceptance of an evolutionary time-line of history and, in particular, their view of mankind within that time-line. If the claims that mankind emerged from the slow process of evolution are true, then the Bible must be wrong, because the biblical record tells us that men were intelligent since the day of their creation (e.g., able to converse with God, able to work, and so on).

Yet our modern society believes we are just reaching the height of human intelligence and capabilities. If we accept this evolutionary view, what do we do with the biblical account? Is it completely unfounded and simply a myth? Or is the Bible true and verifiably so, thus making the evolutionary time-line errant?[2]

Most secular historians have not completely ignored the record of the Bible. However, they cite it as simply a source of information (e.g., a document of men, without God). In doing so, they undermine the authority of Scripture by

---

1. With the ancient man research team from Jackson Hole Bible College
2. For a discussion of philosophical issues of the Bible's truthfulness, see Ken Ham and Bodie Hodge, gen. eds., *How Do We Know the Bible Is True?* Vol. 1 (Green Forest, AR: Master Books, 2011).

not placing the Bible in its rightful place. Many Christians unwittingly accept this abuse of God's Word and furthermore even promote it! When it is assumed that the Bible is only one of many records of early man and it is placed in a time-line alongside the other legends predating it, two key points are missed:

1. God existed before creation and is the infinite, omniscient, and omnipresent Creator and, as such, He is the ultimate authority above all things (Genesis 1:1; Isaiah 40:28; Isaiah 40:14; Proverbs 15:3; Psalm 24:1).
2. The Bible is the inspired, inerrant, infallible, and authoritative Word of God, given to us as God spoke through human writers (2 Peter 1:21; 2 Timothy 3:16).

Therefore, God's account of what happened at the beginning of time, and since then, is accurate and true, and it is fallible man's accounts of history that is subject to error. No matter *when* in human, historic time the Bible was actually penned or by whom, it has priority over any other account. In our book, *The Genius of Ancient Man*,[3] we refer to this idea as the "priority of God in sequence and time." God predates the universe and all human history; He was actually there, and His account (which He revealed to us in His Holy Word) is the accurate one.

What about Legends, Myths, and Pagan Histories?

All non-biblical records and legends of the beginning come from oral (or written) traditions passed down through the descendants of Adam and Eve.[4] They are often mutilated and distorted while still containing some elements of the original truth concerning human history. Unfortunately, some of these accounts are given more historical "credit" because they predate the writing of the Bible. Historians tend to give priority to older documents. Television, movies, books, and modern education continue to undermine the validity and authority of Scripture by quoting the Bible as a late source. Even the Christian world is being fed a secular time-line of historical events. The Bible may be accurately quoted, but it is not given proper authority over all other pieces of historical data.

---

3. Don Landis and a team from Jackson Hole Bible College compiled an in-depth study of ancient man according to the biblical historical record. Their research is presented in the book *The Genius of Ancient Man* (Green Forest, AR: New Leaf Press, 2012).
4. In some cases, there may be completely "homemade" stories to try to counter others of ancient man's day and age, but all false ideas of origins originate in the mind of fallen beings, such as mankind.

For example, secular historians give the Code of Hammurabi superiority over God's Law found in the Pentateuch (the first five books of the Bible, written by Moses). Hammurabi, an ancient Babylonian king, wrote this set of laws about 340 years before Moses.[5] The Code appears to have a moral basis similar to that of the Pentateuch. The assumption is that since Hammurabi wrote before Moses, then Moses's writings are a copy or revision of this previously written moral code. Some historians theorize that Moses even stole or edited many such codes that predated him. So the authority of the Bible is undermined because God is no longer the original author of moral law! Moses is depicted as a compiler of good thoughts and morals that are essentially without truth or integrity. However, if God revealed the truth to Moses, then it was the authoritative, original truth. All the previous allusions to morality or history are distortions of the original and diluted with man's fallible ideas.

If the secular world only presented this occasionally it might not have a wide effect, but we are literally flooded with this idea from different avenues of the media. Without thinking it through, the average Christian subconsciously assumes it is true and thus their confidence in the text of God's Word is devalued. Because Christians have become accustomed to merely accepting these things without challenge, they are in danger of rejecting scriptural authority as a whole.

The study and correct evaluation of ancient man according to the biblical time-line becomes an apologetic vehicle of argument concerning the truthfulness, credibility, and authority of the Scriptures.

Two Views of History

Evolutionary History (Man Is the Authority): If evolution is accurate, then the sequence of life forms transitioning from single-celled organisms to humankind demands simplicity leading to complexity. This means the early animals would be weaker in mental ability and awareness. As early pre-man developed, he would be a simple thinker with limited ability to contemplate life. In modern terms, pre-man would have been stupid and illiterate. Ancient men would have lived as evolution depicts them, eating raw meat and dragging their women around by the hair and living in caves. Then, as man continued to evolve, he became more intellectual and aware and led us to where we are today: sophisticated 21st-century man.

---

5. Hammurabi's law code was written in 1786 B.C. For more information, see Don Landis, "Hammurabi or Moses — Who's the Authority?" *Answers*, January–March 2012, p. 80–81. See also Landis, *The Genius of Ancient Man*, p. 16–17.

Biblical History (God Is the Authority): The first humans were made in God's image and therefore created very intelligent (Genesis 1:27). The early chapters of Genesis tell us that Adam and Eve were moral beings who could communicate with God and each other, rationalize, name things, and work. Their descendants were gardeners (Genesis 4:2), musicians (Genesis 4:21), builders (Genesis 4:17), and metal workers (Genesis 4:22). Man was made in the image of an intelligent, moral, and creative God.

These two opposing views (based on presuppositions and biases) are easy to understand and follow to their logical conclusions. Yet the implications of each are profound. For if evolution is true, then the further back one studies into human history, the simpler and less sophisticated man should be (not to mention that nothing ultimately matters in this worldview). But if we hold that creation is true, then the evidence we find should portray great intelligence and advanced ancient cultures. So what is it that we find through scientific and historical discoveries?

Using Evidence, Which Model of History Is Correct?

The truth is, there is a vast amount of evidence, much of it ignored by scholars who are working from the paradigm of evolution, which clearly shows that early man could build, think, and design very complex cities and empires. They could create with technology that is still unexplainable. They had structured cultures and societies that show an appreciation for beauty and order. They were adept astronomers, fundamentally religious, and dedicated builders.

Ancient man's intelligence is proven by data that is now becoming available to anyone. It directly contradicts the stereotypical view of early barbaric man, dressed in animal skins and searching for the formula for fire. Unfortunately, much of the archeological evidence is basically ignored because it does not fit the evolutionary time-line. There are some who acknowledge the evidence of ancient genius, but they hold the rather mystical view that aliens from outer space endowed ancient peoples with their inexplicable knowledge and ability.[6] But the ever-growing list of new discoveries reveals that the data best fits the biblical paradigm.

Just as the fossil record attests to the authority and accuracy of the biblical text (e.g., a global Flood), so does the study of early man.[7] When the picture of ancient

---

6. Proponents of this theory include Richard Dawkins, David Childress, and Robert Bauval.
7. For further information on how the fossil record supports biblical authority, see Dr. Andrew Snelling, "Order in the Fossil Record," Answers in Genesis, http://www.answersingenesis.org/articles/am/v5/n1/order-fossil-record, and John D. Morris and Frank J. Sherwin, *The Fossil Record: Unearthing Nature's History of Life* (Dallas, TX: Institute for Creation Research, 2010).

man is clearly seen and the evidence evaluated from a proper perspective, there is no alternative: man was intelligent from the beginning just as the Bible indicates.

Examples of Ancient Man's Genius

As more researchers stop ignoring the data, more evidence is being reported and catalogued. The amount of information continues to grow, and we can use it as a good confirmation of biblical history. In light of this new research and evidence, we can confidently state that ancient peoples had exceptional capabilities in construction, astronomy, and transportation. Their architectural skill is still an unsolved mystery. Without the use of modern power tools or machines, early man constructed large buildings with incredible precision. Many of these ancient structures were built in line with astronomical events such as solstices and equinoxes (this is known as "archaeoastronomy"). As far as we know, ancient civilizations did not possess computer technology and yet demonstrated an advanced understanding of the heavens.

The following information gives strong evidences for ancient man's genius around the world.

Puma Punku

Part of a large ancient city known as Tiwanaku in Bolivia, this archeological site displays one of the greatest examples of advanced stone-cutting techniques. The blocks are cut and shaped so well they fit together perfectly. In fact, they are so well cut that even robots today would have trouble making the stones so precise.[8]

Puma Punku
(photo: Wikimedia Commons)

Palace of Knossos

Part of the Minoan civilization on the island of Crete, existing between 2100 B.C. and 1450 B.C., the palace is a highly advanced structure that is perhaps the most impressive ancient structure in Europe; it possesses a water and drainage

Palace of Knossos
(photo copyrights: Ken Zuk)

---

8. See Landis, *The Genius of Ancient Man*, p. 52.

system and was built to withstand earthquakes and to use sunlight to brighten rooms deep within the palace.[9]

La Bastida
(http://www.murciatoday.com/images/
articles/13378_la-bastida-totana_1_large.jpg)

Great Pyramid of Gaza
(photo: Wikimedia Commons)

Baalbek
(photo: Wikimedia Commons)

La Bastida

A fortress located in the Agaric region of Spain dating to around 2200 B.C., it displays that the people who built it possessed advanced military techniques, as well as the oldest arch in the world.[10]

Great Pyramid of Giza

Perhaps the most famous ancient structure in the world, the Great Pyramid is the pinnacle of ancient man's ability to construct advanced buildings. It is not only massive in size; it is precisely aligned with true north within 3/60 of a degree. Its base is only 7/8 of an inch out of level and it covers an area of 13 acres. It, along with the two neighboring pyramids, may be aligned with Orion's belt. Another factor exhibiting its advancement is that the mortar used was stronger than rock, most with less than 1/50 of an inch between them. Over a million stones were used in its construction, averaging 2.5 to 15 tons each. The heaviest weighs around 80 tons![11]

Baalbek

A temple in Lebanon, it was designed to withstand earthquakes.

9. Matthew Zuk, "The Genius of Ancient Man: The Minoan Civilization: Proof of Advanced Nature"; http://geniusofancientman.blogspot.com/.

10. Matthew Zuk, "The Genius of Ancient Man: La Bastida: Europe's Most Formidable City"; http://geniusofancientman.blogspot.com/. http://geniusofancientman.blogspot.com/2013/03/la-bastida.html.

11. See Landis, *The Genius of Ancient Man*, p. 63, as well as the book's blog at www.geniusofancientman.blogspot.com.

The foundation of the temple has no known origin. This site possesses the largest stones ever cut. The three large stones (made of limestone) are labeled the Trilithon stones, and each weighs 800 tons. The lower layers are made up of smaller stones (though still very large), which allowed them to move with the earth during earthquakes, thereby making them stable.[12]

Stonehenge
(photo: Wikimedia Commons)

Stonehenge

Located in England, this is one of the greatest examples of archaeoastronomy in the ancient world. It was likely used to predict when the solstices, equinoxes, and cross quarter days would occur each year. It is yet a mystery as to how these stones were moved, but they are a perfect example of ancient man's knowledge of the sky.[13]

Cuzco
(photo: Wikimedia Commons)

Cuzco

Located in Peru, Cuzco was the first Incan capital. The structures at the site are so well put together not even a knife blade can fit between the stones, yet no mortar is used as a seal. The stones used are also very large and cut at odd angles, but that did not detract from the seamless construction.[14]

City of Alexandria

An example of archaeoastronomy, the entire city of Alexandria was originally laid out so that the sun was aligned with the main street on Alexander the Great's birthday.[15]

City of Alexandria
(photo: Wikimedia Commons)

---

12. See Landis, *The Genius of Ancient Man*, p. 69-71.
13. Ibid.
14. Ibid.
15. Stephanie Pappas, "Ancient Egypt City Aligned With Sun on King's Birthday," Live Science, http://www.livescience.com/23994-ancient-city-alexandria-sun.html (accessed April 18, 2013).

Harappa

Harappa
(photo: Wikimedia Commons)

Located in the Indus valley of Pakistan, it dates back to around 2300–1900 B.C., and it is yet unknown as to why it fell, but it began a rapid decline around 1900 B.C. There are several large domiciles, including a citadel and baths, and large, strong walls. It was primarily a city culture, and used bricks in construction. It also had advanced systems of agriculture, irrigation, and sanitation. There is little evidence for warfare, monarchies, temples or religious deities, slavery, or class distinctions. However, they did have precise measuring systems as well as a form of writing.[16]

Antikythera Mechanism

Antikythera Mechanism
(photo: Wikimedia Commons)

Found off the island of Antikythera, Greece, it dates to around the second century B.C.; it is one of the most advanced artifacts ever found. Around the size of a shoebox, it is believed to have predicted movements of the sun, moon, 12 signs of the zodiac, and possibly five planets. It also tracked the four-year cycle of the Olympic games. Thirty of its gears are still intact, but it may have once had 37.[17]

Ancient Man and the Historic Ice Age

A relatively new and very recent series of discoveries is bringing shock waves to the archeological world. Underwater archeological sites showing evidence of Ice Age civilizations are being discovered at an ever-increasing number.

16. T.A. Kohler, "Week 16: Indus Valley (Harappan) Civilization," Washington State University, http://public.wsu.edu/~tako/Week16.html (accessed April 18, 2013).
17. See Landis, *The Genius of Ancient Man*, p.49.

Since we believe the Bible is true and therefore the Flood of Noah actually took place, we see how perfectly these new discoveries fit into the time-line of the text.

There are studies that indicate that the Flood was followed by a global Ice Age.[18] There are also legends around the world that describe an Ice Age in earth's history.[19] It is theorized that there was a massive buildup of ice in the polar regions of the world during this time, and this would have lowered the water levels of earth's oceans. In Genesis 11, God scattered man because of the rebellion against Him in the building of the Tower of Babel. The city was built to keep man together (Genesis 11:4), directly defying God's command to "fill the earth" in Genesis 9:1. Due to the Ice Age, lower water levels would have allowed man to travel greater distances as the people scattered, settling in new lands, often along subtropical coastlines using land bridges to cross to the Americas, England, Japan, and so on.[20] But these water levels would have risen again as the earth began to warm and the ice caps melted, and slowly covered the coastal cities. This is most likely why many ancient structures have been found largely intact under the earth's oceans.

Examples of underwater sites include Yonaguni near Japan, Dwarka near India, and Yarmuta near Lebanon; there is also evidence of extensive urban civilization off the coasts of both Cuba and Greece.[21] This is a very exciting new field of study that will continue to confirm the truth of Scripture.

The Implications of the Tower of Babel

Along with the truth of intelligent ancient man, the biblical account demands the truth of the city of Babel. The Bible records that mankind gathered together:

> And they said, "Come, let us build ourselves a city, and a tower whose top is in the heavens; let us make a name for ourselves, lest we be scattered abroad over the face of the whole earth" (Genesis 11:4).

18. The Ice Age is not explicitly discussed in the Bible, but there are a few passages that imply there was a cooler climate after the Flood. There is also ample geologic evidence to suggest that it did indeed occur. Also, the possibility of an Ice Age does not conflict with the chronology presented in the Bible. See Michael Oard, "Where Does the Ice Age Fit?" Answers in Genesis, http://www.answersingenesis.org/articles/nab/where-does-ice-age-fit; Dr. Andrew Snelling and Mike Matthews, "When Was the Ice Age in Biblical History?" *Answers*, April–June 2013, p. 46–52; and Landis, *The Genius of Ancient Man*, p. 96–97.
19. See Landis, *The Genius of Ancient Man*, p. 77.
20. Though let's not forget that ancient man was also adept at building boats and likely went to many places by ship. There were the coastline (island or maritime) peoples in Genesis 10:5, and Noah and his sons were excellent ship builders and lived extensively after the Flood, passing along this technology.
21. See Landis, *The Genius of Ancient Man*, p. 71.

In rebellion against God, they formed their own unified government, a counterfeit religion, and a man-centered philosophical system of thought. Some of these concepts were carried throughout the world by those dispersed from Babel.

Thus, the characteristics of Babel are reflected in the ancient empires and cultures all around the globe. The astonishingly advanced civilizations show incredible similarities. Their religious practices such as pagan sacrifice, sun and star worship, and devotion to a false trinity all have their roots in Babel. The pyramids and ziggurats and mounds built around the world are likely examples of man-made mountains, built in rebellion against God, just like what was introduced at the Tower of Babel.[22] It is fascinating to study the ancient cultures and recognize the elements of biblical truth that were present, as well as the perversions that were introduced throughout history.

The Decline of Early Man

Some skeptics might question: if ancient man was intelligent and built such amazing, highly developed civilizations, where are they today? Why is there such a large segment of human history showing men with little ability or technological progress?[23]

It is clearly written in Genesis that Adam and Eve were not created infinite, but "very good." Their sin against God brought an abrupt end to that innocent state, ultimately resulting in death.

When Adam sinned, God placed a curse on the ground that affected the whole universe, a punishment of death instigating a downward spiral to all of creation, including man's being (Genesis 3; Romans 8). Adam and Eve began to die physically (their bodies would deteriorate with age until they died), they died spiritually (they were separated from God), they died mentally (the superior intelligence and capabilities of their minds were weakened), and they died socially (they hid their nakedness from each other). This picture of history is not one of early man moving up a gradual ladder of development via evolution but of the first man, in his created state, rebelling against God and degenerating downhill, "devolving," if you please.

---

22. See presupposition 3 in chapter 2 of Landis, *The Genius of Ancient Man,* for more detail on the evidence of Babel around the earth. A map of the distribution of man-made mountains worldwide is found on p. 65 of *The Genius of Ancient Man.*

23. From history, we know that man did at times live in caves and in a somewhat barbaric fashion. There are records of "stone age" type living conditions and uncivilized cultures. But this does not invalidate the text of the Bible. It is important to remember that where a person lives does not necessarily reflect the intelligence of that person. Was Jesus an illiterate, dumb brute because he had "nowhere to lay His head" (Matthew 8:20)?

The Bible also records that ancient men lived extraordinarily long lives (Genesis 5 and 11). Until the effects of the Curse became more severe and their life expectancy dropped dramatically, they were able to pass on their knowledge to the next generations.

It is true that if one only goes back to the mid-history of early man, there is evidence of a lack of knowledge and skill (often when pagan religions started bearing their fruit and suppressed such things), but if one jumps over this period to even earlier times, the intelligence is remarkable. In our research for *The Genius of Ancient Man,* it became clear that some of the knowledge from these highly advanced, early generations was passed on, although much was eventually lost as time progressed.[24]

Aren't We More Intelligent Now Than We Ever Were?

In present times, we are again *amassing* vast amounts of knowledge and data. In this, modern man takes pride and in fact assumes it is an evidence for evolution. But this is not true. It has taken hundreds of years for our knowledge of technology and science to reach where it is today.

Man's inherent inquisitive nature, evident in an ongoing pursuit of education, testifies that something was lost in Eden. Mankind longs to know things and to discover. He longs for intelligence. He longs to improve himself. This is because he is trying to get back to the way things were (and also hints back to the Fall and man's desire to be like God recorded in Genesis 3).

Though the massive amount of technical data we have accumulated seems impressive, an honest evaluation of our society today still reveals a barbaric inhumanness. For example, in recent times millions were killed by Hitler, Stalin, Lenin, Mao Tse-tung, and other despots.[25] Man is not evolving upward into something better. Rather, these recent events confirm the depraved heart of man and not the ascendency of the human spirit. We think we have reached great heights of technology, but the wisdom of man has led only to an intellectual and moral insanity.

Conclusion

Christians have nothing to be ashamed of when it comes to the time-line of history and ancient man. We need not "hide our heads in the sand" on any truth supposedly "proven" by secular archeology or science or by any discovery

---

24. Reasons for this loss are highly speculative. For more detail about ancient technology and the mystery surrounding it, see chapter 6 in Landis, *The Genius of Ancient Man.*
25. See chapter 5 in this volume on the results of an evolutionary worldview.

— past, present, or future. Observational science and history continue to confirm, support, and validate our faith.

The truth is, man *was* brilliant — brilliant in all the splendor of unspoiled creation, brilliant in intellect and imagination, brilliant in creativity and invention. But with the entrance of sin and the Curse, man began and continues a downward spiral in his rebellion. Without the hope of salvation through the Lord Jesus Christ, man is ultimately doomed to the wrath of God. But we who are believers in Christ have this hope that one day, because of Christ's atoning work, we will again be brilliantly glorified with Him (Romans 8:16–30).

The Bible is true, in far more ways and detail than even imagined by today's believers. Do not undermine its authority. Do not doubt its inerrancy. Stand firm, "Test all things; hold fast what is good" (1 Thessalonians 5:21).

CHAPTER 12

What about Living Fossils?

DR. JOHN WHITMORE[1]

W hen Charles Darwin published the first edition of the *Origin of Species* in 1859, he imagined a large evolutionary "tree" of organisms that were continuously connected by various transitional forms. Furthermore, he envisioned life constantly changing through time as various environmental and climatic conditions changed — with only the fittest and best adapted offspring surviving. At the time, paleontology was still a relatively young science and Darwin realized that the fossil record did not yet support his theory. Subsequently, he predicted that numerous fossil "intermediate links" would be found, gradually leading to the animals that we have today. Darwin did not predict that organisms at the lowest taxonomic levels would remain unchanged for long periods of time.[2] He thought that their morphology (or body shape) would change (or evolve) over time.

What Are Living Fossils?

Initially, the term "living fossil" doesn't make much sense. How could something be alive and a fossil at the same time? "Living fossils" are organisms that

---

1. Professor of Geology, Cedarville University, Cedarville, OH 45314 johnwhitmore@
   cedarville.edu.
2. Carolus Linnaeus developed the system that biologists still use to classify animals:
   kingdom, phylum, class, order, family, genus, and species. These are known as "taxonomic
   levels" and a group(s) within a taxonomic level is referred to as a "taxon" (singular) or
   "taxa" (plural). The species is the most basic taxonomic level and contains only a single
   type of organism or taxon. Genera are similar groups of species. Families are similar groups
   of genera and so on. Most creationists think the Genesis "kind" approximates the family
   level of the Linnaean system of classification.

The classification system of life developed by Carolus Linnaeus.

Kingdom
Phylum
Class
Order
Family
Genus
Species

Many creation biologists believe the "Genesis kind" is near the family level of classification and that the various genera and species that we have today developed from the original Genesis kinds.

can be found both living in the world today and also found preserved in the rock record as fossils, with the living animals showing little if any difference from their fossil counterparts. Studying and comparing fossils to modern organisms is important because we can see how (or if) they have changed over time. The study of these organisms has implications for both evolutionary and biblical models of earth history. An organism is considered a "living fossil" if it has fossil representatives that are from the same taxonomic level — usually in the same genus or species group. Living fossils are impressive from an evolutionary perspective with some animal genera existing for nearly the entire range of the Phanerozoic[3] record — that's more than half of a billion years! From a biblical perspective, no fossils are much older than the time of the Flood, about 4,300 years ago, so a creationist might predict living fossils would be more common. Many famous examples of living fossils are found in the Cenozoic rocks, or ones that were made after the Flood was over.

What Are Some Examples of Living Fossils, and How Many Are There?

Notable examples of living fossil genera (plural for the classification level of a genus that can be further divided into distinct species), that have conserved the characteristics of their genus for millions of years (from an evolutionary perspective, these organisms appeared millions of years ago: MYA), include the ginkgo tree (*Ginkgo*, 252 MYA–present), the coast redwood (*Sequoia*, 151MYA–present), horsetails (*Equisetum*, 361MYA–present), a brachiopod (*Lingula*, 513 MYA–present), an annelid marine worm (*Spirorbis*, 488 MYA–present), the cockroach (*Periplaneta*, 49 MYA–present), the chambered nautilus (*Nautilus*, 340 MYA–present), and a sea mussel (*Mytilus*, 419 MYA–present).[4] Some living genera have very close sister taxa in the fossil record (animals in related groups

---

3. This is a conventional time period lasting from 542 million years ago to the present. It contains the Paleozoic, Mesozoic, and Cenozoic Eras of geological time.

4. When a word is in italics and capitalized it refers to the taxonomic level of the genus. The evolutionary ages are represented as millions of years ago (MYA). The abbreviation "Ma" means millions of years before the present or "mega-annum" and is used in more technical literature. The ranges are conventional ages for these taxa obtained from the Paleobiology Database (pbdb.org).

Coelacanth from the London
Museum of Natural History
(Photo by John Whitmore)

whose body shapes are very similar) including the coelacanth fish (*Latimeria*) with *Coelacanthus* (318–247 MYA), the horseshoe crab (*Limulus*) with *Limuloides* (419–416 MYA), and the Tuatara lizard (*Sphenodon)* with *Cynosphenodon* (190–183 MYA). There are many more examples of living fossils, many of which can be found published in various issues of creationist periodicals.

The standard geological time column is divided up into three main fossil-bearing portions: the Paleozoic, the Mesozoic, and, the most recent period of time, the Cenozoic (which contains the Neogene and Quaternary Periods). Most creation geologists believe the Paleozoic and Mesozoic portions represent rocks that were formed during Noah's Flood and that the Cenozoic represents post-Flood rocks. A recent query of the online Paleobiology Database (pbdb. org) was completed to find how many living fossils have been reported from each of these three periods of time. In this database, the genus is the lowest taxonomic group for which large amounts of data are available. From the Paleozoic, 99 living fossil genera were found; from the Mesozoic, 548 living fossil genera were found; and from the Cenozoic 2,594 living fossil genera were found. This is a total of 3,241 genera that can be found both living today and fossilized in the rock record![5] The database is updated daily by paleontologists as they find new fossils and catalog old ones, so this figure is surely an underestimate. The data were plotted using conventional 10-million-year (Ma) time bins (figure 1). The graph shows a "flat" distribution of living fossil genera during the Paleozoic and Mesozoic[6] and then a "spike" in the number at about the Mesozoic/Cenozoic[7]

---

5. Organisms (genera) were counted if they had a fossil record greater than 2.6 Ma (or older than the Quaternary Period) and their range extended into the present time (or into the Quaternary Period, 2.6 Ma or less).

6. Several statistical techniques were employed to see if there were any significant trends in the Paleozoic and Mesozoic data or in all the combined data. No significant trends could be found (where $R2$ values > 0.90), other than the observation that the number of living fossils increases dramatically toward the present time. Finding $R2$ values is a mathematical technique that can be used to test whether a predictable trend is present or not.

7. A logarithmic or exponential trend can be demonstrated in the Cenozoic data, having $R2$ values of 0.90 or greater. A logarithmic or exponential curve is one that increases rapidly, going from flat to almost vertical.

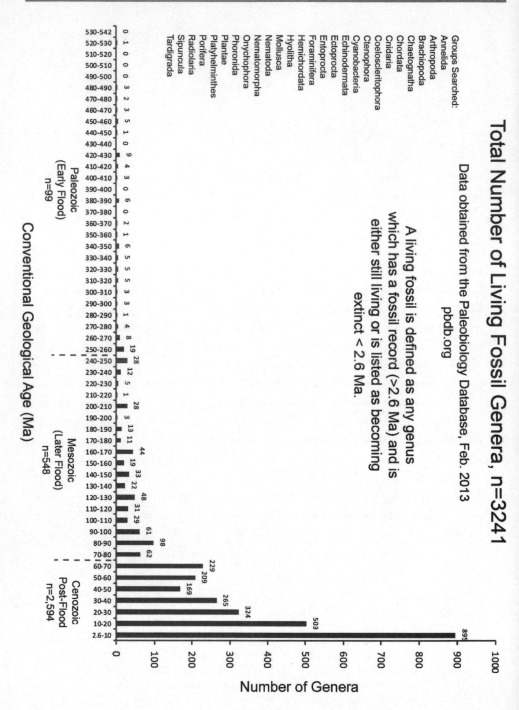

Figure 1

boundary, a time during which most creation geologists think approximately marks the end of the Flood in the rock record.[8]

Do Living Fossils Support the Theory of Evolution?

As mentioned above, Darwin predicted that organisms would change over time. However, the number of living fossil genera (albeit small compared to the large number of extinct fossil genera) is troubling from a naturalistic perspective. Perhaps organisms could resist evolutionary change over long periods of time if their environment or climate did not change; however, this is very unrealistic. From an evolutionary perspective, continents have come together and broken apart several times, there have been several "ice ages," multiple mass extinctions, and many changes in sea level during the time intervals examined. All of these factors have been claimed as impetuses for evolutionary change. In other words, these events have been cited as causes for extinction and evolutionary change every time they occur.[9] Clearly, living fossils do not support the theory of gradual evolution (sometimes called "gradualism") as proposed by Darwin.

To their credit, some paleontologists have recognized that gradualism is not the main pattern in the fossil record.[10] "Stasis" is when organisms remain unchanged and have no recognizable evolutionary change for long periods of time. Gould argued[11] that living fossils might be explained as organisms that have persisted through time and do not have very many different kinds of species within their respective genera and families. Since species diversity was low, the groups therefore lacked the genetic diversity to evolve and the group remained pretty much unchanged through time. This hypothesis might be successful in explaining some small groups like the coelacanths and lungfishes that still look similar after more than 300 million years of geological time. However, there are

8. See J.H. Whitmore and P. Garner, "Using Suites of Criteria to Recognize Pre-Flood, Flood, and Post-Flood Strata in the Rock Record with Application to Wyoming (USA)," in A.A. Snelling (ed.), *Proceedings of the Sixth International Conference on Creationism* (Pittsburgh, PA: Creation Science Fellowship and Dallas, TX: Institute for Creation Research, 2008), p. 425–448.

9. For example see M. Foote and A.I. Miller, *Principles of Paleontology*, 3rd ed. (New York: W.H. Freeman and Company, 2007), or S.M. Stanley, *Earth System History*, 3rd ed. (New York: W.H. Freeman and Company, 2009), or C. Patterson, *Evolution,* 2nd ed. (Ithaca, NY: Comstock Publishing Associates, 1999).

10. Steven Jay Gould (1941–2002) was probably the most prominent paleontologist espousing this view, arguing that stasis in the fossil record was *data* that needed to be explained. See his discussion, for example, on p. 759 of his book *The Structure of Evolutionary Theory* (Cambridge, MA: The Belknap Press of Harvard University Press, 2002). Technically, his evolutionary arguments were for stasis at the taxonomic level of the species.

11. Gould, *The Structure of Evolutionary Theory*, p. 816–817.

two problems with this explanation: 1) smaller groups (like the coelacanths) should consistently be favored for extinction (since they have low diversity[12]), yet somehow they continue to persist for millions of years through many climate changes and extinction events, and 2) the explanation fails to explain why groups that are quite diverse, like the cockroaches (which number over 3,700 described species in multiple genera and families and whose group has been around for 300 million years[13]) fail to evolve. Cockroaches are a group with great genetic diversity; yet living fossils persist within it.

Do Living Fossils Support the Biblical Account of Biology and Geology?

If Paleozoic and Mesozoic fossils primarily represent organisms that were buried during the Flood and if the Cenozoic fossils primarily represent the post-Flood era, several hypotheses can be suggested to explain the patterns in the fossil record of these times. We might predict that rocks deposited during the Flood would lack clear sequences of transitional fossils because most fossils in those rocks would have been from organisms that were alive on the day the Flood began. This could explain the apparent phenomenon of "stasis" that is so common in the fossil record, especially in pre-Cenozoic rocks.[14] We might expect a large number of pre-Flood taxa to become extinct, especially those that lived in marine environments (like trilobites or plesiosaurs) because they were not protected on the ark. Other organisms became extinct because they lived in ecosystems that were permanently destroyed during the Flood (like the floating forests proposed by Wise[15]). Living fossil taxa from the pre-Flood world would then be organisms that found comparable ecosystems in which to live after the Flood and had at least several representatives that survived the Flood. Apparently, not many genera were able to survive the Flood unchanged; there are only 647 Paleozoic and Mesozoic living fossil genera.

---

12. Low genetic diversity within a group is often touted as a cause for extinction.
13. Richard C. Brusca and Gary J. Brusca, *Invertebrates* (Sunderland, MA: Sinauer Associates, 1990).
14. Refer to K. Wise's 1989 paper on reasons for stasis and abrupt appearance in the fossil record: Punc Eq Creation Style, *Origins* v. 16(1): 11-24. Note that I am using the term "stasis" at the genus level (in referring to living fossils), where Wise uses "stasis" at the species level (referring to punctuated equilibrium). It is not yet possible to evaluate stasis at the species level in the paleobiology database (pbdb).
15. See K.P. Wise, K.P., "The Pre-Flood Floating Forest: A Study in Paleontological Pattern Recognition,: in R.L Ivey, Jr. (ed.), *Proceedings of the Fifth International Conference on Creationism* (Pittsburgh, PA: Creation Science Fellowship, 2003), p. 371–381.

In the post-Flood times (the Cenozoic), four times the number of living fossils can be found compared to that of the pre-Cenozoic; and in the immediate post-Flood interval (60–70 MYA) there are more than twice the living fossils of any previous interval. In a Flood model, the Cenozoic would have been the longest period in earth history (lasting more than 4,300 years).[16] The spike in the numbers of living fossils in the Cenozoic may be due to the rapid diversification of organisms immediately following the Flood,[17] and the ability of those organisms to establish themselves in the new niches they were filling. In other words, organisms changed quickly after the Flood (producing many new genera within Genesis kinds[18]) and once they became well-adapted to one of the many new niches after the Flood, change stopped. It is interesting that the graph shows a huge spike in the last interval of time, which may indicate additional diversification due to the climate changes that occurred at the beginning of the "Ice Age" or the Pleistocene Epoch.

Conclusion

From an old earth/evolutionary perspective, "living fossils" are an unexpected problem. Evolutionary change is predicted over time, but some genera remain unchanged for tens or hundreds of millions of years. Furthermore, why are the numbers of living fossil taxa fairly "flat" in the Paleozoic and Mesozoic times with a sudden spike during Cenozoic times? A creation-Flood model might answer this as rapid diversification of organisms following the Flood. Only a few select genera that were alive before the Flood were able to survive with their body shape unchanged. After the Flood, rapid diversification occurred probably because of climate changes and/or the opportunity for organisms to fill new niches. We think that all of these changes happened within the context of the "kinds" God created in Genesis 1. In other words, there was a lot of change, but within Genesis kinds.

---

16. The later part of the Cenozoic, the Quaternary Period, is probably the longest period of earth history from a biblical perspective. The Quaternary Period includes the Pleistocene and Holocene Epochs and is fully contained within the Cenozoic Era. We believe the Pleistocene probably begins after the Tower of Babel since this is the time where we begin to see widespread human fossils in the rock record.

17. For examples see J.H. Whitmore and K.P. Wise, "Rapid and Early Post-Flood Mammalian Diversification Evidenced in the Green River Formation," in A.A. Snelling (ed.), *Proceedings of the Sixth International Conference on Creationism* (Pittsburgh, PA: Creation Science Fellowship and Dallas, TX: Institute for Creation Research, 2008), p. 449–457.

18. It is estimated that there were less than 300 mammal kinds on the ark that diversified into all the mammal species that we have today. See K. Wise, 2009, "Mammal Kinds: How Many Were on the Ark?" in T. Wood and P. Garner (eds.), *Genesis Kinds: Creationism and the Origin of Species*, Center for Origins Research Issues in *Creation*, no. 5, p. 129–161.

Fossils of Organisms also Found Living in the World Today

Sand dollar

Wasp

Brittlestar

Dragonfly

Crab

Fossil photos by
Bodie Hodge

CHAPTER 13

What Is the State of the Canopy Model?

BODIE HODGE

I f there is one thing you need to know about biblical creationists . . . they can be divided on a subject. This isn't necessarily a bad thing. Though we all have the same heart to follow Christ and do the best we can for the sake of biblical authority and the cause of Christ, we can have differences when it comes to details of models used to explain various aspects of God's creation.

When divisions occur over scientific models, this helps us dive into an issue in more detail and discover if that model is good, bad, needs revision, and so on. But note over *what* we are divided; it is not the Word of God nor is it even theology — it is a division over a *scientific model*.

This is where Christians can rightly be divided on a subject and still do so with Christian love, which I hope is how each Christian would conduct themselves — in "iron-sharpening-iron" dealings on a model while still promoting a heart for the gospel (Proverbs 27:17).

The debate over a canopy model is no different — we are all brothers and sisters in Christ trying to understand *what the Bible says and what it doesn't say* on this subject (2 Timothy 2:15). It is the Bible that reigns supreme on the issue, and our scientific analysis on the subject will always be subservient to the Bible's text.

What Is the Canopy Model(s)?

There are several canopy models, but they all have one thing in common.[1] They all interpret the "waters above" the expanse (firmament) in Genesis 1:7 as some form of water-based canopy surrounding the earth that endured from creation until the Flood.

> Then God said, "Let there be a firmament [expanse] in the midst of the waters, and let it divide the waters from the waters." Thus God made the firmament [expanse], and divided the waters which were under the firmament [expanse] from the waters which were above the firmament [expanse]; and it was so (Genesis 1:6–7).

Essentially, the waters above are believed to have formed either a vapor, water (liquid), or ice canopy around the earth. It is the vapor canopy that seemed to dominate all of the proposed models.[2] It is suggested that this canopy was responsible for several things such as keeping harmful radiation from penetrating the earth, increasing the surface atmospheric pressure of oxygen, keeping the globe at a consistent temperature for a more uniform climate around the globe, and providing one of the sources of water for the Flood.

Some of these factors, like keeping radiation out and increasing the surface atmospheric pressures of oxygen, were thought to allow for human longevity to be increased from its present state (upwards of 900 years or so as described in Genesis 5). So this scientific model was an effort to explain several things, including the long human life span prior to the Flood. Other potential issues solved by the models were to destroy the possibility of large-scale storms with reduced airflow patterns for less extreme weather possibilities, have a climate without rain (such as Dillow's model, see below) but instead merely dew every night, and reduce any forms of barrenness like deserts and ice caps. It would have higher atmospheric pressure to possibly help certain creatures fly that may not otherwise.

---

1. This is not to be confused with canopy ideas that have the edge of water at or near the end of the universe (e.g., white hole cosmology), but instead the models that have a water canopy in the atmosphere, e.g., like those mentioned in J.C. Whitcomb and H.M. Morris, *The Genesis Flood* (Phillipsburg, NJ: Presbyterian and Reformed Publishing, 1961); J.C. Dillow, *The Waters Above: Earth's Pre-Flood Vapor Canopy*, Revised Edition (Chicago, IL: Moody Press, 1981); or John C. Whitcomb, *The World that Perished* (Winona Lake, IN: BMH Books, 2009).
2. This is in large part due to the influence of Joseph Dillow, whose scientific treatise left only the vapor models with any potential. He writes on page 422 of his treatise: "We showed that only a vapor canopy model can satisfactorily meet the requirements of a the necessary support mechanism." Dillow, *The Waters Above: Earth's Pre-Flood Vapor Canopy*, .

A Brief History of Canopy Models

Modern canopy models can be traced back to Dr. Henry Morris and Dr. John Whitcomb in their groundbreaking book *The Genesis Flood* in 1961.[3] This book triggered a return to biblical authority in our age, which is highly commendable and much is owed to their efforts. In this volume, Whitcomb and Morris introduce the possibility of a vapor canopy as the waters above.

The canopy models gained popularity thanks to the work of Dr. Joseph Dillow,[4] and many creationists have since researched various aspects of these scientific models, such as Dr. Larry Vardiman with the Institute for Creation Research.

Researchers have studied the possibility of solid canopies, water canopies, vapor canopies, thick canopies, thin canopies, and so on. Each model has the canopy collapsing into history at the time of the Flood. Researchers thought it could have provided at least some of the water for the Flood and was associated with the 40 days of rain coming from the "windows of heaven" mentioned along with the fountains of the great deep at the onset of the Flood (Genesis 7:11).

However, the current state of the canopy models have faded to such an extent that most researchers and apologists have abandoned the various models. Let's take a look at the biblical and scientific reasons behind the abandonment.

Biblical Issues

Though both will be discussed, any biblical difficulties that bear on the discussion of the canopy must *trump* scientific considerations, as it is the authority of the Bible that is supreme in all that it teaches.

Interpretations of Scripture Are Not Scripture

The necessity for a water-based canopy about the earth is not directly stated in the text. It is an *interpretation* of the text. Keep in mind that it is the *text* that is inspired, not our interpretations of it.

Others have interpreted the waters above as something entirely different from a water-based canopy about the earth. Most commentators appeal to the waters above as simply being the clouds, which are water droplets (not vapor) in the atmosphere. For they are simply "waters" that are above.

But most do not limit this interpretation as simply being the clouds, but perhaps something that reaches deep into space and extends as far as the *Third Heaven* or *Heaven of Heavens*. For example, expositor Dr. John Gill in the 1700s said:

---

3. Whitcomb and Morris, *The Genesis Flood.*
4. Dillow, *The Waters Above: Earth's Pre-Flood Vapor Canopy.*

The lower part of it, the atmosphere above, which are the clouds full of water, from whence rain descends upon the earth; and which divided between them and those that were left on the earth, and so under it, not yet gathered into one place; as it now does between the clouds of heaven and the waters of the sea. Though Mr. Gregory is of the opinion, that an abyss of waters above the most supreme orb is here meant; or a great deep between the heavens and the heaven of heavens. . . .[5]

Gill agrees that clouds were inclusive of these waters above but that the waters also extend to the heaven of heavens, at the outer edge of the universe. Matthew Poole denotes this possibility as well in his commentary in the 1600s:

. . . the expansion, or extension, because it is extended far and wide, even from the earth to the third heaven; called also the firmament, because it is fixed in its proper place, from whence it cannot be moved, unless by force.[6]

Matthew Henry also concurs that this expanse extends to the heaven of heavens (third heaven):

The command of God concerning it: Let there be a firmament, an expansion, so the Hebrew word signifies, like a sheet spread, or a curtain drawn out. This includes all that is visible above the earth, between it and the third heavens: the air, its higher, middle, and lower, regions — the celestial globe, and all the spheres and orbs of light above: it reaches as high as the place where the stars are fixed, for that is called here the firmament of heaven Ge 1:14,15, and as low as the place where the birds fly, for that also is called the firmament of heaven, Ge 1:20.[7]

The point is that a canopy model about the earth is simply that . . . an interpretation. It should be evaluated as such, not taken as Scripture itself. Many respected Bible interpreters do not share in the interpretation of the "waters above" being a water canopy in the upper atmosphere of earth.

Stars for Seasons and Light and other Implications

Another biblical issue crops up when we read in Genesis 1:14–15:

---

5. John Gill, *Exposition of the Bible*, Genesis 1:7.
6. Matthew Poole, *A Commentary on the Holy Bible*, Genesis 1:7.
7. Matthew Henry, *A Commentary on the Whole Bible*, Genesis 1:7.

Then God said, "Let there be lights in the firmament [expanse] of the heavens to divide the day from the night; and let them be for signs and seasons, and for days and years; and let them be for lights in the firmament [expanse] of the heavens to give light on the earth"; and it was so.[8]

The stars are intended by God to be used to map seasons. And they were also to "give light on the earth." Though this is not much light, it does help significantly during new moon conditions — that is, if you live in an area not affected by light pollution.

Water

If the canopy were liquid water, then in its various forms like mist or haze, it would inhibit seeing these stars. How could one see the stars to map the seasons? It would be like a perpetually cloudy day. The light would be absorbed or reflected back to space much the way fog does the headlights of a car. What little light is transmitted through would not be sufficiently discernable to make out stars and star patterns to map seasons. Unlike a vapor canopy, clouds are moving and in motion, one can still see the stars to map seasons when they moved through. Furthermore, if it was water, why didn't it fall?[9]

Ice

If it were ice, then it *is* possible to see the stars but they would not appear in the positions one normally sees them, but still they would be sufficient to map seasons. But ice, when kept cool (to remain ice), tends to coat at the surface where other water molecules freezes to it (think of the coating you see on an ice cube left in the freezer). This could inhibit visibility, as evaporated water from the ocean surface would surely make contact — especially in a sin-cursed and broken world.

Vapor

But if an invisible vapor canopy existed in our upper atmosphere, then it makes the most sense. But there could still turn out to be a problem. As cooler vapor nears space, water condenses and begins to haze, though as long as the vapor in the upper atmosphere is kept warm and above the dew point, it could remain invisible. But there are a lot of "ifs." In short, the stars may not serve their purpose to give light on the earth with some possibilities within these models.

---

8. See also Genesis 1:17.
9. Would one appeal to the supernatural? If so, it defeats the purpose of this scientific model that seeks to explain things in a naturalistic fashion.

But consider, if there were a water *vapor* canopy, what would stop it from interacting with the rest of the atmosphere *that is vapor?* Gases mix to equilibrium, and that is the way God upholds the universe.[10] If it was a vapor, then why it is distinguished from the atmosphere, which is vapor?

The Bible uses the terms *waters* above, which implies that the temperature is between 32°F and 212°F (0°C and 100°C). If it was meant to be vapor, then why say "waters" above? Why not say vapor (*hebel*), which was used in the Old Testament?

Where Were the Stars Made?

If the canopy really was part of earth's atmosphere, then all the stars, sun, and moon would have been created within the earth's atmosphere. Why is this? A closer look at Genesis 1:14 reveals that the "waters above" may very well be much farther out — if they still exist today.

The entirety of the stars, including our own sun (the greater light) and moon (lesser light) were made "*in* the expanse." Further, they are obviously not in our atmosphere. Recall that the waters of verse 7 are above the expanse. If the canopy were just outside the atmosphere of the young earth, then the sun, moon, and stars would have to be in the atmosphere according to verse 14.

Further, the winged creatures were flying *in the face of* the expanse (Genesis 1:20; the NKJV accurately translates the Hebrew), and this helps reveal the extent of the expanse. It would likely include aspects of the atmosphere as well as space. The Bible calls the firmament "heaven" in Genesis 1:8, which would include both. Perhaps our understanding of "sky" is similar or perhaps the best translation of this as well.

Regardless, this understanding of the text allows for the stars to be in the expanse, and this means that any waters above, which is beyond the stars, is not limited to being in the atmosphere. Also, 2 Corinthians 12:2 discusses three heavens, which are likely the atmosphere (airy heavens), space (starry heavens), and the heaven of heavens (Nehemiah 9:6).

Some have argued that the prepositions in, under, above, etc., are not in the Hebrew text but are determined from the context, so the meaning in verses 14 and 17 is vague. It is true that the prepositions are determined by the context, so we must rely on a proper translation of Genesis 1:14. Virtually all translations have the sun, moon, and stars being created *in* the expanse, not *above* as any canopy model would require.

---

10. Again, would one appeal to the supernatural? If so, it defeats the purpose of this scientific model that seeks to explain things in a naturalistic fashion.

In Genesis 1, some have attempted to make a distinction between the expanse in which the birds fly (Genesis 1:20) and the expanse in which the sun, moon, and stars were placed (Genesis 1:7); this was in an effort to have the sun, moon, and stars made in the second expanse. This is not a distinction that is necessary from the text and is only necessary if a canopy is assumed.

From the Hebrew, the birds are said to fly "across the face of the firmament of the heavens." Looking up at a bird flying across the sky, it would be seen against the face of both the atmosphere and the space beyond the atmosphere — the "heavens." The proponents of the canopy model must make a distinction between these two expanses to support the position, but this is an arbitrary assertion that is only necessary to support the view and is not described elsewhere in Scripture.

Expanse (Firmament) Still Existed Post-Flood

Another issue that is raised from the Bible is that the waters above the heavens were mentioned *after* the Flood, when it was supposedly gone.

> Praise Him, you heavens of heavens, and you waters above the heavens! (Psalm 148:4).

> So an officer on whose hand the king leaned answered the man of God and said, "Look, if the LORD would make windows in heaven, could this thing be?" And he said, "In fact, you shall see it with your eyes, but you shall not eat of it" (2 Kings 7:2; see also 2 Kings 7:19).

> "Bring all the tithes into the storehouse, that there may be food in My house, and try Me now in this," says the LORD of hosts, "If I will not open for you the windows of heaven and pour out for you such blessing that there will not be room enough to receive it" (Malachi 3:10).

The biblical authors wrote these in a post-Flood world in the context of other post-Flood aspects. So, it appears that the "waters above" and "windows of heaven" are in reference to something that still existed after the Flood. So "the waters above" can't be referring to a long-gone canopy that dissipated at the Flood and still be present after the Flood. This is complemented by:

> The fountains of the deep and the windows of heaven were also stopped, and the rain from heaven was restrained (Genesis 8:2).

Genesis 8:2 merely points out that the two sources were stopped and restrained, not necessarily *done away* with. The verses above suggest that the windows of heaven remained after the Flood. Even the "springs of the great deep" were stopped but did not entirely disappear, but there may have been residual waters trapped that have slowly oozed out since that time; clearly not in any gushing, spring-like fashion.[11]

Is a Canopy Necessary Biblically?

Finally, is a canopy necessary from the text? At this stage, perhaps not. It was promoted as a scientific model based on a possible interpretation of Genesis 1 to deal with several aspects of the overall biblical creation model developed in the mid-1900s. I don't say this lightly for my brothers and sisters in the Lord who may still find it appealing. Last century, I was introduced to the canopy model and found it fascinating. For years, I had espoused it, but after further study, I began leaning against it, as did many other creationists.

Old biblical commentators were not distraught at the windows of heaven or the waters not being a canopy encircling the earth. Such an interpretation was not deemed necessary in their sight. In fact, this idea is a recent addition to scriptural interpretation that is less than 100 years old. The canopy model was a scientific interpretation developed in an effort to help explain certain aspects of the text to those who were skeptical of the Bible's accounts of earth history, but when it comes down to it, it is not necessary and even has some serious biblical issues associated with it.

Scientific Issues

Clearly, there are some biblical issues that are difficult to overcome. Researchers have often pointed out the scientific issues of the canopy model, as well. A couple will be denoted below.

This is no discredit to the *researchers* by any means. The research was valuable and necessary to see how the model may or may not work with variations and types. The development and testing of models is an important part of scientific inquiry, and we should continue to do so with many models to help us understand the world God has given us. So I appreciate and applaud all the work that has been done, and I further wish to encourage researchers to study other aspects to see if anything was missed.

Temperatures

To answer the question about how the earth regulates its temperature without a canopy, consider that it may not have been that much different than the way

---

11. I would leave open the option that this affected the ocean sea level to a small degree but the main reasons for changing sea level was via the Ice Age.

it regulates it today — by the atmosphere and oceans. Although there may have been much water underground prior to the Flood, there was obviously enough at or near the surface to sustain immense amounts of sea life. We know this because of the well-known figure that nearly 95 percent of the fossil record consists of shallow-water marine organisms. Was the earth's surface around 70 percent water before the Flood? That is a question creationist researchers still debate.

An infinitely knowledgeable God would have no problem designing the earth in a perfect world to have an ideal climate (even with variations like the cool of the day Genesis 3:8) where people could have filled the earth without wearing clothes (Genesis 2:25, 1:28). But with a different continental scheme that are remnants of a perfect world (merely cursed, not rearranged by the Flood yet), it would surely have been better equipped to deal with regulated temperatures and climate.

A vapor canopy, on the other hand, would cause major problems for the regulation of earth's temperature. A vapor canopy would absorb both solar and infrared radiation and become hot, which would heat the surface by conduction downward. The various canopy models have therefore been plagued with heat problems from the greenhouse effect. For example, solar radiation would have to decrease by around 25 percent to make the most plausible model work.[12] The heat problem actually makes this model very problematic and adds a problem rather than helping to explain the environment before the Flood.[13]

The Source of Water

The primary source of water for the Flood was the springs of the great deep bursting forth (Genesis 7:11). This water in turn likely provided some of the water in the "windows of heaven" in an indirect fashion. There is no need for an ocean of vapor above the atmosphere to provide for extreme amounts of water for the rain that fell during the Flood.

For example, if Dillow's vapor canopy existed (40 feet of precipitable water) and collapsed at the time of the Flood to supply, in large part, the rainfall, the latent heat of condensation would have boiled the atmosphere!

---

12. For more on this see "Temperature Profiles for an Optimized Water Vapor Canopy" by Dr. Larry Vardiman, a researcher on this subject for over 25 years at the time of writing that paper; http://static.icr.org/i/pdf/technical/Temperature-Profiles-for-an-Optimized-Water-Vapor-Canopy.pdf.
13. Another issue is the amount of water vapor in the canopy. Dillow's 40 feet of precipitable water, the amount collected after all the water condenses, has major heat problems. But Vardiman's view has modeled canopies with 2 to 6 feet of precipitable water with better temperature results and we look forward to seeing future research.

And a viable canopy would not have had enough water vapor in it to sustain 40 days and nights of torrential global rain as in Vardiman's model (2–6 feet of precipitable water). Thus, the vapor canopy doesn't adequately explain the rain at the Flood.

Longevity

Some have appealed to a canopy to increase surface atmospheric pressures prior to the Flood. The reasoning is to allow for better healing as well as living longer and bigger as a result. However, increased oxygen (and likewise oxidation that produces dangerous free radicals), though beneficial in a few respects, is mostly a detriment to biological systems. Hence, antioxidants (including things like catalase and vitamins E, A, and C) are very important to reduce these free radicals within organisms.

Longevity (and the large size of many creatures) before and after the Flood is better explained by genetics through the bottlenecks of the Flood and the Tower of Babel as opposed to pre-Flood oxygen levels due to a canopy. Not to belabor these points, this idea has already been discussed elsewhere.[14]

Pre-Flood Climate

Regardless of canopy models, creationists generally agree that climate before the Fall was perfect. This doesn't mean the air was stagnant and 70°F every day, but instead had variations within the days and nights (Genesis 3:8). These variations were not extreme but very reasonable.

Consider that Adam and Eve were told to be fruitful and multiply and fill the earth (Genesis 1:27). In a perfect world where there was no need for clothes to cover sin (this came after the Fall), we can deduce that man should have been able to fill the earth without wearing clothes, hence the extremes were not as they are today or the couple would have been miserable as the temperatures fluctuated.

Even after the Fall, it makes sense that these weather variations were minimally different. But with the global Flood that destroyed the earth and rearranged continents and so on, the extremes become pronounced — we now have ice caps and extremely high mountains that were pushed up from the Flood (Psalm 104:8). We now have deserts that have extreme heat and cold and little water.

---

14. Ken Ham, ed., *New Answers Book 2* (Green Forest, AR: Master Books, 2008), p. 159–168; Bodie Hodge, *Tower of Babel* (Green Forest, AR: Master Books, 2013), p. 205–212.

Biblical Models and Encouragement

Answers in Genesis continues to encourage research and the development of scientific and theological models. However, a good grasp of all biblical passages that are relevant to the topic must precede the scientific research and models, and the Bible must be the ultimate judge over all of our conclusions.

The canopy model may have a glimmer of hope still remaining, and that will be left to the proponents to more carefully explain, but both the biblical and scientific difficulties need to be addressed thoroughly and convincingly for the model to be embraced. So we do look forward to future research.

In all of this, we must remember that scientific models are not Scripture, and it is the Scripture that we should defend as the authority. While we must surely affirm that the waters above were divided from the waters below, something the Bible clearly states, whether or not there was a canopy must be held loosely lest we do damage to the text of Scripture or the limits of scientific understanding.

CHAPTER 14

Are There Transitional Forms in the Fossil Record?

DR. DAVID MENTON

The central idea of evolution is that all of the kinds of living organisms on earth share a common ancestor and that over time they have evolved one from another by an unplanned and unguided natural process. This unobserved sort of "amoeba-to-man" evolution extending over hundreds of millions of years is called macroevolution to distinguish it from the relatively small-scale variations we observe among the individuals of a species. Evolutionists like to refer to these small variations as "microevolution" with the tacit assumption that over eons of time they add up incrementally to produce macroevolution. Thus, evolutionists look for evidence of these incremental steps, often referring to them as "transitional forms," suggesting that they represent stages of transformation of one organism into a different kind of organism.

Since macroevolution is not observable in the time frame of human observers, evolutionists often invoke microevolution as both evidence for macroevolution as well as its presumed mechanism. But as any animal or plant breeder knows, the limited variation that is observed among the individuals of a species has not been observed to lead to the essentially limitless process of macroevolution. In 1980, a group of evolutionists met in Chicago to discuss the relationship of micro- and macroevolution. Roger Lewin summed up this meeting in the journal *Science* as follows:

The central question of the Chicago conference was whether the mechanisms underlying microevolution can be extrapolated to explain the phenomena of macroevolution. At the risk of doing violence to the positions of some of the people at the meeting, the answer can be given as a clear No.[1]

The lack of a clear relationship between microevolution and macroevolution has continued to be a problem for evolutionists.[2]

No matter what mechanism one might postulate for macroevolution, in the course of presumed evolutionary history there would have been an unimaginably vast number of transitional forms revealing at least some of the incremental stages of macroevolution. Thus evolutionists typically turn to the fossil record in an effort to identify transitional stages in the macro evolutionary process. When this fails, they turn to currently living biological organisms in the hope of "reconstructing" evolutionary transitional stages from living examples. When an appearance of progress is lacking among living organisms and their organs, evolutionists turn to artists who obligingly illustrate what they believe must surely have been the missing transitional stages of evolutionary progress. And, finally, when even artistic imagination fails to produce plausible intermediates of evolutionary progress, some evolutionists simply deny that there even is a vector of progress in evolution! However, evolutionists never question that there is a naturalistic evolutionary process of some kind that explains the origin of all living things.

"Transitional" Fossils – The Missing Links

Evolutionists begin with the unquestioned assumption that evolution has occurred, starting with some primordial life form and progressing over time in a purely naturalistic way to produce all the kinds of living organisms on earth, past or present. Thus for "evidence" of evolution they need only to examine available fossils and attempt to arrange them in a sequence that appears to show progress over time. But a plausible sequential progression of intermediate stages is rarely, if ever, observed in the fossil record, which explains why we hear so

1. Roger Lewin, "Evolutionary Theory Under Fire," *Science* 210, no. 4472 (1980): p. 883–887.
2. D.L. Stern, "Perspective: Evolutionary Developmental Biology and the Problem of Variation," *Evolution* 54, no. 4 (2000): p. 1079–1091; R.L. Carroll, "Towards a New Evolutionary Synthesis," *Trends in Ecology & Evolution* 15, no. 1 (2000): p. 27–32; A.M. Simons, "The Continuity of Microevolution and Macroevolution," *Journal of Evolutionary Biology* 15, no. 5 (2002): 688–701.

much about "missing links." Even Darwin himself was aware of this problem and said in his *Origin of Species*:

> The number of intermediate varieties, which have formerly existed on the earth, [must] be truly enormous. Why then is not every geological formation and every stratum full of such intermediate links? Geology assuredly does not reveal any such finely graduated organic chain; and this, perhaps, is the most obvious and gravest objection which can be urged against my theory.[3]

Why, indeed! For example, no one has observed progressive stages of "prebats" in the fossil record showing a mouse-like mammal gradually evolving into a bat with its long fingered wings. Evolutionists concede that what they consider to be the oldest bat fossils are 100 percent bats with some even showing evidence of sonar navigation.[4] G.K. Chesterton put it simply: "All we know of the Missing Link is that he is missing — and he won't be missed either."

Many evolutionists now concede the dearth of transitional forms in the fossil record and feel obliged to come up with some sort of explanation for it. The late evolutionist Steven J. Gould bluntly admitted, "the extreme rarity of transitional forms in the fossil record persists as the trade secret of paleontology."[5]

Again, Eldridge and Gould noted, "Most species during their geological history, either do not change in any appreciable way, or else they fluctuate mildly in morphology, with no apparent direction."[6]

Gould even goes so far as to concede that not only are transitional stages not found in the fossil record, but in many cases we are not even able to imagine such intermediates:

> The absence of fossil evidence for intermediate stages between major transitions in organic design, indeed our inability, even in our imagination, to construct functional intermediates in many cases, has been a persistent and nagging problem for gradualistic accounts of evolution.[7]

3. Charles Darwin, *The Origin of Species* (1859; repr., New York: Avenel Books, Crown Publishers, n.d.).
4. G. Jepsen, "Bat Origins and Evolution," in *Biology of Bats*, W. Wimsatt, ed. (New York: Academic Press, 1970), p. 1–64; G.L. Jepsen, "Early Eocene Bat from wyoming," *Science* 154, no. 3754 (1966): p. 1333–1339.
5. Stephen J. Gould, "Evolution's Erratic Pace," *Natural History* 86, no. 5 (1977): p. 12–16.
6. N. Eldredge and Stephen J. Gould, "Punctuated Equilibria: The Tempo and Mode of Evolution Reconsidered," *Paleobiology* 3, no. 2 (1977): p. 145–146.
7. Gould, "Is a New and General Theory of Evolution Emerging?" *Paleobiology* 6, no 1 (1980): p. 127.

This conspicuous lack of fossil evidence for intermediate or transitional stages of evolution led Gould to a highly speculative rescuing hypothesis for evolution called "punctuated equilibrium," or as it is sometimes called, the "hopeful monster theory." In this scenario, the lack of fossil transitional forms is explained away by claiming that the transitional stages (hopeful monsters) being both unlikely and unstable occurred rarely and relatively quickly (on a geological time scale) leaving no fossil evidence. So what we actually see is stasis, i.e., no change over long periods of geological time![8] No wonder some evolutionists have argued that ancestor descendent relationships simply cannot be determined from fossils. For example, with regard to human evolution, Richard Lewontin said, "Despite the excited and optimistic claims that have been made by some paleontologists, no fossil hominid species can be established as our direct ancestor."[9]

"Transitional" Living Organisms and Organs – Looking for the Dead Among the Living

When the fossil evidence fails to provide expected transitional stages, evolutionists often turn to living organisms in an attempt to arrange them in a way that appears to show a sequential process of evolution. An advantage of living organisms is that they allow the evolutionist to create an evolutionary scenario for the soft organs of the body. While we are becoming increasingly aware of evidence of soft tissue in fossils, most fossils show only hard tissue such as shells, teeth, and bones. Hard tissues represent a relatively small part of a living organism compared to their soft tissues. So with a bit of imagination, living organisms can sometimes be selectively arranged in a way to give the impression of an evolutionary sequence for soft tissue organs such as eyes, hearts, and kidneys.

In an effort to show evolutionary progress among living organisms, evolutionists look for structures or functions that appear to be intermediate in some way to those of other living organisms. These intermediate structures are then extrapolated to represent "transitional" stages in a sequential evolutionary progress. But while an organ or organism may be considered intermediate in appearance between two other organs or organisms, it does not necessarily mean that it represents an evolutionary transition between the two. Declaring something to be intermediate with regard to some arbitrary structure or character is merely

---

8. Stephen J. Gould, "The Return of the Hopeful Monsters," *Natural History* 86 (1977): p. 22–30.
9. Richard Lewontin, *Human Diversity* (San Francisco, CA: W.H. Freeman & Company, 1995), p. 179.

an organizational decision, whereas declaring it to be transitional presumes an evolutionary or transformational process.

Living organisms are often used in an effort to explain the evolution of the eye. Darwin conceded in *The Origin of Species* that to suppose the eye could have evolved by natural selection "seems absurd in the highest degree," and that to support his theory it would be necessary to demonstrate the existence of "numerous gradations" from the most primitive eyes to the most advanced ones. Since the fossil record provides no evidence for this, evolutionists attempt to arrange the eyes of present-day living invertebrates and vertebrates into what appears to be a progressive evolutionary sequence. For example, in a journal devoted to giving evolutionary support for teachers, Lamb claims to have evidence from living hagfish that the vertebrate eye evolved through numerous subtle changes:

> The great majority of the gradual transitions that did occur have not been preserved to the present time, either in the fossil record or in extant species; yet clear evidence of their occurrence remains. We discuss the remarkable "eye" of the hagfish, which has features intermediate between a simple light detector and an image-forming camera-like eye and which may represent a step in the evolution of our eye that can now be studied by modern methods.[10]

But a recent study of microRNA expression patterns in the hagfish and lamprey showed that the cyclostomes are closely related.[11] This leaves evolutionists arguing whether the relatively simple hagfish eye is really a precursor of the more complex lamprey type eye or a degenerate form of that type eye. From what then did the vertebrate eye evolve? There is a bewildering array of eyes found among the invertebrates. One of the world's most distinguished experts on the eye, Sir Duke-Elder, said in volume one (*The Eye in Evolution*) of his monumental 15-volume work, *System of Ophthalmology*, that the eyes of invertebrates do not show a series of transitional stages:

> The curious thing, however, is that in their distribution the eyes of invertebrates form no series of continuity and succession. Without obvious phylogenetic sequences, their occurrence seems haphazard;

---

10. T. Lamb, E. Pugh, and S. Collin, "The Origin of the Vertebrate Eye," *Evolution: Education and Outreach* 1, no. 4 (2008): p. 415–426.
11. Alysha M. Heimberg et al., "MicroRNAs Reveal the Interrelationships of Hagfish, Lampreys, and Gnathostomes and the Nature of the Ancestral Vertebrate," *PNAS* 107, no. 45 (2010): p. 19379–19383.

analogous photoreceptors appear in unrelated species, an elaborate organ in a primitive species (such as the complex eye of the jelly-fish Charybdea) or an elementary structure high in the evolutionary scale (such as the simple eyes of insects), and the same animal may be provided with two different mechanisms with different spectral sensitivities subserving different types of behavior.[12]

Duke-Elder was not even convinced that we ever will find a solution for the evolution of the eye:

> Indeed, appearing as it does fully formed in the most primitive species extant today, and in the absence of transition forms with which it can be associated unless by speculative hypothesis with little factual foundation, there seems little likelihood of finding a satisfying and pragmatic solution to the puzzle presented by its (the eye's) evolutionary development.[13]

With about 1.5 million named and categorized living species (and possibly several times more species unnamed or categorized) we might reasonably expect to see at least some evidence of a series of transitional stages among living organisms, but such is not the case. In his book *Patterns and Processes of Vertebrate Evolution*, evolutionist Robert Carroll concedes that very few examples of intermediate organisms or organs have been proposed:

> Although an almost incomprehensible number of species inhabit Earth today, they do not form a continuous spectrum of barely distinguishable intermediates. Instead, nearly all species can be recognized as belonging to a relatively limited number of clearly distinct major groups, with very few illustrating intermediate structures or ways of life.[14]

"Transitional" Drawings and Illustrations – Making Your Own Data

When all else fails, there are always artists who will make a picture or model of any missing link the evolutionist might desire. Sadly, laymen are often

---

12. S.S. Duke-Elder, *The Eye in Evolution*, vol. 1, *System of Ophthalmology* (London: Henry Kimpton, 1958), p. 178.
13. Ibid., p. 247.
14. Robert L. Carroll, *Patterns and Processes of Vertebrate Evolution* (New York: Cambridge University Press, 1997), p. 9.

strongly influenced by such fanciful illustrations. Consider the famous "March of Progress" monkey-to-man drawing commissioned by Time Life Books,[15] one of the most famous and recognizable science illustrations ever produced. This drawing presumed to compress 25 million years of imagined human evolution into a row of progressively taller and more erect primates until finally a human walks away with a marine drill sergeant posture and gait.

Many evolutionists have expressed their disapproval over this illustration showing a triumphalist linear progression of evolution that simply does not exist. Nonetheless, this "March of Progress" illustration has probably done more to convince uncritical laymen of the bestial origin of man than any other evidence.

Several years ago, the popular evolutionist Carl Sagan was on a television program where he showed a video clip of a rapid series of cartoon illustrations purporting to show amoeba-to-man evolution while a harpsichord solemnly played in the background. At the conclusion, the audience applauded enthusiastically, seemingly convinced that they had actually seen the whole sweep of amoeba-to-man evolution in a few minutes. We are living in an age where many are careless in distinguishing artistic license from scientific evidence.

But not all pictorial evidence for the imagined transitional stages of evolution is found in the popular literature meant for laymen. Imaginative drawings and illustrations are frequently found in the scientific literature intended for the specialist. An example of artistic license passing for "evidence" of transitional stages of evolution may be seen in efforts to explain the evolution of feathers.

Now that evolutionists are dead certain that dinosaurs evolved into birds (with many insisting that birds are in fact dinosaurs) they are left with the unenviable task of showing how reptile scales evolved into feathers. For years,

---

15. F. Clark Howell, *Early Man* (New York, NY: Time-Life Books, 1965).

evolutionists have insisted that feathers and scales are very similar, but nothing could be further from the truth.[16] Scales are essentially continuous folds in the epidermis while feathers grow from individual follicles. This is why the reptile must shed its entire skin to replace its scales while a bird sheds its feathers individually from feather follicles (in matched left-right pairs in the case of primary feathers). It is hard to imagine two cutaneous appendages more profoundly different than scales and feathers; they share almost nothing in common. In fact, feathers and their follicles show far more similarity to hairs and hair follicles than they do to reptilian scales, but there is no evolutionary scenario that relates the phylogeny of birds to mammals, so this is ignored by evolutionists. So evolutionists are stuck with making feathers out of scales and to do so they must employ artists to illustrate transitional stages not seen in fossils or living creatures.

An attempt was made by Xu et al to show the hypothetical stages of evolution from scale to feather.[17] Their artist illustrates an elongated hollow scale first becoming a frayed or branching structure. This then somehow becomes a compound branching structure (see step II to IIIA below). To accomplish this, a structure with a simple branching pattern (all branching from one node) must implausibly become a compound branching structure (branching from several different nodes). The compound branching structure then undergoes another order of branching to give a superficial resemblance to a feather.

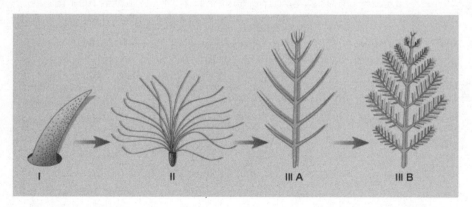

Unmentioned is that in real life, all feather development must occur inside a follicle, where the feather is folded up in a sheath like a ship in a bottle. But then this presents no restrictions for an artist's imagination and drawing.

16. David N. Menton, *Formed to Fly*, DVD (Hebron, KY: Answers in Genesis, 2007).
17. X. Xu, Z. Zhou, and R.O. Prum, "Branched Integumental Structures in Sinornithosaurus and the Origin of Feathers" *Nature* 410, no. 6825 (2001): p. 200–204.

What Do "Transitional" Stages Mean If There Is No Progress?

Can we have transitions or intermediates without progress? Many evolutionists are coming to the conclusion that there is neither purpose nor progress in evolution. In a recent survey of over 150 of the nation's most influential and prestigious evolutionists (all members of the National Academy of Science), it was revealed that nearly 42 percent believe that evolution shows neither purpose nor progress.[18] But if there is no purpose or progress in evolution, how can one identify incremental transitional changes in the process? Another 48 percent of these distinguished evolutionists believe evolution shows progress but no purpose. But how can there be progress without purpose? The English Wordnet dictionary defines progress as "an anticipated outcome that is intended or that guides your planned actions" and the Merriam-Webster dictionary defines progress as "a forward or onward movement as to an objective or to a goal." Since nearly 80 percent of the evolutionists in the survey describe themselves as atheists, it is not surprising that they shun the notion of purpose in evolution. Purpose suggests the Creator (and accountability to the Creator), and that is unthinkable to these professional atheist/evolutionists.

Isn't It Great to Be a Christian and Recognize God's Purpose in Creation?

As Bible-believing Christians, we can gladly recognize the obvious that there is overwhelming evidence of intelligent design and purpose in God's creation. Some evolutionists concede that they are aware of this evidence for design, but as the Bible says, they "suppress the truth in unrighteousness" (Romans 1:18). No better example of this suppression of the truth can be seen than the ardent atheist/evolutionist Richard Dawkins who wrote in the first page of his book titled *The Blind Watchmaker: Why the Evidence of Evolution Reveals a Universe Without Design*:

> Biology is the study of complicated things that give the appearance of having been designed for a purpose.[19]

Dawkins concedes that this obvious appearance of design in biological systems cries out for some kind of explanation:

---

18. G. Graffin, "Evolution and Religion," The Cornell Evolution Project, http://www.polypterus.com/.
19. Richard Dawkins, *The Blind Watchmaker: Why the Evidence of Evolution Reveals a Universe Without Design* (New York: Norton & Company, 1986), p. ix.

The complexity of living organisms is matched by the elegant efficiency of their apparent design. If anyone doesn't agree that this amount of complex design cries out for an explanation, I give up.[20]

But the only explanation the atheist evolutionist can offer is that somehow nature "counterfeits" intelligent design. How sad.

20. Ibid.

CHAPTER 15

Could the Flood Cataclysm Deposit Uniform Sedimentary Rock Layers?

DR. ANDREW A. SNELLING

This is definitely a legitimate question to ask concerning the nature of the evidence one would expect to be left behind by the Flood cataclysm. Because the waters of local floods today are often full of sediments and are fast-moving, it is commonly thought that neat, uniform sediment layers are not deposited under such conditions. So this question needs close examination, starting by looking at what the evidence is that we see in the rock record.

Do We Find Neat Uniform Sedimentary Rock Layers in the Geologic Record?

Whether looking into the Grand Canyon from one of the rim overlooks or traversing through the Grand Canyon on foot or by raft, the answer to this question is obviously yes. The fossil-bearing sedimentary layers deposited by the Flood can be seen exposed in the walls, stacked on top of one another like a huge pile of pancakes. And the view is much the same no matter where one views the Grand Canyon. So at the regional scale in the Grand Canyon area it is clearly evident that the sedimentary rock layers deposited there during the Flood cataclysm are neat and uniform.

Similar observations can be made in many other places across the earth's surface. This pattern is often seen in road cuts and in mountainous areas where erosion has exposed the constituent rock layer sequences. So it is hardly necessary to defend the assertion that the fossil-bearing sedimentary layers that were deposited during the Flood cataclysm are generally neat and uniform and stacked in a sequence that is exposed to view in many places across the earth's continents.

The assertion that these fossil-bearing sedimentary layers were deposited during the Flood cataclysm is easy to defend.[1] The obvious observation to make is that many of these fossil-bearing sedimentary layers contain fossils of creatures that today live on the shallow ocean floors fringing the continents, and not on the continents where countless billions of them are buried in these sedimentary layers. Indeed, sedimentary rock layers containing the same fossils are not found on the ocean floors today, nor are they found in comparable dimensions on the continental shelves fringing the continents. But the vast marine-fossil-bearing sedimentary layers we find spread right across the continents today are thus consistent with the ocean waters having flooded over the continents on a global scale, tearing marine creatures from their shallow ocean floor habitats and picking up sediments, then burying those creatures in those sediments up and across the continents in vast sedimentary layers. This is consistent with the biblical description of the Flood.

Many geologists are already aware that there are six thick sequences of fossil-bearing sedimentary strata, known as megasequences, which can be traced right across the North American continent. This was documented five decades ago in 1963[2] and subsequently verified by numerous observations so that it is now well recognized. In the early 1980s, the American Association of Petroleum Geologists (AAPG) conducted a project in which all the local geologic strata "columns" derived from the mapping of outcrops in local areas, supplemented by drill-hole data, were put on charts to show the sequences of fossil-bearing sedimentary rock layers right across the North American continent (figure 1).[3]

The rationale used to identify these megasequences was based on mapping the preserved rock record across the North American continent. These thick sequences or packages of fossil-bearing sedimentary rock layers were easily identified because they were bounded by erosion surfaces (called unconformities)

1. Andrew Snelling, "What Are Some of the Best Flood Evidences?" in Ken Ham, ed., *The New Answers Book 3* (Green Forest, AR: Master Books, 2010), p. 283–298.
2. Laurence L. Sloss, "Sequences in the Cratonic Interior of North America," *Geological Society of America Bulletin* 74, no. 2 (1963): p. 93–114.
3. F.A. Lindberg, *Correlation of Stratigraphic Units of North America (COSUNA): Correlation Charts Series* (Tulsa, OK: American Association of Petroleum Geologists, 1986).

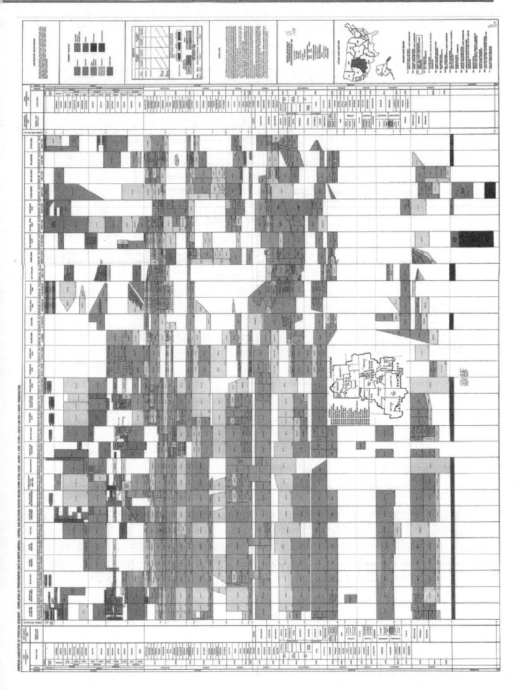

Figure 1. An example of one of the charts produced during the AAPG project showing the local strata columns in the central and southern Rockies region of the USA.

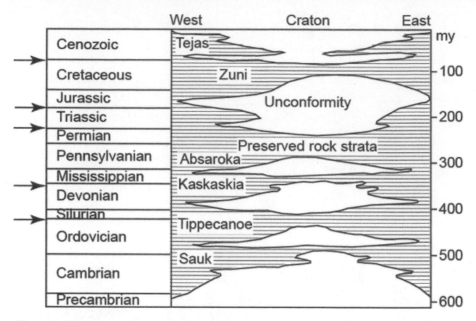

Figure 2. The preserved rock record, consisting of named megasequences, between major unconformities and mass extinctions (arrowed) across the North American continent.

due to the actions of the ocean waters as they advanced over the continent depositing the sedimentary rock layers before retreating again (figure 2).[4] These unconformities therefore coincide with rising and falling water levels as ocean waters oscillated across the continent and back again after depositing their sediment loads, often also coinciding with the mass burial of creatures in what evolutionary geologists have called mass extinctions. Significantly, some of the fossil-bearing sedimentary layers in these megasequences can also be traced beyond North America to other continents.[5]

Within each megasequence are various named strata units. For example, the first (lowermost) of these megasequences, called the Sauk Megasequence, in the Grand Canyon area consists of the Tapeats Sandstone, the Bright Angel Shale, and the Muav Limestone. Thorough geologic mapping was initially only done locally, so the rock units identified and mapped were given names locally. Therefore, even if a rock unit stretched into adjoining local areas and beyond, it often had different names in adjoining local areas. Thus, in the 1980s, when the

4. Leonard R. Brand, *Faith, Reason, and Earth History* (Berrien Springs, MI: Andrews University Press, 1997).
5. Andrew Snelling, "Transcontinental Rock Layers," *Answers* (July–September 2008): p. 80–83.

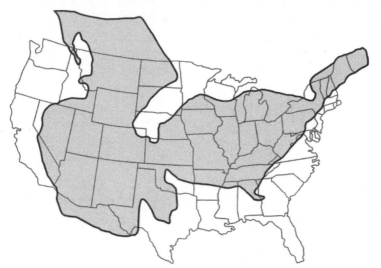

Figure 3. The distribution of the Tapeats Sandstone and its equivalents across North America, constructed from the local geologic columns compiled in the COSUNA charts produced by the AAPG.

American Association for Petroleum Geologists (AAPG) tabulated all the local strata columns across the continent, it became possible to see how some specific rock units, which had been given different names in different local areas, actually were the same unit, which could be traced vast distances across the continent. The Tapeats Sandstone in the Grand Canyon area is one of those units, and it can be traced all across Arizona northward to the Canadian border and beyond, northeastward right across the USA as far as Maine (figure 3).[6] The same sandstone unit in exactly the same geologic strata position is also found in southern Israel, from where it can be traced across to Jordan and into Egypt, and then right across north Africa.[7] Thus the Tapeats Sandstone represents one unit within one megasequence that is easily identified over vast continental scale areas due to its uniform makeup.

However, while some units within megasequences traverse continents, many others are only recognizable and able to be traced over regions, though still vast in extent compared to one's local area. In the Grand Canyon area, for example, the Coconino Sandstone, within the fourth of the megasequences, known as the Absaroka Megasequence, can be traced from northern and central Arizona

6. Andrew Snelling, *Earth's Catastrophic Past: Geology Creation and the Flood* (Dallas, TX: Institute for Creation Research, 2009), p. 1082, figure 45.

7. Andrew Snelling, "The Geology of Israel within the Biblical Creation-Flood Framework of Earth History: 2. The Flood Rocks," *Answers Research Journal* 3 (2010): p. 267–309; available online at http://www.answersingenesis.org/articles/arj/v3/n1/geology-of-israel-2.

across New Mexico into Colorado, Kansas, Oklahoma, and Texas over an area approaching 200,000 square miles, though an isolated remanent in southwestern Arizona indicates the unit previously had a wider distribution that has been reduced by erosion (figure 4).

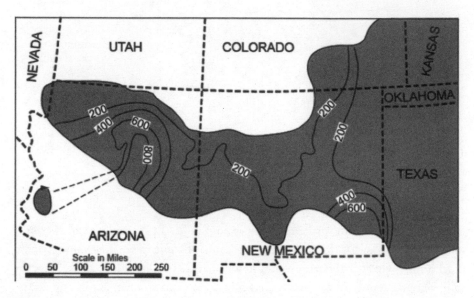

Figure 4. The distribution of the Coconino Sandstone and its equivalents from northern Arizona into adjoining states, showing the variations in its thickness (contour lines in feet) (after Austin[8]).

Nevertheless, not all the strata units are uniform, the character of the rock units changing due to later variations. For example, the Toroweap Formation is a limestone in the Grand Canyon area, but laterally to the southwest it changes into sandstone, along with local variations that include beds of gypsum to the west.[9] Indeed, many strata units change their rock character laterally, which reflects both the type and composition of the sediments within the mixture carried by the ocean waters over the continent to deposit them. Furthermore, not only is the sediment composition related to the source of the sediments, but changes in the sediment composition can occur. As the ocean waters carried sediments up and across the continent, they sometimes eroded underlying

8. Steven A. Austin, *Grand Canyon: Monument to Catastrophe* (Santee, CA: Institute for Creation Research, 1994), p. 36, figure 3.13.
9. Christine E. Turner, "Toroweap Formation," in Stanley S. Beus and Michael Morales, eds., *Grand Canyon Geology*, 2nd ed. (New York, NY: Oxford University Press, 2003), p. 180–195.

sediment layers of different compositions, adding them to their sediment loads before eventually depositing them.

Another aspect of this question is the thickness of the fossil-bearing sedimentary rock layers deposited across the continents. Even on local scales, variations in the thicknesses of strata units can be seen, as well as sometimes even compositional changes. So, for example, even though the Coconino Sandstone averages a thickness of 315 feet in the Grand Canyon area, it changes its thickness through the length of the Grand Canyon, thinning to the west and thickening even up to 1,000 feet toward the southeast (see figure 4). Furthermore, some rock units are made up of beds of alternating compositions, such as within some of the strata units in the Cincinnati area which consist of alternating beds of limestone and shale (figure 5).[10] Sometimes these thinner beds thicken and thin even within the outcrop scale of a road cut. So whereas we do find neat, uniform fossil-bearing sedimentary rock layers across the continents as a record of the Flood, the depositional processes produced and left behind local variations, both in thicknesses of the layers and beds within the named strata units, but also variations in compositions, from local to regional scales.

Were the Fast-Moving Flood Waters Also Churning?

During the Flood cataclysm, there were four main causes for generating the surging flows of water currents that picked up and carried sediments onto and across the continents to deposit the fossil-bearing sedimentary rock layers there.

First, there was the normal ebb and flow of the rising and falling tidal oscillations. The effect of these approximately twice-daily tidal surges would have increased as the Flood waters became global. It has been shown that on a global ocean there would have been a resonating effect by which the tidal surges would have progressively built in height and, therefore, in the strength and impact of each surge, due to the close overlapping of the tidal peaks and troughs in the approximate 12–13 hour spacing between successive highs and lows.[11]

Superimposed on those tidal flows and surges, there would have been repeated tsunamis generated by earthquakes caused by repeated catastrophic earth movements. The "fountains of the great deep" were broken up (Genesis

10. Andrew Snelling, "Cincinnati — Built on a Fossil Graveyard," *Answers* (July–September 2011): p. 50–53.
11. M.E. Clark, and H.D. Voss, "Resonance and Sedimentary Layering in the Context of a Global Flood," in *Proceedings of the Second International Conference on Creationism*, vol. 2, Robert E. Walsh and Christopher L. Brooks, eds. (Pittsburgh, PA: Creation Science Fellowship, 1990), p. 53–63.

Figure 5. Alternating beds of limestone (hard) and shale (soft) in the Fairview Formation in a road cut in the Cincinnati area of northern Kentucky. (Photograph: Andrew A. Snelling)

7:11), initiating the catastrophic plate tectonics that drove the Flood event.[12] The earth's crust was broken up around the globe, producing massive earthquakes, followed by the accelerated motion of the crustal fragments (called plates) across the earth's surface at many-feet-per-second speed. As the Flood event progressed, plates collided with one another, or some plates were pushed under the edges of other plates. All these earth movements would have generated many catastrophic earthquakes that in turn would have repeatedly produced massive tsunamis. As these tsunamis moved, they would have surged toward and onto the continents.

Furthermore, superimposed on the tides and tsunamis would have been the progressive raising of the ocean floor. As the ocean floor plates were pushed apart, molten rock rose from inside the earth to generate new ocean floor rocks. The new warm ocean floor, being less dense, would steadily rise, thus pushing

12. Steven A. Austin, John R. Baumgardner, D. Russell Humphreys, Andrew Snelling, Larry Vardiman, and Kurt P. Wise, "Catastrophic Plate Tectonics: A Global Flood Model of Earth History," in *Proceedings of the Third International Conference on Creationism*, Robert E. Walsh, ed. (Pittsburgh, PA: Creation Science Fellowship, 1994), p. 609–621; Andrew Snelling, "A Catastrophic Breakup: A Scientific Look at Catastrophic Plate Tectonics," *Answers* (April–June 2007): p. 44–48.

up the sea level. This raising of the sea level would have in turn caused a surge of ocean waters toward the continents to flood them.

The net result would have been huge fluctuations in the water levels combined with catastrophic surges of walls of water moving from open ocean areas toward and onto the continents and across them. Yet another force at work driving these surging water currents would have been super-storms. These would have been generated in the atmosphere as a result of the supersonic steam jets at the crustal fracture zones, catapulting ocean waters aloft before they fell back to the earth's surface as global torrential rainfall (the "windows or floodgates of heaven" were opened, Genesis 7:11). It is estimated that such super-storms and their winds moving across the surface of the Flood waters would have driven water currents at speeds of 100 miles an hour or more.[13]

So there is no doubt that there were adequate mechanisms for driving fast-moving, catastrophically powerful water currents and surges from the oceans toward and onto the continents. These were thus capable of carrying the sediments and creatures to be buried in the fossil-bearing sedimentary rock layers deposited across the continents, stacked up in sequence as a result of the fluctuating water levels and the ebb and flow of the water.

Just as is observed today, in the open ocean there are no major effects on the ocean surface from the passage of tsunamis, tidal surges, and fast-moving water currents apart from waves. It is at the base of the water column deep below the surface where the moving and surging water picks up loose sediments from the ocean floor, or scours and erodes sediments from the ocean floor, and then transports them in a slurry of sediment-laden water.

What was happening at the base of the water column of these surging, fast-moving water currents during the Flood would have depended on a number of factors, which in turn would have produced differing results. Though somewhat oversimplified, if the water was flowing over uneven ocean floor topography, then turbulent flow (churning water) could be generated. But if the water was flowing over a flat surface, then the flow would be laminar and sheet-like, and any erosion would result from cavitation, a process in which the fast water flow generates vacuum bubbles that hammer rock surfaces, pulverizing the rock rapidly. If there were loose sediments on the surface being traversed, once the

13. John R. Baumgardner, and Daniel W. Barnette, "Patterns of Ocean Circulation Over the Continents during Noah's Flood," in *Third International Conference on Creationism*, p. 77–86; Larry Vardiman, "Numerical Simulation of Precipitation Induced by Hot Mid-Ocean Ridges," in *Proceedings of the Fourth International Conference on Creationism*, Robert E. Walsh, ed. (Pittsburgh, PA: Creation Science Fellowship, 1998), p. 595–606.

water reached a critical speed it would pick up those loose sediments and carry them. Often, once the process is started, if there is even the slightest of downward slopes on the surfaces being traversed, then gravity takes over to produce debris flows. Many strata units in the rock record bear testimony to having been deposited by gravity-driven underwater debris flows.

The quantity and type of sediments transported would depend on the composition and particle sizes in those loose sediments, so that generally the faster the water flow, the greater the sizes of the particles that could be picked up and transported. Below a critical speed, no sediments would be picked up and carried by the water flows. And that critical speed would likely be lower for turbulent flow and higher for laminar flow, except where gravity is driving the water's ability to pick up sediments to produce debris flows. At higher speeds and carrying more sediment, the water at the base of the water column would become more erosive. The more sediments the water carried, the more they would add to the water's abrasive and erosive power. At the highest water speeds though, when the amount of sediment in the water is greater than the amount of water in the slurry mixture, the density of the slurry is so great that even boulders are transported, suspended in the slurry.

Fast-moving waters are certainly capable of depositing sediments, and many strata layers in the rock record of the Flood would have been deposited in that way, as witnessed by the strata layers that were deposited right across continents. Additionally, once the water started to slow down in its passage over the continents, the water would start to drop the rest of its sediment load and deposit it in more sediment layers, also burying the creatures that had been carried by the water. An example is the postulated progressive simultaneous deposition of the Tapeats Sandstone, Bright Angel Shale, and Muav Limestone across Nevada, Arizona, and New Mexico as the Flood waters advanced, the bottom current speed decreasing in the returning underflow so sediments of decreasing grain sizes were progressively deposited.[14] As the water slowed it would also be less likely to erode previously deposited sediment layers, especially where the surface of those previously deposited sediment layers had started to cohere, and cementation had begun to bind the sediment particles (the first stage of the hardening process).

The net result would be that the Flood waters at the base of the flow would tend to erode in source areas as the current flow increased, and then started switching to depositional mode as the water currents flowed over the continents and started to deposit their loads. Thus, when the water currents subsequently

14. Steven A. Austin, *Grand Canyon: Monument to Catastrophe* (Santee, CA: Institute for Creation Research, 1994), p. 69, figure 4.12.

slowed as they continued further sediment deposition, they would not be eroding at the same time. The outcome would be to deposit uniform sediment layers during their passage across the continents as they progressively spread out and deposited their sediment loads. Of course, there could be lateral variations in sediment types. Sometimes as the waters slowed, the heavier particles would settle out first. Then at slower speeds finer particles would be deposited, so that the sediment particle sizes could change laterally as the one rock unit was deposited across the continent. In some strata layers the grading of the sediment particle sizes is the inverse. But many layers do not exhibit any graded bedding. Instead, the changes between water flow surges meant changes in sediment loads, with sediments of different compositions and types, each consisting of uniform similar particle sizes being deposited, such as lime mud versus quartz sand, as in the example of the Toroweap Formation in the Grand Canyon area being deposited on top of the Coconino Sandstone, as has already been mentioned.

Natural and Experimental Examples

In 1960, Hurricane Donna created surging ocean waves that flooded inland up to 5 miles along the coast of southern Florida for 6 hours.[15] As a result, the hurricane deposited a neat, uniform 6-inch-thick mud layer, with numerous thin laminae within it, across the area traversed by the flood waters. In June 1965, a storm in Colorado produced flooding of Bijou Creek, which resulted in the deposition from the fast-moving waters of new sediment layers containing fine laminations.[16] Then on June 12, 1980, an eruption of Mount St. Helens produced a hurricane-velocity, surging-flow of volcanic ash, which accumulated in less than five hours as a neat, uniform 25-foot-thick layer of laminated volcanic ash, including uniform neat, alternating laminae of coarse and fine sediment grains (figure 6).[17]

In a detailed study of a seven-foot-thick bed within the Redwall Limestone in the Grand Canyon area, Austin[18] has convincingly argued that the evidence

---

15. M.N. Ball, B.A. Shinn, and K.W. Stockman, "The Geological Effects of Hurricane Donna in South Florida," *Journal of Geology* 75 (1967): p. 583–597.

16. E.D. McKee, E.J. Crosby, and H.L. Berryhill Jr., "Flood Deposits, Bijou Creek, Colorado, June 1965," *Journal of Sedimentary Petrology* 37, no. 3 (1967): p. 829–851.

17. Steven A. Austin, "Mount St. Helens and Catastrophism," in *Proceedings of the First International Conference on Creationism*, vol. 1 (Pittsburgh, PA: Creation Science Fellowship, 1986), p. 3–9.

18. Steven A. Austin, "Nautiloid Mass Kill and Burial Event, Redwall Limestone (Lower Mississippian), Grand Canyon Region, Arizona and Nevada," in *Proceedings of the Fifth International Conference on Creationism*, Robert L. Ivey, Jr., ed. (Pittsburgh, PA: Creation Science Fellowship, 2003), p. 55–99.

Figure 6. The 25-foot-thick deposit is exposed in the middle of the cliff. The fine layering within this deposit was produced within hours at Mount St. Helens on June 12, 1980, by hurricane-velocity surging flows from the crater of the volcano. (Photograph: Steven A. Austin)

is consistent with the bed's deposition by a gravity-driven debris flow. In the middle section of this bed, which has been traced over more than 11,600 square miles, are billions of straight-shelled nautiloid fossils of various lengths. Though mostly buried and fossilized horizontally, some are found at various angles, and some are even vertical. These and the ubiquitous vertical fluid evulsion structures are consistent with rapid burial in a debris flow that turbulently tossed some of the nautiloids around during this mass kill event. Yet the bed overall is neat and uniform over this large area.

The three observed examples described above demonstrate that local-regional natural catastrophes do deposit neat, uniform sedimentary rock layers, even though in most instances the flow of water and air respectively was rapid and sometimes turbulent (churning). It should also be noticed that in two of the three examples the surging, fast-moving sediment-laden flows did not erode into the surfaces they flowed over, even though those surfaces consisted of loose materials (soils and sands, and previously deposited volcanic ash, respectively). Instead, the flows left smooth, neat, uniform boundaries at the bases of the neat, uniform sediment layers they deposited. These sediment layers resulting from these local-regional natural catastrophes closely mirror at a smaller scale the neat, uniform sedimentary layers left behind by the Flood waters, stacked up neatly on top of one another with smooth, uniform boundaries between them.

Not only do we have numerous modern examples where local-regional natural catastrophic events have resulted in the rapid accumulation of neat uniform sedimentary layers, but we have numerous laboratory experiments that have allowed researchers to document the same processes. For example, using a circular flume, it was demonstrated that high-velocity water currents sort and deposit sediment grains by weight, density, and shape, and that as the fast-moving current loses its velocity, the segregation of grains produces a succession of thin, parallel laminae in the resultant neat uniform sediment layer.[19] Other linear flume experiments with water swiftly carrying sand grains have demonstrated how a neat uniform sand layer is progressively deposited as the sand-carrying water current advances.[20] These examples demonstrate that water moving at upper (high) flow regime speeds produces planar beds rapidly. Indeed, the results of such flume experiments correlate closely with the observed natural sedimentation processes from swift-flowing water in tidal channels, floods, and other catastrophic events, and also accurately replicate at a smaller scale the features seen in the neat uniform sedimentary rock layers preserved in the continental geologic record.

The difference between the flume experiments and the observed local-regional natural catastrophes on the one hand, and between the observed local-regional natural catastrophes and the global Flood cataclysm on the other, is in both instances the scale of the sedimentation. However, it is a progressive increase in scale from the flume experiments to the observed local-regional natural catastrophes, and then to the scale of the global cataclysmic Flood. Nevertheless, it has been demonstrated that both the flume experiments and the local-regional natural catastrophes produce neat, uniform sediment layers by deposition from the laminar (sheet) flow of fast-moving waters, rather than from turbulent (churning) flow. Thus, because the continental-scale sedimentary rock layers deposited during the Flood cataclysm are neatly uniform across the continents, it is evident that even under global cataclysmic Flood conditions it was the laminar flow of fast-moving waters, and not turbulent or churning

19. P.V.H. Kuenen, "Experimental Turbidite Lamination in a Circular Flume," *Journal of Geology* 74, no. 5 (1966): p. 523–545.

20. Pierre Y. Julien, Yongqiang Lan, and Guy Berthault, "Experiments on Stratification of Heterogeneous Sand Mixtures," *Creation Ex Nihilo Technical Journal* 8, no. 1 (1994): p. 37–50.

waters, that were responsible for the deposition of these neat, uniform sedimentary rock layers.

Conclusion

In answer to the question that was posed, namely, how could neat uniform sedimentary rock layers be deposited during the Flood cataclysm with all the fast-moving waters, we have seen that the observed sedimentation processes in both flume experiments and larger scale (local-regional) natural catastrophes result in neat, uniform sediment layers being deposited from fast laminar (sheet)-flowing waters. Thus it has been argued that the observed neat, uniform sedimentary rock layers found deposited across the continents as a result of the global Flood cataclysm can be envisaged to have also been the result of the same sedimentation processes from similarly fast laminar-flowing waters. In other words, we can confidently extrapolate the orders of magnitude to the enormous scale of the global Flood cataclysm. Though the flume experiments have been conducted at various small scales, the orders of magnitude extrapolation to the observed natural catastrophes over large regions still results in the same observed pattern of uniform sediment layers deposited neatly in succession by fast-moving waters. This makes us confident that at the global scale of the Flood cataclysm the same sedimentation processes would have also been responsible for the neat, uniform sedimentary rock layers we observe to have been stacked on top of one another and preserved in the continental geologic record, even though the Flood waters were often fast-moving.

CHAPTER 16

Should We Be Concerned about Climate Change?

DR. ALAN WHITE

There is good evidence that global temperatures have been slowly climbing for the past four centuries and were slowly declining for many centuries prior to that. But are these temperature changes a serious threat to our way of life or are they just a part of normal variation to which we can readily adjust? Sadly, our lives are going to be affected whether global warming is a real threat or not. Global warming has been blamed for almost every ill in our society.[1] In his State of the Union speech in 2013, President Obama said this:

> It's true that no single event makes a trend. But the fact is, the 12 hottest years on record have all come in the last 15. Heat waves, droughts, wildfires, floods — all are now more frequent and more intense. We can choose to believe that Superstorm Sandy, and the most severe drought in decades, and the worst wildfires some states have ever seen were all just a freak coincidence. Or we can choose to believe in the overwhelming judgment of science — and act before it's too late.[2]

Within this short quote, many of the common issues related to climate change are raised — recent events that are not necessarily indicative of a long-term trend,

1. For example, see Michael E. Mann and Lee R. Kump, *Dire Predictions Understanding Global Warming* (New York: DK Publishing, 2008), p. 108–139.
2. "Transcript of Obama's State of the Union Address," ABC News, http://abcnews. go.com/Politics/OTUS/transcript-president-barack-obamas-2013-state-union-address/ story?id=18480069#.

a claim that the "science" is settled, and a warning that we must act right now. The president followed these words by vowing that, if legislation were not forthcoming, he would do all he could by executive order.

These new policies will almost certainly raise the cost of energy. Higher energy costs will lower the standard of living for all, particularly the poorest among us. Is a disastrous change in the climate looming? Is man responsible? Let's begin our journey to answer those two questions by defining our terms.

What Is Climate Change?

The *Oxford English Dictionary* defines climate change as a change in global or regional climate patterns, in particular a change apparent from the mid to late 20th century onward and attributed largely to the increased levels of atmospheric carbon dioxide produced by the use of fossil fuels. [3] Other dictionary definitions are much more succinct and do not specify cause, direction, or time frame. It is not surprising that there is some disparity in the definitions. With controversial subjects, people often disagree on exactly what the words mean. For the purpose of this chapter, the phrase "climate change" will be used to mean long-term changes in climate (mainly temperature) without implying any cause for, or direction in, the change.

Do *Climate Change* and *Global Warming* Mean the Same Thing?

Some use these phrases interchangeably, and others do not. Those who see the global temperature as going only in one direction often use them interchangeably. However, the phrase "global warming" was much more popular before 2006 and 2007 when the average global temperature declined significantly. "Climate change" is much more commonly used today and seems much less prejudicial. Therefore, "climate change" will be used herein.

How Could There Be So Much Disagreement over a *Scientific* Issue?

When there is a lack of good data and when people view the data from two very different perspectives, it is easy to have disagreement.

A Lack of Good Data

Measuring the average temperature of the earth is very difficult. At any point in time, different parts of the earth are experiencing different conditions; for example, day and night, summer and winter, cloudy and clear, arid and humid, and windy and calm. This level of variability requires frequent measurements

---

3. *Oxford English Dictionary*, s.v. "climate change."

to be made in many places over many years in order to calculate an average global temperature. Temperature measurements have been made at land-based weather stations since 1880. Two main factors have made those measurements less accurate than they need to be — drastic changes in the immediate area around some of these weather stations and poor distribution of weather stations around the earth. These facts led scientists to push for temperature measurements from satellites.

Satellites are able to provide much-improved data over land-based systems. But even the satellite measurements, which began in 1979, are not without their issues. In 2002, the satellite orbits were adjusted so the measurements could be made at a consistent place and time of day.[4] Clearly, only a few years of useful measurements are not enough to give us a good understanding of climate change. That's not even enough time for us to be sure that these new satellite measurements are sufficiently accurate. Lord Kelvin said, "to measure is to know." We will never have a clear understanding of climate change until we are able to accurately measure the earth's temperature for decades, if not centuries.

The lack of accurate measurements has not stopped scientists from interpreting the data they do have. No problem. That is how science works. Scientists do their best to gather accurate data and propose theories based on those measurements. They test those theories by doing further experiments to see if the new measurements are consistent with the latest theory. In the process of using this scientific method, scientists learn how to do better experiments, make more accurate measurements, and propose better theories. The problem here is that we are in a very early stage in the process of understanding climate change. In early stages, researchers have a strong tendency to develop theories based on their own worldview and to run experiments designed to prove their theory rather than test it. The current bias toward global warming will likely lengthen the time required to construct more accurate climate models.

Two Different Views of the World

To those who believe that the universe is the result of the supposed big bang, where invisible particles somehow came into being and randomly organized themselves into atoms, molecules, stars, and planets, there would be no reason to expect that the earth's temperature would be controlled within a specific range. That life exists at all should be considered exceedingly unlikely from this perspective. Stephen J. Gould, an evolutionist, put it this way, "We are here

---

4. Roy W. Spencer, *The Great Global Warming Blunder* (New York: Encounter Books, 2010), p. 13.

because one odd group of fishes had a peculiar fin anatomy that could transform into legs for terrestrial creatures; because the earth never froze entirely during an ice age; because a small and tenuous species, arising in Africa a quarter of a million years ago, has managed, so far, to survive by hook and by crook. We may yearn for a 'higher' answer — but none exists."[5]

To those who believe that the heavens and the earth were designed and created by a "higher" power, there is ample reason to expect that earth's temperature will remain in a range to support life. In fact, God gives us that promise in Genesis 8:22:

> While the earth remains,
> Seedtime and harvest,
> Cold and heat,
> Winter and summer,
> And day and night
> Shall not cease.

Within this worldview it makes perfect sense that the earth would have a temperature control system just like our bodies do, since God designed them both.

Has the Media Accurately Reported on Climate Change?

"When a dog bites a man that is not news, but when a man bites a dog that is news."[6] Likewise, a stable climate is not news, but a dramatically changing one is.

In the late 1970s, numerous popular media outlets were reporting dire warnings about impending climate change. An April 28, 1975 article in *Newsweek* began with this phrase, "There are *ominous* signs that the earth's weather patterns have begun to change *dramatically* and that these changes may portend a *drastic* decline in food production," and ended, "The longer the planners delay, the more difficult will they find it to cope with the climatic change once the results become a *grim reality*" (emphases mine).[7] Sounds familiar, doesn't it? We hear similar pronouncements today. For example, then-Senator Barack Obama said in 2006, "Not only is it [global climate change] real, it's here, and

5. Stephen Jay Gould, quoted in James A. Haught, *2000 Years of Disbelief, Famous People with the Courage to Doubt* (New York: Prometheus Books, 1996), p. 290; or the original reference is S.J. Gould in "The Meaning of Life," *Life Magazine* (Dec. 1988), p. 84.
6. *Bartlett's Familiar Quotations*, 16th ed., ed. Justin Kaplan (Boston, London, and Toronto: Little, Brown, 1992), p. 554.
7. Peter Gwynne, "The Cooling World," *Newsweek*, April 28, 1975; available online at http://denisdutton.com/newsweek_coolingworld.pdf.

its effects are giving rise to a *frighteningly* new global phenomenon: the man-made natural *disaster*" (emphases mine).[8]

The surprising thing is that the *Newsweek* article in the 1970s was referring to global **cooling,** and then-Senator Obama was referring to global **warming**. Yes, that's right. The panic in the 70s was that the earth's temperature was **declining** and would continue to **decline**. Today, the concern is the earth's temperature is **rising** and that it will continue to **rise**.

How Could Predictions about the Direction of Climate Change Be So Different after Only 30 Years?

If, in the 1970s, you considered the data from only the previous 30 years, it would have been possible to conclude that the short-term trend is cooling, particularly if you extrapolate well into the future expecting that trend to continue (figure 1). Interpolation of data, trying to estimate a value within a range you have studied, is challenging enough. But extrapolation of scientific data into a region that you know nothing about is not wise.

If today you again take the perspective of the last 30 years and extrapolate far into the future, it is possible to conclude that the short-term trend is warming (figure 1).[9] Actually, over the last century, it appears that the temperature rose from 1900 to 1940, declined slightly from 1940 to 1970, and increased from 1980 to around 2000. It is easy to make headlines by drawing sweeping conclusions from small ranges of data; however, it is still unclear whether these short-term trends add up to an unprecedented rise in global temperature. Some climatologists claim that the science was not settled in the 1970s and that they were not in agreement with the popular press at that time.[10] Today, those climatologists are convinced that the latest data, now that it has been corrected, is reliable, and the earth is warming.[11]

Very recently, a few people have begun to conclude that we may actually be in the early stages of another cooling trend.[12] Those who suspect this generally

---

8. Barack Obama, "The Coming Storm: Energy Independence and the Safety of Our Planet" (campaign speech, Chicago, IL, April 3, 2006).

9. Data from the Goddard Institute for Space Studies, National Aeronautics and Space Administration. http://data.giss.nasa.gov/gistemp/graphs_v3/Fig.A2.txt. These data are updated from the data in J. Hansen, Mki. Sato, R. Ruedy, K. Lo, D.W. Lea, and M. Medina-Elizade, "Global temperature change," *Proc. Natl. Acad. Sci.*, 103 (2006) 14288-14293, doi:10.1073/pnas.0606291103.

10. Mann and Kump, *Dire Predictions Understanding Global Warming*, p. 45.

11. Ibid., p. 38–39.

12. For example, see http://www.icr.org/article/new-evidence-for-global-cooling/ and http://www.icr.org/article/will-solar-inactivity-lead-global-cooling.

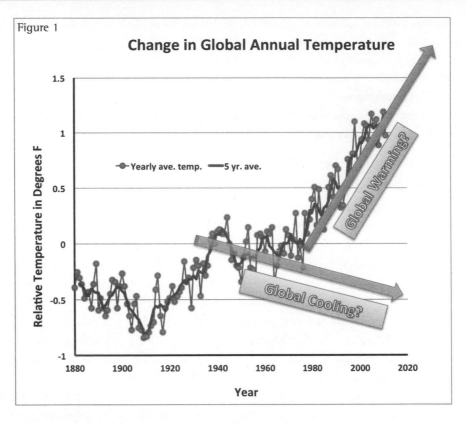

Figure 1

Change in Global Annual Temperature

fall in one of two camps. Some are looking at a specific, narrow range of time (1998 to 2012) where there has certainly been no increase in global temperature. Others are focused on solar activity. They are convinced that the sun is the major factor in determining global temperature. This, of course, is a very reasonable conclusion since almost all our energy comes from the sun. In fact, the number of observed sunspots in this latest sunspot cycle is expected to be the lowest in many decades, and the earth did experience the Little Ice Age at a point in time when sunspot activity was very low.[13] Has the global temperature started to decline after having increased for about 400 years? Only time will tell. Frankly, with our limited understanding of the major factors that affect global temperature, no one should be confident in predicting the future global temperature.

What Are the Politics of Climate Change?

At present a number of expert climatologists and the IPCC (Intergovernmental Panel on Climate Change) appear to be in agreement that the earth's

13. http://solarscience.msfc.nasa.gov/SunspotCycle.shtml

temperature is rising and will continue to rise. However, it is hard to know what the scientific judgment of these individuals would be in the absence of overwhelming political pressure. Their funding and their livelihoods are clearly affected by their stance on this issue.

We scientists want to believe that we are unbiased — that we are strictly interpreting the data and are not swayed by other factors. Are scientists different from all other human beings in this regard? Obviously not. We are swayed by our emotions and our beliefs, just like everyone else. So beware when scientists become emotionally attached to their theories, ignore the uncertainties in their data, or claim that "all reputable scientists agree" or that "the science is settled."[14] When one or more of these is true, you can be sure that the issue being discussed is not purely scientific. When "the science" really is settled, the evidence will be overwhelming, and there will be no need to *claim* that the science is settled.

While investigating any subject, it is interesting to follow the money. There is big money in climate change issues. The person that is the most closely associated with "global warming" is Al Gore. "Critics, mostly on the political right and among global warming skeptics, say Mr. Gore is poised to become the world's first 'carbon billionaire,' profiteering from government policies he supports that would direct billions of dollars to the business ventures he has invested in."[15] "Mr. Gore says that he is simply putting his money where his mouth is."[16] Gore's many multi-million dollar investments in green energy projects and his purchase of a $9M ocean-view home in California are clear evidence of his financial success in this arena. He will certainly have a good vantage point from which to watch a possible rise in sea level!

Is the Truth about Climate Change Really Inconvenient?

It is tempting for each of us to focus only on what has happened in our lifetime. However, for questions related to climate, we need a much longer-term perspective. Have the global temperatures in the last few decades been significantly higher than in the distant past? Unfortunately, there is no way to know for sure. No temperature measurements are available before 1880. Scientists have tried to correlate other scientific data with global temperature, but estimating temperatures in this way is fraught with difficulties. Correlation of ice

---

14. For a similar discussion, see Roy W. Spencer, *Climate Confusion* (New York: Encounter Books, 2008), ch. 2.
15. John W. Broder, "Gore's Dual Role: Advocate and Investor," *The New York Times*, http://www.nytimes.com/2009/11/03/business/energy-environment/03gore.html?_r=0.
16. Ibid.

Figure 2

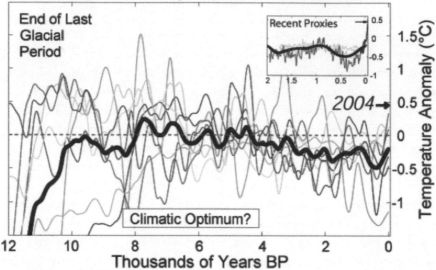

Holocene Temperature Variations

core or tree ring data to global temperatures is full of assumptions that cannot be verified. Figure 2 shows eight different attempts that were made to predict global temperature.[17] The dark line is the average of these data for what they presume to be the last 12,000 years of earth history. Confused as to why anyone would be convinced by these data? You should be. The most recent reconstructions are shown in the insert of figure 2 for the last 2,000 years. These data have led many climatologists to conclude that the climate is much warmer now than in the last 2,000 years.

Historical evidence provides a different perspective on global temperatures during the last two millennia. There is good evidence that the climate in the Northern Hemisphere was warmer about a thousand years ago — the Vikings were able to farm in Greenland. After a few hundred years, they stopped farming due to a cooler climate. The temperature continued to decline for a few hundred more years, and the Thames in London began to regularly freeze.[18] The decline in temperature reversed course in about A.D. 1700. If this warming trend continues, it may again be possible to farm in Greenland, and the sea ice in the north

17. The original literature references for all these data can be found at Wikimedia Commons, "File: Holocene Temperature Variations.png," http://commons.wikimedia.org/wiki/ File:Holocene_Temperature_Variations.png (GNU free documentation license).

18. Spencer, *The Great Global Warming Blunder*, p. 2 and references.

Figure 3

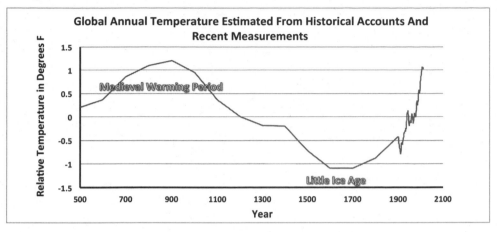

Atlantic may again be scarce. Figure 3 is an estimation of the relative global temperature from historical observations before 1900 and from weather station data after 1990. While we cannot be certain about what was true in ancient times from either historical or scientific data, the historical observations seem more reliable in this instance. From these limited data, it appears that the global temperature cycles around a mean temperature and has been slightly warmer in recorded history than it is today. There is no reason to panic.

Are We the Cause of the Rise in Temperature Since the Little Ice Age?

Many believe that this recent rise in temperature is caused by an increase in carbon dioxide due to our burning of more fossil fuels. Let's look at some facts about carbon dioxide and examine the evidence of its effect on global temperature.

The presence of carbon dioxide in the air is essential to life on earth. Without carbon dioxide, there would be no plant life, and without plant life there would be no animal life. Despite this, Lisa Jackson of the Environmental Protection Agency declared that carbon dioxide was a *pollutant* under the Clean Air Act and deemed that it was a *hazard* to human health.[19] So is CO_2 essential to life or a pollutant? The government apparently thinks that it is both — essential at low levels and harmful at high levels. But is there a level at which CO_2 is too high? As with most government regulations, this regulation preceded our

19. John Broder, "EPA Clears Way for Greenhouse Gas Rules," *The New York Times*, http://www.nytimes.com/2009/04/18/science/earth/18endanger.html.

understanding of the science. While CO_2 does influence the global temperature, the exact relationship has not been established nor has the maximum CO_2 concentration in air.

We do know that carbon dioxide is a greenhouse gas. Greenhouse gases act as a blanket over the earth. When sunlight heats the earth's surface, the warm earth radiates some of that heat into the atmosphere. Greenhouse gases slow the escape of that radiated heat. You have been led to believe that the most important greenhouse gas is carbon dioxide. It is not. Water vapor and clouds are actually responsible for about 80 to 90 percent of the total greenhouse effect. That's right, *at least 80 percent*. That is why clear mornings are usually much colder than cloudy mornings. On clear mornings, we do not have that blanket of clouds to hold in the heat. The percentage of the greenhouse effect attributable to CO_2 is believed to be as high as 20 percent by some and as low as 4 percent by others.[20] Almost everyone agrees that the percent of CO_2 that is man-made is only about 4 percent of total CO_2. Therefore, the greenhouse effect caused by man-made CO_2 is *less than* 1 percent of the total and may be a small fraction of 1 percent.

Despite this, many scientists today claim that the rise in man-made CO_2 is the major cause of the rise in global temperatures over the past century. Just because global temperature and CO_2 concentrations have risen over the past several decades does not mean that one caused the other. Figure 4 shows that the correlation between the CO_2 concentration and global temperature is not strong, particularly between 1900 and 1950. The temperature profile in figure 3 also does not match well with man-made CO_2 levels because man-made CO_2 was not high during the Medieval Warming Period. These data are not convincing.

Is the Global Temperature Nearly Out of Control?

Climatologists' greatest concern is that a temperature increase during the last few decades might be amplified by positive feedback causing the global temperature to spiral out of control. They are worried, for example, that a higher temperature on the earth could melt more of the permafrost, release more CO_2, and cause a greater greenhouse effect. On the other hand, a higher temperature on earth could cause more evaporation, more cloud formation, and more sunlight to be reflected away from the earth. This negative feedback could moderate the global temperature. Which type of feedback is more influential? Scientists

---

20. Spencer, *The Great Global Warming Blunder*, p. 44; G.A. Schmidt, R.A. Ruedy, Ron L. Miller, and A.A. Lacis, "Attribution of the Present-day Total Greenhouse Effect," *Journal of Geophysical Research* 115 (2010): D20106.

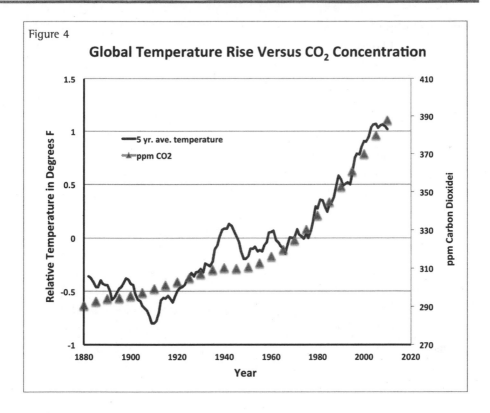

Figure 4

Global Temperature Rise Versus CO$_2$ Concentration

are currently not able to quantify them well enough to know whether the negative feedback outweighs the positive.

Engineers familiar with control systems are well aware that control systems dependent on positive feedback easily go out of control whereas those based on negative feedback generally do not. Since the earth's temperature has been relatively stable for many centuries, it seems more likely that the earth's climate is moderated by more powerful negative feedback systems.

It appears that a brilliant designer has designed a molecule that is both essential to human life and essential for controlling the climate of the earth. Water is a polar molecule that is able to dissolve salts, proteins, and DNA that are essential for our cells to function and for life to exist. Water's other physical properties are just as critical to controlling the earth's climate. It takes more heat to change water from a solid to a liquid or from a liquid to a gas than any other common molecule. The 310,000,000 cubic *miles* of water on the earth's surface are able to hold a tremendous amount of heat and provide great temperature stability to the earth. Water can readily transfer heat from the earth's surface to the air by evaporation and condensation, which is the basis of the hydrological cycle and much of our weather. Cloud formation may also be the key to a negative feedback system that helps moderate temperature changes in the earth's atmosphere. Without water, the range of temperature from day to night and from the earth's surface to the upper atmosphere would be much greater. Clearly water is critical to human life in many, many ways.

How Should We Then Live?

In the first chapter of the first book of the Bible, God commands us to subdue the earth (see Genesis 1:28). Most interpret this to mean that we should take care of the earth and be good stewards of its natural resources. If it were true that the burning of coal, oil, and natural gas did have a significant negative effect on our environment, it would make sense for us to modify our behavior. But it appears that we are just in the upper range of a natural temperature cycle. It is not at all clear that the small amount of additional CO_2 produced by the burning of fossil fuels is detrimental to the environment. It is humbling to remember that when God was judging the earth with a global flood that He was creating inexpensive fuel sources for future generations. Let's obey God's command and use our scientific knowledge to be good stewards of our natural resources and preserve our environment for the next generation until He comes again. [21]

21. For further information on this issue, see Michael Oard, "Is Man the Cause of Global Warming?" in *The New Answers Book 3*, Ken Ham, gen. ed. (Green Forest, AR: Master Books), p. 69–79.

CHAPTER 17

What about Creation, Flood, and Language Division Legends?

TROY LACEY (WITH BODIE HODGE)

Introduction

Nearly every culture around the world has a creation legend and just as many have worldwide flood legends, and, believe it or not, there are even many language division legends around the world in different and diverse cultures.

In today's highly secularized culture, there are attacks on the Bible using these legends. Those who do not trust what the Bible plainly says often speculate that the Bible's discussion about creation, the Flood, and the Tower of Babel are just more legends and determine that the Bible cannot be trusted. What these attackers fail to realize is that these legends are a great confirmation of the Bible and that the Bible retains the true account recorded by God in His Word. From an historical perspective, this makes perfect sense and is consistent with a biblical worldview, but it is hard to explain all these legends from a secular evolutionary worldview — people supposedly evolved and slowly filled the earth with a gradual changing of languages and no global Flood. Why then should we find so many common threads in so many accounts from all over the world? The evolutionary explanation fails to provide a reason for commonality, whereas the biblical one does.

The Nature of "Legends"

Of course, many of these legends have been distorted and have become highly mythologized and embellished over time; and this is to be expected as people dispersed from Babel and the knowledge of God and mankind's early history was forgotten or turned into folklore. Many have common themes, involving mankind being created from clay; a remnant understanding of God (i.e., a "god") as angry with mankind for some reason; large boats (or rafts) being constructed to survive a coming flood, often foretold to the hero by this "god"; animals being collected by the hero in order to survive the coming deluge, and so on. Many of these legends sometimes still bear striking resemblances in many particulars to biblical accounts.

Many, though, are drastically different and show corruption from an original account, as one would expect from an orally passed-down story. Others show details that seem to be in direct contrast to the biblical accounts of creation and the Flood. We see numerous examples of "gods" being killed to create the physical earth and/or heavens; mankind given power by the "gods" to create the animals; mankind re-creating the earth after the Flood; animals that rescue people from the Flood, and so on. Some of these may be the result of distortion over time, while others may be a deliberate attempt by post-Babel peoples to reshape the world and the "gods" in their own image. Romans chapter 1 clearly shows that human hearts and minds willfully suppress the true God and make up one in their own image, or in the image of animals (see also Genesis 8:21; Exodus 32:4–8; 1 Kings 12:28–33; and Jeremiah 17:5–9).

Legends from Genesis 1–11 That Confirm the Bible

There is no way to exhaustively cover this topic in such a short article, as there are literally hundreds of books detailing these creation, Flood, and language division legends. Rather, ten of each will be discussed in the following tables.

Creation Legends

	Who	Where	Quote
1	Mosotene	Bolivia, South America	"Dobitt created the world. He made it in the shape of a great raft which floats in space supported by innumerable spirits. Then Dobitt created mankind to live in the world. He made images out of clay and gave them life, and then went off to live in the sky. Later Dobitt returned and made animals and birds. He

			carried a big basket full of water and spilled it out here and there over the earth to make the rivers." Authority: Leach[a]
2	Lenape or Delaware Native Americans	United States, North America	"In the beginning, forever, lost in space was the Great Manito. He made the earth and the sky. He made the sun, moon, and stars. He made everything move in harmony. Then the wind blew violently, it became lighter and water flowed strongly and from afar, and groups of islands emerged and remained. Once again the Great Manito spoke, one Manito to other Manitos, to mortal creatures, spirits and all. All creatures were friendly with one another at that time." Authority: Maclagan[b]
3	Zuni Native Americans	United States, North America	"The creator Awonawilona conceived in himself the thought and the thought took shape and got out into space, and through this it stepped out into the void, into outer space and from this came nebulae of growth and mist, full of power and growth." Awonawilona then made "mother-earth" and "father-sky." Authority: Maclagan
4	Ona	Argentina, South America	"Temaukl always existed. He created the earth and sky, and there was no time when Temaukl was not. Kenos was the first man, sent into the world by Temaukl to put things in order. So Kenos created the plants and animals and gave the Ona their land." Authority: Leach
5	Ekoi	Nigeria, Africa	"One day in the beginning of the world, Obassi Osaw made a man and a woman and brought them down to live upon the earth. He placed them here in the green world and then went back into the sky. He returned to see how they were getting along. 'What have you eaten? What have you had to drink?' Obassi asked them. 'Nothing' they replied. Then Obassi dug a ditch, drew forth a jar full of water and poured the water into the ditch. This was the first river. The next thing he did was to plant a palm kernel which he carried in his hand. 'Drink the water. Take care of the Palm tree.' So the man and woman watched the palm tree grow and tended it with care and love. After a while great clusters of yellow fruit ripened. When Obassi saw this, 'This is your food' he said to the man and woman." Authority: Leach

6	Lozi	Zambia, Africa	"In the beginning, Nyambi lived on earth with his wife Nasi-lele. As god, he made the birds and all of the animals and fishes. One thing Nyambi made was different, and it was a man. The first man's name was Kamonu. One day Kamonu fixed a spear for himself. He killed an antelope and did not stop there. He killed again and again. 'Man!' Nyambi shouted 'What you do is wrong. You are killing your brothers' So Nyambi gave him a place to plant and grow things to calm man." Authority: Hamilton[c]
7	Norse	Scandinavia and Northern Europe	"In Norse mythology, a foggy void between the lands of fire (Muspell) and ice (Niflheim) produced a primeval cow Audumbla, and the Frost Giant Ymir. The cow licked at ice and eventually uncovered the 'god' Buri. Ymir produced frost giants as he slept, and Buri married one of Ymirs daughters. Ymir was later killed by Odin, a grandson of Buri. Ymir's flesh became the earth, his bones the mountains, his teeth became rocks and his blood became rivers, lakes, and seas. Mankind was created later by three gods; Odin gave them life, Vili gave them intelligence, and Ve gave them the five senses." Authority: Cotterel and Storm[d]
8	Babylon	Middle East	"Apsu (primeval water) and Tiamat (chaos and salt-water) created the great gods, who begat other gods. These gods danced and made noise, so that Apsu wanted to destroy them so that he and Tiamat could rest. One of the gods Ea cast a spell on Apsu which caused him to sleep, and then Ea killed him. Tiamat produced monsters so that they could avenge Apsu on the gods. Ea's son Marduk promised to kill Tiamat if he was given supreme power by the other gods. They agreed and Marduk trapped Tiamat in a net and killed her with an arrow and a whirlwind. He cut her body in half and with the two halves, made the sky and the earth. Later he made man out of the blood of Tiamat's second husband Kingu." Authority: Hamilton

9	Tahitians	Polynesia	"Ta-aroa lived alone in a shell shaped like an egg. The egg revolved in dark empty space for ages. Then came a new time when Ta-aroa broke out of the egg. Being so by himself, he made the god Tu. Tu became Ta-aroa's great helper in the wonderful work of creation. Ta-aroa and Tu made gods to fill every place. They made the universe and they brought forth land and creatures. Last, they created man to live on the earth." Authority: Hamilton
10	Greece	Southern Europe	"In the days of old there was only chaos. Out of chaos arose the earth Gaia, and out of earth rose Uranus the sky god with whom she mated to produce the Titans who ultimately deposed Uranus." The Titans were later led by Cronos who was overthrown by Zeus and the rest of the classical Greek pantheon of gods. Much later, a Titan named Prometheus created man out of clay and water; while even later, Zeus ordered Hephaistos to create woman, more or less as a punishment for mankind for having been given fire by Prometheus. Authority: Leach; Cotterell and Storm

a. Maria Leach, *The Beginning: Creation Myths Around the World* (New York: Funk and Wagnalls, 1956), p. 127–139, 234–235.
b. David Maclagan, Creation Myths: Man's Introduction to the World (London: Thames and Hudson, 1977), p. 15, 78–79.
c. Virginia Hamilton, *In the Beginning: Creation Stories from Around the World* (New York: Harcourt, Inc., 1988), p. 65–67, 83–85, 101–103.
d. Arthur Cotterell and Rachel Storm, *The Ultimate Encyclopedia of Mythology* (Lanham, MD: Anness Publishing, 1999).

Flood Legends

1	Aztec	Central America	"Humanity was wiped out by a flood, but one man Coxcoxtli and one woman Xochiquetzal escaped in a boat, and reached a mountain called Colhuacan." Authority: Sheppard[a]
2	Hindu (Sanskrit)	India	"The God Brahma, in the form of a fish told Manu who had cared for him many years: 'the dissolution of all moving and unmoving things of earth is near. This deluge of the worlds is approaching . . . all ends in violent water. A boat is to be built by you, furnished with a sturdy cord. There with the seven Rsis, sit Great Manu and take with you all

			the seeds, preserving them in portions.'" Manu did as instructed and waited in the boat after it was built, and he and the Rsis were preserved in the boat by Brahma while the entire earth was flooded. The boat landed on a peak of the Himalayas. Authority: Martin[b]
3	Karina	Venezuela South America	"The sky-god Kaputano came down to the kingdom of the Karina. 'Children, hear me well. Soon a great rain will fall on the earth and will cover all with water.' Only four couples listened, as the rest scoffed, declaring that there wouldn't be any flood. Kaputano and the eight people began building a very large canoe, and when they were done they went around gathering two of every animal to put on board. They also brought seeds from every plant on earth. Once they were done they got on board and it began to rain, and it rained for many, many days. Soon the entire earth was flooded. Eventually the rain stopped and the water began to recede and the land began to dry. The four couples exited their canoe but the world was destroyed. Kaputano asked how the Karina would like the world remade, and they asked for rivers and hills and trees, which Kaputano made for them." Authority: Martin
4	Babylon	Middle East	Utnapishtim related to Gilgamesh how the god Ea told him to build a boat to escape a worldwide flood the other gods were sending to wipe out mankind. It was to be a 30x30 cubit boat in the shape of a cube. He was instructed by Ea to also bring two of every animal, and water and provisions. He obeyed and after loading the boat, with his cargo, his wife and a captain to pilot the boat, the rains came and lasted for 7 days. All, the earth was flooded and destroyed, but 12 days later dry land began to appear. Utnapishtim waited 7 more days then sent out a dove, then a swallow which both returned, then a raven which did not. After this, Utnapishtim unloaded all the animals from the Ark. He offered a sacrifice to the gods and he and his wife were granted immortality. Authority: Martin

5	Bahnars	China	"Once a crab and a kite had an argument. The kite pecked the crab so hard that he pierced the crab's shell. To avenge this great insult, the crab caused the waters of the sea to swell. They swelled so much that everything on earth was destroyed, except for a brother and a sister, who survived by locking themselves in a huge chest. Because they were afraid that everything would perish forever, they brought on board two of every animal. After 7 days they heard a rooster crowing outside the chest (which the ancestors had sent) and knew it was safe to come out." Authority: Martin
6	Greece	Southern Europe	"One Day Prometheus came to Deucalion and told him 'Zeus was going to destroy all the men of this bronze age. Build yourself a chest of wood so that you and your wife may survive.' Deucalion did just that and after he had provisioned it, took his wife aboard with him. Zeus caused a great flood which destroyed everything." Authority: Martin
7	Hareskin Tribe	NWT, Western Canada	"Kunyan (Wise Man) resolved to build a great raft. When his wife asked him why he would build it, he said 'If there comes a flood, as I foresee, we shall take refuge on the raft.' He told his plan to other men on the earth and they laughed at him saying, 'If there is a flood we shall take refuge in the trees.' But Kunyan made a great raft, joining the logs together by ropes made of roots. Suddenly there came a flood such that the like of it had never been seen before. Men climbed up into trees, but the water rose after them and all were drowned. But Kunyan, his wife and his son floated safely on his strong raft. As he floated he thought of the future, and he gathered two of all the animals he met with on his passage. 'Come up on my raft, for soon there will be no more earth' he said. Indeed the earth disappeared under the water. The Wise Man told a beaver to dive down into the waters and see what he could find. The beaver returned with a piece of mud. Kunyan took the mud into his hand and breathed on it and it began to grow. So he laid it on the water, kept it from sinking and watched as it continued to grow.

			Later, after a long time, it grew to the size of the land as it was before the flood. Then Kunyan, his wife and son, and all the animals came off the raft and repopulated the world." Authority: Frazier[c]
8	Rotti	West Timor, Indonesia	"Once, the sea-god became angry with mankind and decided to flood the whole earth. In fact the entire earth was destroyed except for the peak of one mountain. A man and his sister along with several animals had escaped to the high mountain and there survived. However, there was nowhere to go, so they asked the sea-god to bring the waters back down. He refused unless they could find a creature whose hairs he could not number. After throwing into the waters a pig, goat, dog, and hen, all of whose hairs the sea-god could number, they finally threw in a cat and the sea-god gave up and agreed that the waters could recede. He then caused an osprey to fly over the mountain, sprinkling dirt on the water. The dirt became dry land and the man, his sister, and the animals were able to descend the mountain." Authority: Martin
9	Montagnais Tribe	Quebec and Labrador, East Canada	"A race of giants was destroying the earth, and God, angry with them for it, commanded a man to build a very large canoe. The man did as he was told and as soon as he entered in the water rose on all sides until no land could be seen in any direction. Bored with the scenery, the man told an otter to dive down into the waters and see what he could find. The otter returned with a piece of earth. The man took the earth into his hand and breathed on it and it began to grow. So he laid it on the water, kept it from sinking and watched as it continued to grow. As it grew the man saw that it was becoming an island. The man decided that the earth was not yet large enough so he continued to blow on it. In time all of the lakes, mountains, and rivers were formed, and the man knew it was time to leave the canoe." Authority: Martin

10	Lake Tyers Aborigines	Victoria, Australia	"Once upon a time, a huge frog swallowed all the water of the world and everyone was thirsty. Because of this all the animals took a poll and decided that the best way to make the frog give the water back was to make him laugh. So they all took turns playing pranks and cutting up in front of him. They were so hilarious that everyone else would have died laughing, but the frog did not even smile. Finally, as a last resort the eel wriggled about dancing and swaying as it stood on its tail. Not even the glum frog could watch this without laughing. He laughed and laughed until tears ran down his cheeks. The water poured from his mouth and soon became a flood. The waters rose killing many people. In fact all of mankind would have drowned, if the pelican had not paddled about in a canoe, rescuing survivors as he went." Authority: Martin

a. Pam Sheppard, "Tongue Twisting Tales," Answers in Genesis, http://www.answersingenesis.org/articles/am/v3/n2/tongue-twisting-tales.

b. Charles Martin, *Flood Legends: Global Clues of a Common Event* (Green Forest, AR: Master Books, 2009), p. 126–129, 131–143.

c. James George Frazier, *Folklore in the Old Testament: Studies in Comparative Religion* (Whitefish, MT: Kessinger Publishing, 2010), p. 310–312.

Language Splitting/Tower of Babel Legends

1	Maidu Natives	Western North America	"suddenly in the night everybody began to speak in a different tongue except that each husband and wife talked the same language. . . . Then he called each tribe by name, and sent them off in different directions, telling them where they were to dwell." Authority: Sheppard[a]
2	Quiches	Central America	"when the tribes multiplied and left their old home to a place called Tulan. Here the language changed, and the people sought new homes in various parts of the world as a result of not being able to understand each other." Authority: Sheppard
3	Wa-Sania	East Africa	"that of old all the tribes of the earth knew only one language, but that during a severe famine the people went mad and wandered in all directions, jabbering strange words, and so the different languages arose." Authority: Sheppard.

4	Mikir	Northeastern India	"Higher and higher rose the building, till at last the gods and demons feared lest these giants should become the masters of heaven, as they already were of earth. So they confounded their speech, and scattered them to the four corners of the world. Hence arose all the various tongues of mankind." Authority: Sheppard
5	Greece	Southern Europe	"for many ages men lived at peace, without cities and without laws, speaking one language, and ruled by Zeus alone. . . . At last Hermes introduced diversities of speech and divided mankind into separate nations." Authority: Sheppard
6	Polynesia	Pacific Island of Hao	"they made an attempt to erect a building by which they could reach the sky, and see the creator god Vatea [Atea]; but the god in anger chased the builders away, broke down the building, and changed their language, so that they spoke diverse tongues." Authority: Sheppard
7	Sumerians	Middle East	"In those days . . . the whole universe, the people in unison. . . . Enki, the Lord of abundance. . . . Changed the speech in their mouths, and [brought?] contention into it, Into the speech of man that [until then] had been one." Authority: Sheppard
8	Gaikho	Southeast Asia	"In the days of Pan-dan-man, the people determined to build a pagoda that should reach up to heaven. . . . When the pagoda was half way up to heaven, God came down and confounded the language of the people, so that they could not understand each other. Then the people scattered, and Than-mau-rai, the father of the Gaikho tribe, came west, with eight chiefs, and settled in the valley of the Sitang." Authority: Sheppard
9	Greece	Southern Europe	"In the days of old the gods had the whole earth distributed among them by allotment. There was no quarrelling; for you cannot rightly suppose that the gods did not know what was proper for each of them to have, or, knowing this, that they would seek to procure for themselves by contention that which more properly belonged to others. They all of them

			by just apportionment obtained what they wanted and people to their own districts. . . . Now different gods had their allotments in different places which they set in order."[b]
10	Inca	Western South America	"In the story of the creator god Virachocha, he created the second race of human beings from clay — the earth. Having painted his creations with distinctive clothes and given them different languages and customs that would distinguish them, he breathed life into them and caused them to descend into the earth and disperse."[c]

a. Pam Sheppard, "Tongue Twisting Tales," Answers in Genesis, http://www.answersingenesis.org/articles/am/v3/n2/tongue-twisting-tales.

b. Plato, *Critias, in Great Books of the Western World*, vol. 7, ed. Robert Maynard Hutchins (Chicago, IL: University of Chicago, 1952), p. 479.

c. David M. Jones, *The Lost History of the Incas* (Leicester: Hermes House, 2007), p. 198.

Conclusion

The Bible records the true account of creation, the Flood, and the Tower of Babel. The more we find legends from cultures around the world that contain elements of these actual events, the more excited the Christian should be to connect these confirmations to the Bible's truth. As people left Babel, they took their history with them. Therefore, we would expect to find cultures with this history of Creation, Catastrophe, and Confusion, and we would expect it to be corrupted, unlike the Bible, whose word will never pass away (Luke 21:33).

Even many atheists have a massive flood legend. The problem with their flood legend is that it is said to have happened on Mars, while insisting that there is not enough water on earth for a global Flood! The primary reason they reject a global flood on earth is because it gives credence to truthfulness of God's Word, which they do not want due to their religious convictions.

CHAPTER 18

How Big Is the Universe?

DR. DANNY R. FAULKNER

Introduction

The universe appears to be very large — billions of light years across. Since this is far larger than a few thousand light years, people frequently ask how we can see objects this far away if the universe is only thousands of years old, as the Bible seems to imply. This is a very good question — so good that we have given this question a name: the light travel time problem. There are a number of proposed solutions to this problem, but I will not discuss those here.[1] Instead, I will address the question of whether the universe really is as big as is often claimed. The short answer is, yes, the universe most certainly is that large. To explain this conclusion, I will describe some of the methods astronomers use to measure distances of astronomical bodies.

Distances

I emphasize that there are three realms of astronomical distances: those within the solar system, those within the galaxy, and those of objects outside of our galaxy. The techniques used in these realms are different, and there is little overlap between the techniques used in those realms. The first distance measurements in astronomy were within the solar system, and they were done by geometric means as planets orbited the sun. This largely was replaced by more accurate radar measurements in the latter half of the 20th century. I will not

---

1. See Chapter 21 in this volume for more on the distant starlight models.

discuss solar system distances, for the light travel times involved here amount to mere hours at most, and thus are not a problem for recent creation. The sun and all the stars that we can see are members of the Milky Way galaxy, a vast collection of more than 100 billion stars spanning nearly 100,000 light years. The term "stellar distance" normally refers to measuring distances of stars within the galaxy. The first stellar distance measurement was in 1838. There are billions of many other galaxies, each of them being millions or even billions of light years away. We say that the distances of other galaxies are extra-galactic. The first extra-galactic distance measurement was in 1924.

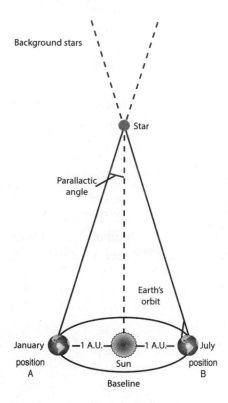

Figure 1. An illustration of parallax

The first stellar distance measure used trigonometric parallax. Trigonometric parallax employs the principle of the apparent shifting position of an object due to our changing location from where we view the object. You can illustrate this by looking at your upheld thumb at arm's length. Close one eye and note the position of your thumb with respect to background objects. Now open that eye and close the other eye. You'll notice that your thumb appears to shift position. We call this apparent shift in position parallax. If you hold your thumb closer to your eyes or if you try this with a more distant object, you will discover that the amount of parallax depends upon the distance of the object — the greater the distance, the less the parallax. The amount of parallax also depends upon the length of the baseline, in this case the distance between your eyes. For a given distance, a greater baseline produces a larger parallax. Surveyors have long used this technique to measure the distances of faraway objects and altitudes of mountains. They set up a transit (in ancient times a dioptra) to view a distant object and measure the angles that the object made at either end of the baseline. Using the baseline and angles, one can use simple trigonometry to measure the distance to the object.

In similar manner, astronomers use the baseline of the earth's orbit around the sun to measure the apparent shift in the positions of nearby stars with respect to more distant stars. An astronomer at location A on one side of the earth's orbit measures the position of a star. Six months later, when the astronomer has arrived at position B on the other side of the earth's orbit, he re-measures the position of the star. The total shift in apparent position is a very small angle, so we normally express it in seconds of arc.[2] Notice that the baseline is the diameter of the earth's orbit, which is twice the distance of the earth from the sun. The average distance of the earth from the sun is a standard unit of distance that astronomers call the astronomical unit (AU for short). Astronomers express the baseline as one AU, so the parallax angle is defined to be one-half the total measured shift. The closest star, Proxima Centauri, has the largest parallax, but its parallax is less than one arc second. And its distance is about 26 trillion miles, so use of normal trigonometric relationships would be quite cumbersome. To avoid this and use a very simple formula, astronomers have defined their own units. If d is the distance of the star and π is the parallax, then the formula is:

$$\pi = 1/d$$

Note that π here is a variable and does not refer to the ratio of the circumference of a circle to its diameter. For this equation to work, astronomers have defined a new unit of distance, the parsec (abbreviated pc). The parsec is the distance that a star would have if its parallax were one second of arc.[3] Since we normally measure the parallax and then compute the distance, we can re-write the equation:

$$d = 1/\pi$$

Friedrich Bessel was the first to measure a star's parallax in 1838 (the star was 61 Cygni). In the early 20th century, astronomers began to use photography for parallax work. The techniques of the time allowed reasonably accurate measurements of stellar distances (within 20 percent) out to about 20 pc (65 light years) and thus included a few hundred stars. The primary limitation of this work was the blurring of the earth's atmosphere. To avoid this problem, the European Space Agency (ESA) launched the Hipparcos satellite in 1989. The Hipparcos mission accurately measured the parallaxes of more than 100,000 stars, providing good distances to about 600 light years. ESA has scheduled the launch of

---

2. A degree is divided into 60 minutes of arc, and each minute is divided into 60 seconds, so there are 3,600 seconds in one degree.

3. The name comes from parallax of one second of arc. A parsec is 3.26 light years.

Gaia, a much-improved mission, in late 2013. If successful, Gaia will accurately measure distances of millions of stars to tens of thousands of light years. Obviously, parallax data obtained so far are not a problem for recent creation, but the Gaia data could be a problem for a creation that is only 6,000 years old.

Trigonometric parallax is the only direct method of measuring stellar distances, but astronomers have developed other indirect means. Many of these indirect methods involve the use of "standard candles." A standard candle is a star or other object for which we have a good idea of how bright it actually is. Astronomers use magnitudes to express stellar brightness. A star's apparent magnitude, m, is how bright a star appears to us. Its absolute magnitude, M, is a measure of how bright a star actually is, defined to be the apparent magnitude a star would have if it were ten pc away. A star's apparent magnitude depends upon the star's absolute magnitude and its distance. We can directly measure m, and if we think that we know M, we can form the distance modulus m – M. We can find the distance, d, in pc, by inserting the distance modulus in the following formula:

$$d = 10^{(m-M+5)/5}$$

The best example of a standard candle is the use of Cepheid variables. Cepheid variables are pulsating giant and super giant stars with temperatures similar to the sun. As these stars pulsate, their diameters alternately increase and decrease while their temperatures cyclically change. The changes in size and temperature cause a Cepheid regularly to vary in brightness over a definite period. The periods of Cepheid variables range from two days to two months. About a century ago, the astronomer Henrietta Leavitt discovered that Cepheid variables follow a period-luminosity relation. That is, the longest-period Cepheid variables have the greatest average brightness. In observing a Cepheid variable, an astronomer obtains the star's average m and period. Knowing the period, the period-luminosity relation reveals the Cepheid variable's absolute magnitude,

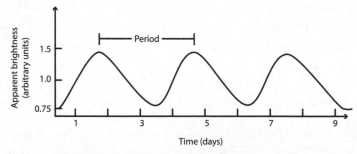

Figure 2. A Cepheid variable light curve showing the period

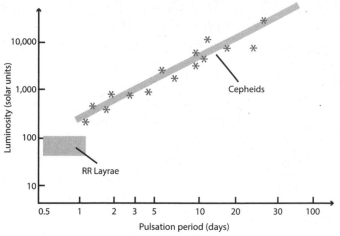

Figure 3. The period-luminosity diagram

which yields the distance modulus and hence the distance. Astronomers had used some other indirect methods to calibrate the period-luminosity relation, but now the Hipparcos mission has allowed direct calibration, in good agreement with the indirect methods. How do we know that a particular variable star indeed is a Cepheid? Cepheid variables have unique characteristics, such as their temperature and the shape of their light curves. The physics of the pulsation is well understood, and from the theory we would expect them to follow the period-luminosity relation.

In addition to standard candles, astronomers can compute distances of stars by estimating their intrinsic luminosities. The spectra of stars contain dark absorption lines that form in the atmospheres of stars. Absorption lines normally are very narrow, but various mechanisms can broaden spectral lines. One of the most important broadening mechanisms in stellar spectra is pressure broadening. The physics of pressure broadening is well understood, with the result being there is an inverse relationship between the amount of pressure broadening and the size of a star. That is, the largest stars have the narrowest lines. Astronomers can estimate the size of a star (expressed by radius, R) by how broad its spectral lines are. We can also determine a star's temperature, T, expressed in Kelvin, a number of different ways. The total luminosity, L, of a star may be expressed as:

$$L = 4\pi R^2 \sigma T^4$$

In this equation, σ is the Stefan-Boltzmann constant. When combined with a model atmosphere, we can convert the luminosity to an absolute magnitude. If we measure the star's apparent magnitude, we know the distance modulus, and we can use the previous equation to find the distance of the star.

Figure 4. Crab Nebula
(Shutterstock.com)

There are some specialized distance determination methods. A good example of this is use of the expansion rate of the Crab Nebula to find its distance. The Crab Nebula is the remnant of a supernova that the Chinese recorded seeing on July 4, 1054. Modern photographs taken a few decades apart reveal that knots of material near the periphery of the remnant are moving outward. Measurement of the motion of those knots allows astronomers to estimate the age of the remnant, an age consistent with the known age. In addition, emission lines in the spectrum of the remnant have both positive and negative Doppler motions along our line of sight. The negative Doppler motion comes from gas moving toward us on the near side of the remnant, while the positive Doppler motion comes from gas on the far side moving away from us. We combine this Doppler motion with the aforementioned expansion of the knots to measure the size and distance of the Crab Nebula. This last step assumes that the expansion is uniform in all directions. The nebula is elongated on photographs, showing that the expansion is not exactly uniform, but this simple assumption probably introduced less than 25 percent error in the final results. We find that the Crab Nebula is about 6,000 light years away.

It is most fortunate that the Crab Nebula also contains a pulsar. Pulsars are radio sources that periodically flash radiation with very regular periods. Astronomers think that pulsars are rapidly spinning neutron stars. There are now more than 2,000 known pulsars, with periods ranging from

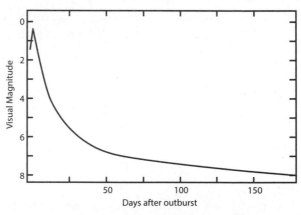

Figure 5. A nova light curve

about a thousandth of a second to a few seconds. Pulsar timings are done in the radio spectrum, and astronomers have found that the pulses are slightly delayed, or dispersed, depending upon the frequency of observation. Dispersion is a well-understood phenomenon, and in addition to dispersion depending upon the frequency, dispersion also depends upon the number density of electrons, n, in the interstellar medium (ISM). The dispersion of the Crab Pulsar and its known distance allow astronomers to measure the average value of n in the ISM along our line of sight to the Crab Nebula. Given the great distance of the Crab Nebula, this appears to be a good average of n in the ISM, which in turn allows radio astronomers to measure the distance of any pulsar with dispersion measurements. This has been done with nearly all pulsars. One of the closest is PSR J0108-1431, about 400 light years away. Pulsars are found

throughout the galaxy, with distances up to tens of thousands of light years. Furthermore, astronomers have found pulsars in the Large and Small Magellanic Clouds, two small satellite galaxies of the Milky Way, about 160,000 and 200,000 light years away.

The various methods of finding distances within the Milky Way galaxy help establish the size of the Milky Way, about 100,000 light years across. Since these distances are greater than 6,000 light years, there is some tension between recent creation and these distances. I now turn my attention to extra-galactic distances. Since Cepheid variables are such bright stars, we see them in other galaxies, so this is the one overlap between these realms. The only difference between

Figure 6. Milky Way over the desert of Bardenas, Spain (Shutterstock.com)

galactic Cepheids and extra-galactic Cepheid variables is that the ones in other galaxies are much fainter than the ones that we see in our own galaxy. It follows from their faint apparent magnitudes that these Cepheid variables, and hence their host galaxies, are millions of light years away.

In addition to Cepheid variables, astronomers have developed other standard candles for extra-galactic use. They include:

1. Novae
2. Bright super giant stars
3. Bright Globular star clusters
4. Bright HII regions
5. Type Ia supernovae

Novae are eruptions on white dwarf stars in close binary systems, and they have a large range in brightness. But the brightest, classical novae appear to have a narrow range in maximum absolute magnitude. If we happen to observe a nova in another galaxy near its peak brightness, we can measure the apparent magnitude, find the distance modulus, and use the distance formula to find the distance. In similar manner, it appears that the brightest super giant stars in galaxies of the same type have about the same absolute magnitude, allowing an estimate of distances. Large spiral galaxies like the Milky Way have about 200 globular star clusters. The largest and brightest have about the same absolute magnitude. In addition, globular clusters have some appreciable diameter, so that they show up as extended objects on photographs. The largest globular clusters have about the same diameter, so their apparent size can be used as a method of finding distances to them and hence their host galaxies. HII regions are glowing clouds of ionized hydrogen gas surrounding hot, bright stars. While HII regions vary in size and brightness, like globular clusters, there appears to be uniformity among the biggest and brightest ones. These methods now work out to a distance of nearly 50 million light years. Within this range, astronomers like to use several methods and average the results. The variance gives an idea of the errors involved.

Type Ia supernovae characteristics are distinctive from other types of supernovae, so they are easy to identify. In recent years, they have stood out as one of the most powerful methods of

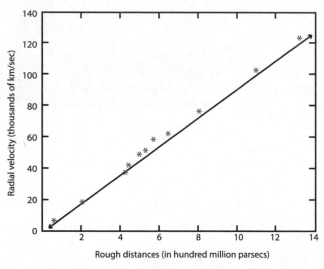

Figure 7. Hubble relation

finding extra-galactic distances. Astronomers think that a type Ia supernova results from the disintegration of a white dwarf star in a close binary system. The white dwarfs involved in this scenario are so similar that the resulting explosions are nearly identical. This means that at peak brightness all type Ia supernova have the same absolute magnitude, so mea-

Figure 8. Globular cluster
(Shutterstock.com)

surement of the apparent magnitude easily yields the distance. Supernovae are rare events in any particular galaxy, but in recent years astronomers have automated robotic telescopes to look for type Ia supernovae in other galaxies. This has resulted in the discovery of a vast number of these supernovae and hence distances to the host galaxies. In 2013, the HST detected a type Ia supernova about ten billion light years away. In 1999, data from type Ia supernovae played a key role showing that the rate of expansion in the universe may be speeding up, an effect attributed to dark energy. The only restriction on this method is that it works only for galaxies that have type Ia supernova that we happen to observe.

Finally, since Edwin Hubble's 1928 discovery of the expansion of the universe, astronomers have used the Hubble relation to find the distances of galaxies. Redshift is a measure of how much the lines in the spectrum of a galaxy are shifted toward longer (more red) wavelengths.[4] Hubble showed that there is a relationship between redshift and distance, something that one would expect if the universe is expanding. There is some scatter in the data, but the trend generally holds. Mathematically, we can represent the Hubble relation as:

$$v = Hd$$

In this equation, v is redshift expressed as velocity in km/s, d is the distance in Mpc (megaparsec = one million pc), and H is the Hubble constant. This is the

---

4. People often liken the redshift due to expansion to a Doppler effect of an object moving away from us. Though they observationally are not distinguishable, they are not the same thing.

equation of a line with H being the slope. H is difficult to determine, but once we get that, we can find distances by re-writing the Hubble relation:

$$d = v/H$$

As long as there is enough light to obtain a spectrum of a galaxy, we can measure the galaxy's redshift, and we may use the Hubble relation to find its distance.

Conclusion

I have described here some of the simpler and more often used methods of finding distances to galaxies. In each case, they produce distances that are millions and even billions of light years. While all of these methods suffer from error, those errors would not reduce the distances down to just thousands of light years. The universe is very large, much larger than people can really comprehend. Douglas Adams probably said it best in *The Hitchhiker's Guide to the Galaxy*:

> You just won't believe how vastly hugely mind-bogglingly big it is. I mean, you may think it's a long way down the road to the chemist, but that's just peanuts to space.[5]

Many recent creationists worry about the light travel time problem and entertain possibilities of the universe being far smaller than generally thought as a way out of this dilemma. But this stumbles over something that ought to be obvious. Only a truly powerful Creator could conceive and make such a large universe. It is as if He created the world so large that we finite creatures upon seeing His handiwork ought to fall down prostrate in worship of Him. It may not be possible for a mere human to truly grasp the immensity of the universe, and understanding the power required to create such a universe is infinitely beyond that, but we creationists accept that fact. Yet we so often stumble over how God could have brought the light here so that we could see the universe. Compared to creation, the light travel time problem is trivial. Chapter 21 briefly discusses some of the proposed solutions to the light travel time problem.

---

5. Douglas Adams, *The Hitchhiker's Guide to the Galaxy* (New York: Ballentine Books, 2005), p. 76.

CHAPTER 19

Could Noah's Ark Have Been Made of Wood?

TIM LOVETT

There's a biblical ark that rode out the Flood, and it was no bathtub. Noah built it somehow, with or without some mysterious ancient technology or extreme gopherwood. Does this mean God had to suspend the laws of physics to keep Noah afloat?

Let's say He didn't. In that case, could Noah get through the whole ark operation?

Building the Ark

Constructing an ark of biblical proportions would take time, resources, and know-how.

Time: Noah had plenty of time — 120 years in fact. In Genesis 6:3, the Lord said, "My Spirit shall not strive with man forever, for he is indeed flesh; yet his days shall be one hundred and twenty years." Some take this as God setting the human lifespan to 120 years. There's a problem with that: every patriarch from Noah to Amram broke God's new "ruling." Noah made it to 950 years of age, his son Shem was 600, and even Abraham died "full of years" at 175.

It's not about lifespans, but about God giving Noah 120 years warning of the Deluge. That's a long time to build a boat; too long, in fact. At that pace, Noah would still be chipping away at the stern while the bow had been exposed to the weather for a century. It makes more sense that Noah spent a lot of this time in preparation until, with everything prepared, he organized a serious barn-raising.

This is where the pitch comes in. The pitch for Noah's ark was probably not bitumen but the gum-based resins extracted from certain trees (such as pitch pine). Wooden ships were routinely waterproofed in this way. The difference here is that God directed Noah to apply the icky goo *inside* as well as out. That's a lot of pitch, so no doubt God had a good reason. Here are two: pitch stabilizes the moisture content of the wood and acts as a preservative. This is ideal for a larger-than-average wooden ship that takes a decade or more to assemble, not just the typical year or so.

Resources: Did Noah need help? A pit-sawing team (of two) would take many decades to cut the wood for one ark. That's cutting it close. Noah and sons had other things to focus on, so it makes sense that labor was hired, or that processed materials like sawn lumber were purchased. Noah should have been extremely wealthy having lived 480 years before the project even began, probably with the help of his grandfather Methuselah,[1] who lived to see the ark constructed.

His world had abundant resources (particularly timber and food), and bronze and steel technology had been around for generations ever since Tubal-Cain first got into working bronze and iron (Genesis 4:22). With such long life spans, technology could rapidly increase in the 1,656 years from Adam to the Flood.

But let's not get too carried away. There are limits to the technology of the pre-Flood world. The ark was made of wood, not metal, which is better for ship hulls. There were also no other survivors in ships (or space-stations for that matter!). The civilizations immediately after the Babel dispersion give us some clues. They excelled at building big things in difficult materials but were not industrialized in the modern sense. An appropriate estimate for the level of technology in Noah's day might be something on par with ancient Egyptians, Greeks, Romans, Chinese, etc. The Egyptians could drill and cut granite, the Greeks could build huge ships with furniture-like precision. These were very ingenious, accomplished builders, experts in crafting metals, ceramics, and other materials — but without the industrialized manufacturing made possible with electricity and heat engines (i.e., steam or combustion engines) implying high-precision machine tools.

We will treat such industrialization as missing from the pre-Flood world as we describe the following construction materials and techniques.

---

1. Methuselah, the oldest man recorded in the Bible, died at 969 in the same year as the Flood (Genesis 5:21–27; 1 Chronicles 1:3). Dr. Henry Morris said his name may mean, "When he dies, judgment."

Permitted materials and hardware: (Technology of ancient civilizations) Wood: Accurately sawn to fixed sectional dimensions. An up/down saw driven by flowing water or animal draft power, for instance. Sawing is a key technology. Metals: bronze and iron (cast and/or hand forged). Ceramics: fired and glazed pots, oil lamps, stoneware, small glass panes. Other: leather, bone, animal, and resin glues. Fasteners: wooden pegs, metal rods, spikes, and straps. Basic processing/cooking/distilling of pitch/glues. Hand tools in bronze and iron: Drilling auger or spade bit, hand saws, axes, chisels. Measurement: basic surveying, water levels. Lifting and carrying devices: cranes, winches, wheels, rollers, rope, and pulleys. Special long lead-time methods: Planting and harvesting old-growth trees, training trees into shapes (arborsculpture), breeding and training of animals.

Excluded materials and hardware: (Technology after the Industrial Revolution) Electrical power machines, heat engines (steam or internal combustion), threaded bolts and screws, rolled steel plate, metallic films and sheet, processed polymers, highly oxidizing metals like aluminum and titanium, stainless steel, electronics, advanced chemical processing, engineered wood products such as finger jointed and glulam beams, bulk dressed lumber (planed), plate glass (laminated or tempered), steel rope and drawn steel wire, advanced adhesives like epoxy.

Know-how: There are many examples in Scripture where God called people to tackle things outside their expertise, so Noah may not have had much experience in shipbuilding. This is rather unlikely at age 480, but on a 120-year project he could afford to do decades of research.

Having lived for around five centuries, Noah may have been perfectly capable of designing the ark all on his own. The ark is briefly specified in only three verses (Genesis 6:14–16), even lacking crucial data such as the number of animals or amount of food. Perhaps Noah was given more detail, just like Moses received the tabernacle instructions that included exact dimensions and even the number of curtain rings. There's a hint given in Genesis 6:22: "Noah did *everything* just as God commanded him" (NIV), which strongly parallels Exodus 39:32: "The Israelites did *everything* just as the LORD commanded Moses" (NIV). Perhaps this "everything" was more than three verses we have recorded for our benefit, or maybe this is all he had to go on.

Either way, Noah had to get it right the first time — there were no second chances. As far as miracles are concerned, there is one "miracle" recorded; God gave instructions, however brief.

Launching the Ark

The launch of the ark was not meant to be an extreme sport. Noah needed a safe way to launch during earthquakes and strong currents.

The Flood started suddenly when "on that day, all the fountains of the great deep were broken up, and the windows of heaven were opened" (Genesis 7:11). Any flood that rapidly inundates the world (in 40 days or less) will involve massive high-speed currents that would dwarf any modern tsunami. In fact, no modern flood lays down sediments anything like the huge, fossil-filled rock layers deposited all over the world. Such a sudden inundation would pulverize everything in its path, including all shipping and coastal settlements.

How could the ark survive? One solution is to launch from the highest point. This keeps Noah out of the violence of the initial inflows of ocean water as predicted by the Catastrophic Plate Tectonics model.[2] The Flood went on to drown every mountain in the pre-Flood world (Genesis 7:19). Since modern oceans contain enough water to drown the planet to a depth of about 1.8 miles (2.85 km),[3] the pre-Flood terrain was probably limited to within this elevation.[4] By the time the water reached the ark, the currents would have slowed to manageable levels before the launch.

Noah, whether by acumen or divine guidance, may have selected an elevated site where temperate conditions could support a pine forest. Pine, a possible candidate for the mysterious "gopherwood," is especially suited to both shipbuilding and pitch production. This original location is unknown to us today because "the ark moved about" (Genesis 7:18) before finally coming to rest in the Middle East. Gopherwood doesn't have to be a desert acacia, or even a cedar of Lebanon. The very fact that gopherwood is never mentioned again suggests the wood had vanished too. It may have been alive and well on the other side of the world, be it Douglas fir, yellow pine, or even teak.

Here is a quick rundown of a possible construction plan.

---

2. John Baumgardner. Email correspondence. May 3, 2004. "In regard to the pre-Flood topography, my strong suspicion was that there were highland areas that were not destroyed until late into the cataclysm. . . . It is my feeling that the wave action where the water was shallow was extremely violent throughout the 40 days. It would seem to me that however the ark was launched, it had to get into deeper water very quickly to avoid being destroyed by such violent wave activity."

3. S L Polevoy, *Water Science and Engineering* (UK: Chapman Hall, 1996), p. 192.

4. A. Snelling, ". . . it is likely the pre-Flood hills and mountains were nowhere near as high as today's mountains, a sea level rise of over 3,500 feet (1,067 m) would have been sufficient to inundate the pre-Flood continental land surfaces."

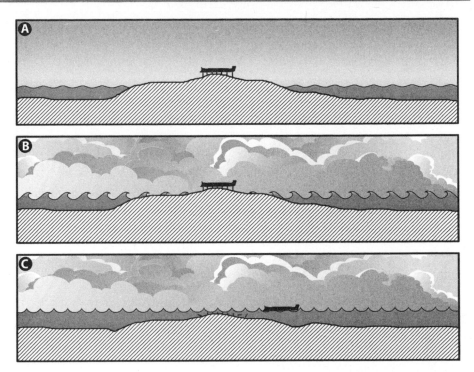

Figure 1. (A). The ark constructed at a high elevation (by pre-Flood standards). (B). Violent inundation devastates lowlands. (C). Water surface less severe once oceans meet.

Noah clear-cuts the hilltop expanse. A foundation is prepared with massive stone walls running transversely to support the hull. Large stones give resistance to strong currents, and tapered ends avoid snagging. Besides all that, don't ancient people always seem to baffle us with their stonework — oversized and outrageously precise? Those ancient civilizations were not a great many generations after Noah himself (Genesis 10).

The three keels laid on the foundation walls help to:

- form a base to erect frames while the bottom can still be planked from underneath;
- hold the hull upright without shoring (handy when planking multiple layers);
- absorb earth tremors and turbulent water (sliding at wall/keel interface);
- reduce rocking in waves (increased roll damping);

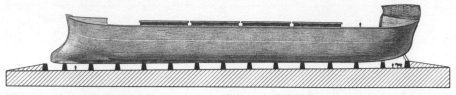

Figure 2. The ark built on pedestal walls to provide underside access and a safe launch.

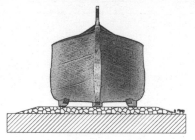

Fig. 3. Ark built on pedestal walls: very heavy stonework to resist erosion during launch.

- improve direction-keeping in winds (keel gets deeper toward the stern);
- resist abrasion (multiple sacrificial layers — false keel/keel shoes);
- keep the ark level when beached (sloping floors would be annoying for seven months!).

These massive keels are built up by laying beams and pinning them together (edge bolted). The lower members within the keels are not scarfed in order to manage stresses.[5]

Ships are normally launched on a slipway, but in Noah's case "the waters increased and lifted up the ark" (Genesis 7:17). Extra safeguards would be prudent, such as releasable mooring ropes to keep the ark from moving away until properly buoyed. There should be no solid obstacles higher than the skid platform — including tree stumps.

The Ark on the Floodwaters

Once afloat, the depth of the water would average almost two miles (three km),[6] shielding the ark from tectonic activity. Deep water is safe in a

---

5. As it rides over waves, the hull acts as a longitudinal beam under alternating bending (hogging and sagging). The bending stress increases with distance from the center (neutral plane), so the lowermost keels and uppermost skylight should be deliberately flexible or discontinuous to avoid overstressing them.

6. "Ocean Facts: Did you know?" http://www.ocean-expeditions.com/ocean-facts/. "If all the land in the world was flattened out, the earth would be a smooth sphere completely covered by a continuous layer of seawater 2,686 metres [over a mile] deep."

tsunami.[7] The ark had to survive the ocean surface, not the massive sediment flows at the seabed.

But the surface was no picnic either. Later in the voyage, God sent a wind (Genesis 8:1), and wind creates waves, so rough seas are at least part of the five-month voyage. Since the proportions of the ark (Genesis 6:15) are ideal[8] for an ocean-going vessel, it was obviously meant to behave like a ship. With such proportions, the necessary stability and sea kindliness can be achieved even for extreme seas,[9] by a suitable coordination of hull shape and load distribution.

But is it even possible for a wooden vessel as large as Noah's ark to survive the stresses at sea?

The Trouble with Carvel Hulls

The largest wooden ships in recent history (1800s and early 1900s) tended to flex in rough seas, making them prone to leakage. These ships were carvel-built, a plank-on-frame construction method that lacks inherent resistance to racking.[10] The stiffness of the hull depended almost entirely on the tightness of caulking between planks.

Figure 4. Racking: Without bracing, a plank-on-frame structure distorts to a parallelogram under shear loading.

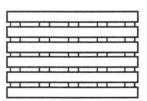 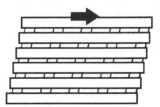

Carvel[11] planking dominated wooden shipbuilding in the last few centuries. The method was simple and quick, but a new ship did not stay a "tight ship" for

7. "What You Should Do," National Weather Service, http://www.nws.noaa.gov/om/brochures/tsunami6.htm. "If there is time to move your boat or ship from port to deep water. . . ."

8. S.W. Hong et al. "Safety Investigation of Noah's Ark in a Seaway," *CEN Technical Journal* 8(1) (1994):26–36. Comparison of 12 arks of various proportions showed the biblical specification (300x50x30) gave the optimal combination of stability, seakeeping, and strength.

9. Ibid., figure 5: Vertical accelerations (43 m significant wave height), figure 6: Roll stability (47.5 m)

10. D.L. Dennis, *The Deficiencies of Wooden Shipbuilding* (London, UK: Mariner's Mirror, 1964), p. 50, 62–63.

11. A carvel hull is formed by parallel horizontal planking fixed to parallel vertical frames (usually by spikes, trunnels, or bolts) to form a smooth outer surface. Lengthwise joints between the planks are typically caulked with fiber and sealed.

very long. Even fitting two pins in each plank gave little improvement.[12] Larger ships were subject to higher forces, accelerating the loosening of the caulked planks. This led to reinforcement with iron straps.

These diagonal straps certainly helped improve a bad design and gave the single layer of carvel planking some much-needed shear resistance. But the steel straps were pinned (bolted) to softer wooden frames, a considerable stress concentration, especially at the ends of the straps.

This led to the next patch-up — steel plates at the top and bottom to secure the diagonal bracing. That kept the hull sides intact, but now the problem was transmitted to extremities, like the top deck.[13]

Later, during World War I, steel was scarce and wooden supply ships[14] were being built in a hurry. Naval architects revisiting the carvel hull-bending problem made big increases to keelson depth[15] and upper deck reinforcement (using clamp and shelf strakes).[16] One design aimed to "produce a boat which will have strength equivalent to that of a steel hull without using excessive amounts of timber."[17] It had a double layer of diagonal planking under the standard planks. That is not a carvel hull, it is cold-molded just like the wooden minesweepers built in the 1990s.[18]

12. H.R. Milner and J. Peczkis, "Wooden Ship Hulls as Box Girders with Multiple Interlayer Slip," *Journal of Structural Engineering* 133, no. 6 (June 2007): 855–861. "In frame-built construction, there is usually no direct lateral plank-to-plank connection: There is only the friction provided by the oakum rammed between the planks . . . even carvel construction that employs two rows of densely spaced fasteners (instead of the usual single row) fails to achieve complete composite action."

13. Milner and Peczkis, "Wooden Ship Hulls as Box Girders with Multiple Interlayer Slip," p. 859. ". . . the asymmetric cross section of traditionally built wooden hulls, in which too much timber is already situated in the sides and bottom, and not enough in the deck 'flange.'"

14. Harvey Cole Estep, *How Wooden Ships Are Built: A practical treatise on modern American wooden ship construction, with a supplement on laying off wooden vessels* (Cleveland, OH: The Penton Publishing Co., 1918).

15. Ibid., figure 36, 37.

16. Ibid., p. 6.

17. Ibid., figure 40.

18. The last Avenger-class wooden minesweeper was commissioned in 1994. The 224-foot (68 m) hull was framed in wood and planked with diagonal layers of fir, then covered with fiberglass. Wood was used to minimize the magnetic signature of the vessel. USS *Guardian* (MCM-5), launched in 1987, and ran aground near the Philippines on Tubbataha Reef on January 17, 2013. The hull was holed but remained intact for months before being cut into sections and lifted off the reef by crane ships by March 30, 2013.

So the shortcomings of a carvel hull are not easily corrected.[19] A better way is to use a planking system with inherent shear strength, akin to a house frame braced with plywood instead of clapboards (lap siding or weatherboards).

The claim that Noah's ark is an impossible size for a wooden ship is based on the apparent limiting size of documented wooden ships of the 1800–1900s; around 330 feet (100 m) even with iron bracing. In comparison, using one of the most reliable ancient cubits, the Royal Egyptian Cubit at 20.6 inches (0.523 m), Noah's ark would be 515 feet long, 86 feet wide, and 51.5 feet high (157 m x 26 m x 15.7 m).

That makes it about 50 percent longer than the longest wooden ships in modern records.

Working with Wood

Is this proof positive that the laws of physics must be suspended to keep Noah afloat? This assumes that Noah's ark is built like a carvel hull, or worse. Wood may be an ancient building material, but it still has a competitive strength-to-weight ratio, even compared to metals. For large structures like buildings, bridges, and ships, the problem is not the strength properties of the wood itself, but the manner of *joining*.[20]

Using the strength properties of wood, calculations can determine the required thickness for a vessel the size of Noah's ark operating in extreme seas. Naval architects at the world-class ship research center KRISO (renamed MOERI in 2005) in Korea, studied Noah's ark in 1992 and declared the biblical specifications sound. They used a planking layer 12 inches (0.3 m) thick, taken as a shear resistant "plate structure." Internal structural framework comprised of beams 20 inches (0.5 m) square.

This structure was assessed to determine the stresses on the hull under increasingly severe ocean conditions, with irregular (random) waves up to 30 meters (98 feet).

---

19. A. Shimell (SP-High Modulus) and H. Ten Have (Dykstra & Partners Naval Architects), Symposium paper: "Structural Design of S/Y Dream Symphony: The Largest Wooden Ship Ever Built," 22nd International HISWA Symposium on Yacht Design and Yacht Construction, Nov. 13, 2012. Referring to steel reinforcement of large carvel hulls, "But even with these reinforcements, the lack of rigidity was never fully solved."

20. Ibid., p. 4. "The main reason for these problems lies in the traditional carvel-planking building method of these ships. As their size increased, the thickness of their members also grew. However, being limited to pin or nail connections, the stresses around the joints and connections became very high. This caused the wood to crack and give way around the connections of members and seams of the shell, resulting in large deflections and ultimately structural failure."

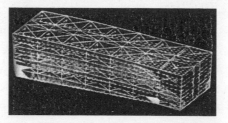

Figure 5. Lattice of 2 feet (0.5m) square beams. The ark may well have been constructed by joint structures of frames and plates. The frame structure of thick beams (50 cm x 50 cm) could have been installed in longitudinal, transverse, and diagonal directions, and connected to each other at each end. The plate structure may have been attached to the frame structure to make the shell, deck, and compartments using thick boards (30cm).

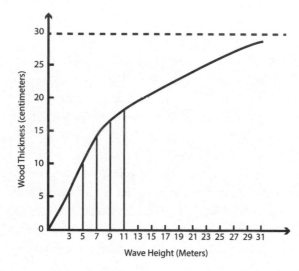

Figure 6. Plate structure (planking) thickness vs. wave height. To calculate the voyage limit from the structure viewpoint, the required thickness of the wood was plotted for varying wave heights. This showed that the ark's voyage limit was more than 30 meters if the thickness of the wood was 30 cm, which was quite a reasonable assumption.

Planking

There are several ways to create this integrated "plate structure." Carvel is not one of them:

- **Diagonal planking.** The definitive way to build a strong wooden hull is to use multiple diagonal layers. Used for U.S. Navy minesweepers (1990s) and PT boats (1940s),

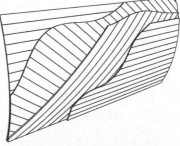

Figure 7. Diagonal planking

diagonal planking also appeared in the design of World War I wooden steamers.[21] However, the British beat them to it with multi-layered diagonal planking in Aberdeen ships such as *Vision*[22] (1854), *Schomberg*[23] (1855), and *Chaa-Sze*[24] (1860), and even "Queen Victoria's new yacht." In 1998, another old ship, the USS *Constellation*, was switched from carvel to diagonal planking to avoid clumsy steel beams to fix hogging strains.[25] In 2012, naval architects proposed a wooden hull laminated in diagonal layers for the 463 feet (141 meters) yacht *Dream Symphony.*[26]

- **Mortise and tenon planking.** A spectacular (almost unbelievable) solution to shearing between planks includes mortise and tenon attachments. Characteristic of Greek and Roman ships, this method was in use well before the 14th century before Christ,[27] then faded away around A.D. 500 to be forgotten until recently rediscovered through underwater archaeology. This lends credence to the records of ark-sized wooden ships of antiquity. For example, *Athenaeus* discussed a large warship that was 427 feet (130 m) long. It

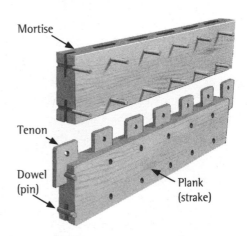

Figure 8. Mortise and tenon planking

21. Estep, *How Wooden Ships Are Built*, p. 3., fig 4, with description on p. 5.
22. *Vision* (diagonal planked), built in 1854 by A. Hall & Co., Aberdeen, *Aberdeen Journal*, 11/10/1854: "The New Principle of Building Wooden Vessels Diagonally."
23. http://www.dpcd.vic.gov.au/heritage/maritime/shipwrecks/victorian-shipwreck-dive-sites/schomberg-shipwreck.
24. *Chaa-Sze* built in 1860 by A. Hall & Co., Aberdeen. Diagonal build. Laid down as a steam whaler. The teak frames were from 4–6 ft. apart with a triple thickness of planking binding the whole together in 9 inches of solid teak. The planking was fastened with screw-treenails (patented in June 1853).
25. Andrew Davis and Keith Gallion, "A Cold Molded Shell for the USS *Constellation*," http://www.maritime.org/conf/conf-davis.htm, October 21, 2007.
26. A. Shimell and H. Ten Have, *Structural Design of S/Y Dream Symphony:* Length overall 141m, beam 18m.
27. Lionel Casson, *The Ancient Mariners*, second edition (Princeton, NJ: Princeton University Press, 1991) p. 108. The practice of joining planks with mortise and tenon joints "certainly goes back to the 14th century B.C. and very much likely before that."

was built by Ptolemy Philopater around 250–200 B.C.[28] It proved itself worthy, even in war. Then there was the *Leontifera* — based on the specification of 8 tiers of oarsmen, it is estimated at about 393 feet (120 m) long.[29]

- **Multiple layers of planking.** Simple but effective. This method was clearly used by Chinese shipbuilders,[30] which would include the treasure ships of Zheng He (A.D. 1400s), with a reported length of 444 chi (137m or 450 feet). It was also seen in Greek and Roman ships (80s B.C.).[31] More recently (A.D. 1800s) multiple layers were employed for impact with floating ice.[32] Each successive layer of overlapping planking dramatically increases the shear resistance of the planking system. Even a double layer is "vastly superior to single carvel."[33]

- **Edge bolted.** The easy way to do mortise and tenon is to use vertical pins (drift bolts) to connect horizontal members (strakes) together. By the sixth century A.D., iron spikes had replaced the painstaking mortise and tenon for edge joining of planks.[34] This technique was used by American shipbuilders[35] to fasten ceiling strakes and keelsons together.[36]

---

28. Athenaeus, *The Deipnosophists*, trans. Charles Burton Gulick, Loeb Classical Library 208 (Cambridge, MA: Harvard University Press, 1987), Book 5, Section 203f–204b, (2:421–425).
29. Memnon, *Excerpts*, c. 14, 15, as cited by James Ussher, *The Annals of the World*, second printing, trans. Larry and Marion Pierce (Green Forest, AR: Master Books, 2003), p. 354.
30. G. Deng, *Maritime Sector, Institutions, and Sea Power of Premodern China* (Westport, CT: Greenwood Publishing Group, 1999). "Chinese ships were maintained once a year by adding a layer of planks to the hull. As a rule, when six layers were added, the ships were half-retired from the ocean-going fleet to coastal services due to the ship's loss of speed." Claims of an ark-like scale of Zheng He's treasure ships have drawn skepticism (mostly by non-Chinese commentators), but it is agreed they were built with two or three layers of planks.
31. Lionel Casson, *Ships and Seamanship in the Ancient World* (Baltimore, MD: The Johns Hopkins University Press, 1995). "The Mahdia wreck had double planking with bands of impregnated cloth between the layers."
32. Loney, *Wrecks Along The Gippsland Coast.*
33. David H. Pascoe, "Surveying Wood Hulls, Part 3: Appendix," http://marinesurvey.com/surveyguide/wood3.htm. "Double Planked: Same as carvel only uses light inner layer with heavier outer layer, parallel longitudinal. Vastly superior to single carvel. Much less prone to leaking, working, and fastener failure."
34. Casson, *Ships and Seamanship in the Ancient World*, p. 208.
35. *Rules Relative to the Construction of Lake Sail and Steam Vessels, 1866.* "Ceiling on sides of vessels of 300 tons and upward, must be edge-bolted between each frame"; http://www.maritimehistoryofthegreatlakes.ca/Documents/Rules1866/default.asp.
36. Estep, *How Wooden Ships Are Built*, p. 13. "In modern wooden vessels built on the coasts of the United States, considerable use is made of edge-bolting to fasten the various keel

Figure 9. Multi-layered planking

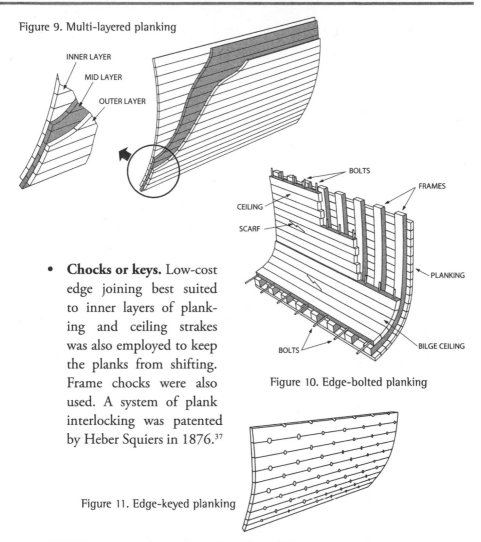

INNER LAYER

MID LAYER

OUTER LAYER

BOLTS

FRAMES

CEILING

SCARF

PLANKING

BOLTS

BILGE CEILING

- **Chocks or keys.** Low-cost edge joining best suited to inner layers of planking and ceiling strakes was also employed to keep the planks from shifting. Frame chocks were also used. A system of plank interlocking was patented by Heber Squiers in 1876.[37]

Figure 10. Edge-bolted planking

Figure 11. Edge-keyed planking

and keelson elements and the strakes of ceiling together. Edge bolting means fastening the pieces together longitudinally. In other words, the ceiling strakes are bolted through and through to each other, as well as being bolted to the frame timbers. There is no doubt that this form of fastening adds greatly to the strength of the hull structure, particularly in a longitudinal direction, offering resistance to hogging strains. In fact, some experts go as far as to say that the edge-bolting is all that prevents the largest of wooden ships from breaking-up in a seaway. This is probably an exaggeration, although it has been demonstrated that timbers well edge-bolted at least approximate the strength of single pieces of the size of the members so combined."

37. Heber Squier, "Heber Squier's New Method of Fastening and Strengthening Wooden Ships : patented, Aug. 29th, 1876. Gives the Most Strength for the Least Money, and Applies Equally well to Vessels Old and New," Grand Haven, MI, August 1877 (Clarke Historical Library Central Michigan University).

Internal Framing

The Hong study (see footnote 8) also included frames and beam members (50 cm x 50 cm) in their structural analysis. These beams need to be joined together somehow, a critical detail especially in joints that could undergo completely reversed loading. Due to the wave loadings and accelerations at sea, joints that normally sustain compression forces can also go into tension. These joints are the most difficult to achieve in wood, but the full tensile strength of a 0.5 m square beam is an unlikely requirement. Joints must be designed to handle various combinations of compression, tension, twisting (torsion), and possibly bending.

There are a number of structural options for joining large beams. All are held together by metal rods (called bolts) driven into pre-drilled holes, or spikes (large nails). Metal fasteners are also found in large ancient ships.

- **Knees.** A knee is a reinforcing elbow made from a natural bend, typically in large oak branches (crooks). A hanging knee, based on American clippers, used iron "bolts" driven through and clenched.
- **Clamps and Shelves.** A shelf was reinforced with thick longitudinal beams (shelf/clamp) bolted through both frames and beams. Detail based on WWI wooden motor ship.
- **Straps.** A cast or hand-forged bronze strap was held by spikes to opposing members to take tensile forces. Iron straps (or stirrups) were typically used to reinforce connections where axial forces dominate (such as stanchion to deck beam). Straps can also accommodate complex members like diagonal braces.
- **Lamination.** A shear wall performs the dual role of bracing the frame and tying framing members together. This is also the most effective form of bracing.

Each of these framing joints has its own merits and is suitable for different tasks, so several of these methods can be found on any one ship.[38]

The familiar mortise and tenon framing joint is conspicuously absent in primary ship structures. It is too weak, especially in tension.

---

38. Estep, *How Wooden Ships Are Built*, p. 6, fig 7, "Midship Section: Standard Wooden Steamer for Government."

Figure 12. Knee type framing joint

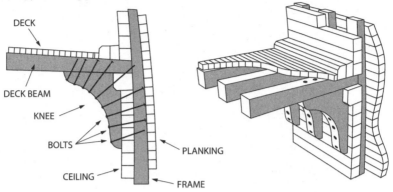

Figure 13. Clamp type framing joint

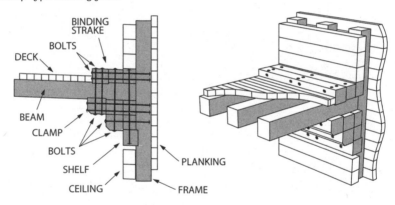

Figure 14. Strap type framing joint

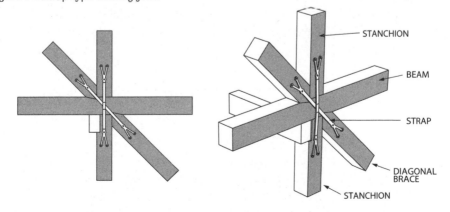

Figure 15. Bulkhead type framing joint

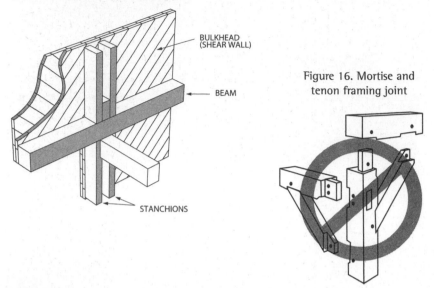

Figure 16. Mortise and tenon framing joint

BULKHEAD (SHEAR WALL)

BEAM

STANCHIONS

Bulkheads

Another problem for these "oversized" carvel ships was weak frames[39] or "ribs." The curved frame profiles were built up of many short segments bolted together, but this made them flex and go out of shape. Modern wooden frames are laminated, but the best fix is to use bulkheads — lateral shear walls at regular intervals along the hull. The Chinese were doing that at least 12 centuries[40] before Benjamin Franklin suggested it in 1787.

Extensive use of internal walls actually suits the ark. It was never meant to have a cavernous interior; in fact, quite the opposite. Noah was directed to build "nests" for the animals, not cattle yards. Private enclosures are appropriate for the transport and care of live animals as it helps to keep them calm. From a structural viewpoint, this could mean plenty of bulkhead structures (walls) in both transverse and longitudinal directions. This all adds to the structural integrity of the hull.

39. Milner and Peczkis, "Wooden Ship Hulls as Box Girders with Multiple Interlayer Slip," p. 856. "Frames consisting of many small timbers bolted together are readily deformed, and have frequently been identified as a major weakness of traditional wooden ships."
40. L. Xi, X. Yang, and X. Tang, eds., *The History of Science and Technology in China: Transportation.* (Beijing, China: Science Press, 2004), p. 58. "It can now be deduced that the first watertight bulkheads appeared around 410." The Chinese design was a deliberate shear wall, complete with dowel pins and ledges for shear resistance and even limber holes for maintenance. They form watertight compartments to keep the boat afloat if damaged.

Conclusion

While 330 feet (100 m) may well be the practical limit for a carvel-built hull with a single layer of planking, more appropriate construction methods would extend that boundary by at least 50 percent.

As for the compulsory miracles: God gave instructions to Noah, He brought the animals, He closed the door, and He even sent a wind. But was supernatural intervention the only thing holding Noah's ark together?

Not necessarily. Maybe Noah used ancient bulkheads and ancient planking to build a ship that was more than able to withstand the stresses it faced during the Flood.

CHAPTER 20

What about Environmentalism?

DR. E. CALVIN BEISNER[1]

Introduction

Environment and economy: One of the great difficulties of addressing these two challenges together is that many people think economic development puts the created environment at risk, on the one hand, and environmental protection puts economic development at risk, on the other hand. And indeed, sometimes economic development does cause environmental damage, and sometimes environmental protection does impede economic development. The great challenge is learning how to pursue both at once, for the benefit of men, women, and children, and for the good of animals and plants, of earth, water, and air, all to the glory of God our loving, wise, all-powerful Creator.

While some, like Dr. Michael Nortcott, think — as he expresses it repeatedly in his recent book *A Moral Climate: The Ethics of Global Warming* — that we must choose between people's rising out of poverty and protecting the environment, as if either prevented the other (a bifurcation fallacy), we believe the two are not exclusive alternatives but mutually interdependent. A clean,

---

1. Dr. Beisner is the national spokesman for the Cornwall Alliance for the Stewardship of Creation. This chapter is based on a lecture presented originally at Creation Care Colloquium: Perspectives in Dialogue, Southeastern Baptist Theological Seminary, Wake Forest, North Carolina, August 28, 2009.

healthful, beautiful environment being a costly good, and wealthier people being able to afford more of a costly good than poor people, it follows that growing wealth — accompanied by ethics and values informed by Scripture, and in the context of a just civil social order — can protect and improve our surroundings (the real meaning, by the way, of the word *environment*) rather than degrade them.

While Dr. Northcott and others prescribe abandonment of industrial civilization, or what Dr. Northcott calls "the machine world," and a return to a hunter-gatherer, or at most a "primitive," subsistence agricultural social order, as the solution to environmental problems,[2] we believe a technologically advanced society and ecological well-being can co-exist, and indeed that they must co-exist if humanity is to fulfill the stipulation of Genesis 1:28 to multiply and to fill, subdue, and rule the earth — a stipulation not repealed after the Fall but repeated in God's covenant with Noah (Genesis 9:1–17).[3]

Let us look at some foundational principles in Scripture, beginning at the beginning, with the biblical record of creation and early history in Genesis 1–9. It will be impossible to touch on, let alone to expound in detail, all the relevant truths in these chapters, but we can notice some of the most prominent.

The Doctrines of Creator and Creation

"In the beginning God created the heavens and the earth. . . . [and] God saw all that He had made, and behold, it was very good" (Genesis 1:1, 31).[4] The

---

2. Michael S. Northcott, *A Moral Climate: The Ethics of Global Warming* (Maryknoll, NY: Orbis Books, 2007), p. 113, 124–126, 129–130, 175, 232–241, and elsewhere.

3. I argued for this complementarity rather than opposition of economic development and environmental stewardship in my books *Prospects for Growth: A Biblical View of Population, Resources, and the Future* (Wheaton, IL: Crossway Books, 1990) and *Where Garden Meets Wilderness: Evangelical Entry into the Environmental Debate* (Grand Rapids, MI: Eerdmans/Acton Institute, 1997), and in a monograph published by the Institute on Religion and Democracy and available online titled *What Is the Most Important Environmental Task Facing American Christians Today?* (Washington, DC: Institute on Religion and Democracy, 2008), and similar arguments have been made by such scholars as Julian L. Simon and Indur Goklany: Julian L. Simon, *Population Matters: People, Resources, Environment, & Immigration* (New Brunswick, NJ: Transaction Publishers, 1990), Simon ed., *The State of Humanity* (New York and London: Blackwell, 1995), and Simon, *The Ultimate Resource 2* (Princeton, NJ: Princeton University Press, 1996); Ronald Bailey, ed., *The True State of the Planet* (New York: Free Press, 1995); Indur M. Goklany, *The Improving State of the Planet: Why We're Living Longer, Healthier, More Comfortable Lives on a Cleaner Planet* (Washington, DC: Cato Institute, 2007).

4. Scripture quotations in this chapter, unless otherwise identified, are from the *New American Standard Version*.

first and last verses of Genesis 1 immediately set forth the eternity, omnipotence, and sovereign righteousness of God the Creator and the temporality, finitude, and dependence of all created things. They affirm all of creation, material and spiritual alike, as God's work and therefore neither evil — contrary to Gnosticism and much Eastern philosophy, such as that underlying yoga, which sees nature, or *pakruti*, as evil because it traps the soul, *parusa* — nor value neutral, as presumed by the materialist worldview.[5] Between those verses we have a record of God:

1. creating light and, separating it from darkness, establishing the cycles of day and night (verses 2–5);

2. making sky and sea, with their liquid and gaseous waters, and separating them from each other (verses 6–8);

3. gathering the waters of the sea into one place, separating them from the dry land, and causing vegetation to sprout from the land (verses 9–12);

4. establishing the heavenly bodies, especially sun and moon, to rule and separate day and night (verses 13–19);

5. making living creatures and separating their domains into water and sky (verses 20–23); and finally

6. making living creatures to inhabit the dry land, and, on that same day, making mankind and separating it from all other living creatures by endowing it with His own image.

On that sixth day, having made man, male and female, in His image, crowned with glory and honor (as we learn from Psalm 8), God "blessed them; and God said to them, 'Be fruitful and multiply, and fill the earth, and subdue it; and rule over the fish of the sea and over the birds of the sky and over every living thing that moves on the earth'" (verse 28). The verse is pregnant with implications.

The first implication is that human beings are different from all other creatures on earth. *Like* all other creatures, they're not God, they're creatures. But *unlike* all other creatures, they are God's image. *Like* all other living things, they are to reproduce after their kind. But *unlike* all others, they are to fill not just "the waters in the seas" (fish, verse 22), not just the air (birds, verse 20), but the whole earth (verse 28). And *like* all other living things, they are to obey their

---

5. Vishal Mangalwadi, " 'Cap-and-Trade' Legislation: Secularizing Sin?" draft paper, October 27, 2009.

Creator (implicit in His commanding them), but *unlike* all others, people are to have rule over other living creatures, and over the earth itself.

And what is it for them to bear the image of God? It is partly what we have just noticed: to rule over other creatures. And from the New Testament and elsewhere we learn that it is for them to have rational and moral capacity (Ephesians 4:24; Colossians 3:10). But we must not neglect what the immediate context reveals about the image of God in man. It is what it reveals about God Himself in verses 1–25: that He is a Maker — indeed, a prolific, even extravagant Maker. People, too, are to be makers — not makers of things *ex nihilo*, "out of nothing," which is the province of God alone, but *ex quispiam*, "out of something." That is, people, made in God's image, are to make new things out of what God puts before them — and, as God made all things of nothing, so people more fully express this creative aspect of His image as they make more and more out of less and less.

The second implication is that the earth and the various living creatures in it — in its seas, in its air, on its ground (*ha-adamah*, related to the name for man; *adam*, who was taken from it, fashioned by God, who then breathed into him the *neshamah hayyim*, the breath of life) — the earth and all in it, while "very good" (verse 31), were not yet as God intended them to be. They needed filling, subduing, and ruling.

Was this because there was something evil about them? No. We have already seen that the biblical doctrine of creation rules out notions of the inherent evil of the material world, whether derived from the Hindu and Buddhist view of matter and spirit as antithetical (in opposition), or from the Platonic and neo-Platonic doctrine of a hierarchical "great chain of Being" from God (who has most being) to nothing (which has none). It was not that there was something evil about the earth and its non-human living creatures. It was that they were designed as the setting, the circumstance — the *environment*, if you will (that word coming from the French *environner*, "to surround") — they were designed as the *surroundings* in which Adam and Eve and their descendants are to live out their mandate as God's image bearers.

As God created it, the earth and all its constituents were very good. They were perfect — not terminally perfect, but circumstantially perfect, perfectly suited as the arena of man's exercise of the *imago Dei* (image of God) in multiplying, filling, subduing, and ruling according to the knowledge and righteousness that most essentially constitute the *imago*.

Already we can recognize some important distinctions between a biblical ethic of creation stewardship, on the one hand, and secular and pagan religious environmentalisms, on the other.[6] The common environmentalist vision of human beings as chiefly consumers and polluters, using up earth's resources and degrading it through their waste (a view expressed by Paul Ehrlich and others in the famous formula I=PAT, that is, environmental impact [which is always harmful] is a function of population, affluence, and technology). They claim that an increase in any of those factors inevitably brings more harm to the earth. This vision of man as essentially consumer and polluter confronts the biblical view that people are designed to be producers and stewards, capable of transforming raw materials into resources through ingenuity and hard work, making more resources than they consume, so that each generation can pass on to the next more of the material blessings than it received, and through godly subduing and ruling of the earth actually improving the environment.

In Genesis 2, a parallel account of creation that focuses more specifically on mankind on day 6, we learn that God placed Adam in the Garden of Eden, stipulating that he was to "cultivate it and keep it" (2:15). Almost as an aside, both this and the mandate of 1:28 to multiply and to fill, subdue, and rule the earth are not *solely* commands but *also* stipulations — God's speaking to them ensuring their fulfillment just as surely as His saying "Let there be light" ensured that light would be.

We should note that this means God's intention that mankind multiply and fill, subdue, and rule the earth, and that he cultivate and keep the Garden, is not conditioned on mankind's remaining morally perfect. We *shall* multiply, we *shall* fill, we *shall* subdue, we *shall* rule, we *shall* cultivate, and we *shall* guard — none of that is uncertain. *How* we shall do these things — *that* is what is in question: whether we shall do them wisely and righteously, or foolishly and wickedly. Our Fall into sin unquestionably influences *how* we do these things, but it neither does nor can prevent our doing them or relieve us of the duty imposed by these mandates.

Although some Christian environmental writers attempt to use Genesis 2:15's stipulation of cultivating and keeping the Garden to define Genesis 1:28's stipulation of subduing and ruling the earth, that is surely mistaken, for

---

6. For example, Pantheism, and Gnostic, illusionist, and Manichaean dualisms, and Platonic idealism and Aristotelian materialism, and modern Marxist and secular humanist naturalisms — all of these fall before this biblical worldview. Epistemological and moral relativism, antinomian utilitarianism, existentialism's claim that we define morality by our choice, postmodernism's rejection of hierarchy and transcendence and enduring meaning — these, too, fall.

two reasons. First, the Garden is not the whole earth; it is a specific, limited geographical location, "toward the east, in Eden" (2:8). Just as we saw separation of light from darkness, heavens from earth, waters from land, life from non-life, animal life from vegetable, and human life from non-human life, so also there is a separation of Garden from the rest of the earth — a distinction that will later be developed between wilderness and Promised Land.

Second, the language in the stipulations differs radically. In 1:28, God told Adam and Eve to "subdue and rule" (*kabash* and *radah*), the words meaning, respectively, to subdue or bring into bondage, and to have dominion or rule. In 2:15, God told Adam to "cultivate and keep" (*abad*, and *shamar*), the words meaning, respectively, to work or till, and to keep, watch, or preserve. What God assigned Adam to do in the *Garden* (to cultivate and keep) was not the same thing He assigned him to do in the *earth* (to subdue and rule). Some environmental writers have also suggested that the command to cultivate, or till, the Garden should be translated "to serve," and then, by equating Garden with earth, have inferred that humankind is to serve the earth. But this is not only to equate Garden and earth, which Scripture expressly distinguishes, but also to misuse the Hebrew *abad*, which, although it *may* bear the sense of serve when followed by an accusative of *person*, does *not* bear that sense when followed by an accusative of *thing*.[7]

From these two stipulations — to subdue and rule the earth, and to cultivate and keep the Garden — it follows:

1. that humans are not aliens, much less a cancer or a plague on the earth, but its rightful, God-ordained rulers;
2. that it is not wrong in principle but right that they should subdue and rule the earth;
3. that their *cultivating* the Garden (to increase its fruitfulness) and *keeping* it (to protect it against degradation) are not mutually exclusive but complementary; and
4. that their cultivating and keeping are not antithetical to but additional and complementary to their subduing and ruling the earth and everything in it.

It follows also that the beliefs, common among many environmentalists, that "nature knows best," that nature is best untouched by human hands, that nature's unaided fruitfulness is all that is right and sufficient for mankind, and

---

7. Francis Brown, S.R. Driver, and Charles A. Briggs, eds., *A Hebrew and English Lexicon of the Old Testament* (Oxford: Clarendon Press, 1907, 1953, 1978), s.vv.

that, as Dr. Northcott puts it in *A Moral Climate,* "the move from the hunter-gathering lifestyle of Eden to the agrarian life on the plains [was] a fall from grace,"[8] are all contrary to the biblical worldview and to the binding stipulations/commands given to mankind at creation.

Adam and Eve did not abandon their post in the Garden and strike out into the wilderness of their own accord and so come under God's judgment. Rather, they disobeyed the probationary command not to eat of the fruit of one particular tree in the Garden, and in response God banished them from the Garden into the wilderness — where, consistent with the stipulatory character of the commands to multiply and to fill, subdue, and rule the earth, they would indeed do so.

Indeed, Dr. Northcott's assertion that Edenic society would have been hunter-gatherer rather than agrarian is explicitly contradicted by the command to *cultivate* the Garden. His claim, again, that "Just as the story of Genesis is that of a Fall from the Garden to an imperious and idolatrous urban culture, so the story of redemption in Exodus is of an urban prince who leads his people in a revolt against the slavery imposed by the city, back out to the levelling nomadic lifestyle of the wilderness,"[9] is also mistaken, for Israel's destination in the exodus was not the *wilderness*, where God forced it to spend 40 years as chastisement for its rebellion, but the *Promised Land*, where the Israelites would possess and settle in cities and houses that they did not build (Deuteronomy 19:1).

And contrary to the common environmentalist notion that cities are essentially bad, God names some of them as places of refuge (Deuteronomy 19:1–10); chooses one city, Jerusalem, as the special abode of His Temple; and ultimately describes the completed and perfected Church, the Bride of Christ, as the holy city, the New Jerusalem, descending out of heaven (Revelation 21:2, 10). Thus, the biblical history of creation, Fall, Curse, redemption, and consummation begins in a Garden, makes its way through a wilderness, and ends in a Garden City, and it becomes clear that the command/stipulation of Genesis 1:28 to multiply and to fill, subdue, and rule the earth was a command/stipulation to go forth from the Garden of Eden into the rest of the earth to transform wilderness into Garden City.[10]

---

8. Northcott, *A Moral Climate: The Ethics of Global Warming*, p. 233.
9. Ibid., p. 235.
10. Indeed, as I have argued in *Where Garden Meets Wilderness*, it was precisely by doing this that mankind were to guard, or keep, the Garden, for what threatened it — even before Adam and Eve's fall into sin — was encroachment by the wilderness.

Thus far we have taken only little notice of a very significant statement at the end of God's creative activity: Genesis 1:31, "God saw all that He had made, and behold, it was very good." We have seen that this does not entail that it was *terminally* perfect but that it was the perfect setting for man's probation and for his exercising the *imago Dei*. Let's draw one other implication from this brief and simple sentence. A crucial element of the environmentalist worldview is that the earth and its habitats and inhabitants are extremely fragile and likely to suffer severe and perhaps even irreversible damage from human action. Let us for now ignore the implicit assumption here that humans are aliens, that they alone among all living things are prohibited from transforming their surroundings. Rather, what are we to think of the explicit thrust: that the earth and its various ecological subsystems are fragile? That element of environmentalism contradicts this verse. It is difficult to imagine how God could have called "very good" the habitat of humanity's vocation in a millennia-long drama if the whole thing were prone to collapse like a house of cards with the least disturbance.

Now, I have encountered an objection to this reasoning, pointing out that, after all, some things in this world *are* fragile — a fly's wing, for instance. But there are two mistakes in this rejoinder. First, it confuses the part with the whole. That some inhabitants of the earth are fragile doesn't entail that the whole earth is, and that the wings of individual flies are fragile doesn't entail that therefore the genus *Drosophila*, or even the species *Drosophila melanogaster*, is fragile. Though many individual flies lose their wings and all flies die, the genus and even the species endure.

Second, it neglects that, seen in proportion, what deprives a fly of its wing is not, in proportion to the fly and its wing, a tiny disturbance. The fly's wings serve quite well for their normal purposes and in the absence of *proportionally* overwhelming impingement. To speak of the whole biosphere, or even of extensive ecosystems, as extremely fragile is both to neglect the force of Genesis 1:31 and to ignore the testimony of geologic history, which includes the recovery of vast stretches of the Northern Hemisphere from long coverage by ice sheets several miles thick — which certainly wiped out more ecosystems more thoroughly than human action has come close to doing — not to mention the recovery, according to Genesis, of the whole earth from a Flood that destroyed all air-breathing, land-dwelling life but the few representatives rescued in Noah's ark and the curse in Genesis 3.

Let me apply this insight to the most controversial environmental issue of our day — indeed, of the whole history of environmentalism to date – anthropogenic global warming. Briefly put, the fear is that human emissions of carbon dioxide and other "greenhouse gases" (a sadly misleading metaphor since greenhouses work not by absorbing infrared radiation, as do these gases, but by preventing the movement upward of warm air) — that our emissions of these gases have caused, by increasing the rate of absorption of infrared radiation bouncing back from earth's surface toward space, or will soon cause, sufficient warming of the earth's surface to set off a series of positive feedback mechanisms (for example, more evaporation and hence more water vapor, which then absorbs yet more infrared radiation). The feedbacks will warm the surface still more, thus instituting a positive feedback loop that leads to a runaway greenhouse effect that eventually makes the earth uninhabitable, at least to human beings, and particularly to human beings living in modern civilization. (As an aside, one wonders why those environmentalists who despise industrial society mourn the prospect of its collapse due to global warming. One would expect them to celebrate it as judgment instead.)

Clearly, this scenario rests upon precisely the assumption of the fragility not of individual elements but of the whole of the bio-/geosystem. That an increase in carbon dioxide from one molecule in every 3,704 in the atmosphere to one molecule in every 2,597 — from 270 to 385 parts per million — from 0.027 percent to 0.0385 percent — should cause catastrophic damage to the biosphere, or even set off a positive feedback loop ("runaway global warming") that will cause such damage — particularly when carbon dioxide's infrared absorption is logarithmic (each new unit absorbing less than the previous one) — is fundamentally inconsistent with the biblical worldview of the earth as the "very good" product of the infinitely wise Creator. That biblical worldview instead suggests that the wise Designer of the earth's climate system, like any skillful engineer, would have equipped it with balancing positive and negative feedback mechanisms that would make the whole robust, self-regulating, and self-correcting.[11]

Perhaps more importantly, they should prompt Christians to praise God for the way in which the earth, like the human body, is "fearfully and wonderfully made" (Psalm 139:14). In some senses this planet, like the eye, may be fragile, but overall it is, by God's wise design, more resilient than many fearful environmentalists can imagine even in a sin-cursed world.

---

11. For more on global warming and climate change, please see chapter 16 in this volume and chapter 7 in the *New Answers Book 3*. See also *A Renewed Call to Truth, Prudence, and Protection of the Poor: An Evangelical Examination of the Theology, Science, and Economics of Global Warming* (Burke, VA: Cornwall Alliance, 2009; online at http://www.cornwallalliance.org/docs/a-renewed-call-to-truth-prudence-and-protection-of-the-poor.pdf).

The Doctrines of Fall, Curse, and Redemption

As we move along in these early chapters of Genesis, we come to the account of mankind's fall into sin. It is not, as we have already noted, a sin of moving from the idyllic hunter-gatherer life of the Garden on the mountain to the urban life of the plain (against which God had given no command, and "sin is lawlessness" [1 John 3:4]), but disobedience to a specific command: not to eat of the fruit of the tree that was in the midst of the Garden. The aetiology (study of causation) of this sin is significant for our discussion of environmental ethics: it came about when Eve, who as bearer of the *imago Dei* was supposed to rule over every living thing that moved on the earth, abdicated her rule and instead bowed to the serpent, "more crafty than any beast of the field which the LORD God had made" and then Adam, to whom Eve was to be a helper rather than a ruler, bowed to Eve (Genesis 3:1–6). The rejection of human rule over the animal world, common to many environmentalists, reflects Eve's abdication, and it is not right. This ultimately led to Adam's sin as well.

In response to their sin, God pronounced judgment on Adam and Eve: pain for her in childbirth, and a frustrated desire to rule over her husband; pain for him in cultivating the ground; and death for both of them (Genesis 3:16–19). Yet at the very same time, "God said to the serpent, 'Because you have done this, cursed are you . . . and I will put enmity between you and the woman, and between your seed and her seed; he shall bruise you on the head, and you shall bruise him on the heel" (verses 14–15), and "God made garments of skin for Adam and his wife, and clothed them" (verse 21), spilling the blood of animals to cover over the now-embarrassing nakedness of these sinners, typifying the sacrificial system of Judaism and the ultimate sacrifice of His incarnate Son on the cross.

Judgment and the promise of redemption met in that moment. And then "God sent him [that is, the man generically — Adam and Eve together, the human race] out from the garden of Eden, to cultivate the ground from which he was taken" (verse 23). Despite the Fall, the God-ordained vocation of cultivation remained — only now it would be cultivation in a more difficult, less cooperative environment — instead of the Garden, the wilderness, a term consistently associated in Scripture with curse. Yet the stipulation that Adam and Eve should multiply and fill, subdue, and rule the earth, transforming wilderness into Garden, remained, and indeed the next chapter recounts the beginning of the fulfillment of that stipulation in Adam and Eve's bearing of children; the eruption of enmity between the seed of the woman and the seed of the serpent in the farmer Cain's murder of his sheep-herding brother Abel; a new pronouncement of curse on Cain, frustrating his cultivation of the earth and making him "a vagrant and a wanderer on the earth" (a description that well fits the hunter-gatherer life admired by some environmentalists), and yet again God's gracious extension of life despite sin (Genesis 4:1–17).

For space's sake let's skip over the detailed accounts of the descendants of Cain and Seth and come to Noah, in whose day the wickedness of mankind reached such a height that God "was sorry that He had made man on the earth, and He was grieved in His heart," and He said, "I will blot out man whom I have created from the face of the land, from man to animals to creeping things and to birds of the sky; for I am sorry that I have made them," for "the earth was corrupt in the sight of God, and the earth was filled with violence" (Genesis 6:6–7, 11). "But Noah found favor in the eyes of the LORD" (verse 8), i.e., God looked on him with grace, and God instructed him to construct an ark to rescue remnants of all flesh from the Flood He decreed.

God then rained His judgment on the earth and wiped out all air-breathing land-dwelling life, excepting only those few on the ark. It must be admitted that the event brought ecological devastation on a scale unmatched by anything man has done. And yet that devastation was done by God due to disobedience to God's Word. This, it seems to me, is difficult to reconcile with environmentalist notions of inherent as opposed to imputed value in nature and the condemnation of any action that harms any of it.

Following the Flood, we read, Noah built an altar to God and sacrificed birds and animals on it, and God "smelled the soothing aroma; and the LORD said to Himself, 'I will never again curse the ground on account of man, for the intent of man's heart is evil from his youth; and I will never again destroy every living thing, as I have done. While the earth remains, seedtime and harvest, and cold and heat, and summer and winter, and day and night shall not cease" (Genesis 8:18–22). The Hebrew poetic *merism* in verse 22 uses pairs of opposites to express the inclusion of all things of the sort mentioned. The implication is that God has promised to Himself that He will sustain the cycles on which human and other life on earth depend as long as the earth itself remains. This promise of God to Himself is, it seems to me, difficult to reconcile with fears that some human action will send the climate into irreversible, catastrophic disruption, threatening mass species extinctions and the destruction of human civilization or perhaps even human extinction.

And then God makes a promise to Noah and his sons, repeating the command/stipulation first given to Adam and Eve in Genesis 1:28: "Be fruitful and multiply, and fill the earth." But this time He continues, "The fear of you and the terror of you will be on every beast of the earth and on every bird of the sky; with everything that creeps on the ground, and all the fish of the sea, into your hand they are given. Every moving thing that is alive shall be food for you; I give all to you, as I gave the green plant" (Genesis 9:1–3). This passage forever invalidates the claim that vegetarianism is ethically superior to meat eating. God has permitted people to kill and eat "every moving thing that is alive." The Apostle Peter would later write of "unreasoning animals, born as creatures of instinct to be captured and killed" (2 Peter 2:12).

And finally, God re-establishes His covenant with Noah and, through him, the whole human race, and even with "every living creature": ". . . all flesh shall never again be cut off by the water of the flood, neither shall there again be a flood to destroy the earth." He ordains the rainbow as the sign of the covenant, and says, "when I bring a cloud over the earth . . . the bow will be seen in the cloud, and I will remember My covenant . . . and never again shall the water become a flood to destroy all flesh" (Genesis 9:9–15). We find this language reflected later in Psalm 104:5–9, which says that after the Flood God "set a boundary, that [the waters] may not pass over, so that they will not return to cover the earth."

Conclusion

In a stunning passage, the prophet Jeremiah compares the stubborn and rebellious people of Judah with the waves of the sea (Jeremiah 5:21–25) due to their lack of fear of the Lord. Just as the sea could not overcome the boundaries God set for it following the Flood, so the people of Judah could not overcome the boundaries God had set for them. Rage against His laws as they might, they would still face His judgments. I will conclude with two observations on this passage.

First, like Psalm 104:5–9, what it says about the boundaries God has set for the sea is difficult to reconcile with fears of catastrophic sea level rise. While there is evidence that sea level was once much higher than what it is now, the sea has never again prevailed against the land. This is best interpreted in the light of the Flood of Noah's day — a never-to-be-repeated, cataclysmic judgment of God that would have been followed by an ice age (accompanied by much reduced sea level as water was stored in vast ice sheets on land) as the atmosphere lost its high water vapor content and so cooled rapidly, and then a gradual recovery as water vapor (which accounts for over 95 percent of the greenhouse effect) rose to approximately its present concentration (accompanied by a gradual sea level rise to near-present levels as the continental glaciers melted).

This does not mean that sea level cannot rise (and likewise fall) gradually over long periods as earth warms and cools through natural cycles. But it is inconsistent with the fear of catastrophic sea level rise driven by anthropogenic global warming, which also finds no support in sound science. The IPCC reduced its estimate of likely 21st-century sea level rise from about 35 inches in its 2001 report to just 17 inches in its 2007 report, in which it also projected that there would be no significant melting of the Greenland ice sheet for several millennia — and then only if the world remained at least 2°C warmer than today throughout those millennia (an unlikely scenario granted historical temperature cycles driven by cycles in solar radiance). While the IPCC included no sea level experts among its authors, one of the world's leading experts on sea level, Nils-Axel Mörner, head of the sea level commission of the International Union for Quaternary Research, concluded in the study "Estimating Future Sea Level Changes from Past Records" that 21st-century sea level rise would be much lower than even the revised IPCC estimates:

> In the last 5000 years, global mean sea level has been dominated by the redistribution of water masses over the globe. In the last 300 years, sea level has been [in] oscillation close to the present with peak rates in the period 1890–1930. Between 1930 and 1950, sea [level] fell. The late 20th century lack[ed] any sign of acceleration. Satellite altimetry indicates virtually no changes in the last decade. Therefore, observationally based predictions of future sea level in the year 2100 will give a value of + 10 ± 10 cm (or +5 ± 15 cm) [0 to + 7.88 inches, or –3.94 to + 7.88 inches], by thus discarding model outputs by IPCC as well as global loading models. This implies that there is no fear of any massive future flooding as claimed in most global warming scenarios.[12]

Recent data from sea level monitoring stations around the southwest Pacific confirm that sea level rise during the last 30 years, despite widespread claims to the contrary and fears of the impending submersion of island nations like Tuvalu and Kiribati, has been slight to nonexistent and certainly not significantly greater than its long-term rate.[13]

---

12. Nils-Axel Mörner, "Estimating Future Sea Level Changes from Past Records," *Global and Planetary Change* 40 (2004): p. 49–54.
13. Cliff Ollier, "Sea Level in the Southwest Pacific is Stable," *New Concepts in Global Tectonics Newsletter*, no. 50 (June 2009), accessed online September 7, 2009, at http://nzclimatescience.net/images/PDFs/paperncgtsealevl.pdf.

Second, God's words through Jeremiah make it clear what is the real root of fears of natural catastrophes like droughts: the absence of the fear of the Lord, manifested in persistent sins like those named so frequently throughout Jeremiah: idolatry (1:16; 2:5; 3:6; 7:9, 18; 8:19; 10:2; 11:10; 16:18; 17:2), forsaking God (Jahweh) and worshiping pagan gods, which God called spiritual adultery (1:16; 2:11, 17, 20; 3:1, 2-3, 9, 20; 5:7, 18; 7:30; 9:2, 13; 11:10, 17; 13:10, 25, 27; 14:10; 15:6; 16:11), prophets speaking in the name of false gods (2:7), absence of the fear of God (2:19), rejecting and killing God's prophets (2:30), forgetting God (2:32), murder (2:34; 4:31; 7:9), injustice (5:1; 7:5), falsehood and lies (5:1, 12; 6:13; 7:9; 8:8, 10; 9:3), deception (9:8), oppression (5:25–29, 6:6; 7:6; 9:8; 17:11), fraud (5:27), false priests and prophets "and My people love to have it so" (5:30; 14:15), rejection of God's Word (6:10, 19; 8:9; 9:13; 11:10; 13:10), covetousness (6:13; 8:10), religious formalism and presumption (7:3-4), stealing (7:8–9), sexual adultery (7:9; 9:2), general disobedience to God's law (7:28), child sacrifice (7:31), worship of nature (8:2), covenant breaking (11:3), general wickedness (12:4), complaint against God (12:8), pride (13:8), trusting in man instead of in God (17:5), and Sabbath breaking (17:21).

It is significant that, in contrast to some Christian environmentalists' claims that God sent Israel and Judah into exile because they defiled the land, never once do the prophets describe the sins for which God punishes them as unsustainable farming practices, pollution, or similar things. Oh, the people defile the land, true. But how? "[T]hey have polluted My land: they have filled My inheritance with the carcasses of their detestable idols and with their abominations" (16:18). It is precisely because the people of Judah do not fear God (and so practice all kinds of sin) that they come to fear that the spring and autumn rains will fail.

Fear of environmental catastrophe grows out of the lack of the fear of God. That, I would argue, is the real root of the environmental scares that have plagued the modern world.[14] And such fears will continue — with or without scientific basis[15] — until people repent and fear the Lord. "Cursed is the man

14. For catalogues and exposés of such, see Julian L. Simon, ed., *The State of Humanity* (New York and London: Blackwell, 1995); Aaron Wildavsky, *But Is It True? A Citizen's Guide to Environmental Health and Safety Issues* (Cambridge, MA: Harvard University Press, 1995); Ronald Bailey, *Eco-Scam: The False Prophets of Ecological Collapse* (New York: St. Martin's Press, 1993); Christopher Booker and Richard North, *Scared to Death: From BSE to Global Warming: Why Scares Are Costing Us the Earth* (London: Continuum, 2007).

15. Charles Mackay, *Extraordinary Popular Delusions and the Madness of Crowds* (1841; reprint ed., Hampshire, UK: Harrman House Ltd., 2007); Booker and North, *Scared to Death: From BSE to Global Warming: Why Scares Are Costing Us the Earth*.

who trusts in mankind, and makes flesh his strength, and whose heart turns away from the LORD. . . . Blessed is the man who trusts in the LORD and whose trust is the LORD. For he will be like a tree planted by the water, that extends its roots by a stream, and will not fear when the heat comes; but its leaves will be green, and it will not be anxious in a year of drought nor cease to yield fruit" (Jeremiah 17:5, 7–8).

A Christian should be aware of the unchristian roots and philosophies underlying the environmental religious movement today. It is important to get back to God's Word as the ultimate authority and rely on God and His Word as the solution to such issues.

CHAPTER 21

What about Distant Starlight Models?

DR. DANNY R. FAULKNER AND BODIE HODGE

D istant starlight is seen as one of the biggest difficulties to trusting God's Word about a young universe and earth. When adding up genealogies back to creation week, there are about 4,000 years from Christ to Adam.[1] With six normal-length days in creation week, there is no room for the idea of billions of years (Exodus 20:11)!

In *The New Answers Book 1*, astrophysicist Dr. Jason Lisle tackled the subject of distant starlight by looking at the various assumptions behind the issue.[2] This complementary chapter discusses the various models that have been proposed for distant starlight by creationists in an effort to show how this alleged problem can be overcome.

But we would like to give some background to make sure that readers understand the issues at stake.

Why Is Distant Starlight a Problem in the First Place?

Usually, the way this issue is couched to Bible-believing Christian is this: "So how do you get starlight billions of light years away to earth in only about 6,000 years?"

1. Bodie Hodge, "How Old Is the Earth?" in *The New Answers Book 2*, Ken Ham, gen. ed. (Green Forest, AR: Master Books, 2008), p. 41–52.
2. Jason Lisle, "Does Distant Starlight Prove the Universe Is Old?" in *The New Answers Book 1*, Ken Ham, gen ed. (Green Forest, AR: Master Books, 2006), p. 245–254.

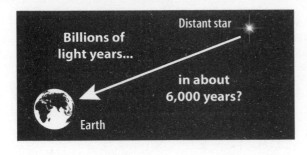

Most Christians are at a loss as to how to answer this question. Some try to say that the distances are not that accurate. But we would disagree. The distances really are that far.[3] That should give you an inkling of the mind of God!

There are ways to measure the distances such as parallax and the Hubble relation. We will not belabor these points, as they are already discussed in chapter 18 in this volume.

But the issue is even more difficult than many may think. We are not just trying to get light billions of light years away to earth in only 6,000 years, but we are trying to get light to earth in only two days. Why? The stars were created on day 4, and Adam was created on day 6. Starlight needs to arrive for Adam to be able to use the stars to mark the passage of time, which is one of the purposes of stars listed in Genesis 1:14.

The Secularists Have the Same Sort of Problem

The opposition rarely realizes that they have a starlight problem, too. In the big-bang model, there is the "Horizon Problem," a variant of the light-travel time problem.[4] This is based on the exchange of starlight/electromagnetic radiation to make the universe a constant temperature.

In the supposed big bang, the light could not have been exchanged and the universe was expected to have many variations of temperature, but this was not the case when measured. Such problems cause many to struggle with the big-bang model, and rightly so.

(1) Early in the alleged big bang, points A and B start out with different temperatures.

(2) Today, points A and B have the same temperature, yet there has not been enough time for them to exchange light.

---

3. See Danny Faulkner, "Astronomical Distance Determination Methods and the Light Travel Time Problem," *Answers Research Journal* 6 (2013): p. 211–229, http://www.answersingenesis.org/articles/arj/v6/n1/astronomical-distance-light-travel-problem.

4. Robert Newton, "Light-Travel Time: A Problem for the Big Bang," *Creation*, September–November 2003, p. 48–49, http://www.answersingenesis.org/articles/cm/v25/n4/light-travel-time.

Inflation

How did secularists try to solve it? In laymen's terms, they appealed to "inflation of the universe" in big-bang models as an *ad hoc* explanation. In other words, very quickly after

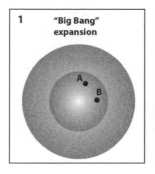

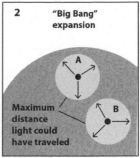

the big bang, the fabric of space in the universe supposedly expanded very quickly (faster than the speed of light), then instantly slowed to the rate we see today. But what caused all that?

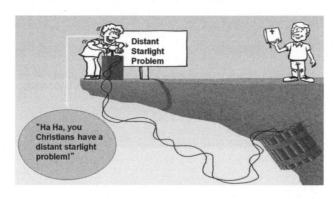

They suggest that some field existed that caused inflation. There is no direct evidence of inflation; that is, there is no independent evidence. Inflation was invented to solve the horizon problem and another problem (the flatness problem, but that will not be addressed in this chapter).

Researchers recognize there are problems with inflation and the big bang. Some physicists and astronomers have been "jumping ship" from the big-bang model in recent times, and this movement has continually gained steam since an open letter with respected signatories was published in the magazine *New Scientist* in 2004.[5] However, the majority of old universe believers still adhere to the big bang.

The hope of many who opposed the big bang was to revise the big bang and inflation to avoid the many problems. More recently, *New Scientist* ran an article called "Bang Goes the Theory."[6] The article quotes two leading cosmologists, Drs. Paul Steinhardt and Max Tegmark:

---

5. Eric Lerner, "Bucking the Big Bang," *New Scientist*, May 22, 2004, p. 20. To view the signers of this statement, visit http://www.cosmologystatement.org.
6. Amanda Gefter, "Bang Goes the Theory," *New Scientist*, June 30, 2012, p. 32–37.

We thought that inflation predicted a smooth, flat universe. . . . Instead, it predicts every possibility an infinite number of times. We're back to square one.[7]

Inflation has destroyed itself. It logically self-destructed.[8]

To boil it down, some researchers recognize there are problems with inflation and the big bang, and they are questioning aspects of these ideas, such as:

1. the big bang and its type
2. nothing to something
3. what started and stopped inflation
4. the starlight problem and recognizing how bad it is

Inflation and the big bang have their problems, and honest scientists fully admit this.

Potential Models to Solve the Problem

Interestingly, biblical creationists have known about the distant starlight problem for a while and have been working on solutions. The popular ideas include:

1. Light in transit (or mature creation)
2. Speed of light decay (cdk[9])
3. Relativistic models
4. Alternate Synchrony Conventions
5. *Dasha* Solution

Let's take a look at each of these in brief.

Light in Transit

Light in transit: This is the idea that God created the universe mature, or fully functioning. The functions of the stars (Genesis 1: 14–17; Psalm 19:1–2) required that Adam see them right away, so God created starlight in transit when He created the stars. Many reject this particular model today.

The reason many do not accept the light in transit idea is because starlight contains a tremendous amount of detailed information about stars. For instance, stars have been known to blow up into supernovas like *SN 1987a*.

---

7. Ibid., p. 35.
8. Ibid., p. 35.
9. cdk = c decay, where c is the symbol that physicists use for the speed of light.

Had this merely been starlight in transit, then what we saw would *not* have represented a star or a supernova, but instead merely light arriving at our eye to *appear* as a star and then a supernova. In other words, the star that was observed before the supernova could not have come from the actual star. If the light in transit idea is correct, then the light was encoded on the way to earth to make it look like an actual star. In that case, the supernova itself did not really happen but amounted to an illusion, sort of like a movie.

Many have suggested that if this were the case, then most stars are not stars. The implication is that God would be deceptively leading us to believe they were stars, when in fact they are illusions of stars. The idea of light in transit was widely popular among creationists for some time, but now many reject this idea because it seems far too deceptive.

Speed of Light Decay (cdk)

Speed of light decay (spearheaded by Barry Setterfield): This is the idea that the speed of light was much faster in the past and has been slowing down primarily in a uniform fashion (but possibly in steps) to what we observe today.

Most creationists reject this idea now, but we encourage researchers to keep working on it. In the end though, it appears to have problems with other constants in the universe that are tied to it. If the speed of light were to change, then these constants would change, too. Those constants govern the structure of matter so that matter would drastically change as the speed of light changed.

Evidence for a reduced speed of light decay is also lacking and in centuries past, the accuracy of such measuring devices has been limited. Furthermore, as people really researched the speed of light over the past three centuries, it really was not changing as previously thought, but has remained largely the same.[10]

In recent times, secularists such as John Moffat, Andreas Albrecht, and Joao Magueijo have appealed to the speed of light decay (VSL or Variable Speed of Light) as a possible solution to the secular starlight problem.[11] Perhaps as secular scientists do further research, they will see that there are some problems with this model. Either way, creation scientists are "light years" ahead of them in the research (pun intended).

---

10. Gerald A. Aardsma, "Has the Speed of Light Decayed?" Institute for Creation Research, http://www.icr.org/article/has-speed-light-decayed/ (accessed June 17, 2013).

11. Andrew Sibley, "Variable Speed of Light Research Gets a Boost," *Journal of Creation* 20, no. 1 (2006): p. 16–18, http://creation.com/images/pdfs/tj/j20_1/j20_1_16-18.pdf.

Relativistic Models

White Hole Cosmology[12]

Dr. Russell Humphreys has a model dubbed the "White Hole" cosmology. A white hole is like a black hole, except that matter flies outward from a white hole whereas matter falls into a black hole. Near the boundary of a black hole or a white hole, space and time are distorted. According to Einstein's theory of general relativity, this distortion can be described as stretching the fabric of space, and time progresses at different rates depending upon where you are.

So this theory plays off general relativity to solve the distant starlight problem with gravitational time dilation. From an overview perspective, Dr. Humphreys challenges the commonly held assumption that the universe has no boundary. Running a bounded cosmos through general relativity results in a model that is not at all like the big bang and consistent with biblical creation.

Essentially, in the White Hole cosmology, all the matter in the universe flew out of this "white hole." This would have occurred during creation week, and the white hole would have vanished some time during that week. As matter left the white hole, gravitational time dilation occurred. The earth was near the center of the white hole, so time on earth passed much more slowly than time near the boundary of the white hole.

Though there are still problems with this issue, such as blue shifts and red shifts not matching what they should be,[13] this model also holds some promise, and so we encourage further work on this model.

Hartnett Model (Carmelian Physics)[14]

A method solution utilizing Carmelian physics (named for Moshe Carmeli) was proposed by physicist Dr. John Hartnett. In a different approach to Humphrey's White Hole cosmology where the bounded universe was in four dimensions, this has assumed five dimensions (utilizing Carmeli's approach) and was still bounded.

Like the Humphreys model, the Hartnett model also relies on time dilation — a massive amount on earth. He postulates that most of this occurred on day

---

12. D. Russell Humphreys, *Starlight and Time* (Green Forest, AR: Master Books, 1994).
13. John G. Hartnett, "Look-back Time in Our Galactic Neighbourhood Leads to a New Cosmogony," *Technical Journal* 17, no. 1 (2003): p. 73–79.
14. Hartnett, "A New Cosmology: Solution to the Starlight Travel Time Problem," *Technical Journal* 17, no. 2 (August 2003): 98–102; Hartnett, "Starlight, Time, and the New Physics," in Proceedings of The Sixth International Conference on Creationism, Andrew A. Snelling, ed. (Pittsburg, PA: Creation Science Fellowship, Inc., and Institute for Creation Research, 2008), p. 193–204.

4 of creation week resulting from space expansion as God was creating galaxies. So time was running at different rates with six days passing on earth but more time passing elsewhere. Much of this dilation of time would have occurred during creation week, as opposed to Humphrey's model where it occurred all along at a more steady rate. Hartnett has produced some interesting results. Both the Humphreys and the Hartnett models are still being developed.

Alternate Synchrony Conventions

Lisle-Einstein Convention[15]

This model derives from passages like Genesis 1:17 that states that the stars were to "give light on the earth." For a God who created all things, having distant stars give light on earth is no problem. Astrophysicist Dr. Jason Lisle (also writing under the pen name of Robert Newton) led the research on this model.

From the concept of light being given from stars to light the earth, Dr. Lisle derived the Lisle-Einstein Synchrony Convention, otherwise known as the Anisotropic Synchrony Convention (ASC), which is based on an alternative convention that is *position-based* physics as opposed to *velocity-based* physics. Einstein left open both options but did most of his work on velocity based, and so have most physicists since him.

Einstein pointed out that time is not constant in the universe, so our simple equation [Distance = Speed x Time] is not so simple anymore. But this starlight model is based on something quite "simple." Dr. Jason Lisle built on this position-based physics and the *one* direction speed of light (which cannot be known), and it solves distant starlight.

In laymen's terms, think of it like this: You leave on a jet from New York at 1 P.M. and you land in L.A. at 1 P.M. But you might say, "The flight took about five hours on the jet." Here is the difference: according to Einstein, when you approach the speed of light, time goes to zero. So if you rode on top of a light beam from a star that was billions of light years away from earth, it took *no time* for you to get here. So that five-hour flight was a "no hour" flight for light. It was an instantaneous trip.

---

15. For more, see Robert Newton, "Distant Starlight and Genesis: Conventions of Time Measurement," *Technical Journal* 15, no. 1 (April 2001): p. 80–85, http://www. answersingenesis.org/articles/tj/v15/n1/starlight; Jason Lisle, "Anisotropic Synchrony Convention — A Solution to the Distant Starlight Problem," *Answers Research Journal* 3 (2010): p. 191–207, http://www.answersingenesis.org/articles/arj/v3/n1/anisotropic-synchrony-convention; Lisle, "Distant Starlight — Anisotropic Synchrony Convention," Answers, January–March 2011, p. 68–71, http://www.answersingenesis.org/articles/am/v6/n1/distant-starlight.

Based on this convention-based model, light left distant stars and arrived on earth in no time. This fulfills God's statement that these lights were to give light on the earth in Genesis 1:14. Of course, the physics is more complicated than this, but this analogy should give you an idea of how this model might work. However, it does not appear that we could perform an experiment to see if the ASC solution is true.

Dasha Solution

We would leave open miraculous options (as this was creation week). One particular form is by co-author Dr. Danny Faulkner (astronomer) dubbed the *Dasha* Solution.[16] *Dasha* is the Hebrew word for "sprout" as found in Genesis 1:11. Many processes during creation week were done at rates uncommon today.

While some things were created *ex nihilo* (out of nothing) during creation week (Genesis 1:1), many things during that week probably were made of material created earlier in the week. For instance, the day 3 account tells us something about how God made plants (Genesis 1:11–12). The words used there suggest that the plants shot up out of the ground very quickly, sort of like a time-lapse movie. That is, there may have been normal growth accomplished abnormally quickly. The result was that plants bore fruit that the animals required for food two to three days later. The plants had to mature rapidly to fulfill their function.

God made stars on day 4, but to fulfill their functions the stars had to be visible by day 6 when Adam was on the scene. As the normal process of plant development may have been sped up on day 3, the normal travel of starlight may have been sped up on day 4. If so, this rapid thrusting of light toward earth could be likened to the stretching of the heavens already mentioned.

Some people may want to equate this stretching of starlight with some physical mechanism such as cdk or relativistic time effects, but this would not explain the abnormally fast development of plants on day 3. This also overlooks the fact that much about the creation week was miraculous, hence untestable today. If one were to attempt to explain the light travel time problem in terms of a physical mechanism, one might as well look for a physical mechanism for the virgin birth or Resurrection.

---

16. Danny Faulkner, "Astronomical Distance Determination Methods and the Light Travel Time Problem," *Answers Research Journal* 6 (2013): p. 211–229, http://www. answersingenesis.org/articles/arj/v6/n1/astronomical-distance-light-travel-problem.

Conclusions

When all is said and done, this alleged problem of distant starlight does not seem as problematic for the biblical creationist. Researchers have several options that can solve this problem, so it is not a problem for a young universe. Furthermore, we want to encourage researchers currently working on these projects.

But from a big picture standpoint, no one outside of God completely understands all the aspects of *light* (or *time* for that matter). It acts as a particle and in other instances acts as a wave, but we simply cannot test both at the same time. This dual behavior is still an underlying mystery in science that is simply accepted in practice. The more light is studied, the more questions we have, rather than finding answers.

Such things are similar in the theological world with the deity of Christ (fully man and fully God). Even the Trinity is a unique yet accepted mystery (Father, Son, and Holy Spirit; one God but three persons). And in science, there is the "triple point" of water, where at one temperature and pressure, water is solid, liquid, and gas at the same time.

Light is truly unique in its makeup and properties, and with further study perhaps we can be "enlightened" to understand this issue in more detail. Regarding the distant starlight issue, there are plenty of models that have some promising elements to solve this alleged problem, and we would leave open future models that have not been developed yet (and we would also leave open the miraculous).

But as we consider the light travel time problem, we frequently overlook the immensity of the creation itself. The sudden appearance of space, time, matter, and energy is a remarkable and truly miraculous event. This is something that we humans cannot comprehend at all. Compared to creation, the light travel time problem is not very big at all.

CHAPTER 22

What Are the Tactics of the New Atheists?

DR. ELIZABETH MITCHELL[1]

Following the April 29 opening of their documentary *The Unbelievers* at Toronto's Hot Docs Film Festival, outspoken atheists Richard Dawkins and Lawrence Krauss discussed the merits of their approaches to "ridding the world of religion." In a recent interview with Steve Paikin,[2] they made it clear that, despite their sometimes different personas, they have the same agenda — getting people to get rid of their belief in God. Yet they both say that Christians should not feel "threatened" by their efforts to expunge religion from human history.

The Goal of *The Unbelievers* Documentary

Evolutionary biologist Dawkins and theoretical physicist Krauss recounted that when they first met they had a heated debate about, as Dawkins said, "Whether we should have a kind of full-on attack on religion or whether we should, as Lawrence preferred, seduce them."[3] Krauss explained that this is really

---

1. Footnotes are by Bodie Hodge.
2. http://ww3.tvo.org/video/190768/rise-new-atheists.
3. Of course, Dawkins means all religions but his own. He is very religious, being a secular humanist. He is a signer of the Humanist Manifesto III. Humanism comes in various flavors like "agnosticism," "traditional atheism," "new atheism," etc. When someone says he is "not religious" in this context, it is a fancy way of saying he adheres to the religion of humanism in one form or another. Dawkins' religious viewpoint is "new atheism," distinguished from traditional atheism in that it actively proselytizes for the atheistic viewpoint, whereas adherents of traditional atheism believe that nothing matters and so see no reason to proselytize.

Outspoken atheists Lawrence Krauss and Richard Dawkins, costars of the documentary *The Unbelievers,* discuss their strategy for ridding the world of religion in general and Christianity in particular. They consider Christianity "demeaning" and wish to re-design society "the way we want it." (Image:screen shots from interview with Steve Paikin on http://ww3.tvo.org/video/190768/rise-new-atheists.)

"a strategic question."[4] They agree that both approaches have merit depending on the nature of the people being targeted. However, expressing general agreement with the more confrontational approach of the often-irascible Dawkins, Krauss said, "You've got to confront silly beliefs by telling them they are silly," adding, "If you're trying to convince people, pointing out that what they believe is nonsense is a better way to bring them around."[5]

---

4. We have known about their strategic attacks for some time. They have tried to force the religion of humanism in the classroom and now elsewhere. In 1983, humanist John Dunphy also spoke of this strategy — to put their atheistic religion into schools — when he said: "I am convinced that the battle for humankind's future must be waged and won in the public school classroom by teachers who correctly perceive their role as the proselytizers of a new faith: a religion of humanity that recognizes and respects the spark of what theologians call divinity in every human being. These teachers must embody the same selfless dedication as the most rabid fundamentalist preachers, for they will be ministers of another sort, utilizing a classroom instead of a pulpit to convey humanist values in whatever subject they teach, regardless of the educational level — preschool, daycare, or large state university. The classroom must and will become an arena of conflict between the old and the new — the rotting corpse of Christianity, together with all its adjacent evils and misery, and the new faith of humanism." John Dunphy, "A Religion for a New Age," quoted in John Dunphy, "The Book that Started It All," Council for Secular Humanism, http://www.secularhumanism.org/index.php?section=library&page=dunphy_21_4.

5. Yet these atheists do not realize the silliness of their own views. Dawkins himself admits that it is possible that aliens designed and seeded life on earth — yes, really! Krauss and Dawkins both believe that all people ultimately came from a rock — clearly this is in violation of the law of biogenesis. Both believe that everything is material; therefore, from their view, logic, truth, and knowledge, which are non-material, cannot exist. By thus laying claim to logic, truth, and knowledge, they inadvertently borrow from a Christian worldview — how silly for their religion to borrow from its enemy! Dawkins argues there is no morality and then tries to say Christians are immoral. Both believe that nothing ultimately matters; yet they both seem to think it matters a great deal to force this belief on others. Neither Krauss nor Dawkins seem to realize that in an atheistic worldview, the atheist is actually claiming to be "God" (because to know there is no God, one must be omnipresent and omniscient, which are attributes of God alone), which refutes their own atheism. This short list should suffice. Such silliness should be embarrassing to an atheist.

Despite their great hostility toward religious beliefs (other than their own) and avowal that they hope this film will help in their efforts to eradicate all religion worldwide, the atheist pair indicates that belief or non-belief in a deity is not what really matters to them. Krauss declares that what is actually important to them is that "everything should be open to question and that the universe is a remarkable place."[6] By contrast, he says, "This is more important to us than not believing in God — that's not important at all." Dawkins and Krauss both expressed grudging tolerance for evolutionists who want to keep their religious beliefs in order to keep the good things religion offers them — "spirituality," "consolation," and "community" — so long as they do not then reject evolution.[7] They said that people are "hard-wired" to seek something spiritual, but by "spiritual" they refer to a sort of emotional high. And they declare that science offers a better kind of spirituality, "a sense of oneness with the universe."[8] Therefore science,[9] they maintain, can meet the inmost needs of people better than religion of any sort.

"Spirituality is a sense of awe and wonder at something bigger than oneself,"[10] Krauss explained, adding that being "insignificant is uplifting."[11] And while some people cling to their religion to satisfy some spiritual need,[12] he says, "The spirituality of science is better than the spirituality of religion because

---

6. Interestingly, Christians believe in asking questions and seeking answers to all sorts of tough questions — including the scientific and the theological. And Christians certainly recognize that the universe is a remarkable place, but we know it was created by God. So the opposition to Christianity on this ground is completely without warrant by their own criteria.

7. Evolution (and millions of years, or geological evolution) is the real key. These are tenets of the Humanist Manifestos, so humanists do not want to give up this key aspect. They must fight for this in their religion. But underlying all of this is the idea that man is the ultimate authority, not God.

8. "Oneness with the universe" is a tenant of Buddhism, which is strange, considering they are arguing to oppose Buddhism along with all other religions.

9. What they mean by "science" here is not the observable and repeatable science that makes discoveries about how things work and applies that knowledge, but instead a "science" that embraces naturalism and evolution as absolutely axiomatic. Therefore, what Dawkins and Krauss mean when they say science is not just how things work but their own naturalistic, unverifiable, dogmatically held ideas about where everything came from. By science, they really mean their religion of humanism.

10. If one believes there is something greater than oneself in atheism, then it means that he is not atheistic. Hence, this is self-refuting.

11. If being insignificant is so great, then why waste time seeking popularity by speaking out against Christianity by making documentaries?

12. This is oddly similar to what the religious atheist is doing, per the very context.

it is real."[13] Both of course vigorously deny that their own atheistic position is one of "belief," saying "we don't define ourselves by what we don't believe in."

Dawkins and Krauss Want to Rid the World of All Religion Except Their Own

Like most atheists, Dawkins and Krauss fail to recognize the worldview-based nature of the interpretations they define as "real." They repeatedly refer in the interview to accepting the "evidence of reality" concerning origins when they are actually equating their worldview-based interpretations with reality. Furthermore, the atheistic belief that there is no God is actually a "religion."

There really is no such thing as a person without a religion — you either believe that there is or is not a god. You are either for Christ or against Him (Luke 11:23), and you base your interpretation of origins, morality, and the meaning of life on that belief. The belief that there is or is not a god is essential to how one explains existence, the nature of authority, and our place in the universe. Krauss's belief that the atoms in his body originated billions of years ago in stardust, for instance, is the "religious" way he explains his existence without God and the way he experiences what passes for spirituality by knowing the "fantastic" truth that he is "intimately connected to the cosmos."

Atheists do claim to be non-religious, but they use their set of beliefs as a way to explain life without God — they worship and serve the creation (e.g., the universe) rather than the Creator (Romans 1:25). Krauss extols the profound sense of wonder he gets studying the cosmos and Dawkins enjoys the "poetry of science," but they tie their love for science to their belief in atheistic evolution and their sheer joy in shaking their fists at the possibility of a Creator's existence.

The Reason Behind the Hostility toward Religion

And frankly, the point here is not whether a person defines his worldview as a religion or not, or whether he believes in a "god." Christianity is unique — it is the truth — and, perhaps for that reason as much as any other, is the especial target for Dawkins and most others. Those who love "darkness" (e.g., sin, rebellion against God, and rejection of Jesus Christ) will naturally attack the light (John 3:19–21). Based on Scripture, we know that God looks at the heart to see how each person stands in relation to Jesus Christ (Romans 10:9–10; cf.

---

13. This is a "No True Scotsman" fallacy, meaning that the arguer has defined the terms in a biased way to protect his argument from rebuttals.

1 Samuel 16:7). Again, Jesus made clear that a person is either for or against Him (Matthew 12:30, 25:46).

Dawkins and Krauss reserve their greatest hostility for young-earth creationists. They indicated that all debate about origins has been completely and unequivocally settled by "Darwin and his successors"[14] or else by big-bang cosmology,[15] which Krauss describes as "the last bastion of God — I mean there are some fundamentalists of course who say the earth is 6,000 years old and don't believe in evolution — but rational 'theologians' have moved away from that debate."[16]

Design in Nature

Furthermore, even Dawkins admits that nature — in particular, biology — appears to be specially designed. We see, for instance, precise irreducible complexity everywhere we look, from major anatomical features to biological processes at the molecular level. Dawkins agrees that "special creation" is "intuitive" — a look at nature in essence screams that there must have been a Creator. But Dawkins says that he is thankful to Darwin for coming up with a very "*non-intuitive*" way to explain nature without God. Darwinian belief basically builds a theoretical guess about biological origins by appealing to a series of billions of tiny, unobservable changes over billions of unobserved years.[17] Yet neither Darwin nor his successors have through scientific observation shown how either abiogenesis or the evolution of biological complexity is possible.

Dawkins explains that both biology and physics (cosmology) are complementary fields that supplant belief in God.[18] But he indicated that biology,

---

14. It is sad that they appeal to Darwin, a racist, who went so far as to say that the more evolved Caucasians would eventually exterminate everyone else (Charles Darwin, *The Descent of Man* [New York: A.L. Burt, 1874, 2nd ed.], p. 178). Even James Watson, a co-discoverer of the structure of DNA, also has underlying racist attitudes. But note that they appeal to man as the ultimate authority.
15. Which big-bang model (open models, closed model) do they think is true, and why are the others wrong?
16. The atheists simply do not like the fact that Christians actually believe God when He speaks. They really want us to compromise God's Word with theirs like Eve did in the Garden and to deny God's Word in Genesis in favor of their fallible sinful words. The issue is not mere distaste for creationists, but rather their distaste for God's Word. Note this: the conflict is not between atheists and creationists; it is between atheists and God.
17. Note what replaced God in their religion. It was time, chance, and death. Without these, evolution is meaningless. These are the "god" for an evolutionary worldview.
18. Yet science comes out of a Christian worldview, where God upholds the universe in a particular fashion, and this all-knowing God has told us so (e.g., Genesis 8:22 and others). In the humanistic view, how can man know that the laws in the universe will be the same

because design is so apparent, was the first battleground in the war against a Creator:

> Historically biology, I suppose, has been the most fertile ground for those who wish to make a supernatural account because living things are so fantastically complicated and beautiful and elegant, and they carry such an enormous weight of apparent design. They really look as though they're designed.

> So historically biology has been the most fertile ground for theological arguments. That's all solved now. Darwin and his successors solved that.

> I think the spotlight in a way has shifted to physics and to cosmology where we're less confident I think about how the universe began — in one way more confident because there's a lot of detailed mathematical modeling going on — but there are some profound questions remaining to be answered in that field and that's where cosmologists like Lawrence come in. We are complementary.

In typical fashion, Krauss and Dawkins believe that anyone who disagrees with their own interpretations about origins is irrational and out of touch with reality. And as happens with most lay people, anything that can be "mathematically modeled" is accepted as truth because numbers surely do not lie. Yet mathematical models concerning cosmology (like the big bang) and the long-age interpretations ascribed to radiometric dating are based on unverifiable, worldview-based assumptions.[19] Dawkins and Krauss say that they hope that viewers of their film will be inspired by the wonders of science to critically evaluate their beliefs and to acknowledge that they are "silly." As discussed below, however, from a biblical worldview, a careful study of the wonders of science only affirms what God reveals in the Bible and actually glorifies the Creator (Psalm 19:1; Colossians 1:16–17).

Biblical creationists understand that God created all the various kinds of living organisms about *6,000 years ago* (based on the genealogies listed in the Bible). According to Genesis 1, God equipped each to reproduce "after their kinds." There is no indication in Scripture that God used evolutionary processes

---

in the future? According to man, from the big bang to today, the laws have changed. How does one know they will not change tomorrow? If one says, "Because they always have," he is arbitrarily begging the question.

19. Such methods are classic cases of begging the question; they are using long-age assumptions to prove long ages. We could just as easily do the same thing by using young-age assumptions to prove a young earth, but this simply shows the arbitrariness of their uniformitarian claims.

or that He made organisms able to evolve through random processes into new and increasingly complex kinds of creatures. We also do not see this happen in biology. As many articles on the Answers in Genesis website explain, organisms vary within their kinds (e.g., variations in dogs or in cats) but do not evolve into new, more complex kinds of organisms (e.g., amoebas into dogs or cats). Bacteria remain bacteria, canines remain canines, apes remain apes, and humans remain humans — though there is much biodiversity among each *created kind*. This diversification within kinds is observable. But evolution of new kinds is not, and biological observation can offer no actual *mechanisms* by which *this can happen*.[20]

Further, biological observation confirms that living things do not spring into existence through the random interaction of non-living components, despite evolutionary claims about abiogenesis. This is consistent with the biblical account of our origins. Thus, biblical history — God's eyewitness account of what He did when He created us and what sort of biology He put in motion — does *not* differ from biological observations. There is nothing "irrational" about recognizing that observable science is consistent with biblical history.[21]

Can Dawkins and Krauss Really "Rid This World of Religion"?

The interviewer concluded by asking the pair, *"Is it your hope or expectation that you can, in your words, rid this world of religion?"*

"I'm not sure how soon," Dawkins answered. "I think that religion is declining, that Christianity is declining throughout Christendom."[22] Looking to the future, he adds, "And I think that that's going to continue. If we look at

---

20. The two proposed mechanisms of evolution are called: (1) natural selection, a creationist concept by the way, and (2) mutations. In both cases, they are losing information (i.e., it is going in the wrong direction for evolution). For example, natural selection filters out already existing information; mutations lose information quickly, or in many cases it remains nearly neutral. See http://www.answersingenesis.org/articles/nab/is-natural-selection-evolution and http://www.answersingenesis.org/articles/nab2/mutations-engine-of-evolution.

21. Isn't it fascinating that humanists who are materialistic by their very admission appeal to logic and claim we are irrational, when rational thought is only possible if nonmaterial things exist like concepts, truth, logic, and so on? Yet these atheists (materialists, humanists) must reject it because if they leave open an immaterial realm (i.e., a spiritual realm), then God could exist and they cannot be atheistic or humanistic (i.e., humans are the ultimate authority).

22. Yet Christianity is still the fastest growing religion. Please see http://fastestgrowingreligion.com/numbers.html; it is merely declining or stagnant in certain places, like Western Europe and the United States.

the broad sweep of history, it's clear that the trend is going in the right direction. I'm not so optimistic that it will be in my lifetime, but it will happen."[23]

And what do Dawkins and Krauss hope to accomplish by getting rid of Christianity? Why do they care what others believe? Why are they so eager to expedite God's exit from human history? Dawkins summed up the proud position of humanism when he said that he wants to see us "intelligently design our society, our ethics, our morality — so that we live in the kind of society we want to live in rather than in the kind of society that was laid down in a book written in 800 B.C."[24] Krauss added that accepting the ideas of "Iron Age peasants" is "demeaning."[25]

Though Dawkins and Krauss disparage the ideas of biblical peasants, their notions of social planning really sound very much like the post-Flood population who built the Tower of Babel in rebellion against God's command to replenish the earth. In their pride (Psalm 10:4; Proverbs 16:8), those people said, "Let us make a name for ourselves" (Genesis 11:4). Indeed, how arrogant does a person have to be to assume that everyone who disagrees with him is either ill-informed or irrational? Is it any wonder that God hates pride, for through humanistic pride people not only reject God's ways but "suppress the truth" (Romans 1:18) of His very existence?

Dawkins and Krauss seem to want to redesign the world and society for the rest of us according to their own vision, making certain that God is written out of the picture. Yet those of us who know and trust God and accept the Bible as His revealed Word believe wholeheartedly that Jesus Christ, our Creator and Savior, possesses all true wisdom and knowledge (Colossians 1:16–17, 3:2). And we not only accept the history in God's Word but also God's declaration that we

23. Did you catch that Dawkins just made a prophecy? He predicted that religion would cease. God disagrees with him (Matthew 16:18; Daniel 2:44).
24. Satan, in the Bible, sinned with his pride of wanting to ascend to God's position (Isaiah 14:14). It appears clear that Dawkins wants to replace God, too, as the "intelligent designer" no less, albeit of society rather than the universe. (We suppose even Dawkins knows he has some limitations!) Interestingly, Dawkins does seem to believe in a form of intelligent design because he has said he considers it a possibility that aliens designed life here (per his comments in the documentary *Expelled* with Ben Stein, not in this interview). Furthermore, it is unclear what book Dawkins is talking about, though he is surely alluding to the Bible with a prejudicial conjecture about the timing. The Bible was written over the course of about 1450 B.C. to about A.D. 68–95. (Christians do debate this.) Take note of the irony here though; Dawkins wants people to follow what he says in his books, but not follow God's book! Again, he is trying to replace God (2 Corinthians 2:11), and in his own mind, he already has.
25. Note the straw man fallacies these atheists are committing. They are trying to make Christianity look silly, but because they cannot even get basic facts correct, they look silly by default.

are all sinners in need of the grace of Jesus Christ. By contrast, those who, like Dawkins and Krauss, refuse to even acknowledge the testimony of the "design" they themselves see in nature (Romans 1:18–22) and their own consciences (Romans 2:12–16), much less God's Word, are — according to God — "fools" (Psalm 14:1, 53:1). *"Professing to be wise, they became fools"* (Romans 1:22).

In answer to the interviewer's final question about the prospects for the imminent demise of religion, Krauss said, "I would have thought that by now religion would be gone. I thought religion was on the way out [in the 1960s], so I was kind of surprised and disappointed in some ways by the resurgence of fundamentalism in my country [the United States]."[26] Speaking of the future he expects, he adds, "But I do think that it's obvious that access to information and knowledge is decreasing" the number of people who say they are religious worldwide and that "inevitably knowledge and wonder of the real universe will supplant" religion.[27] Answers in Genesis exists to make knowledge available to help people make informed decisions about the claims of atheistic evolutionists so that they will see that they can trust God's Word from the very first verse.

Both Krauss and Dawkins think it unreasonable that people feel "threatened" by their efforts to rid the world of religion.[28] Dawkins said, "Where religion is concerned if you speak clearly it sounds threatening" and "if you say something clearly and distinctly and truthfully there are people who will take that as threatening." He said that religion is so entrenched that it "gets a free ride" and that "very mild criticism" and "questioning" shouldn't be regarded as threatening.[29]

---

26. This is reminiscent of atheist Friedrich Nietzsche who declared "God is dead" several times in the 1800s. It is sad that atheists like Krauss know so little about God's Word that they fail to realize a dominating principle: the power of God in the Resurrection. When the Jews had Christ crucified, even Christ's disciples thought the Son of God was dead. But God is known for His Resurrection. Though Nietzsche is dead, God continues to live and gives to all life and breath. And Christianity continues to grow by the power of the Holy Spirit.

27. Note here that Krauss has now prophesied the same sort of thing as Dawkins. He is predicting that universe worship, like his atheistic view, will come to destroy religion. But this would naturally fail, as atheism and universe worship are a form of religion, making Krauss's prediction inherently contradictory.

28. Actually, Christians should find it a blessing. Matthew 5:11 says, "Blessed are you when they revile and persecute you, and say all kinds of evil against you falsely for My sake."

29. Again, Christians do not fear questioning, nor do we get a free ride or mild criticism. Christians in various parts of the world are murdered for their beliefs, attacked and beaten for their beliefs, abused for their beliefs, and lied about because of their beliefs. If one is not a Christian, like Dawkins, why assume such people actually adhere to the Ten Commandments, which say not to lie? Dawkins claimed that there is no morality in his debate with Lanier. So why trust him to tell the truth? With this in mind, notice Dawkins's deception here. He wants the freedom to question, but he does not want us to respond. Nor does he want Christians to question things like evolution or the big bang —

Conclusion: Man's Word vs. God's Word

Krauss and Dawkins repeatedly refer to the "evidence of reality" in this interview. Yet they, like other evolutionary scientists, fail to distinguish between testable scientific reality — experimental science — and the untestable, unobservable, and unverifiable assumptions on which the scientific claims of evolutionary origins science are based. What they claim as "reality" is interpreted through their own worldview, a worldview that is clearly hostile toward God.[30] And while they oppose "all" religion, it is clear they particularly oppose Christianity and the Bible. They firmly believe that anyone who fails to accept their worldview is irrational. They admit that religion meets the needs of some people for "spirituality," but their concept of spirituality is a purely emotional response.[31]

And lest this "response" be deemed defensive (a point made not only in this interview but also by a number of atheists who have recently written in to this ministry), let me hasten to point out that if "just asking a question" should not be seen as "threatening," then neither should just answering one. If saying "something clearly and distinctly and truthfully" should not be seen as threatening when Dawkins speaks, then neither should the truth from God's Word be taken that way. It should not be threatening when we question evolution, big bang, millions of years, humanism, or even Dawkins and Krauss themselves. In fact, they would welcome it in every forum, if they were consistent.

Krauss and Dawkins do have one thing in common with most biblical creationists — a sense of awe and wonder at what we can learn from experimental science about the world around us. Krauss and Dawkins appreciate the "poetry of science," but superimpose their own rhapsodic notions about the

---

especially in classrooms! If he did welcome responses, he would be happy for Christians to question evolution, the big bang, naturalism, and so on, and to respond to his false claims about Christianity in a proper forum, like the classroom, which is a place for learning. But Dawkins is adamant that Christians should have no say, no response, and no questioning of the evolutionary view in the state schools. Dawkins wants only his religion taught in schools and only his religion is permitted to question others. This is a double standard.

30. Remember, they assume long ages to prove long ages — an arbitrary begging-the-question fallacy.

31. They are trying to demote all religions to being materialistic (underlings to their religion). This is why they say spiritual is not immaterial, but merely emotion (e.g., chemical reaction in the brain). They are trying to change the definition of spirit and spiritual. They want to make God (who is spirit, John 4:24) into part of the universe or place Him in a position that is lower than the universe. Hence, the universe can be the unofficial "god" to the atheist, next to *man*, of course.

atoms in our bodies being derived from stardust billions of years old.[32] Biblical creationists, however, examine the actual facts of science — the observable and repeatable ones, not evolutionary story telling and conjectures — in light of God's revealed truth and see that there actually is no contradiction between the history revealed in the Bible and science (Romans 1:18–22).

Krauss and Dawkins hope their film will prompt Christians to ask questions and to critically examine their beliefs in light of science. At Answers in Genesis we encourage people — both believers and unbelievers — to ask questions and to critically examine scriptural revelation and scientific facts. We provide help in finding answers to those questions. Sadly, one example Dawkins provided was a young-earth creationist who came to his lectures on evolution and was very impressed, having never heard the evolutionary point of view. We do not encourage ignorance about evolutionary positions[33] but instead want to equip people with the information they need to discern the difference between *observable experimental science and historical science*, between that which can be tested and that which can only be imagined, between what can actually be seen in the world through science and the claims of evolutionists.

We want to equip children, teens, and adults with the tools they need to help them trust God's Word and see through false religions like atheism, so that they will then be able to trust Jesus Christ as their Savior and the Lord of their lives. The very name of our ministry, Answers in Genesis, makes it clear we are not encouraging people to have blind faith. On the contrary, we are providing reasonable, scientific, and biblical answers for questions on origins. And we do so with confidence that the Bible has the answers to explain the world we live in — scientifically, morally, and theologically.

---

32. When Krauss attacks the Bible with his famous mantra, "Forget Jesus, the stars died so you can be here today," he is promoting a mere fairy tale and stories to satisfy a meaningless atheistic worldview.

33. This is why we teach people about each evolutionary view and its problems. In brief, there are five main views: (1) The Epicurean evolutionary view, which has its roots in Greek mythology. This is where evolution came from. The newer forms we have today are just rehashes of this mythology that Paul refuted in Acts 17. (2) Lamarckian evolution, which taught that animals can acquire new traits through interactions with their environments, and then pass them on to the next generation. (3) Traditional Darwinism, where natural selection and time are the primary factors for change. (4) Neo-Darwinism, where natural selection and time are combined with mutations as the primary factors for evolution. (5) Punctuated Equilibrium, which tries to explain the lack of fossil evidence for transitional forms. This view assumes that evolution occurred in bursts and is not recorded in the fossil layers; it still relies on natural selection, mutations, and time. For more, see Roger Patterson and Dr. Terry Mortenson, "Do Evolutionists Believe Darwin's Ideas about Evolution?" *New Answers Book 3*, Ken Ham, gen. ed. (Green Forest, AR: 2010), p. 271–282.

The Bible attests not only to the true history of our origins but also the truth about humanity's rebellious and sinful nature.[34] Dawkins and Krauss consider biblical truth restrictive and demeaning. The Bible does make it clear that all people are sinners who have rebelled against the omniscient, omnipotent, and holy God. Dawkins and Krauss personify this rebellious spirit in declaring their desire to redesign the world the way "we" — in other words, "they" — want it to be. But evil men and seducers will, according to Scripture, get worse and worse (2 Timothy 3:13), so much so that Jesus said *"Nevertheless, when the Son of Man comes, will He really find faith on the earth?" (Luke 18:8).* As Christians, meanwhile, we are commanded to respond to the "nonthreatening threats" volleyed at us by skeptics and by sincere questioners by providing answers (1 Peter 3:15, KJV; 2 Timothy 2:22–26), including the answer to people's sin problem (Romans 3:23, 6:23) — salvation through the shed blood of Jesus Christ. But the final end of humanity's destiny is not the end prophesied by Dawkins and Krauss, for the same Jesus Christ that rose from the dead will indeed come again (Revelation 22:20). Dawkins and Krauss may be leading the charge to eradicate Christianity, but it is the Lord Jesus Christ who will surely have the last word.

For more information:

http://www.answersingenesis.org/articles/aid/v4/n1/morality-and-irrationality-evolutionary-worldview.

http://blogs.answersingenesis.org/blogs/georgia-purdom/2011/10/04/the-magic-of-reality-or-unreality/.

http://www.answersingenesis.org/articles/am/v5/n2/variety-within-kinds.

http://www.answersingenesis.org/articles/arj/v5/n1/evolution-myth-biology.

http://www.answersingenesis.org/articles/2011/06/03/feedback-search-for-historical-adam.

---

34. It is important to note that in the beginning, God called His creation "very good" (Genesis 1:31; Deuteronomy 32:4). It is because of man's sin that death, suffering, and disease came into the creation. God did not make the world like it is today (full of suffering) but subjected it to this due to man's sin. We have essentially been given a taste of what life is like without God. But Christ did not leave us to perish; instead, He took the punishment that we deserve on the Cross, once for all. Christ, the God-man, took the infinite punishment that is demanded by the very nature of God, who is infinite. God then offers the free gift of salvation, and promises a new heavens and new earth that will not be subjected to death, suffering, and decay. See http://www.answersingenesis.org/articles/2009/04/21/what-does-it-mean-to-be-saved.

http://www.answersingenesis.org/articles/2012/06/01/feedback-evolutionary-call-to-arms.

http://www.answersingenesis.org/articles/2011/06/24/feedback-huffing-and-puffing.

http://www.answersingenesis.org/articles/2012/04/12/teacher-protection-academic-freedom-act.

http://www.answersingenesis.org/articles/2012/08/30/bill-nye-crusade-for-your-kids.

http://blogs.answersingenesis.org/blogs/ken-ham/2013/01/08/teaching-on-hell-worse-than-child-sexual-abuse/.

http://blogs.answersingenesis.org/blogs/ken-ham/2013/02/14/biblical-creation-and-child-abuse/.

http://blogs.answersingenesis.org/blogs/ken-ham/2012/09/18/origins-and-child-abuse/.

http://www.answersingenesis.org/articles/nab2/does-big-bang-fit-with-bible.

http://www.answersingenesis.org/articles/nab/is-natural-selection-evolution.

http://www.answersingenesis.org/articles/nab2/do-rock-record-fossils-favor-long-ages.

http://www.answersingenesis.org/articles/am/v5/n1/order-fossil-record.

http://www.answersingenesis.org/articles/am/v4/n3/radiometric-dating.

http://www.answersingenesis.org/articles/am/v4/n4/assumptions.

http://www.answersingenesis.org/articles/am/v5/n1/patterns.

http://www.answersingenesis.org/articles/am/v1/n1/radioactive-dating.

http://www.answersingenesis.org/store/product/does-biology-make-sense-without-darwin/.

**Thanks to Bodie Hodge, AiG–U.S., for his helpful and insightful additions in the footnotes.

CHAPTER 23

Were There Any Volcanoes, High Mountains, and Earthquakes before the Flood?

DR. ANDREW A. SNELLING

The Scriptures are silent on the issue of whether there were any volcanoes or earthquakes in the world before the Flood, but we do know there were mountains. The opening chapters of Genesis only have an abbreviated description of the earth's early history (only six chapters describing more than 1,650 years). However, it is still possible to glean hints from the scriptural record, and to a subordinate extent infer details from the geologic record, to demonstrate that the pre-Flood earth was likely very stable with no major catastrophes.

Springs and Rivers

We are told in Genesis 7:11 that the Flood began with the breaking up of "the fountains of the great deep," a vivid description of catastrophic geologic activity. This implies that whatever caused this "breaking up" was restrained in the pre-Flood world. While the Hebrew phrase translated "the great deep" is used in Scripture to refer to and describe sub-oceanic waters, some uses also refer to subterranean waters (Isaiah 51:10 and Psalm 78:15, respectively).[1]

1. David M. Fouts and Kurt P. Wise, "Blotting and Breaking Up: Miscellaneous Hebrew Studies in Geocatastrophism," in *Proceedings of the Fourth International Conference on Creationism*, Robert E. Walsh, ed. (Pittsburgh, PA: Creation Science Fellowship, 1998), p. 217–228.

So "the fountains of the great deep" in Genesis 7:11 would have likely been primarily oceanic springs, although the possibility of these also including terrestrial springs that tapped waters residing within the earth's crust cannot be ruled out. Thus, the geologic activity referred to by the term "breaking up" must imply deep fracturing of the earth's crust accompanied by dramatic earth movements, volcanic eruptions, and devastating earthquakes. Such catastrophic geologic activity on a global scale must therefore have been restrained and thus absent in the pre-Flood world.

Genesis 2:6 describes a mist that went up from the earth and watered the whole face of the ground. The Hebrew word usually translated as "mist" is *ed*, but old translations such as the Septuagint, Syriac text, and the Vulgate all translate the word as "spring."[2] Such a translation would seem relevant in the light of other biblical evidence for the existence of terrestrial and oceanic springs. In Revelation 14:7, an angel declares, "Worship Him who made heaven and earth, the sea, and the springs of waters," which suggests that fountains or springs were an integral part of the created earth. It would have been the same fountains that were then "broken up" at the beginning of the Flood (Genesis 7:11, "all the fountains of the great deep were broken up"). The connotation in both the Greek and Hebrew words used in these verses, respectively, is of gushing springs where water burst forth from inside the earth. It is also the connotation of a different Hebrew word used in Job 36, usually translated as "springs."

Some have contended that Genesis 2:5 implies that there was definitely rain in the pre-Flood era, just no rain before Adam was created, as stated in the verse. They have thus suggested that the river that flowed through the Garden of Eden to water it, and then split into four rivers (Genesis 2:10–14), was fed by these fountains or springs.[3] Of course, the biblical record does not specifically say that there was a connection between these fountains or springs and the rivers on the pre-Flood earth. However, since the existence of these springs and fountains on both the land surface and the ocean floor are clearly mentioned in the Scriptures, then it is not unreasonable to expect that at least some of the

2. Gordon J. Wenham, Genesis 1–15, vol. 1, *Word Biblical Commentary* (Waco, TX: Word Books, 1987), p. 58; Victor P. Hamilton, *The Book of Genesis: Chapters 1–17, The New International Commentary on the Old Testament* (Grand Rapids, MI: William B. Eerdmans, 1990), p. 154.
3. Joachim Scheven, "The Geological Record of Biblical Earth History," *Origins* (Biblical Creation Society UK) 3, no. 8 (1990): 8–13; Joachim Scheven, "Stasis in the Fossil Record as Confirmation of the Belief in Biblical Creation," in *Proceedings of the Second International Conference on Creationism*, vol. 1, Robert E. Walsh and Christopher L. Brooks, eds. (Pittsburgh, PA: Creation Science Fellowship, 1990), p. 197–215.

rivers on the pre-Flood earth were fed by springs. Furthermore, even though the Hebrew word *ed* in Genesis 2:6 is probably correctly translated as "mist," the existence of springs and fountains on the pre-Flood earth is clearly mentioned in other passages.

Nevertheless, we cannot be dogmatic that there was no rain for the entire pre-Flood era, even though Genesis 2:6 indicates that the mist "watered the whole face of the ground." In this way, the pre-Flood land surface must have been well watered and have produced lush vegetation. The latter is, of course, attested to by the huge volume of fossilized vegetation in the coal beds in the geologic record, which was destroyed and buried by the Flood.[4] Thus, climatic conditions in the pre-Flood era would seem to have been ideal for animal and human habitation across the face of the earth and must have been generally warm and humid. Though the Scriptures are silent on the subject, it could perhaps be inferred that there may not have been the same extremes of weather conditions that we experience on today's post-Flood earth. If this were the case, then it might also be inferred that there were not the same extremes in topography across the pre-Flood earth as there are today, because high mountains do affect weather patterns and conditions, for example, causing "rain shadows" and inducing snowfalls.

Topography and Mountains

While we are given no specific statements about the topography of the pre-Flood earth and how much it varied, we are given some hints. For example, the Garden of Eden must have been at a relatively high elevation, because we are told that the river flowing from it divided into four other rivers as it flowed downhill (Genesis 2:10–14). Furthermore, that there were mountains on the pre-Flood earth's land surface is clearly specified in Genesis 7:19–20, where we are told that the Flood waters prevailed exceedingly on the earth so that all the high hills under the whole of the heaven were covered, and then the mountains were covered. The difference between these topographic terms "hills" and "mountains" are somewhat subjective and arbitrary, but they do indicate a difference in sizes and elevations. So while we cannot be specific about the elevation differences on the pre-Flood land surface, we could potentially infer from all these descriptions that the topographic relief then was, for instance, not as enormously different and varied as it is today, and therefore was much more subdued. After all, today's high mountain ranges were produced during and

---

4. Andrew A. Snelling, "How Did We Get All This Coal?" *Answers* (April–June 2013): p. 70–73.

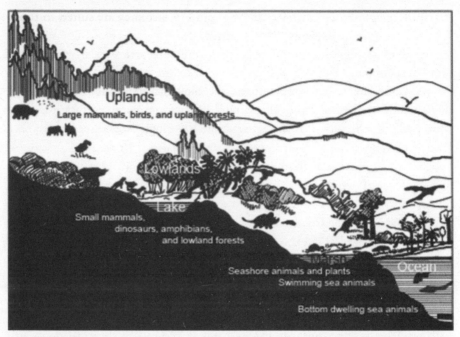

Figure 1. Diagrammatic presentation of likely ecological zonation in the pre-Flood world, illustrating how animals and plants could then be buried in a roughly predictable order by the rising Flood waters.

soon after the Flood catastrophe, because they often consist in part of Flood-deposited, fossil-bearing sedimentary rock layers that have been buckled due to catastrophic crustal plate collisions during the Flood, followed immediately by major rapid uplift due to post-Flood isostatic (vertical crustal weight balance) adjustments.[5]

Other clues not only come from the text of Scripture, but also from the geologic record of the Flood. It has been amply argued that the fossil-bearing sedimentary rock layers in the geologic record resulted from the Flood waters rising up over the continents and progressively burying different pre-Flood eco-systems and biological communities (figure 1).[6] Just as today there are different

5. Steven A. Austin, John R. Baumgardner, D. Russell Humphreys, Andrew A. Snelling, Larry Vardiman, and Kurt P. Wise, "Catastrophic Plate Tectonics: A Global Flood Model of Earth History," in *Proceedings of the Third International Conference on Creationism*, Robert E. Walsh, ed. (Pittsburgh, PA: Creation Science Fellowship, 1994), p. 609–621.
6. Harold W. Clark, *The New Diluvialism* (Angwin, CA: Science Publications, 1946); Harold G. Coffin, *Origin by Design* (Hagerstown, MD: Review and Herald Publishing

biological communities at different elevations because they are suited to those different micro-climates, it was likely the same in the pre-Flood world. Today, the rims of the Grand Canyon are covered in pine forests with squirrels, deer, and other animals, but as one hikes down into the canyon, with the loss in elevation and increasing temperatures, the biological communities gradually change, until at the bottom of the canyon the predominant vegetation is cacti typical of a desert, with different animals, such as ringtails, and seasonally, big-horn sheep.

In the fossil record, for example, dinosaur fossils are primarily found only in association with "naked seed" plants (gymnosperms) that do not have flowers, such as cycads and gingkoes. Flowering plants (angiosperms) are only rarely found fossilized with dinosaurs, and instead are found higher in the fossil record buried with mammal fossils. This potentially suggests that in the pre-Flood world there was a mammal-angiosperm biological community at higher elevations, geographically separated from a dinosaur-gymnosperm biological community at lower elevations.[7] We can conclude this difference in elevations between these two different biological communities (biomes) in the pre-Flood world because the dinosaur-gymnosperm biome would have been buried first as the Flood waters rose higher over the continents. Also, this difference in elevations between these two biomes thus likely not only reflects different elevations, but different climatic conditions for each biological community.

Furthermore, it is clear from the description of Adam's life in the Garden of Eden that the garden contained fruit trees (angiosperms) and beasts of the field that he named (mainly mammals). As well, the inference has already been noted that the garden was at a higher elevation, because the river running through it flowed downhill out of it and divided into four other rivers. Thus the mammal-angiosperm biological community must have been at the generally cooler higher elevations in the pre-Flood world. That would have meant the geographically separated dinosaur-gymnosperm biological community was

Association, 1983); Andrew A. Snelling, "Doesn't the Order of Fossils in the Rock Record Favor Long Ages?" in *The New Answers Book 2*, Ken Ham, gen. ed. (Green Forest, AR: Master Books, 2008), p. 341–354; Kurt P. Wise, "Exotic Communities Buried by the Flood," *Answers* (October–December 2008): p. 44–45; Andrew A. Snelling, "Order in the Fossil Record," *Answers* (January–March 2010): p. 64–68; Andrew A. Snelling, "Paleontological Issues: Deciphering the Fossil Record of the Flood and Its Aftermath," in *Grappling with the Chronology of the Genesis Flood*, Steven W. Boyd and Andrew A. Snelling, eds. (Green Forest, AR: Master Books, 2013).

7. Kurt P. Wise, *Faith, Form, and Time* (Nashville, TN: Broadman and Holman Publishers, 2002), p. 173–174.

likely found in generally warmer lowland areas. Of course, the Scriptures are clear that dinosaurs and humans lived at the same time, because dinosaurs as land animals were created on day 6 of the creation week, just before man was created.

So based on all of this discussion of what we can glean from Scripture and from the geologic record about the pre-Flood world, we can answer part of the posed question. Clearly, there were mountains in the pre-Flood world, because it was those mountains that Genesis 7:20 describes as being eventually covered by the Flood waters. However, while we cannot dogmatically say that those mountains were not high, the scriptural evidence would suggest that the pre-Flood mountains were not as high as today's mountains. The latter were formed and thrust up to their current elevations by the catastrophic mountain-building processes during the Flood, when some fossil-bearing Flood-deposited sedimentary rock layers were buckled and then elevated. The hints in Scripture suggest that there were conducive climatic conditions around the globe to support the lush vegetation worldwide that was subsequently buried *en masse* and fossilized to form the coal beds during the Flood. This would likely have precluded high mountains and major elevation and climate differences in the pre-Flood world, as would also the lack of mention of any ice or snow in the Scriptures describing the pre-Flood world.

Volcanoes and Earthquakes

The issue of whether there were any volcanoes and earthquakes in the pre-Flood world is a lot harder to discern because there is no mention of them in the scriptural account, unlike the mountains. Today volcanic eruptions and earthquakes often result in destruction and loss of life, including *nephesh*-bearing animal life. However, prior to the Fall and the resultant Curse, we would have to assert that there were no physical events that would have resulted in the death of any *nephesh*-bearing creatures. In Genesis 1:31, at the end of day 6 of the creation week, God declared that all He has made was "very good," with animals and man eating only plants. And Paul reminds us in Romans 8:20–22 that today's world is subject to corruption and death because of man's sin. So these scriptural details would seem to preclude the possibility of volcanoes and earthquakes in the pre-Flood world.

It is certainly true that there are no fossils of *nephesh*-bearing animals in the geologic record below the fossil-bearing sedimentary rock layers that represent such powerful evidence of the Flood cataclysm, when the ocean waters flooded over the continents and all land-dwelling, air-breathing, *nephesh*-bearing animals outside the ark perished (Genesis 7:17–24). However, the geologic record may still give us some clues.

The rocks found below where the evidence of the Flood begins are very thick and extensive. They are foundational to the structure of today's continents. Yet they also represent the astounding results of God's creative activity during the creation week to build the land on which would be man's home, followed by the minor, non-destructive geologic activity of the pre-Flood world. Obviously, there could not have been any catastrophic geologic activity across the earth after God created the dry land on day 3 of the creation week, because any such catastrophic geologic activity would have impacted the sea creatures, the land creatures, and man that God created on days 5 and 6. This matches the lack of any such fossils in the geologic record of the creation week and pre-Flood eras.

What we do see in some pre-Flood era sedimentary rocks that is relevant to understanding the topography and environmental conditions in the pre-Flood world are occasional fossilized stromatolites, layered structures probably built by algal mats.[8] Today's rare living stromatolites are usually found in intertidal zones and on the shallow sea floor where the algal mats trap and bind sediment particles to build these structures. The fossilized stromatolites found in pre-Flood era sedimentary rocks usually occur in thick sequences of limestones and related rocks, including cherts, unusual rocks likely produced from hot water springs. Thus, it has been proposed that in the pre-Flood world there could have been a unique ecosystem consisting of stromatolite reefs built in association with hydrothermal springs on the shallow ocean floor some distance from, and fringing, the coastline of the pre-Flood supercontinent and enclosing a wide, shallow lagoon inhabited by now-extinct unusual marine invertebrates.[9] Confirming evidence of just such a stromatolite reef has been documented in what have been interpreted as pre-Flood shallow ocean floor sedimentary rock layers now exposed in the eastern Grand Canyon.[10]

8. Georgia Purdom and Andrew A. Snelling, "Survey of Microbial Composition and Mechanisms of Living Stromatolites of the Bahamas and Australia: Developing Criteria to Determine the Biogenicity of Fossil Stromatolites," in *Proceedings of the Seventh International Conference on Creationism*, Mark F. Horstemeyer, ed. (Pittsburgh, PA: Creation Science Fellowship, 2013).

9. Kurt P. Wise, "The Hydrothermal Biome: A Pre-Flood Environment," in *Proceedings of the Fifth International Conference on Creationism*, Robert L. Ivey, ed. (Pittsburgh, PA: Creation Science Fellowship, 2003), p. 359–370.

10. Kurt P. Wise and Andrew A. Snelling, "A Note on the Pre-Flood/Flood Boundary in the Grand Canyon," *Origins* (Geoscience Research Institute) 58 (2005): p. 7–29.

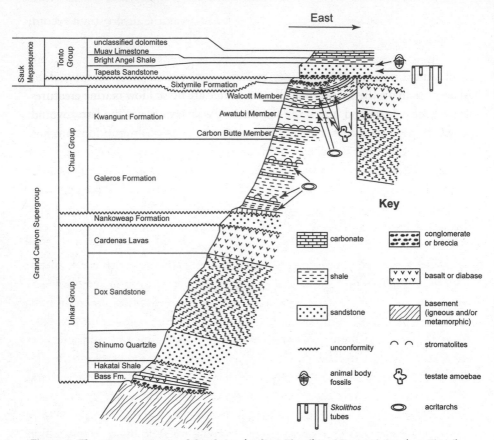

Figure 2. The strata sequence of Cambrian (earliest Flood) and Precambrian (pre-Flood) sedimentary rock layers of eastern Grand Canyon, schematically showing the relative position of the Cardenas Basalt lavas and the strata thicknesses to scale.

However, none of these details from both Scripture and the geologic record precludes the possibility of minor volcanic eruptions of a non-explosive nature on the deeper ocean floor of the pre-Flood world, well away from the creatures that inhabited the shallow ocean floor surrounding the pre-Flood supercontinent. For example, in the eastern Grand Canyon exposed among the pre-Flood rocks are lava flows of the Cardenas Basalt (figure 2).[11] They outcrop not

---

11. Steven A. Austin and Andrew A. Snelling, "Discordant Potassium-Argon Model and Isochron 'Ages' for Cardenas Basalt (Middle Proterozoic) and Associated Diabase of Eastern Grand Canyon, Arizona," in *Proceedings of the Fourth International Conference on Creationism*, p. 35–51; J.D. Hendricks and G.M. Stevenson, "Grand Canyon Supergroup: Unkar Group," in Stanley S. Beus and Michael Morales, eds., *Grand Canyon Geology*, 2nd ed. (New York, NY: Oxford University Press, 2003), p. 39–52.

far below the pre-Flood/Flood boundary in the Grand Canyon strata record. Above the Cardenas Basalt lava flows are the sedimentary rock layers containing evidence that they accumulated on the pre-Flood ocean floor, including the fossilized stromatolite reef originally built by algal mats on the shallow sea-floor adjacent to hydrothermal springs. Because there are no shallow marine creatures in the rocks above and below the Cardenas Basalt lava flows, the latter would appear to have erupted on the deeper ocean floor. As basalt eruptions are not explosive and these erupted on the deep ocean floor, then no destruction of animal life would have resulted. So there would have been no impact from these volcanic eruptions on the pre-Flood land surface to affect land animals and man.

Nevertheless, earthquakes usually accompany the lead-up to volcanic eruptions, due to the molten rock moving up inside the earth into the throat of the volcano. It is because of such earthquakes that volcanologists are able to predict and warn of impeding volcanic eruptions. Thus, since there were likely such volcanic eruptions during the pre-Flood era, we cannot rule out the possibility of accompanying earthquakes. Whether they were felt by the people living at the time, we have no indication whatsoever. But if such volcanic eruptions were only on the deep ocean floor, far away from the pre-Flood supercontinent, then it is not likely the people noticed any of the accompanying earthquakes. From what we can glean from the scriptural comments about life in the pre-Flood era, people were so engrossed in the pursuit of pleasure and sin (Genesis 6:5, 11–12), as well as the normal routines of living (as Jesus said in Matthew 24:37–39; Luke 17:26–27), ignoring Noah's preaching (2 Peter 2:5), that they had no premonition of the Flood coming from any earthquakes or volcanic eruptions until it was too late — "the Flood came, and took them all away" (Matthew 24:39).

Conclusions

While the Scriptures are silent on the issue of whether there were any volcanoes or earthquakes in the world before the Flood, we do know there were mountains. Since all the high hills and mountains are specifically mentioned as being inundated by the waters of the Flood as they prevailed during the first 40 days of that global cataclysm, then mountains must have existed in the pre-Flood world. But those mountains were likely not nearly as high as today's mountains (formed out of buckled Flood-deposited rock layers that were then uplifted), because the pre-Flood mountains were evidently upland areas like the Garden of Eden inhabited by flowering plants, mammals, and people.

On the other hand, we have to infer rather sketchily from the geologic record that there were likely some volcanic eruptions accompanied by earthquakes in the pre-Flood world, but these occurred far away from human habitations out on the deep ocean floor, where they had no impact on people or animals. In all probability, there were no mountainous volcanoes across the pre-Flood land surface like we have scattered across today's world, and thus no devastating earthquakes and volcanic eruptions. Since there are no fossils of *nephesh*-bearing creatures in pre-Flood rocks, the pre-Flood earth was likely very stable with no major catastrophes.

CHAPTER 24

What about Beneficial Mutations?

DR. GEORGIA PURDOM

Many claim that beneficial mutations provide examples of "evolution in action." These mutations supposedly result in the formation of "major innovations" and "rare and complex traits"[1] that over time have resulted in the evolution of all living things from a common ancestor. However, analyses of these mutations show they only result in variations in *pre-existing* traits, traits that organisms already possess, and cannot result in the *origin of* novel traits necessary for molecules-to-man evolution.

All You Need Is Novelty!

For a simple, single-celled ancestor to evolve into a human over billions of years, novel traits must be gained. New anatomical structures — like brains, arms, and legs — and new functions — like cardiovascular and muscle activities — must be acquired. Regardless of whether this is proposed to occur through beneficial mutations that result in the addition of new DNA, changes in existing DNA, or through other mechanisms, there must be a way to add novel traits. However, all observed mechanisms, including beneficial mutations, do just the opposite — they cause the loss of or slight variation in *pre-existing*

---

1. Bob Holmes, "Bacteria Make Major Evolutionary Shift in the Lab," *New Scientist* (June 2008), http://www.newscientist.com/article/dn14094-bacteria-make-major-evolutionary-shift-in-the-lab.html.

traits.[2] Beneficial mutations and other mechanisms cannot account for the *origin of* novel traits of the type necessary for molecules-to-man evolution. In a paper entitled "A Golden Age for Evolutionary Genetics? Genomic Studies of Adaptation in Natural Populations," the authors (who are evolutionists) agree that the lack of mechanisms to add novel traits is a problem: "Most studies of recent evolution involve the loss of traits, and we still understand little of the genetic changes needed in the origin of novel traits."[3]

In this paper, the scientists give many examples of variations in organisms such as pattern changes in butterfly wings, loss of bony structures in stickleback fish, loss of eyes in cavefish, and adaptations to temperature and altitude. But none of these examples involve the *origin of* novel traits necessary to evolve into a different kind of organism. Again, they realize this problem and state, ". . . over the broad sweep of evolutionary time what we would really like to explain is the gain of complexity and the origins of novel adaptations."[4]

Their frustration with the lack of evidence for "novelty-gaining" mechanisms like beneficial mutations sinks to apparent desperation when they state, "Of course, to some extent the difference between loss and gain could be a question of semantics, so for example the loss of trichomes [hair-like appendages on flies] could be called gain of naked cuticle."[5] The authors have decided that the whole loss/gain issue is merely one of semantics! In order to get the gain required by molecules-to-man evolution they will just change the wording and say it is a "gain of loss."

That's equivalent to a person who has suddenly lost all their money saying, "I've not lost money; I've just gained poverty!" While it makes the person sound optimistic, it doesn't change the fact that they have lost all their money. In the same way, an organism doesn't gain novel traits needed to evolve into something else — instead, organisms lose traits or develop variations in *pre-existing* traits. It doesn't matter how evolutionists choose to say it; there is still no mechanism that results in the *origin of* novel traits required for molecules-to-man evolution.

---

2. Kevin L. Anderson and Georgia Purdom, "A Creationist Perspective of Beneficial Mutations in Bacteria," in the *Proceedings of the Sixth International Conference on Creationism* (Pittsburgh, PA: Creation Science Fellowship, 2008): p. 73–86.
3. Nicola J. Nadeau and Chris D. Jiggins, "A Golden Age for Evolutionary Genetics? Genomic Studies of Adaptation in Natural Populations," *Trends in Genetics* 26 (2010): p. 484–492.
4. Ibid.
5. Ibid.

Do Beneficial Mutations Exist?

While beneficial mutations may not result in the *origin of* novel traits necessary to go from molecules to man, they do exist . . . sort of. Let me explain. It is more appropriate to say that some mutations have beneficial *outcomes* in certain environments. Mutations are context dependent, meaning their environment determines whether the outcome of the mutation is beneficial. One well-known example of a proposed beneficial mutation is antibiotic resistance in bacteria.[6] In an environment where antibiotics are present, mutations in the bacterial DNA allow the bacteria to survive. However, these same mutations come at the cost of damaging the normal functions of the bacteria (such as the ability to break down nutrients). If the antibiotics are removed, the antibiotic resistant bacteria typically do not fare as well as the normal (or wild-type) bacteria that have not been affected by mutations. Thus, the benefit of any given mutation is not an independent quality, but rather a dependent quality based on the environment.

Another common example of a supposed beneficial mutation, this time in humans, is individuals that are resistant to infection with HIV. These people have a mutation that prevents HIV from entering the white blood cells and replicating, making them unlikely to develop AIDS. However, studies have shown these individuals may be at a higher risk of developing illness associated with West Nile virus[7] and hepatitis C[8] (also caused by a virus). Again, we see that the mutations are only beneficial in a given environment, such as if the person were exposed to HIV. It is possible that the mutations would not be beneficial in other environments such as if the person were exposed to West Nile virus. The benefit of any given mutation is a dependent quality based on the environment.

There is no question that mutations can be beneficial in certain environments, but do they lead to the *origin of* novel traits of the type necessary for molecules-to-man evolution? Let's look at several examples commonly used to support this idea and the problems with them.

---

6. Georgia Purdom, "Is Natural Selection the Same Thing as Evolution?" in *The New Answers Book 1*, ed. Ken Ham (Green Forest, AR: Master Books, 2006), p. 271–282.
7. William G. Glass et al., "CCR5 Deficiency Increases Risk of Symptomatic West Nile Virus Infection," *The Journal of Experimental Medicine* 203 (2006): p. 35–40.
8. Golo Ahlenstiel, et al., "CC-chemokine Receptor 5 (CCR5) in Hepatitis C- at the Crossroads of the Antiviral Immune Response?" *Journal of Antimicrobial Chemotherapy* 53 (2004): 895–898.

Proposed Beneficial Mutations in Bacteria

Richard Lenski and the Citrate Mutation in *E. coli*

In 1988, Dr. Richard Lenski, an evolutionary biologist at Michigan State University, began culturing 12 identical lines of *Escherichia coli* (a common gut bacteria). Over 50,000 generations and 25 years later, the experiment continues. Lenski has observed many changes in the *E. coli* as they adapt to the culture conditions in his lab. For example, some lines have lost the ability to break down ribose (a sugar),[9] some have lost the ability to repair DNA,[10] and some have reduced ability to form flagella (needed for movement).[11] In other words, they've gotten lazy as they've adapted to life in the lab! If they were grown in a natural setting with their wild-type (normal) counterparts, they would not stand a chance in competing for resources.

In 2008, Lenski's lab discovered another change in one of their lines of *E. coli*. A *New Scientist* writer proclaimed, "A major innovation has unfurled right in front of researchers' eyes. It's the first time evolution has been caught in the act of making such a rare and complex new trait."[12] But was this change really the formation of "a rare and complex new trait"?

Normal *E. coli* has the ability to utilize citrate as a carbon and energy source when *oxygen levels are low*. They transport citrate into the cell and break it down. Lenski's lab discovered that one of their *E. coli* lines could now utilize citrate under *normal oxygen levels*.[13] It's easy to see that this was not "a major innovation" or the "making of a rare and complex new trait" because the normal *E. coli* already has the ability to transport citrate into the cell and use it! This was simply a beneficial outcome of mutations that changed under what conditions citrate was used by *E. coli*.[14] The mutations caused the alteration of a *pre-existing* system, not the *origin of* a novel one. There is a lot of citrate in the medium that the bacteria are grown in, and since other

9. Vaughn S. Cooper et al., "Mechanisms Causing Rapid and Parallel Losses of Ribose Catabolism in Evolving Populations of *E. coli* B," *Journal of Bacteriology* 183 (2001): 2834–2841.
10. Paul Sniegowski et al., "Evolution of High Mutation Rates in Experimental Populations of *E. coli*," *Nature* 387 (1997): 703–705.
11. Tim F. Cooper et al., "Parallel Changes in Gene Expression after 20,000 Generations of Evolution in *E. coli*," *PNAS* 100 (2003): 1072–1077.
12. Holmes, "Bacteria Make Major Evolutionary Shift in the Lab."
13. Zachary Blount et al., "Historical Contingency and the Evolution of a Key Innovation in an Experimental Population of *Escherichia coli*," *PNAS* 105 (2008): 7899–7906.
14. Zachary Blount et al., "Genomic Analysis of a Key Innovation in an Experimental *Escherichia coli* Population," *Nature* 489 (2012): 513–518.

carbon sources are not plentiful, the bacteria have merely adapted to the lab conditions.

Lenski stated, "It is clearly very difficult for *E. coli* to evolve this function. In fact, the mutation rate of the ancestral strain . . . is immeasurably low. . . ."[15] If developing the ability to utilize citrate under different conditions by altering the *pre-existing* citrate system is so rare, then how much more improbable is it to believe that similar beneficial mutations can lead to the *origin of* novel traits necessary for dinosaurs to evolve into birds!

Nylon-Digesting Mutation in Bacteria

In the mid-1970s, bacteria (*Arthrobacter* sp. K172) were discovered in ponds with wastewater from a nylon factory that could digest the byproducts of nylon manufacture. Nylon is a synthetic polymer that was first produced in the 1940s, thus, the ability of bacteria to break down nylon must have been gained in the last few decades. Many evolutionists touted that the bacteria's ability to break down nylon occurred through the gain of new genes and proteins. In a 1985 article entitled "New Proteins Without God's Help," the author explained testing that supposedly showed the bacteria's ability to break down nylon was due to the formation of new proteins, not the modification of pre-existing ones.[16] In conclusion he stated, "All of this demonstrates that . . . the creationists . . . and others who should know better are dead wrong about the near-zero probability of new enzyme formation. Biologically useful macromolecules are not so information-rich that they could not form spontaneously without God's help."[17]

Does this mean that biblical creationists should run screaming and stick our heads into the sand? No. In 2007, genetic analyses of *Arthrobacter* sp. K172 showed that no new genes or proteins had been added that resulted in the ability of the bacteria to break down nylon.[18] Instead it was discovered that mutations in a *pre-existing* gene resulted in a protein that is capable of breaking down nylon. The protein, known as EII, normally breaks down a substance very similar to nylon. Slight alterations in what is called the "active site" of the protein (where the activity of breaking down the substance occurs) changed its

---

15. Blount et al., "Historical Contingency and the Evolution of a Key Innovation in an Experimental Population of *Escherichia coli*," 7899–7906.
16. William M. Thwaites, "New Proteins without God's Help," *Creation Evolution Journal* 5 (1985): 1–3.
17. Ibid.
18. Seiji Negoro et al., "Nylon-oligomer Degrading Enzyme/Substrate Complex: Catalytic Mechanism of 6-aminohexanoate-dimer hydrolase," *Journal of Molecular Biology* 370 (2007): 142–156.

specificity such that it could now also break down nylon. No changes occurred of the type necessary to go from molecules to man, just a "tweak" in a gene and protein whose normal function is to break down something very similar to nylon. Again, we see the alteration of a *pre-existing* gene and protein, not the *origin of* new ones. Information-rich molecules like DNA and protein cannot spontaneously form — they do need "God's help."

Barry Hall and the *ebg* Mutation in *E. coli*

Beginning in the 1970s and continuing into the 1990s, Dr. Barry Hall, professor emeritus of the University of Rochester, New York, did extensive work in the field of what has been termed adaptive or directed mutations. According to evolutionary ideas, mutations are random changes in the DNA that may or may not be beneficial to an organism in its environment. However, research from scientists like Hall has indicated that adverse environmental conditions, like starvation, may initiate mechanisms in bacteria that result in mutations that *specifically* allow the bacteria to survive and grow in a given environment. These changes do not appear to be random in respect to the environment, thus the term directed or adaptive mutations.

There are two reasons why adaptive mutations are problematic for evolution. First, the mechanisms in bacteria for generating adaptive mutations are specifically responding to the environment. The changes are goal-oriented, allowing the organism to adapt and survive by alteration of *pre-existing* traits. A second reason is that the mechanisms resulting in adaptive mutations (which appear to be a very common type of mutation in bacteria) set limits on the genetic change possible and cannot account for the *origin of* novel traits.

E. coli can break down the sugar lactose to use as a food source. Hall was able to mutate a strain of *E. coli* such that it lost the ability to break down lactose.[19] He then put the mutant *E. coli* in a starvation situation where lactose was the only food source. In order to survive, the *E. coli* either had to develop the ability to break down lactose or die. After a period of time, *E. coli* developed the ability to break down lactose. How did *E. coli* do this? Were new genes and proteins added to allow this to happen?

No. Genetic analyses showed that mutations had occurred in a group of *pre-existing* genes named *ebg*. These genes are in normal *E. coli* and produce proteins that very weakly break down lactose. The genes were also present in

---

19. Georgia Purdom and Kevin L. Anderson, "Analysis of Barry Hall's Research of the *E. coli ebg* Operon," in the *Proceedings of the Sixth International Conference on Creationism* (Pittsburgh, PA: Creation Science Fellowship, 2008): p. 149–163.

Hall's mutant *E. coli* (he mutated only the primary set of genes used for lactose breakdown *not* the *ebg* genes). In response to the starvation conditions, mechanisms were initiated in the bacteria that resulted in mutations in the *ebg* genes that produced proteins with enhanced ability to break down lactose well enough that the mutant bacteria could survive. No new or novel traits were gained, there was merely the alteration of a *pre-existing* trait that allowed the bacteria to adapt and survive.

Interestingly, Hall theorized that if both the primary set of genes needed for lactose breakdown and the *ebg* genes were made non-functional (through mutations) that adaptive mutations would occur in *other* genes resulting in *E. coli* once again developing the ability to break down lactose.[20] However, "despite extensive efforts," Hall was unable to get *E. coli* that could survive on lactose. They did not survive because adaptive mutations only make *limited* changes. *Ebg* genes in *E. coli* already possess the ability to break down lactose, adaptive mutations enhanced this ability. Adaptive mutations cannot make possible the *origin of* lactose breakdown from genes whose functions are not as similar.

Despite the evidence, Hall concluded this aspect of his research by saying, "Obviously, given a sufficient number of substitutions, additions, and deletions, the sequence of any gene can evolve into the sequence of any other gene."[21] But Hall's own experiments showed otherwise — a gene cannot just become a completely different gene; adaptive mutations are limited. Mutations can cause changes in *pre-existing* traits, but observable mechanisms, such as adaptive mutation, cannot account for the *origin of* novel traits necessary for molecules-to-man evolution.

Proposed Beneficial Mutations in Animals

TRIM5-CypA Mutation in Monkeys

The *TRIM5* gene is found in humans, monkeys, and other mammals. The protein produced from this gene binds to the outer covering (capsid) of retroviruses (like HIV) and prevents them from replicating inside cells, thus essentially preventing the spread of infection. A portion of the *TRIM5* gene (C-terminal domain) seems especially variable and may confer resistance to different types of viruses.[22] In 2004, it was discovered that owl monkeys (*Aotus* sp.) have a unique

---

20. Barry G. Hall, "Evolutionary Potential of the *ebgA* Gene," *Molecular Biology and Evolution* 12 (1995): 514–517.
21. Ibid.
22. Welkin E. Johnson and Sara L. Sawyer, "Molecular Evolution of the Antiretroviral *TRIM5* Gene," *Immunogenetics* 61 (2009): 163–176.

version of the *TRIM5* gene that appears to be a fusion of this gene to the nearby *CypA* gene.[23] The *CypA* gene can produce a protein that also binds to the outer covering of viruses, including HIV. Thus, the *TRIM5-CypA* fusion protein has the antiviral activity of *TRIM5* coupled to the HIV recognition of *CypA* and the fused protein was able to prevent infection from HIV. (A similar fusion gene/protein has also been discovered in certain species of macaques.)[24]

New Scientist writer Michael Le Page in an article entitled "Evolution Myths: Mutations Can only Destroy Information," stated in regard to this mutation, "Here, a single mutation has resulted in a new protein with a new and potentially vital function. New protein, new function, new information."[25] But is this really a new protein with a new function?

No. *TRIM5-CypA* is the fusion of two *pre-existing* genes producing a fused protein. The fusion doesn't change the function of *TRIM5* or *CypA*, so there is no new function. The addition of *CypA* merely allows *TRIM5* to recognize a different group of viruses and exert its antiviral activity against those viruses. This fusion does not result in the *origin of* a novel trait of the type necessary for molecules-to-man evolution.

Gene Duplication, Mutation, and "New" Genes and Functions

Evolutionists often cite gene duplication, followed by subsequent mutation of the duplicated gene, as a mechanism for adding new genes with new functions to organisms. The idea is that the duplicated gene is free to mutate and gain new functions because the original copy of the gene can still perform the original function. Evolutionary biologist Dr. Sean Carroll, referring to his work on gene duplication in yeast, stated, "This is how new capabilities arise and new functions evolve. This is what goes on in butterflies and elephants and humans. It is evolution in action."[26] However, a deeper look at a couple of examples of gene duplication and mutation show exactly the opposite — the complete impotence of these mechanisms to explain the *origin of* novel traits necessary for molecules-to-man evolution.

---

23. Sébastien Nisole, "A Trim5-cyclophilin A Fusion Protein Found in Owl Monkey Kidney Cells Can Restrict HIV-1," *PNAS* 101 (2004): 13324–13328.
24. Cheng-Hong Liao et al., "A Novel Fusion Gene, *TRIM5-cyclophilin A* in the Pig-tailed Macaque Determines Its Susceptibility to HIV-1 Infection, *AIDS* 21 (2007): S19–S26.
25. Michael Le Page, "Evolution Myths: Mutations Can only Destroy Information," *New Scientist*, April 2008, http://www.newscientist.com/article/dn13673-evolution-myths-mutations-can-only-destroy-information.html.
26. Terry Devitt, "A Gene Divided Reveals Details of Natural Selection," *University of Wisconsin-Madison News*, October 10, 2007, http://www.news.wisc.edu/14276.

RNASE1 and *1B* in Monkeys

The diet of most monkeys consists of fruit and insects; however, the colobine monkeys predominantly eat leaves. These monkeys have a special foregut that harbors symbiotic bacteria that help in the digestion of the leaves. *RNASE1* is a digestive enzyme in colobines that breaks down RNA from the bacteria in the foregut. This results in the efficient recycling of phosphorus and nitrogen that are used in the production of the monkey's own proteins and nucleic acids like DNA and RNA.

It has been shown that some colobines have two RNASE genes—*RNASE1* and *RNASE1B*.[27] *RNASE1B* is proposed to be a duplication of the gene *RNASE1*. There are several differences in the genes and the proteins produced, however, the function remains the *same*. Both enzymes break down RNA, but the changes in RNASE1B allow it to break down RNA in more acidic conditions such as those found in the foregut of the monkeys. The authors of one study of the *RNASE1* genes commented, "Gene duplication has long been thought by evolutionary biologists to be the source of novel gene function. . . . We believe our data to be another example that do not support this hypothesis."[28] Other authors of similar research indicate: "Taken together, our results provide evidence of the important contribution of gene duplication to adaptation of organisms to their environments."[29] The differences (caused by mutations) in the *RNASE1B* gene appear to enhance the *pre-existing* function of the original *RNASE1* gene, resulting in adaptation, and do not represent the type of mutation necessary for the *origin of* novel traits needed for molecules-to-man evolution.

Antifreeze Proteins in Fish

Antifreeze proteins (AFPs) prevent the growth of ice crystals in organisms that live in very cold environments such as the Arctic and Antarctica. There are five classes of these proteins found in fish. AFP type III is found in the Antarctic zoarcid fish. The *AFPIII* gene is proposed to be a duplication of a portion of the *SAS* (sialic acid synthase) gene.[30] The *SAS* gene is responsible for the synthesis

27. John E. Schienman, et al., "Duplication and Divergence of 2 Distinct Pancreatic Ribonuclease Genes in Leaf-eating African and Asian Colobine Monkeys," *Molecular Biology and Evolution*, 23 (2006): 1465–1479.
28. Ibid.
29. Jianzhi Zhang, et al., "Adaptive Evolution of a Duplicated Pancreatic Ribonuclease Gene in a Leaf-eating Monkey," *Nature Genetics* 30 (2002): p. 411–415.
30. Cheng Deng, "Evolution of an Antifreeze Protein by Neofunctionalization under Escape from Adaptive Conflict," *PNAS* 107 (2010): 21593–21598.

of sialic acids (found on cell surfaces) but *also* has an antifreeze function. Mutations in the *AFPIII* gene (a duplicate copy of a portion of the *SAS* gene) appear to have further enhanced the antifreeze function.

One of the authors of the study on the formation of the *AFPIII* gene commented, "This is the first clear demonstration . . . [of] the underlying process of gene duplication and the creation of a completely new function in one of the daughter [duplicate] copies."[31] But the *AFPIII* protein does not have a "completely new function"! Instead the *AFPIII* gene is likely the result of a duplication of a portion of the *pre-existing SAS* gene with mutations that enhanced the *SAS* gene's *pre-existing* antifreeze function. Once again, we see that the differences (caused by mutations) in the *AFPIII* gene appear to enhance the *pre-existing* antifreeze function of the original *SAS* gene resulting in adaptation to the environment and do not represent the type of mutation necessary for the *origin of* novel traits needed for molecules-to-man evolution.

Beneficial Mutations from a Biblical Creation Perspective

The previous examples show that there can be beneficial outcomes to mutations. However, these mutations can only alter *pre-existing* traits; they cannot result in the *origin of* novel traits necessary for molecules-to-man evolution. In every example, it appears that the mutations help organisms in adapting to a specific environment. This is easily seen in bacteria when they are faced with limited food choices and must gain the ability to break down a different nutrient or die. It is also seen in animals like monkeys and fish that have essentially become more specialized for eating a particular diet or living in a particular environment.

But are these mutations random in respect to the environment? On the Evolution 101 website, sponsored by the University of California Museum of Paleontology, it states:

> The mechanisms of evolution — like natural selection and genetic drift — work with the *random* variation generated by mutation. (emphasis in original)
>
> For example, exposure to harmful chemicals may increase the mutation rate, but will not cause more mutations that make the organism resistant to those chemicals. In this respect, mutations are random —

---

31. Diana Yates, "Researchers Show how One Gene Becomes Two (with Different Functions)," University of Illinois at Urbana-Champaign News Bureau, January 12, 2011, http://www.news.illinois.edu/news/11/0112genes_cheng.html.

whether a particular mutation happens or not is generally unrelated to how useful that mutation would be.[32]

The basis of molecules-to-man evolution is random mutation in conjunction with other mechanisms like natural selection. However, mutations with beneficial outcomes do not appear to be random or at least the mechanisms generating the mutations are not random. From a biblical creation perspective, this could be a type of adaptive variation that God has designed in organisms to allow them to survive in a world dramatically changed by the Fall and Flood. Rather than the changes being random, organisms have been "pre-programmed" to change in response to their environment.

These types of adaptive traits may be the result of what creationists have termed *mediated design*. Several creation scientists describe it this way:

> God specifically designed the created kinds with genes [in the DNA] that could be turned on to help them adapt to new environments. In other words, the Creator continues to accomplish His purpose for organisms after creation, not by creating something new, but by working through existing parts that were designed during Creation Week. An analogy is the manufacturer of a fully equipped Swiss army knife, who stores within the knife every tool a camper might need as he faces the unknown challenges of wilderness living.[33]

God designed adaptive traits to be expressed only under certain conditions to allow microbes, animals, plants, and humans to fill the earth as environments changed over time (Genesis 1 and 8:16–19). Thus, God programmed organisms with mechanisms that would be triggered under certain conditions that would then modify *pre-existing* traits to allow organisms to survive and thrive in new environments. Possible mechanisms to accomplish this are seen in the previous examples with directed mutations (*ebg* and *E. coli*) and duplication followed by mutation (*RNASE1* and *1B* in monkeys). Another exciting area of modern genetics research is the role of epigenetics in modifying how genes and, thus, the physical traits, are expressed. Epigenetic markers, chemical tags on DNA, have been shown to be heritable and may be a way to pass on modified traits to future generations (see postscript). Understanding the God-given ability of organisms to change and adapt is an active area of creation research.

---

32. "Mutations Are Random," Evolution 101, http://evolution.berkeley.edu/evosite/evo101/ IIIC1aRandom.shtml.

33. Tom Hennigan, Georgia Purdom, and Todd Charles Wood, "Creation's Hidden Potential," *Answers*, January–March 2009, p. 70–75.

But what adaptive variations can't do is change one kind of organism into a completely different kind of organism because they do not result in the *origin of* novel traits needed for this type of change. This is consistent with Scripture because God created animals and plants according to their kind (usually at the family level in modern classification schemes).[34] The inference from Scripture is that animals were to reproduce according to their kind (Genesis 1, 6, and 8). We observe mechanisms that allow animals and plants to adapt but not evolve into different kinds of organisms.

So why, in spite of all the evidence to the contrary, do many scientists, who are unbelievers, argue that beneficial mutations are a valid mechanism (as evidenced by their quotes) to account for the *origin of* novel traits resulting in molecules-to-man evolution? Paul says that God can be known through what He has created (Romans 1:20), but just before that Paul states why people don't acknowledge God as the Creator: "For the wrath of God is revealed from heaven against all ungodliness and unrighteousness of men, who *suppress the truth in unrighteousness*" (Romans 1:18, emphasis added). Just as Pharaoh hardened his heart repeatedly (1 Samuel 6:6), today, people's hearts have been hardened in their willful rebellion against God. They want to continue in their sin and will go to extremes to "deny the obvious" and reject God as the Creator.

God, in His mercy, compassion, and grace, designed living organisms with the ability to adapt and fill, survive and thrive in a fallen world. We look forward to the day when all life will be restored to perfection and the wolf will live with the lamb, the lion will eat straw like an ox, and a baby will play by the cobra's hole (Isaiah 11:6–8).

Postscript: Epigenetics – Inheriting More Than Genes

All our lives, we've heard that our physical makeup is determined by our genes, not environment. But the science of epigenetics is forcing scientists to rethink their assumptions.

You're probably familiar with the phrase, "You are what you eat." But did you know that you are also what your mother and grandmother ate? The budding science of epigenetics shows that our physical makeup is about much more than inheriting our mother's eyes or our father's smile.

We are accustomed to thinking that the only thing we inherit from our parents are genes — packets of information in DNA that give instructions for

---

34. Jean K. Lightner et al., "Determining the Ark Kinds," *Answers Research Journal* 4 (2011): 195–201.

proteins. These genes determine our physical traits such as hair and eye color, height, and even susceptibility to disease.

But we also inherit specific "modifications" of our DNA in the form of chemical tags. These influence how the genes express our physical traits. The chemical tags are referred to as "epigenetic" markers because they exist outside of (*epi-*) the actual sequence of DNA (*-genetics*).

Let me use an analogy to explain. The following sentence can have two very different meanings, depending on the punctuation used. "A woman, without her man, is nothing" or "A woman: Without her, man is nothing." Perhaps it's a silly illustration, but it gets the point across.

The words of both sentences are the same, but the meaning is different because of the punctuation. The same is true for DNA and its chemical tags. The sequence of DNA can be identical but produce different results based on the presence or absence of epigenetic markers. For example, identical twins have the same DNA sequence but can have different chemical tags leading one to be susceptible to certain diseases but not the other.

Parents can pass down epigenetic markers for many generations or their effect can be short-lived, lasting only to the next generation. Either way, the changes are temporary because they do not alter the sequence of DNA, just the way DNA is expressed.

What does this mean in practice? Your behavior, including the food you eat, could change how your body expresses its DNA. Then those changes — for good or bad — could be passed to your children! If you do something to increase your susceptibility to obesity or cancer or diabetes, your children could inherit that from you.

In one experiment, mice from the same family, which were obese because of their genetic makeup, were fed two different diets. One diet consisted of regular food. The other diet consisted of the same food but contained supplements that were known to alter the chemical tags on DNA.

Normally when these mice eat regular food they produce fat offspring. However, the mice that ate the same food with the supplements produced offspring that were normal weight. The parents' diet affected their offspring's weight!

Scientists are still trying to understand the details. The epigenetic markers that were modified by the food supplements appear to have "silenced" genes that encourage appetite. The parents' environment — in this case, the food they ate before becoming parents — affected the weight of their offspring.

Certain types of medicine have also been suspected of causing changes in epigenetic markers, leading to cancer in the offspring of women who took the

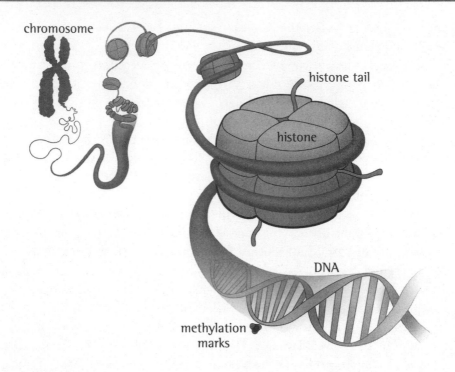

chromosome

histone tail

histone

DNA

methylation marks

medicine. For example, a type of synthetic estrogen prescribed to prevent miscarriages has been linked to an increased number of cancers in their daughters' and granddaughters' reproductive organs.

Studies point to changes in the epigenetic markers related to the development of reproductive organs, which the mothers passed down to their daughters. This finding affirms the adage that "you are what your mother — or grandmother — ate."

Tagalongs to Our Genetic Code

Our DNA includes additional components, which may sometimes be passed from parent to child at the same time as the genetic code. First are molecules attached to the DNA, called methylation marks, that turn genes on and off. Second are balls of proteins composed of histones, which the DNA wraps around. Histones and a portion of these proteins, called histone tails, regulate how the DNA is folded (and thus what is turned on or off).

The food you eat and other aspects of your environment can change these tagalongs. Then they can be passed down to your children and even your grandchildren, affecting the genes that are turned on.

Epigenetics: A Problem for Evolution?

Until these findings, many evolutionists dismissed the ideas of Charles Darwin's contemporary, Jean-Baptiste Lamarck, who believed that animals could acquire new traits through interactions with their environment and then pass them to the next generation. For instance, he believed giraffes stretching their necks to reach leaves on trees in one generation would cause giraffes in the next generation to have longer necks. Many science textbooks today reject Lamarck's ideas, but epigenetics is a form of Lamarckianism.

Of course this is contrary to classic Darwinian evolution. The theory of evolution is based on random changes or mutations occurring in DNA. If a change happens to be beneficial, then the organism will survive via natural selection and pass this trait to its descendants.

Although evolutionists do not deny the reality of epigenetics, its existence is hard to explain! Epigenetic changes are not random; they occur in response to the environment via complex mechanisms already in place to foster these changes.

These non-random epigenetic changes imply that evolution has a "mind." Creatures appear to have complex mechanisms to make epigenetic changes that allow them to adapt to *future* environmental challenges. But where did this forward-thinking design come from? Evolution is mindless; it cannot see the future. So how could it evolve mechanisms to prepare for the future?

But God does! God is omniscient (all-knowing), and He foreknew Adam and Eve would sin. He would judge that sin (Gen. 3) and the world would be cursed (Rom. 8:22). God knew that organisms would need the ability to adapt in a world that was no longer "very good." God likely designed organisms with epigenetic mechanisms to allow them to change easily and quickly in relation to their environment. These types of changes are much more valuable than random mutation and natural selection because they can produce immediate benefits for offspring without harming the basic information in the actual sequence of DNA.

Although we often hear that "nothing in biology makes sense except in the light of evolution," it should be said that "nothing in biology makes sense without the Creator God." Epigenetics is an exciting field of science that displays the intelligence and providence of God to help organisms adapt and survive in a fallen world.

CHAPTER 25

What about the Hebrew Language and Genesis?

DR. BENJAMIN SHAW

Introduction

A number of years ago, I heard a noted New Testament scholar relate a story about teaching a Sunday school class. As would be expected, he was using an English translation. At one point, one of the students in the class asked, "What does it say in the Greek?" The teacher's response was, "The same thing it says in the English." His point was not that there is no difference between Greek and English; only that in that passage the English gave an accurate and adequate presentation of the Greek.

It is the same in the Old Testament with Hebrew. Often, the Hebrew text says just what it does in English. That is not to say that there are not differences between Hebrew and English. There are, and frequently those differences pose difficulties for the translator. But in many places that is not the case. That is the reason that if you take a number of the more literal English translations (such as the KJV, NASB, NKJV, and ESV) and compare them verse-by-verse you will often see very little difference among them.

Why Are the Original Languages Important in Studying Genesis?

Vocabulary

To qualify my opening statement, there are many differences between Hebrew and English, and those differences can make it difficult to convey some of the subtleties of Hebrew in an English version. These differences are of various kinds. Some of them have to do with vocabulary. Two examples here might suffice.

One is the Hebrew word *hesed*. It can be translated "steadfast love," "lovingkindness," "mercy," "faithfulness," and some other words as well. According to *Strong's Concordance*, the KJV translates it into about 12 different words or phrases. The point is that the range of meaning for *hesed* is wider than that of any of the English words used to translate it.

A second example is the word *shalom*. It is usually translated "peace" in English versions, but again, the range of meaning of the Hebrew word is much wider. It can mean health, well-being, and satisfaction, as well as simply absence of conflict (at least seven different English words are used to translate it in the KJV).

Grammar and Syntax

Other differences have to do with grammar and syntax. Grammar, as I use it here, has to do with the form and function of words, whereas syntax has to do with the structure of sentences. As an example for the differences in grammar, the English verb system is time-based. That is, English has past, present, and future tenses (and variations on each of those), and the primary consideration is *when* the action took place. Hebrew verbs, on the other hand, have an aspect-based system. That is, the verb form can vary depending on whether the action is viewed as a whole, or viewed as incomplete or repeated. Thus, a particular verb in Hebrew may be translated past tense, present tense, or even future, depending on the context. The one consistency among the three would be that in each case the aspect from which the action is viewed is of primary importance. Hebrew verbs do have tense, but it is simply indicated by the context rather than by the form of the word. English tense is indicated (usually) by the form of the word. We know that "see" is present tense, while "saw" is past tense.

Another example would be in the use of the definite article (the). Hebrew will sometimes use the article in places where English would not, and vice versa. So, for example, in Genesis 28:10 the English says, "So he came to a certain place." In Hebrew, it says, "and he came to the place." In English, the use of "the" in such a context implies that the place had already been introduced, whereas that is not the case in Hebrew. In Hebrew, the definite article is regularly used to refer to something that has not been previously introduced but is definite in the mind of the narrator. This explains the English rendering "a certain place" in Genesis 28:10.

As for syntax, the normal word order in English is subject-verb-object: John (subject) saw (verb) the ball (object). In Hebrew, the normal word order, at least in narrative, is verb-subject-object. If that word order is changed, it is a clue to the reader that something other than straightforward narrative is taking place, or that some explanatory comment is being inserted into the narrative.

These differences between Hebrew and English vocabulary, grammar, and syntax mean that there are always some subtleties that are lost in translation. We find this in the Greek New Testament as well. As an example here, in John 2:4, Jesus says to Mary, "Woman, what does your concern have to do with Me?" For most English readers, that may sound as if Jesus is being rude to His mother. But in fact, He is simply being formal. Understanding this is largely a matter of vocabulary, knowing the various nuances that the noun "woman" may have in a particular context. For these reasons, in any detailed study of the Bible, it is important to have recourse to the original languages.

Problems That Arise in Today's Debates Due to Lack of Hebrew Knowledge

Today, there are many study helps and lexicons that can aid a layman and professional scholar. I suppose in some sense that the real problems here are not so much due to a lack of knowledge of Hebrew, though that may often be the case with laymen, nor with scientists who are knowledgeable in their own field but ignorant in the biblical languages.

Rather, the most serious problems are with those who know Hebrew, many of them fluent in it, yet because Genesis 1–2 is special (especially in today's debate over millions of years and evolution), all the ordinary rules of Hebrew vocabulary, grammar, and syntax seem to be thrown out the window! Essentially, it seems that outside ideas are influencing people to reinterpret Genesis 1–2 instead of reading it in a straightforward fashion in the normal sense of grammar, syntax, and vocabulary. Let's define some non-traditional, modern views of Genesis:

1. Day-Age: Days of Genesis are long periods of time to accommodate the secular concepts of long ages.
2. Framework Hypothesis: Days 1–3 parallel days 4–6 in many aspects, so this sets up a literary style so Genesis 1 is denoting importance, not history, and long ages can therefore be incorporated into Genesis 1.
3. Gap Theory: Separate Genesis 1:1 and 1:2 and put a large gap of time between these verses to accommodate long ages.

4. Theistic Evolution: Essentially reinterpret Genesis 1–11 as myth with some truth value and replace it with an evolutionary world-view, picking up the biblical narrative with Abraham.

Matters Having to Do with Vocabulary

Yom/Day

We might as well begin here with the common "problem" of the definition of "day" (*yom* in Hebrew). According to the Brown-Driver-Briggs Hebrew lexicon (dictionary), *yom* has six basic uses in the Old Testament. The first is day as opposed to night as in Genesis 1:4, where the light period is called "day," and the dark period is called "night." The second is day as a division of time, so for example, "three days journey" as in Genesis 30:36 or Exodus 3:18. Under this sense, day is defined by evening and morning, where the dictionary cites Genesis 1–2.

Third is the particular phrase "the day of the Lord." Fourth is the use of the plural "days" to refer to the life of someone (Genesis 6:3; Deuteronomy 22:19). Fifth is the use of the plural to indicate an indefinite period (Genesis 27:44, 29:10). Finally, there is the use of "day" (again, primarily in the plural) to indicate "time." So, for example, in Proverbs 25:13, "the day of harvest" refers to harvest time, not to a single day. See also Genesis 30:14 or Joshua 3:15. Other Hebrew dictionaries, including the most recent, set out essentially the same range of meanings for the word *yom*.

It is clear from the discussion in the dictionary that *yom* in reference to the days of creation discussed in Genesis 1–2 refers to ordinary days. However, many scholars are unwilling to take it in that sense because of the "special" character of these chapters as viewed by modern scholars and their response to things like "millions of years."

In part, this contributed to the development of the day-age view of Genesis 1 (as well as other long-age views). It gave the developers of the view a way of reading Genesis 1 that allowed them to hold to the old age of the earth that was being put forth by secular geologists at that time.

It is important to note, however, that the definition of day in Genesis 1 as an ordinary day is not limited to the standard dictionaries. It is also the case with many of the classic commentaries on Genesis such as John Gill, John Calvin, Jamieson-Fausset-Brown, H.C. Leopold, and others. This is also true of some modern commentators. For instance, Gordon Wenham, commenting on Genesis 1:5, says,

There can be little doubt that here "day" has its basic sense of a 24-hour period. The mention of morning and evening, the enumeration of the days, and the divine rest on the seventh show that a week of divine activity is being described here.[1]

Claus Westermann doesn't even discuss the possible range of meaning of *yom*. He says,

> What is essential for P [sadly, *Westermann presumes that this part of Genesis has come from the so-called "Priestly source" from the outdated and refuted Documentary Hypothesis*] is only the chronological disposition of the works of creation. The alternation between night and day is not conceived as a period of 24 hours, as a unity with a precise beginning; the 24 hours comprise two parts. The constantly recurring sentence which concludes the work of each day plots the regular rhythm of the passage of time, and gives P's account of creation the character of an event in linear time which links it with history.[2]

In short, the interpretation of *yom* in Genesis 1 as anything other than an ordinary day appears to be special pleading on the part of interpreters in an attempt to avoid the clear implication of the passage that what we have here is an ordinary week at the very beginning of time.

Firmament/Expanse

Another term that comes in for frequent discussion is the word "firmament." In Hebrew, the word is *raqiya'*. It is derived from a verb that means "to hammer out" or "to flatten." It is usually used in reference to metal that has been flattened out by hammering or beating. As a result, most scholars take the view that the *raqia'* is a solid expanse. Westermann says, "In earlier times the heavens were almost always regarded as solid."[3] However, it may also be the case that what is in view is the idea of something being stretched out. Psalm 104:2 refers to God as the one "who stretch[es] out the heavens like a curtain." A different verb is used here than in Genesis 1:6, but the idea is the same. In verse 8,

---

1. Gordon Wenham, *Word Biblical Commentary* (Dallas, TX: Word Incorporated, 1987), Genesis 1–15, p. 19.
2. Claus Westermann, *Genesis1-11: A Commentary*, trans. J.J. Scullion (Minneapolis, MN: Augsburg Publishing House, 1984), p. 115. For an explanation of the Documentary Hypothesis, see *How Do We Know the Bible Is True?* Volume 1, Ken Ham and Bodie Hodge, gen. eds. (Green Forest, AR: Master Books, 2011), chapter 8: "Did Moses Write Genesis?" p. 85–102.
3. Ibid., p. 117.

the firmament is called "heavens." Thus, while it may be the case that ancient societies saw the heavens as something solid, it does not appear that that view is necessarily being taught in Genesis 1:6. Many translations today use the word "expanse" to denote this.

One other element having to do with vocabulary should also be discussed here. That is the use of a figure of speech called a "hendiadys." The word comes from Greek and literally means one-through-two. It is the use of two related terms to identify one idea. Some examples in English are: law and order, assault and battery, and kith and kin.

In the Bible, there are numerous examples. In Leviticus 24:47, the phrase "stranger and sojourner" means "resident alien." In Lamentations 2:9, the phrase "destroyed and broken" means "totally ruined." In Genesis 1, there is one important example of hendiadys. In verse two, the phrase "without form and void" does not indicate two separate things, but one thing. Wenham translates it as "total chaos" and makes the following comment: " 'Total chaos' is an example of hendiadys."[4] Similarly, Westermann says, "E.A. Speiser describes the phrase as 'an excellent example of hendiadys'; it means the desert waste and is used as the opposite of creation."[5]

If this phrase is indeed a hendiadys, it seriously undercuts one aspect of the framework hypothesis.[6] The framework hypothesis generally takes the phrase as two separate words, the first meaning "unformed" and the second meaning "unfilled." Days 1–3 then deal with the forming of the various elements of creation, while days 4–6 deal with their filling. Such hair-splitting of the terms is unlikely.

Matters Having to Do with Syntax

Here the primary syntactical observation is the use of what is called the vav-consecutive in Hebrew (sometimes denoted as a "waw-consecutive"). As was mentioned above, Hebrew verbs function somewhat differently than do English verbs. The vav-consecutive is a verb construction that is the ordinary verb form used for relating a narrative. The verb form also appears in poetry, but it is a matter of dispute among Hebrew grammarians whether the form has the same function in poetry as it does in narrative. It is conceded by all that Genesis 1 is

---

4. Wenham, *Word Biblical Commentary*, p. 15.
5. Westermann, *Genesis1-11: A Commentary*, p. 103.
6. For a refutation of the framework hypothesis, see *How Do We Know the Bible Is True?* Volume 1, Ken Ham and Bodie Hodge, Gen. Eds., "Chapter 17: Framework Hypothesis?" (Green Forest, Arkansas: Master Books, 2011), pp. 189–200.

narrative. Some want to qualify that by calling it "poetic narrative" or "elevated narrative." However, it is still narrative.

Not only does the repeated use of the vav-consecutive indicate that a passage is narrative, but it also indicates sequence. That is, the action of the second verb follows the action of the first verb in sequence; the third follows the second, and so forth. That is the standard character of the vav-consecutive in other biblical narratives, such as the stories in the books of Samuel and Kings. The vav-consecutive appears approximately 50 times in Genesis 1:1–2:4. This emphatically characterizes the passage as narrative, and it traces an extended sequence of actions throughout the section. This consideration is particularly damaging to the framework hypothesis, which sees days 1–3 as paralleled in days 4–6. Thus, days 4–6 do not follow days 1–3 in sequence, but take place at the same time. If that were the case, there would be no good reason for the repeated use of the vav-consecutive, since there would be no sequence of events to report.

A second consideration having to do with syntax deals with the transition from Genesis 1:1 to Genesis 1:2. Though the gap theory[7] probably originated in some form well before the 19th century, it became popular in that century as a way to provide concordance between the reading of Genesis 1 and the idea of an old earth (much older than five or six thousand years) that was being put forward by the secular geologists of the day. It later gained great popularity, particularly in fundamentalist circles, through its inclusion in the *Scofield Reference Bible*.

An essential element of this theory is the idea that there is a gap between Genesis 1:1 and Genesis 1:2. Genesis 1:1 is taken as a statement regarding the original creation of the totality of the universe. Verse two is then translated "and the earth *became* formless and void." The idea is that there was an original creation, perhaps many millennia ago, perhaps even millions of years ago. Then, in more recent time, the earth became formless and void.

Part of the defense of this view is the use of the identical phrase in Jeremiah 4:23, where the formless and void state is a result of judgment. This consideration is strengthened by the fact that in Jeremiah 4:23 there is the additional statement that the earth had no light. The reasoning then is that the earth being dark, formless, and void in Genesis 1:2 is the result of some catastrophic judgment. From that point, gap theorists develop an explanation of what took place in that "gap" period to bring about such a catastrophic judgment that the earth had to be entirely recreated.

---

7. For a discussion on the problems with the gap theory, see *The New Answers Book 1*, Ken Ham ed. (Green Forest, Arkansas; Master Books, 2006), chapter 5: "What about the Gap and Ruin-Reconstruction Theories?" p. 47–63.

There are two fundamental problems with this view. The first is that it makes Genesis 1:2 dependent on Jeremiah 4:23, while the opposite is the case. Genesis was written well before the time of Jeremiah, and Jeremiah is borrowing the imagery from Genesis to express the severity of the judgment that is about to befall the nation of Judah. The people have persisted in their idolatry and their rebellion against God, and He is about to bring judgment on the land. The judgment will be so severe that it is as if the earth will be returned to its primordial state, before God began to order the creation.

The second problem is with the translation of the verb as "became." The verb used here can indeed mean become, or come into being, as in Genesis 2:7, "and man became a living being." More commonly, however, it simply means to happen. The definition of the verb itself does not answer the question. The issue here is the syntax. How does this verb relate to the verb in the preceding verse? In English, we do not often think of how one verb may be related to preceding or following verbs. English is full of adverbs and prepositions that indicate how one statement relates to preceding or following statements.

This is similar in the case of Greek, too. So, for example, the reader may well have heard a preacher say that when we see a "therefore" in one of Paul's letters, we need to ask what it's there for. Hebrew does not have the same structure as English, and it does not have the large number of conjunctions, adverbs, and prepositions that English has.

Instead, the relation of one verb to preceding and following verbs is regularly indicated by two things. Hebrew indicates the relationship between clauses and sentences first by the form of the verb; and second, by the placement of the verb in the sentence. The verb "created" in Genesis 1:1 is in the perfect state (not to be confused with the perfect in English), as is ordinarily the case with the beginning of a narrative. We would then expect the next verb to be at the beginning of the next sentence, and to be the vav-consecutive form. This would indicate the continuation of the narrative sequence. However, neither of those two things is true of the verb "was" in Genesis 1:2.

First, the verb is not in first place in verse two. In verse 2, the subject comes first (and the earth). Second, the verb is in the perfect state. The combination of these two factors indicates that verse 2 is a descriptive clause about the noun (usually referred to as a nominal clause). It is making some further statement about the last element in verse 1 before the narrative sequence is continued. Thus, verse 2 is very closely related to verse 1, and this close relationship does not allow for the gap needed by the gap theory.

An expanded translation of the two verses, indicating this relationship, would be something like this: *"In the beginning God created the heavens and the earth. As for the earth, it was without form and void. . . ."* The narrative begins with a general statement about the heavens and the earth. It then moves to focus on the earth, giving the reader information about the state of the earth at the very beginning of time. In order for the gap theory to work at this point, the reader would simply have to ignore this standard element of Hebrew syntax. As Wenham says, "And + noun (=earth) indicates that v 2 is a disjunctive clause. It could be circumstantial to v 1 or v 3, but for reasons already discussed the latter is more probable."[8]

Limitations to the Use of Hebrew Grammar and the Work of Hebrew Experts

In the material already discussed, there has been a fair amount of unity in the views of Hebrew experts. However, Hebrew experts are not agreed on all matters Hebrew. For example, while most view "without form and void" as a hendiadys, not all do.

It is at this point, for example, that I would take issue with the NKJV. It translates the beginning of verse 2 this way: "The earth was without form, and void." By putting the comma between the two words, the translators indicate that they do not see the two words as a hendiadys. In this, it follows the KJV, but it is the only modern translation to do so.

In Genesis 1, however, the deepest disagreement among Hebrew experts has to do with the way the first three verses are translated. Aside from the issue of "formless and void," the NKJV is representative of most modern English versions. It translates verses 1–3 as follows:

In the beginning God created the heavens and the earth. ²The earth was without form, and void; and darkness *was* on the face of the deep. And the Spirit of God was hovering over the face of the waters. ³Then God said, "Let there be light"; and there was light.

Some other translations will give the reader a sense of the different ways some translators understand the verses.

When God began to create the heavens and the earth — ²the earth was without shape or form, it was dark over the deep sea, and God's wind swept over the waters — ³God said, "Let there be light." And so light appeared. (Common English Bible)

---

8. Wenham, *Word Biblical Commentary*, p. 15.

In the beginning when God created the heavens and the earth, ²the earth was a formless void and darkness covered the face of the deep, while a wind from God swept over the face of the waters. ³Then God said, "Let there be light"; and there was light. (New Revised Standard Version)

When God began to create heaven and earth — ²the earth being unformed and void, with darkness over the surface of the deep and a wind from God sweeping over the water — ³God said, "Let there be light"; and there was light. (Tanak: The New Jewish Publication Society translation)

A careful reading of these versions shows that the Hebrew is being read differently by Hebrew experts. All of them are grammatically and syntactically possible, though each of the three after the NKJV require some playing around with the text. It demonstrates that the translation and interpretation of a Bible passage does not depend on a knowledge of vocabulary, syntax, and grammar alone. As I sometimes tell my Hebrew students, "A detailed knowledge of Hebrew grammar will not answer all your questions."

It's important for the reader to know what is going on with above variant translations. This explanation is summarized from that of Wenham, who gives a clear and fair presentation of the evidence.[9]

There are four ways of understanding the syntax of Genesis 1:1–3 that have been defended by various Hebrew experts. The first is that verse 1 is a temporal clause that is subordinate to verse 2, which is the main clause. That is, "When God created . . . the earth was without form." The second view is that verse 1 is a temporal clause subordinate to the main clause in verse 3, while verse 2 is a parenthetical comment. That is, "When God created . . . (the earth being formless and void) . . . God said." The third view is that verse 1 is a separate main clause, serving as a title to the remainder of the section. The actual creation then begins with verse 2. The last view is that verse 1 is the main clause. It indicates the first act of creation, which is then continued in the following verses.

The first view was first set forth by one of the medieval Jewish rabbis by the name of Ibn Ezra, but not many have adopted his view. The second view was adopted by the medieval rabbi Rashi, though it may have been set out earlier. It is represented by all three of the alternate translations given above. The third and fourth views are represented by the standard translations such as the NKJV, the NASB, and the ESV. View three and four are distinguished only by interpretation, not by translation.

The third and fourth views clearly do not understand verse 1 as a temporal clause, while the other two do. The main point of contention is the very first word in the verse, which is usually translated as "in the beginning." Some grammarians have observed that the first word in verse 1 does not have the definite article (the). As a result, in their view it should be translated as the start of a temporal clause ("when God began to create," or, more literally, "in beginning of God's creating"). However, there are other examples where this same word is used without a definite article, yet it is clearly definite in sense (see Isaiah 46:10, where even the NRSV translates: "declaring the end from the beginning").

The idea that Genesis 1:1 should begin with this kind of temporal clause (when God began to create) has also been defended by the fact that one of the Babylonian creation myths, the *Enuma Elish*, begins "when the heavens had not been named." The idea here is that the author of Genesis (not Moses, in the view of those who hold to this theory) was influenced by the way in which the Babylonian myths began. However, more recent scholarship has seen little influence of Babylonian mythology on the organization of Genesis 1. Further, the ancient translations, such as the Septuagint (the Greek translation of the Old Testament that was done before the time of Christ), translate Genesis 1:1–3 in just the same way as our modern, literal translations do.

The grammar and syntax of the Hebrew in Genesis 1:1–3 allow for the differing translations provided above. However, the first two options at least leave room for, and probably demand, the idea of matter existing before creation. That is, God and matter are both eternal. However, that view is inconsistent with the theology taught in the remainder of the Scriptures — that God is the sole source of all that is, and that nothing existed but God before creation (e.g., Exodus 20:11; Nehemiah 9:6; Colossians 1:16). That leaves us, then, with the traditional translation of Genesis 1:1–3 as best representing the vocabulary, grammar, and syntax, as well as the theology, of the Hebrew text.

Conclusion

A knowledge of Hebrew vocabulary, grammar, and syntax is important for providing the basis for an accurate understanding of what the opening chapters of the Bible teach. The standard, traditional Christian understanding of the teaching of these chapters is not based on English mistranslations and misinterpretations. Instead, it has a solid foundation in the Hebrew language itself. But it is important for the reader who knows only English to realize that faulty theology can be as damaging to understanding Genesis as a faulty understanding of Hebrew. It is only when we are faithful to the teaching of the whole Bible that we can be confident that we have not misrepresented the teaching of any one part.

CHAPTER 26

The Recapitulation of Recapitulation: Does Embryology Prove Evolution?

DR. ELIZABETH MITCHELL

Introduction

Do human embryos replay the evolutionary history of their species as they develop? This idea has led many people to believe that what is in a woman's womb is merely an animal that can be simply disposed of by abortion at its fish stage. The false portrayal of embryonic development has tragically convinced countless people that the evolutionary worldview must be true, that humans are just highly evolved animals, and that abortion is acceptable.

Summed up in many textbooks by the popular and pithy declaration "Ontogeny recapitulates phylogeny," *recapitulation theory* (also known as the *biogenic law*) was popularized by evolutionist Ernst Haeckel's famous (or infamous) 19th-century illustrations intended to demonstrate how embryos pass through stages reminiscent of their evolutionary ancestors.

While the inaccuracy of Haeckel's drawings became apparent almost immediately, they have continued to be presented in textbooks, museums, and the secular media as "proof" of evolution even into this century. Evolutionary biologists who freely acknowledge the inaccuracy of the drawings continue to debate the validity of the "theory"[1] and its variants. Applications of recapitulation

---

1. A theory in science usually has little if anything against it, and a scientific "law" should have no exceptions. In light of this, recapitulation is more like a failed hypothesis since

theory are widely accepted in other disciplines such as linguistics and developmental psychology.

To many people, the evolutionary principles underlying recapitulation theory are fundamental truths, so the theory retains its authority in their thinking even when it requires substantial modification to exist alongside observable facts. Moreover, in recent years even Haeckel's evolutionary critics have shifted gears and begun to rehabilitate his reputation and his work. Forgiving the "liberties" he took, some now consider him positively brilliant for manufacturing pictures to prove what he "knew" must be true.

Many creationists are under the impression that evolutionists have abandoned recapitulation theory. Its persistence in the educational system, however, testifies to its usefulness even in the hands of those who believe that it has some problems. It remains a tool to explain evolutionary principles to students and to convince them that evolution is true.

Furthermore, many still believe that recapitulation theory (in some form or other) is sufficiently true to count as convincing evidence for evolution. And in the world of professional evolutionists, while some debate which variations of it they accept, others consider it a valid predictor of evolutionary stages and use it to unravel the secrets and subtleties of an evolutionary past shrouded by deep time and an incomplete fossil record. Thus, recapitulation theory continues to fuel the evolutionary thinking of students from the cradle to college, the lay public, and many academic professionals.

Big Words

"Ontogeny recapitulates phylogeny." The way that phrase rolls off of the tongue, combined with the compelling visual images that usually accompany it, appeal to the ear, the eye, and the mind. After all, how could big words that rhyme so well convey an untruth? But what do all those big words mean?

Ontogeny

Ontogeny means development from the earliest stages to maturity. In biology, *ontogeny* is roughly synonymous with embryologic development. Certainly, a fertilized egg must pass through a number of stages as it develops into a mature organism ready for life outside its mother's womb or its egg. A developing embryo changes its shape dramatically as it grows and morphs into its mature form.

---

it has so much against it. But since this is the recognized terminology, we will continue to refer to "recapitulation theory" and the "biogenic law" in this chapter for the sake of understanding.

Some anatomical structures first appear in the embryo in an apparently simple form and develop complexity. (That morphological simplicity is generally only a superficial impression, but the illusion of simplicity fits the evolutionary story that embryology supposedly tells.) Some embryonic anatomical structures disappear completely or remain only as *vestiges* (literally, "footprints") in the final mature product. *Vestigial organs* are commonly (and erroneously) viewed as "useless" anatomical structures leftover from our evolutionary past.

Phylogeny

Phylogeny refers to evolutionary ancestry. It is based on the presumption that all living organisms evolved from simpler forms through natural processes. The phylogenetic tree of life is a metaphor for the branching of the earliest life forms into stem branches, which, through the ongoing development of complexity and continued divergence into more and more branches, eventually produced the life forms we see today. Moreover, Haeckel, like many evolutionists then and now, maintained that this phylogeny is *monophyletic* — that all animal life can be traced back to a single common ancestor.

Recapitulation

Recapitulation refers to summarizing, repeating, or restating something. Thus, "ontogeny recapitulates phylogeny" is the claim that the developing embryo goes through stages that resemble, at least structurally, the various animals on that organism's ancestral trip up the tree of life.

Simply stated, Haeckel claimed that the embryonic forms of an animal resembled the adult organisms in its evolutionary ancestry. Because observation shows that developing embryos do not resemble the adults on the evolutionary tree of life, a modified form of the theory holds that an embryo only resembles the embryos of its evolutionary ancestors. A more recent reinterpretation of Haeckel's claims credits him with only claiming recapitulation applies to individual traits, rather than to entire embryonic stages.[2]

Seen and Unseen

Ontogeny is observable. Embryonic development of an organism can be studied through the lens of actual scientific methodology. Even the development of the human embryo has been studied in great detail.[3] The anatomy of

---

2. M. Richardson and G. Keuck, "Haeckel's ABC of Evolution and Development," *Biological Reviews of the Cambridge Philosophical Society* 77 no. 04 (2002): p. 495–528.
3. "Feedback: Embryo Protection" Answers in Genesis (July 22, 2011) http://www.answersingenesis.org/articles/2011/07/22/feedback-embryo-protection.

each stage of human embryonic development and that of many animals has been examined, sketched, and photographed.

When Haeckel's embryo drawings were published, they purportedly showed a comparison of the embryos of a number of vertebrates. Some see Haeckel's illustrations as blatant frauds, and others say he took artistic liberties to emphasize a point. Regardless, the images were almost immediately shown to be inaccurate by comparison with observable reality.

Phylogeny is *not* observable. No amount of scientific achievement makes it possible to see back through time to observe the purported upward evolution of life. Neither does biological research reveal any mechanism by which a simpler kind of organism can acquire the genetic information to become a more complex kind of organism.

Furthermore, no such transformation has ever been observed. Fossils labeled "transitional forms" are actually just animals with a variety of characteristics interpreted through an evolutionary imagination that connects the dots through time.

Thus, phylogeny is a figment intended to explain life without God. The claim that "ontogeny recapitulates phylogeny" is a claim that the observable steps in embryonic development are similar to and therefore reveal the unobservable evolutionary past of that organism.

Because the unobservable evolutionary past is not amenable to scientific examination, it is impossible to "test" the recapitulation claim. But because "evolution" is presented to students and to the public and held by the majority of mainstream scientists to be indisputable fact, recapitulation theory becomes a tool for education, a visually appealing bit of evidence, and a paleontological predictor to order fossils into the "right" lineages.

History

While Haeckel's drawings are the expression of recapitulation theory most familiar to modern schoolchildren, college students, and adults, the idea did not originate with Haeckel or even with Darwin. The germs of recapitulation theory can be found in the ancient world, but it gradually acquired its more modern form in the 19th century, with contributions by J.F. Meckel (1811), Karl Ernst von Baer (1828), Charles Darwin (1859), and finally Ernst Haeckel (1866).

Haeckel was a professor of zoology in Germany. He was particularly moved by Darwin's *Origin of Species,* and actively promoted Darwinian evolution to the public and to academia. As he taught how humans gradually developed

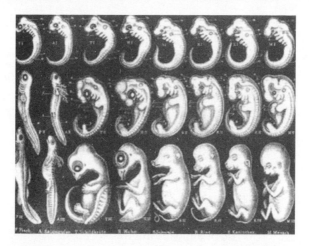

Haeckel's famous (infamous) set of 24 drawings purporting to show eight different embryos in three stages of development, as published by him in *Anthropogenie*, in Germany, 1874. This is the version of his drawings most often reproduced in textbooks. Left to right are shown embryos of a fish, salamander, turtle, chicken, pig, cow, rabbit, and human. Top to bottom depicts three stages of development. The drawings contain errors intended to emphasize embryonic similarity and support recapitulation theory. IMAGE: from M. Richardson and G. Keuck, "Haeckel's ABC of Evolution and Development," *Biological Reviews of the Cambridge Philosophical Society*, 77 no. 04 (2002): p. 495–528.

through upward evolution along a tree of life, he presented hypothetical simple organisms as if they were real, an ape-man for which he had no evidence, and his infamous doctored embryo sketches.

Haeckel's version of the "biogenetic law" held that embryos looked like the adult forms of their evolutionary forebears. He wrote that embryonic development paralleled phylogenetic (evolutionary) history — that "embryonic development is a short and rapid re-run, or recapitulation, of evolution."[4] To support his claim, in his book *Natürliche Schöpfungs-geschichte* (Germany, 1868; published in English in 1876 as *The History of Creation*), Haeckel included sketches of embryos substantially altered to make his point. "His drawings are also highly inaccurate, exaggerating the similarities among embryos, while failing to show the differences," explains embryologist Michael Richardson, lead author of a famous 1997 article refuting Haeckel's claims.[5]

4. Richardson and Keuck, *Biological Reviews of the Cambridge Philosophical Society*, p. 495–528.
5. M. Richardson et al., "There is no highly conserved embryonic stage in the vertebrates: implications for current theories of evolution and development," *Anatomy and Embryology* 196 no. 2 (1997): p. 91–106.

Soon after publication, Haeckel's 19th-century contemporaries spotted the fraud and publicized it. For instance, in 1874, William His, after critiquing Haeckel's ideas and demonstrating that many of the embryo figures were "invented," concluded, "The procedure of Professor Haeckel remains an irresponsible playing with the facts even more dangerous than the playing with words criticized earlier."[6]

For over a century, criticism from the evolutionary scientific community has continued. "Scientific objections to Haeckel's drawings . . . include charges of:

(i) doctoring (the alteration of images during copying);

(ii) fabrication (the invention of features not observed in nature); and

(iii) selectivity (the use of a misleading phylogenetic sample)."[7]

The most generous and gracious modern assessments have been unable to allay charges of falsification, and Haeckel even admitted to some of the accusations. For instance, to the charge that he printed a woodcut of a single turtle embryo three times, altered to represent three different species, he confessed to "an imprudent folly" necessitated by a shortage of time.[8]

Despite the almost immediate rejection of Haeckel's evidence by much of the scientific community, his rather impressive fabrications did their job: they found their way into textbooks as evidence illustrating evolutionary claims for over a century. Countless children and adults — and young women coaxed to proceed with abortion — have been told that the human embryo goes through a fish stage, an amphibian stage, and a reptilian stage. Attesting to the sometimes-disputed fact that these fraudulent "teaching tools" persisted in the educational system despite their known errors and general rejection in the scientific community, leading evolutionist Stephen Gould in the year 2000 wrote:

> Haeckel had exaggerated the similarities by idealizations and omissions. He also, in some cases — in a procedure that can only be called fraudulent — simply copied the same figure over and over again. At certain stages in early development, vertebrate embryos do look more alike, at least in gross anatomical features easily observed

6. Richardson and Keuck, *Biological Reviews of the Cambridge Philosophical Society*, p. 495–528.

7. Ibid.

8. Ibid.

with the human eye, than do the adult tortoises, chickens, cows, and humans that will develop from them. But these early embryos also differ far more substantially, one from the other, than Haeckel's figures show. Moreover, Haeckel's drawings never fooled expert embryologists, who recognized his fudgings right from the start.

At this point, a relatively straightforward factual story, blessed with a simple moral story as well, becomes considerably more complex, given the foils and practices of the oddest primate of all. Haeckel's drawings, despite their noted inaccuracies, entered into the most impenetrable and permanent of all quasi-scientific literatures: standard student textbooks of biology. . . . We should therefore not be surprised that Haeckel's drawings entered nineteenth-century textbooks. But we do, I think, have the right to be both astonished and ashamed by the century of mindless recycling that has led to the persistence of these drawings in a large number, if not a majority, of modern textbooks![9]

In a succinct summation of Haeckel's work, Gould concluded that Haeckel, who used his doctored diagrams as data to support his scientific hypotheses, committed the "academic equivalent of murder."[10]

A 1997 study of comparative embryology, published in the journal *Anatomy and Embryology* by embryologist Michael Richardson, then of London's St. George's Hospital Medical School, also called attention to the persistent acceptance of Haeckel's fraudulent diagrams. He found that Haeckel had resized embryos and eliminated limb buds and heart bulges to enhance similarity. He wrote, "These drawings are still widely reproduced in textbooks and review articles, and continue to exert a significant influence on the development of ideas in this field."[11] Gould quotes Richardson saying, "I know of at least fifty recent biology textbooks which use the drawings uncritically."[12]

While some excuse Haeckel's diagrams as mere schematics, these "schematics" were clearly meant to systematically and deceptively improve on nature. For instance, he selectively removed limbs on one of his embryos while rendering

---

9. Stephen Jay Gould, "*Abscheulich!* (Atrocious!)," *Natural History*, 109 no. 2 (2000): p. 44–45. Quoted in Revisiting Those Pesky Embryo Drawings — Evolution News & Views http://www.evolutionnews.org/2010/06/revisiting_those_pesky_embryo035741.html.
10. Richardson and Keuck, *Biological Reviews of the Cambridge Philosophical Society*, p. 495–528.
11. Richardson et al., *Anatomy and Embryology*, p. 91–106.
12. Stephen Jay Gould, *Natural History*, p. 44—45.

others perfectly, commenting that they were similar with "no trace of limbs or 'extremities' in this stage."[13] According to Richardson, the "intent [of these systematic alterations] is to make the young embryos look more alike than they do in real life."[14]

Despite overwhelming evidence that has been used to refute Haeckel's claims and the manufactured data he used to support them, Richardson and colleagues write, "The idea of a phylogenetically conserved stage has regained popularity in recent years."[15] To assess the merits of recapitulation theory and Haeckel's work, they conducted a systematic examination of embryos from all sorts of vertebrates, noting that modern textbooks typically confine their attention to the frog, the chick, and the "typical" mammal.

They compared the most *phylotypic* stage of each — the stage at which vertebrate embryos possess comparable characteristics such as a notochord, pharyngeal arches ("gill slits"), a neural tube, somites (segments of undifferentiated blocks of embryonic mesoderm), and a postanal tail (a posterior extension of the embryo's developing musculoskeletal structures beyond the anus).

Richardson et al. in 1997 confirmed that even the earliest stages of embryonic development vary greatly between vertebrate species. They attributed these differences to evolution, as they hold an evolutionary worldview. But their paper demonstrated, on the basis of rigorous comparative embryology, that the "biogenetic law" as commonly understood is false.[16]

A quick Internet search today will produce many references to recapitulation theory as "inadmissibly simplified,"[17] "outdated" and "buried,"[18] "refuted," "defunct" and "largely discredited." Haeckel's drawings are recognized by many as "fraudulently modified"[19] "misinformation."[20] Embryologist Michael Richardson was quoted in a 1997 issue of *Science* magazine saying Haeckel's work was "turning out to be one of the most famous fakes in biology."[21] So has

13. Ernst Haeckel, *Anthropogenie oder Entwickelungsgeschichte des Menschen. Keimes- und Stammesgeschichte* (Engelmann, Leipzig, 1903); quoted in Michael Richardson and Gerhard Keuck, "A Question of Intent: When Is a 'Schematic' Illustration a Fraud?" *Nature* 410 no. 144 (2001).
14. Ibid.
15. Richardson et al., *Anatomy and Embryology*, p. 91–106.
16. Ibid.
17. http://www.frozenevolution.com/haeckel-s-recapitulation-theory.
18. http://education.stateuniversity.com/pages/2026/Hall-G-Stanley-1844-1924.html.
19. http://www.thematrix.co.uk/texttopic.asp?ID=31.
20. https://en.wikipedia.org/wiki/Recapitulation_theory.
21. E. Pennisi, "Haeckel's Embryos: Fraud Rediscovered," *Science* 277 (1997):1435. Quoted in http://home.uchicago.edu/~rjr6/articles/Haeckel--fraud%20not%20proven.pdf.

Haeckel's work — so heavily criticized even in the evolutionary community — dropped off the scene? No. Why is that?

Despite over a century of widespread acknowledgement that Haeckel faked his pictures, Haeckel's claims and even colorized adaptations of his diagrams still show up in the popular press and even textbooks. For instance, the cover story of *Time* magazine (November 11, 2002) reported that the human embryo at 40 days "looks no different from that of a pig, chick or elephant. All have a tail, a yolk sac and rudimentary gills."[22] Even 21st-century textbooks perpetuate this 19th-century fraud. Sylvia Mader's 2010 edition of *Biology*, for instance, features colorized Haeckel-ish embryos and teaches, "At these comparable developmental stages, vertebrate embryos have many features in common which suggests they evolved from a common ancestor."[23]

In a world where evolutionary educators decry any effort to "teach the controversy" in public schools — allowing students to be exposed to facts that reveal problems with evolutionary dogma — the convenient foot-dragging on the removal of this compelling lie from curricula is telling.

Those Fishy Gill Slits

Our embryonic "gill slits" are possibly the most oft-cited anatomical "proof" of our fishy ancestry. *Inside the Human Body*, a popular 2011 BBC1 program hosted by Dr. Michael Mosley, provides a typical example. The program features a state-of-the-art high-quality video of human embryonic development called "Anatomical clues to human evolution from fish."[24] The video was produced by digitally splicing scans taken in early pregnancy. Mosley interprets the developing features as anatomical proof of fish in our evolutionary past. Among these are "gill-like structures," a reference to the "gill slits."[25]

The poorly named "gill slits" in human embryos are not anything at all like gills and are not even slits, just folds of tissue destined to develop into various anatomical parts of the head and neck. They never have a function or a structure remotely resembling gills. They don't even turn into anything having to do with the lungs. Never in the course of development does a human embryo absorb oxygen from water as fish do with gills.

---

22. *TIME*, November 11, 2002, http://www.time.com/time/magazine/article/0,9171,1003653,00.html.
23. "Current Textbooks Misuse Embryology to Argue for Evolution," *Evolution News Views*, http://www.evolutionnews.org/2010/06/current_textbooks_misuse_embry035751.html.
24. Available online at http://www.bbc.co.uk/news/health-13278255.
25. See "Vestigial Hiccups, Folding Fish-eyes, and Other Fables: Our Fishy Forebears . . . Again!" at http://www.answersingenesis.org/articles/aid/v6/n1/fishy-fables.

Evolutionist Steven Jay Gould writes, "In Haeckel's evolutionary reading, the human gills slits *are* (literally) the adult features of an ancestor" (emphasis in original).[26] In later writings, Haeckel did not ascribe a respiratory function to these structures in the non-fish embryo. He still maintained that there were actual gill slits and gill arches in the non-fish embryos but that they had evolved into other structures. He wrote in 1892 that "we never meet with a Reptile, Bird or Mammal which at any period of actual life breathes through gills, and the gill-arches and openings which do exist in the embryos are, during the course of their ontogeny, changed into entirely different structures, viz. into parts of the jaw-apparatus and the organ of hearing."[27] And by 1903 he wrote of the "total loss of respiratory gills," saying that "in the embryos of amniotes there is never even a trace of gill lamellae, of real respiratory organs, on the gill arches."[28]

Evolutionists consider homologies in fish gills, fish jaws, reptilian jaws, and mammalian ear bones to be sequential evolutionary developments that demonstrate the common evolutionary ancestry of fish, reptiles, and mammals. *Homologous* structures are the different anatomical structures that form from a similar embryonic structure. Meckel's cartilage, for instance, has different destinies in different creatures. Meckel's cartilage supports the gills in cartilaginous fish. It ossifies to form the jaws of bony fish and reptiles. And in mammalian embryos, Meckel's cartilage helps shape the middle ear bones and the mandible; then it virtually disappears. But each creature has its own kind of DNA directing the process, and at no time in science do we see DNA of one creature mutating to produce new information that can change the organism into a new kind. And at no point do these so-called mammalian "gill slits" have anything to do with gills or respiratory structures.

Mammalian "gill slits" are folds in the region of the tiny embryo's throat. By the 28th day of life, the embryo's brain and spinal cord seem to be racing ahead of the rest of the body in growth. Therefore, for a time, the spinal cord is actually longer than the body, forcing the body to curl and flexing the neck area forward. (This curled embryo with the long spinal cord is mistakenly accused by

26. Stephen Jay Gould, *Ontogeny and Phylogeny* (Cambridge, MA: Belknap Press, 1977), p. 7.
27. Ernst Haeckel, *The History of Creation* [translation of the 8th German Edition of *Natürliche Schöpfungsgeschichte*]. (ed. E.R. Lankester) (Kegan Paul, London: 1892). Quoted in Richardson and Keuck, "Haeckel's ABC of Evolution and Development," *Biological Reviews of the Cambridge Philosophical Society*: p. 495–528.
28. Ernst Haeckel, *Anthropogenie oder Entwickelungsgeschichte des Menschen*; Quoted in Richardson and Keuck, "Haeckel's ABC of Evolution and Development," *Biological Reviews of the Cambridge Philosophical Society*: p. 495–528.

some people of having an animal's tail.) Just as many people develop a double chin when bending the neck forward, so the embryo has folds in its neck area due to this flexing.

Gill slits, thus, is a misleading name, since these folds are neither gills nor slits. Another popular name, *branchial arches*, is just as deceptive because *branchial* comes from the Greek word for "gills." Somehow the name *neck folds* just isn't fancy enough for our scientific minds, so these folds are called *pharyngeal arches*, since they are arch-shaped folds near the throat. (*Pharyngeal* is the scientific word for things having to do with the throat. When you say you have a sore throat, your doctor says you have pharyngitis.) The creases between the folds are called *pharyngeal clefts*, and the undersides of the folds are called *pharyngeal pouches*. The pouches and clefts are not connected by an opening. Each fold shapes itself into specific structures, none of which are ever used for breathing. The outer and middle ear as well as the bones, muscles, nerves, and glands of the jaw and neck and even the immune system's thymus gland develop from these folds as tissues differentiate in compliance with the blueprint in human DNA.

Nevertheless, the meaning-packed terms *gill slits* and *gill-like structures* persist. But mammalian pharyngeal arches are no more related to gills — ancestrally or otherwise — than stars are to streetlights.

Even texts that refer to these folds by correct names sometimes perpetuate the powerful gill slit myth. For instance, Mader's *Biology* (2007 edition) correctly describes the ultimate anatomic destiny of each pharyngeal arch component and then asks:

> Why should terrestrial vertebrates develop and then modify such structures like pharyngeal pouches that have lost their original function? The most likely explanation is that fishes are ancestral to other vertebrate groups.[29]

What "lost original function"? No one has ever documented that pharyngeal pouches in the embryos of terrestrial vertebrates function as gills or that adult terrestrial vertebrates ever had gills. Preserved in textbooks and the media, the fishy ancestral myth persists. Our unseen and unverified fishy past still surfaces regularly in the assumptions that the pouches/folds/slits, or whatever-they-get-called, are leftovers from a fish ancestor.

In a chilling application of this misinformation, many abortionists have used Haeckel's embryologic falsehoods to assuage the guilt of women seeking

---

29. Sylvia Mader, *Biology*, 9th ed. (New York: McGraw-Hill, 2007), p. 97.

abortion, telling them they're only removing something like a fish, not a baby. The late Dr. Henry Morris observed, "We can justifiably charge this evolutionary nonsense of recapitulation with responsibility for the slaughter of millions of helpless, pre-natal children — or at least for giving it a pseudo-scientific rationale."[30]

The Current Debate

Given all the data researchers have used to refute recapitulation theory, do real scientists still cling to its discredited notions? After all, it's one thing to foist a fabricated over-simplified bit of evolutionary evidence on the gullible public and generations of children and college students, but do professionals hang on to these notions, too?

While some professional evolutionary scientists have given up on recapitulation theory altogether, many continue to cling to various permutations of it.

Some distance the beloved recapitulation dogma from Haeckel and look back a bit further to Karl Van Baer's 1828 version that claimed embryonic stages only recapitulate the embryonic stages of their evolutionary ancestors. Neither version has ever truly explained embryologists' observations, however. And as Richardson's work has clearly demonstrated, vertebrate embryos have discernible differences even at the earliest stages, an observation that finally strips the underpinnings of both versions. Thus to make the theory work, some evolutionary biologists who wish to keep it have modified it, choosing which parts they can make the best case for.

Ernst Mayr's modification, laid out in "Recapitulation Reinterpreted: The Somatic Program," appeared in 1994 in the *Quarterly Review of Biology.* He wrote that despite "the disrepute into which Haeckel's claims had fallen . . . every embryologist knew that there was a valid aspect to the claim of recapitulation."[31] A 2012 paper co-authored by Richard Lenski, "Ontogeny Tends to Recapitulate Phylogeny in Digital Organisms," notes that Mayr's "sentiment is still widely held today, and the idea that ontogeny recapitulates phylogeny in some form has its modern proponents."[32]

---

30. Henry Morris, T*he Long War Against God* (Ada, Michigan:Baker Book House, 1989), p. 139.
31. Ernst Mayr, "Recapitulation Reinterpreted: The Somatic Program," *Quarterly Review of Biology* (2002).
32. J. Clune et al., "Ontogeny Tends to Recapitulate Phylogeny in Digital Organisms," *The American Naturalist*, 180 no. 3 (2012): p. E54–E63.

Making It Work

Recapitulation theory is just too appealing to abandon for many evolutionists. Lenski's group wrote, "At a minimum, the fact that the debate has continued for so long lends credence to Mayr's view that there is at least some validity to recapitulation."[33]

Perhaps the most dramatic rehabilitation of Haeckel has come at the hands of one of his best-known modern critics, Michael Richardson. In the 2002 paper "Haeckel's ABC of Evolution and Development," published in *Biological Reviews of the Cambridge Philosophical Society,* Richardson and Gerhard Keuck re-examined Haeckel's work. They wrote:

> Haeckel recognized the evolutionary diversity in early embryonic stages, in line with modern thinking. He did not necessarily advocate the strict form of recapitulation and terminal addition commonly attributed to him. Haeckel's much-criticized embryo drawings are important as phylogenetic hypotheses, teaching aids, and evidence for evolution. While some criticisms of the drawings are legitimate, others are more tendentious. . . . Despite his obvious flaws, Haeckel can be seen as the father of a sequence-based phylogenetic embryology.[34]

Richardson and Keuck conclude that the biogenetic law is valid after all, if applied to the evolution of "single characters only" and not entire embryonic and evolutionary stages.[35] In other words, so long as only single traits are followed through evolutionary time and embryonic development, Richardson is now aboard the recapitulation bandwagon.

Richardson and Keuck's analysis of Haeckel's work was not able to expunge the charge of falsification, but they clearly have granted him absolution. They and others support "Haeckel's practice of filling in gaps in the embryonic series by speculation,"[36] even though "Haeckel presented the embryo drawing as data in support of his hypotheses"[37] and not just helpful teaching aids.

Haeckel's artistic liberties are clearly not the result of any lack of observation skills or artistic ability. One of his latter-day apologists has even praised Haeckel's diagrams of single-celled radiolarians, noting their resemblance to

---

33. Ibid.
34. Richardson and Keuck, *Biological Reviews of the Cambridge Philosophical Society*, p. 495–528.
35. Ibid.
36. Ibid.
37. Ibid.

modern light microscope images and electron micrographs.[38] Haeckel was a skilled illustrator able to render what he observed with accuracy and detail when he wanted to. But when real observation failed to confirm what he needed to be true in order to support his worldview-based beliefs about the evolutionary past and its parallels in the present, he opted to draw his own version of "reality."

The ultimate excuse for Haeckel's graphic concoctions has come from those who wish to honor what they see as his cognitively pure prescience coupled with a somewhat liberal view of the purpose of scientific illustration. "Haeckel's own views on art stressed the primacy of interpretation over pure observation,"[39] write Richardson and Keuck. They note that Haeckel's own writings reveal that he knew early embryos of various species have a lot of differences. They assert that Haeckel therefore never intended for his pictures to depict his actual observations but rather to show what he deemed to be "a true reproduction of the really existing natural produce."[40] And fabrications though some of these drawings clearly were, Haeckel intended them as support for his recapitulation theory. Yet because Richardson and Keuck maintain that recapitulation theory is true so long as it is viewed in a certain way — one trait at a time, with allowances for traits that have disappeared over time — they believe "Haeckel's embryo drawings are important as phylogenetic hypotheses, teaching aids — *even scientific evidence*" (emphasis ours).[41]

But Why?

What recapitulation believers still struggle with, however, is some reason recapitulation should be true. What evolutionary advantage would it have? If embryos really recapitulate their evolutionary past, what is the evolutionary advantage of anatomic structures that develop and ultimately don't get used? Why would unused "gill slits," for instance, stick around across the evolutionary time scales through organisms that did not need gills until they could evolve a non-respiratory purpose?

Some embryologic structures only serve temporary purposes in the embryo and then disappear or regress. If these represent footprints of an evolutionary

---

38. Ibid.
39. Ibid.
40. Ernst Haeckel, (1904). *Kunstformen der Natur. Bibliographisches Institut, Leipzig und Wien*; quoted in M. Richardson and G. Keuck, "Haeckel's ABC of evolution and development," *Biological Reviews of the Cambridge Philosophical Society*, p. 495–528.
41. Richardson and Keuck, *Biological Reviews of the Cambridge Philosophical Society*, p. 495–528.

past, why would structures that don't get used in the mature organism persist purposelessly through millions of year of evolutionary history?

In an attempt to answer this question, some expand on Gould's idea of "terminal addition," proposing that successful earlier evolutionary innovations are not lost but allowed to keep functioning while new developments are added. To undo earlier developments before they have served their place-holding purpose in the newly evolving organism would disrupt subsequent add-ons. While this describes exactly what happens in a developing *embryo* whose development is directed by its DNA blueprint, however, how can mindless random evolution "know" it needs to keep a useless structure in place for millions of years?

Phylogeny and the Return of Haeckel

Haeckel's diagrams do not represent observable embryologic reality, and Haeckel knew that they didn't when he made them. Nevertheless, he intended them — doctored though they were — to be data in support of his evolutionary ideas. He intentionally falsified scientific observations in order to use "embryonic resemblance as proof of evolution"[42] and "recapitulation as proof of the Biogenetic Law."[43] Yet he receives praise for his insight into the evolutionary past and his ability to reconstruct the observable present to prove what evolutionists believe.

Rigorous comparative embryology confirms "there is no evidence from vertebrates that entire stages are recapitulated."[44] Thus, Haeckel's claims about embryonic development are not supported by actual observation. Even if embryonic development did proceed as he claimed, of course, it would not prove anything about a hypothetical evolutionary past.

But that aside, why are evolutionary scientists and educators so keen to use inaccurate diagrams for "phylogenetic hypotheses, teaching aids, and evidence for evolution"? Why do Haeckel's modern apologists strain at his work, re-packaging it to show how it could be true so long as it is viewed a certain way, such as one trait at a time?

Embryology, because it outlines successful steps that produce fully functional, mature organisms, tells the evolutionist what to look for. And because whole organisms don't often fill the needs of the evolutionary story, evolutionists can now justify tracing single traits through deep time and seeking parallels in embryology. A fossil that seems to possess a trait in any of the ways it appears

42. Ibid.
43. Ibid.
44. Ibid.

in an embryological developmental sequence can be claimed as a representative of its evolutionary sequence and assigned its spot in history.

If fossils seeming to fit the step-wise nature of different embryological stages can be found, they are lined up as evidence for evolution. But fossils do not demonstrate evolutionary transitions. Neither do embryologic stages. Yet by claiming that both actually do represent evolutionary sequences, evolutionists concoct visually compelling evidence and tie it together through a comforting knot of circular reasoning.

The controversy about the evolutionary origin of the turtle shell illustrates both of these points. Evolutionists have long debated the origin of the turtle shell. Until recently all the turtle fossils found had been fully equipped with modern-appearing shells. Therefore, evolutionists have debated whether the shell evolved over millions of years by following the sequence seen inside the turtle egg or whether it evolved as a modification of external scales.

Now that two varieties of turtle with seemingly less developed parts of the shell have been identified, evolutionary researchers have noted that these shell variations more or less mirror shell developmental stages in the embryo. They therefore are asserting that turtle embryology predicted those forms successfully, proving on the one hand that those turtles are genuine transitional forms and on the other hand that ontogeny of turtle shells really does recapitulate phylogeny.[45]

In reality, no evolution from non-turtles is seen here, only two varieties of turtles. What these turtle fossils reveal is not a series of non-turtles evolving into turtles but just varieties of turtles. Mutations alter genetic information, and it is likely that these two extinct turtles are merely variations that developed from the original turtle kind God created about 6,000 years ago. Finally, as teaching aids, teachers and textbook manufacturers can now once again return in good conscience to teaching the mantra, "ontogeny recapitulates phylogeny," that is — those that ever actually stopped in the first place. For many who accept evolution as unquestioned fact, any evidence that can be used to indoctrinate the young or the gullible is acceptable, even fraudulent concoctions from a man who was in the habit of manufacturing whatever counterfeits and forgeries he needed in order to promote evolution with the evangelistic zeal of a missionary.

Thus, despite their inaccuracies, Haeckel's sometime critic-turned-defender concludes, "Haeckel's embryo drawings are important as phylogenetic

45. "Turtle in the Gap," Answers in Genesis (June 29, 2013), http://www.answersingenesis.org/articles/2013/06/29/turtle-gap.

hypotheses, teaching aids — even scientific evidence. . . . The drawings illustrate embryonic similarity, recapitulation, and phenotypic divergence."[46]

Recapitulation's Future

Just because something is proven blatantly false, like recapitulation theory, doesn't mean people are *persuaded*. These controversies can be expected to continue, not because there is proof that all life evolved from simpler ancestral forms, but because there is a popular widespread worldview-based belief in molecules-to-man evolution.

Believing that life must be explained as the product of natural evolutionary processes, evolutionary scientists must seek natural explanations wherever they can. Yet embryonic development is observable, and evolutionary phylogeny is not. Their supposed parallelism and the notion that such parallelism would constitute evolutionary proof are popular and powerful lies.

The observable wonders of embryology — surely a showcase of God's design — were hijacked by Haeckel and continue to be much too valuable components of the evolutionary toolkit to relinquish. Recapitulation has therefore been resurrected and repackaged to teach and to convince. Haeckel's "liberties" are excused with a nod that would never be extended to any modern scientist who faked his findings.

Recapitulation theory will doubtless continue to serve a prominent place in classrooms and on television documentaries aimed at convincing the public of the "obvious" truth of evolution. Moreover, as illustrated by the case of the turtle shell, highly trained evolutionary scientists, seeking to answer not "whether" things evolved but "how," will find recapitulation theory to be a convenient tool to provide the circular reasoning to justify the theory of the moment.

46. Richardson and Keuck, *Biological Reviews of the Cambridge Philosophical Society*, p. 495–528.

CHAPTER 27

Is Speciation Evidence for Creation or Evolution?

DR. GARY PARKER

I n a debate at a major Texas university, the creationist was challenged with this claim: Hawaiian fruit flies that could once all interbreed had changed into numerous reproductively isolated species, and that, said the challenger to considerable applause, "proved evolution." The creationist responded (also to considerable applause) that such a change would be the opposite of evolution. Losing the ability to interbreed, each "new species" would have less genetic variability, less ability to meet changes in its existing environment, and less ability to explore new environments — all suggesting decline and demise rather than the expansion of genetic potential required for what Darwin called "the production of higher animals."

Which of these views is more consistent with our present understanding of genetic science and with the biblical record of earth history?

Basic Genetics

The Bible records several key events in early earth history that suggest concepts geneticists can test scientifically. Genesis 1 states that God created many distinct "kinds." We infer from a plain reading of Scripture that animals and plants were created to reproduce within the boundaries of their kinds (Genesis 1, 6, and 8). A created kind is typically equivalent to the level of family in modern classification schemes as many members of a family can interbreed and produce offspring. The kinds were also "to fill" (scatter, move into) earth's varied environments (Genesis 1:22, 8:17). Multiple biological mechanisms accounted for this filling and resulted in variation within kinds, or speciation. Do these fundamental concepts in God's Word — discrete created kinds, or baramins (Hebrew: *bara* = create and *min* = kind), having broad but limited variability — help scientists understand the genetic changes in organisms and speciation found in God's world? Indeed, they do!

The complete set of DNA specifying a kind is called its genome. The human genome includes approximately 20,000 to 25,000 protein-coding chromosomal segments commonly called genes. The genes and the information they encode are largely responsible for the set of biological traits that distinguish human beings from other kinds of life. All humans have essentially the same genes, and they are over 99 percent similar in all seven billion of us; hence, geneticists refer to the human genome and have concluded that we are all members of one race, the human race (as the Apostle Paul preached in ancient Greece, Acts 17:26).

The similarity among all human beings is obvious, but so is the tremendous variation! The genes we share in the human genome make us all the same (100 percent human); but different versions of these shared genes, called alleles, produce the spectacular variation that makes each individual unique. For any given gene, God could have created it in four different allelic varieties (two in both Adam and Eve). Genetic alterations occurring since sin corrupted creation have introduced many new alleles, but no new genes.

The human genome, for example, has genes for producing hair and controlling its shape; allelic versions of these genes result in individuals with straight, wavy, curly, and tightly-curled hair; all variations within the human kind. Although, genetically speaking, skin color is more complex, the variation in human skin tone can be described as the action of two pairs of genes with different alleles (A/a and B/b) that influence the production of the skin pigment melanin. As shown in figure 1,[1] two people with medium-brown skin tone and genes AaBb could have children with the full range of skin tones — from very dark (AABB), to dark (AABb or AaBB), to medium (like AaBb), to light (like Aabb), to very light (aabb). That would certainly be "change through time" but a lot of change in a little time (one generation!) With no genes added, this is just variation within a kind.

Mutations, changes in DNA that occurred after man's sin corrupted God's creation, do not produce new genes. Rather, mutations only produce alleles, variations in pre-existing genes. Alleles are not different genes in the sense that

---

1. Gary Parker, *Building Blocks in Life Science* (Green Forest, AR: Master Books, 2011), p. 9.

A couple with **melanin** control genes
AaBb (Adam and Eve?)
would have "**medium**" skin tone, and each
would make four kinds of reproductive cells,
as shown along top and side of this
"genetic square":

genes in mother's egg cells

		AB	Ab	aB	ab
genes in father's sperm cells	AB	AA BB	AA Bb	Aa BB	Aa Bb
	Ab	AA Bb	AA bb	Aa Bb	Aa bb
	aB	Aa BB	Aa Bb	aa BB	aa Bb
	ab	Aa Bb	Aa bb	aa Bb	aa bb

Each box in the larger "Punnett square" shows the gene
combination possible in a child.

As shown in the pictures below,
children of "medium" parents could have
most to least melanin and
color darkest to lightest with 4, 3, 2, 1, 0 "capital letter"
genes indicated with each picture.

Figure 1. Inheritance of melanin skin color

genes for skin color and genes for making sickle-cell hemoglobin (resulting in sickle cell anemia) are. Similarly, the sickle-cell gene is a different allele (version) of the hemoglobin gene in the sense that it was not present at creation, but it is only a different harmful version of a *pre-existing* gene. In fact, the allele for sickle-cell hemoglobin differs in sequence in only one position out of several hundred from the normal gene for making hemoglobin. Again, we see mutations leading to different versions of *pre-existing* genes resulting in a variety of alleles but not the creation of brand new genes encoding novel proteins with novel functions of the type necessary for molecules-to-man evolution.

Variation within a Kind

All the genes in one generation available to be passed on to the next are called the gene pool. Members of the same kind may also be defined as organisms that share the same gene pool. The number of genes for different kinds of traits, the number in a complete genome, can be called the depth of the gene pool. The human gene pool is around 20,000–25,000 genes deep. The width of the gene pool refers to the amount of its allelic variation. Among dogs, for example, the width of a greyhound's gene pool is very narrow; crossing purebred greyhounds just gives you more greyhounds, all very similar in speed, color, intelligence, hair length, nose length, etc. Crossing two mongrels, however, can give you big dogs and small dogs, dark and light and splotchy-colored dogs, dogs with long and short hair, yappy and quiet dogs, mean and affectionate dogs, and the list goes on! The width of the mongrel's gene pool (its allelic variability) is quite large compared to the greyhound's, but the depth of the gene pool (the number of genes per genome) is the same for both dogs.

A kind is defined in terms of depth of the gene pool, which is the total number of different genes in a genome and a list of traits they encode for. Variation within a kind is defined in terms of the width of the gene pool, the number of possible alleles at each gene site (locus).

Geneticists call the shuffling of *pre-existing* genes recombination. Perhaps you have played a game with a common deck of 52 cards that includes four groups (hearts, diamonds, clubs, and spades), each with 13 different numbers or "faces" (2–10 plus J, Q, K, A). In a game called bridge, each of four players gets a "hand" of 13 cards. You can play bridge for 50 years (and some people do!) without ever getting the same group of 13 cards. The hands you are dealt are constantly changing, and each is unique — but the deck of cards remains always the same.

Although the comparison is not perfect, a deck of cards illustrates the concept of variation within a created kind. The bridge hands dealt are unique, different, and constantly changing, like the individual members of a population. But the deck of 52 cards remains constant, never changing, always the same, like the kind. Individual variation plus group constancy equals variation within a created kind.

Faith in Man Versus Faith in God's Word

Based on faith in Darwin's words, evolutionists assume that all life started from one or a few chemically evolved life forms with an extremely small gene pool. For evolutionists, enlargement of the gene pool by Darwinian selection (struggle and death) among random mutations is a slow, tedious, grim process that burdens each type with a staggering "death load" and "genetic load" of harmful mutations and evolutionary leftovers. Based on faith in God's Word, creationists assume each created kind began with a large gene pool, designed to multiply and fill the earth with its tremendous ecological and geographic variety.

Neither creationists nor evolutionists were there at the beginning to see how it was done, of course, but the creationist can build on the Word of the One who was there "in the beginning" (Genesis 1:1; John 1:1–3). Furthermore, the creationist mechanism is consistent with scientific observation. The evolutionary mechanism doesn't work, and is not consistent with present scientific knowledge of genetics and reproduction. As a scientist, I prefer ideas that do work and do help to explain what we can observe, and that's biblical creation!

Since animals were commanded to multiply and fill the earth, we can infer that the created kinds were "endowed by their Creator" with tremendous allelic variability and allelic potential in very wide gene pools. Geneticists now know, for example, that alleles for the full range of normal human variation — darkest to lightest skin tone, Pygmy to Watusi heights, wide to thin lips, hair from straight to wavy to curly to tightly-curled, eyelids producing round to oval shapes, etc. — are possible, beginning with just two people. Genetics problems solved by high school students (figure 1) show how such parents could produce children with traits from darkest to lightest, shortest to tallest, with hair of any style, and eyes and lips of any shape in just one generation — all with NONE of the deep time, chance mutations, and ceaseless struggle to the death that evolutionists use to explain variation in beak sizes in finches or amounts of black pigment in moth wings.

What Does This Awesome Variability within Kinds Mean?

For one thing, such awesome variation reflects God's creativity. God created the first man from the dust of the ground and the first woman from a rib from his side (Genesis 2:7, 21–22). Then, God rested from His creative acts at the end of the creation week (Genesis 2:1–2). But we still see God's creativity unfolding before our very eyes in a different way in the birth of each child. As they relate to the genetic potential God created in our first parents, we may not yet have seen the fastest runner or the greatest mathematical or musical genius. Genes were not produced one at a time by evolutionary processes — time, chance, mutations, struggle, and death over millions of years. This unfolding of genetic variability in *pre-existing* genes is all stunning variation within a kind, but it is NOT the formation of new genetic information of the type required for molecules-to-man evolution.

As the descendants of each created kind multiplied to fill the earth, we see their genetic potential unfolding. God created the bear kind, for example. But as bears moved into different environments around the world after the Flood, their built-in variability and ability to genetically change came to visible expression in black bears, brown bears, grizzly bears, polar bears, etc. The created dog kind diversified into specialized subtypes: wolves, coyotes, domestic dogs, etc. Think also about the tremendous genetic variability brought to visible expression in the cat kind, rose kind, tomato kind, etc.

There is a strong tendency, both in nature and in experimental breeding, for generalized, adaptable organisms to produce a variety of specialized, adaptable subgroups. Figure 1, discussed earlier, showed that if Adam and Eve, for example, had a variety of alleles for skin tone (AaBb) they could have children with skin tones from darkest to lightest. However, some of that initial genetic variability would be lost when subgroups of the human population moved apart and remained reproductively isolated, as they did at the Tower of Babel (Genesis 11). Some language groups may have included only A and B alleles, losing a and b; in such AABB subgroups, parents could only have children with very dark skin. Subgroups without the A and B alleles (only a and b) would produce only very light-skinned children, and either AAbb or aaBB subgroups would always be medium brown. AaBb subgroups would continue to produce the entire color range, like some groups in India still do today.

Darwin thought otherwise, but scientists now recognize that people groups who express only part of the full range of melanin color variation (such as very dark skin) are 100 percent human. But among animals and plants, both in nature and from selective breeding, subgroups of some kinds may become so different (e.g., size, courtship ritual, mating season, chromosomal rearrangements, aggressiveness, etc.) that they can no longer interbreed (even though their identity as members of the same created kind can still be confirmed by genetic testing). Such reproductive isolation was once used as the key criterion for defining species.

What? Two or more specialized species descended from one generalized ancestral kind? Doesn't that prove evolution after all! Exactly the opposite.

Speciation, yes; evolution, no. Molecules-to-man evolution requires a net *increase* in novel genetic information, the addition of genes for new trait categories to a genome. Reproductive isolation and subsequent speciation results in a *loss* of genetic variability (alleles), converting a large gene pool into subgroups with smaller gene pools (i.e., "new species" with less ability to meet changes in their environment, restricted ability to explore new environments, and reduced prospects for long-term survival). Indeed, evolutionists now regularly use the term "over specialization" in speciation as an explanation for extinction versus evolutionary progress.

The Florida panther, for example, is considered an endangered species. What endangers it? The small, inbred population was so riddled with mutations that no cubs could survive to reproductive age. The cure? Since it is only a species within a kind, it was bred with western panthers (members of the same kind) having different post-Fall mutations. The former Florida panther is now recovering from its flirt with extinction and being restored to health.

Distinctive genetic diseases and abnormalities characterize many purebred dogs, which have often reached the end of the line, genetically speaking. Each has all the genetic information in its genome to be 100 percent dog (so each has the same gene pool depth), but the allelic variability (gene pool width) could be reduced ultimately to 0 percent (only one allele per locus in a population). Therefore, crossing purebred poodles with poodles, for example, would produce only poodles and would not be a promising path for recapturing the ancestral wolf or generalized dog kind. If a "poodle plague" wiped out the poodle, however, poodles could be brought back again over several generations through breeding wolves or mongrel dogs. Even the quagga, an extinct subspecies of zebra, is being brought back through cross breeding varied members of the horse kind.

The Wrong Kind of Change

Speciation is moving in the wrong direction to support the evolutionary belief in upward changes between kinds, or molecules-to-man evolution. Speciation produces only variation within kinds as a result of the subdivision and/or alteration of *pre-existing* genetic variability. Speciation also brings to visible expression the magnificent variability and potential for variation that God programmed into the members of each of the original created kinds.

After man's sin, mutations introduced many "negative variations," helping scientists to explain the origin of birth defects and disease. Evolutionists had hoped mutations would provide the new genetic information required to move organisms up the so-called evolutionary tree. But mutations only produce variation in *pre-existing* genes, which are alleles that only make a gene pool wider rather than deeper. So mutations result in variation within a kind and not the formation of new and different kinds, which Darwin called the "production of higher animals."

Uncritical acceptance of evolution has so stunted scientific thinking that people give mutations god-like qualities. They act as if a cosmic ray striking a cell can cause a mutation that somehow assembles over 1,500 DNA nucleotides into a brand new gene, regulators and all, that suddenly begins producing a brand-new protein responsible for a brand-new trait, raising the lucky mutated organism to the next higher limb on the evolutionary tree! NOTHING remotely like that has ever been observed, nor will it be!

Mutations are NOT genetic "script writers"; they are merely typographic alterations in a genetic script that has already been written. Typically, a mutation changes only one letter in a genetic sentence averaging 1,500 letters long. To make evolution happen — or even to make evolution a theory fit for scientific discussion — evolutionists desperately need some kind of genetic script writer to create novel genetic information, increasing the size of a genome and the depth of a gene pool. Mutations have no ability to compose genetic sentences, no ability to produce novel genetic information, and, hence, no ability to make evolution happen, at all.

Yet molecules-to-man evolution requires phenomenal expansion of genetic information. It would take thousands of mutations adding novel information to change simple cells into invertebrates, vertebrates, and mankind. The evolutionist's problem is with the fundamental nature of information itself. The information in a book, for example, cannot be reduced to nor derived from the properties of the ink and paper used to write it. Similarly, the information in the genetic code cannot be reduced to nor derived from the properties of matter or the allelic variations caused by mutations. Its message and meaning originated instead in the mind of its Maker, Jesus Christ, the Author of life (John 1:1–3). What we see in God's world agrees with what we read in God's Word.

CHAPTER 28

Are Genetically Modified Organisms (GMOs) Wrong?

DR. ANDREW FABICH

I don't like food, I love it!" — Anton Ego in *Ratatouille*

W e all like food. Some of us like food more than others. Food is more popular today than it was 20 years ago. There are even several TV channels devoted to food and a full-length animated film about food. Unfortunately, our love of food goes to many unhealthy extremes. So we have organizations like the Food and Drug Administration (FDA) to help oversee our food supply. The FDA is supposed to make sure our food is safe to eat, even providing guidelines on what to eat or what not to eat. Even with FDA approval, we have an abundance of "safe" food products. Occasionally, the FDA has to move things from the safe list to the unsafe list.

About ten years ago, the food battle waged against artificial sweeteners like those found in Sweet'N'Low (i.e., the chemical aspartame). In addition to tasting bad, some claim that Sweet'N'Low causes cancer. More recently, the FDA has appropriately recalled foods like beef tainted with deadly *E. coli*. Warnings have been placed on cigarettes, which cause lung cancer. In those instances, the FDA has acted responsibly by removing food products and labeling foods that are dangerous to eat. But there has been a shift in food battles lately. Today's food battle typically wages against seemingly wholesome foods containing "corn, soybean, cotton, wheat, canola, sorghum, and sugar cane seeds."[1] What

---

1. http://www.monsanto.com/products/Pages/default.aspx, accessed 04-12-13.

is common to all these seemingly wholesome foods is that they typically are genetically modified in the US — their DNA has been changed. Currently, the FDA has no requirement to label foods made with these ingredients and there have been no recalls. But have they acted in a safe and responsible fashion? Or is there anything really wrong with these common "all natural" products?

Let me give you some background. In the old days, farmers used to breed plants together and make "hybrids" — think of a corn hybridized from crossing two different varieties of corn. This was done to enhance the corn to make it bigger or healthier and so on. They would do this with other farm commodities like breeding various cattle together as well. But corn is a great example. Corn is found in the American food supply in the form of high fructose corn syrup. We find this high fructose corn syrup in many household products as a general additive. To understand how much high fructose corn syrup you are consuming, just check the ingredients label in your pantry. (Really, if you're reading this and haven't ever looked, quickly carry your book to the pantry and look for yourself.) The ingredients are listed in the order of abundance, so the first ingredient is most abundant in the food you eat. You may be surprised to find all the products that have high fructose corn syrup in them (let alone how much of it) — especially soft drinks. Even the ethanol additive in our gasoline at the gas pump was produced from corn products! You may begin wondering: what doesn't have corn in it?

The biggest surprise for most people is that most Americans have consumed a vegetable product, including corn, that has been genetically altered . . . without even knowing it. This brings us to *genetically modified organisms* (GMOs).[2] They are any organism (like plants — specifically here, corn) that has been modified with DNA from another organism. Instead of cross-pollinating corn to make it better, like the old days, they are now taking genes from one organism and forcing them into the DNA (or genome) of a different organism to make it better. Essentially, scientists have added some genes from something else to improve the crop (e.g., to make food grow bigger, taste better, etc.). For the sake of this chapter, I will focus on the GMOs in the American food supply.

There are large lobbies interested in whether GMOs should be in the food supply or not.[3]

---

2. For our discussion in this chapter, we will primarily be looking at GMOs that involve the artificial transfer of genetic information from one kind of organism to another. This is the area that raises the most ethical concerns and is the primary focus of the GMO food debate.

3. I receive no benefits from any GMO producers or from any non-GMO organizations. My primary concern is for the future ecosystem and the health of my children.

1. The first lobby interested in GMOs is for the use of GMOs and includes major corporations like Monsanto. Monsanto is one of the largest agricultural companies that sells "seeds, traits developed through biotechnology, and crop protection chemicals." They have been at the center of some recent U.S. Supreme Court decisions (e.g., Bowman v. Monsanto Company).[4]

2. The second lobby interested in GMOs is against the use of GMOs and includes the Non-GMO Project. "The Non-GMO Project is a non-profit organization committed to preserving and building sources of non-GMO products, educating consumers, and providing verified non-GMO choices."[5]

3. The third lobby that should be interested in GMOs is the unaware majority of Americans having already consumed a GMO without knowing it.

But is ignorance bliss? As a trained scientist who has done the research and also as a dad, let me first scrutinize these GMOs using the Scriptures then scientifically evaluate GMOs to determine if there is anything wrong with using them.

Do Scriptures Teach against GMOs?

Since the structure of the DNA double helix was discovered only recently (1953), the human authors of the Bible could not use the term "genetically engineered" like we use it today. The lack of GMOs in Scripture does not invalidate Scripture nor does it mean that these genetic engineering concepts are not addressed in Scripture, leaving us without a guide through the 21st century. (Keep in mind that the word *dinosaur* was not invented until the 1800s and so it, too, is not found in Scripture even though God created dinosaurs.)

To the contrary, some important words that also define biblical Christianity and yet do not appear in Scripture include (but are not limited to) the Trinity and the hypostatic union. Significant words always discussed in the GMO debate like "drought-resistant crops" and the active herbicide found in RoundUp™ (the chemical glyphosate) are hardly found in normal people's vocabulary and were not in our vocabulary until recently. But even though

---

4. For reference, see http://www.monsanto.com last accessed 06-18-13 and http://www.nytimes.com/2013/05/14/business/monsanto-victorious-in-genetic-seed-case.html?_r=0 last accessed 06-18-13.

5. http://www.nongmoproject.org.

drought-resistant crops and the herbicide glyphosate are certainly not biblical, they are directly related to the biblical subject of man's dominion over the earth.

Both the image of God and man's dominion are first mentioned in Scripture simultaneously. When God creates the first humans on day 6, Scripture tells us:

> Then God said, "Let Us make man in Our image, according to Our likeness; let them have dominion over the fish of the sea, over the birds of the air, and over the cattle, over all the earth and over every creeping thing that creeps on the earth." So God created man in His own image; in the image of God He created him; male and female He created them. Then God blessed them, and God said to them, "Be fruitful and multiply; fill the earth and subdue it; have dominion over the fish of the sea, over the birds of the air, and over every living thing that moves on the earth" (Genesis 1:26–28).

It is abundantly clear that these verses teach what is traditionally referred to as the dominion mandate. God gave the dominion responsibility to those who bear His image and to nothing else. Since we bear His image, we must understand the responsibility of dominion over organisms, their seeds, and their DNA so that we act according to God's desires. Furthermore, we must guard against the abuse and misuse of God's creation.

> The works of the Lord are great, studied by all who have pleasure in them (Psalm 111:2).

> You have made him to have dominion over the works of Your hands; You have put all things under his feet (Psalm 8:6).

When using any part of God's creation, we must be found good stewards. Our dominion should be taken seriously, but also not neglected (cf. Luke 19:11–27). Since we are entrusted with creation, we have the God-given responsibility to care for it. Some people have taken Leviticus 19:19, "You shall not sow your field with mixed seed," out of context to interpret seed to mean the genetic material of one organism should not be mixed with that of another organism. The text says mixing *seeds* (kil'ayim, which also appears in Deuteronomy 22:9 in the same context) is wrong, not the mixing of *kinds* (miyn) (where the biblical term kind is usually synonymous with the family level in modern classification schemes). While the word "seeds" falls in the semantic range encompassed by the word "kinds," the converse is not true (i.e., "kinds" are not "seeds").

In today's modern technological world, we often find ourselves enjoying God's creation because of different technologies. But as any technology changes new challenges arise. When Noah built the ark, the technology included tools made of stone, bronze, and/or iron. When Moses was writing the Law, the Egyptians were repairing devastation. Nebuchadnezzar finished his hanging gardens during the lifetime of Daniel. All roads were headed to Rome while Jesus walked this planet. Everyone should realize that using technology is not wrong in and of itself, but can be problematic when someone uses the technology in a *wrong* way (e.g., Nazis' inventions for the destructions of Jews, Poles, Slavs, and others). Building pyramids, hanging gardens, and road construction are technologies in their own right, but can this be true for scientists today genetically modifying our food?

Since technological innovations are developed by real-world, problem-solving scientists, then Christians should not be afraid of properly using technology (e.g., cell phones, spaceships, or the computer I used to write this chapter). GMOs are intended, like any technology, to potentially improve humanity when used properly, but they may also bring harm.

So picking on GMOs because they are new technology is a bad argument because there have been new technologies since the beginning of time. In fact, is it any wonder that it has taken us this long since Adam to invent GMOs? Of all people, today's Christians live with more information available, have the complete Word of God, and so should "have an answer" (1 Peter 3:15) for GMOs because they directly relate to the dominion mandate. Essentially, GMOs are like any technology that should be used consistent with what the Scriptures teach. While there is no specific verse teaching against GMOs, is there a scriptural principle that teaches GMOs violate the dominion mandate?

Do Scriptural Principles Teach against GMOs?

The Bible contains several very interesting examples of biotechnology without using the words DNA or GMOs. Genesis 30 records an exchange between Jacob and his father-in-law Laban. The exchange includes Jacob negotiating Laban's daughter to be his wife for an unusual price. The unusual price was for taking care of Laban's livestock; in exchange, Jacob would marry one of Laban's daughters. At the same time, Jacob was cunning enough to secure some livestock to provide for his future wife. All newlyweds start off with very little wealth and so Jacob asked for Laban's undesirable livestock to provide for his future wife. In exchange for those undesirable livestock, Jacob also promised to take care of Laban's desirable livestock. Specifically, the undesirable livestock that Jacob requested were "speckled and spotted among the goats, and brown among the lambs" (Genesis 30:33). Even though Jacob was deceived, he made the best of the situation by performing an odd technique that we still do not understand today: "Jacob took for himself rods of green poplar and of the almond and chestnut trees, peeled white strips in them, and exposed the white which was in the rods" (Genesis 30:37). This passage about using "rods of green poplar" (among others) implies that Jacob was artificially selecting (i.e., breeding) desirable traits from his newly acquired undesired animals. While Jacob worked with animals, the techniques he used are based on the same principles used to make GMOs.[6] So Jacob used the biotechnology of his day to artificially select certain desirable traits among his livestock (similar to dog breeding today). Not exactly a GMO by today's definition, but Jacob never compromised the dominion mandate in what he did.

Later in the New Testament, Paul writes to the Romans to describe important heavenly truths using an earthly example from the science of plant cultivation. Paul uses the term "graft" six times in Romans 11 to describe the spiritual truth that the Gentiles were to spiritually flourish essentially because God did so with the nation Israel. When Paul was writing in the first century, the term "graft" was often used to describe taking a slice of an olive branch and placing the cut branch into a fresh olive tree. GMOs and grafting are similar because they combine two separate sources of DNA. Grafting was a common practice in the ancient world and still used today to cultivate particular foods like seedless grapes. Paul used common language about grafting biotechnology (GMOs) to convey a spiritual truth.[7] Since olive trees do not bear the image of God and cutting a tree branch does not cause them to go extinct, then Paul's point did not suggest an abuse of the dominion mandate.

These two biblical examples of common practices when the Scriptures were written demonstrate that the concepts of genetic engineering and biotechnology do not necessarily violate any biblical principles. Modern genetic engineering principles and biotechnology practices are modified forms of

---

6. The way in which GMOs relate to animal breeding is that we look within a population of traits and select the ones we're interested in for breeding purposes. While this example of Jacob's goats explicitly refers to the same species, it is relatively easy to discuss movement of traits within a biblical kind. The trait does not necessarily have to be identified by its DNA in one species before moving it to another species — all within a created kind. The term GMO is usually set at the species level. Further discussion of moving genes between created kinds is discussed in subsequent sections with regard to grafting and previously discussed in terms of seeds/kinds.
7. See footnote 4 for the logic, but applied to grafting.

ancient animal breeding and plant grafting (as described in Scripture), which are simply a form of artificial selection. Scripture never says artificial selection is wrong, but actually uses examples of artificial selection to convey spiritual truths. No one can point to any verse or idea to suggest that artificial selection is wrong, let alone GMOs. Therefore, nothing is wrong with the process of genetically modifying any organism, even in a "very good" creation, so long as it glorifies God (all the more so now that we live in a fallen world). Whether Noah or Adam "artificially selected" anything is purely conjecture because Scripture is silent, but it is interesting to speculate nonetheless. In one sense, the animals were brought on Noah's ark due to a form of supernatural selection that gave us variation in the original gene pool necessary for all species existing today (cf. Genesis 7:16). So there is no specific verse teaching against GMOs, nor is there a biblical principle being violated. But is producing GMOs a valid scientific endeavor?

Is the Science Supporting GMOs Flawed?

Making a GMO is a long process that begins by identifying a feature of an organism to improve. Knowing which feature to improve then simplifies finding another organism with the desirable feature. Before we go further, let's hypothetically consider faster-growing crops as the feature we desire in our slower-growing crops. Let's continue, hypothetically, saying that we know certain weeds grow fast because of a faster-growing gene, and farmers could potentially benefit from placing the faster-growing weed gene into corn seeds to produce faster-growing corn (see figure 1 for a general overview of the process to make a GMO). To make this hypothetical situation happen, we first need to make copies of the faster-growing weed gene before introducing it into the slower-growing corn. Once the faster-growing weed gene is introduced into the slower-growing corn, we officially have our genetically modified corn and the corn is then tested in a controlled situation. Simply because the hypothetically faster-growing corn has a weed gene does not make it a weed and vice versa (see the previous comment about Leviticus 19:19). No one selling a GMO is going to under-deliver on the benefits claimed for their new product (in this case, faster growth of the corn). So the hypothetical company tests their product in controlled conditions until they feel it is safe. But when the faster-growing corn is sold, will it overtake all the traditional corn (not genetically modified) in the world?

To understand whether faster-growing corn is bad science depends on our understanding of natural selection and artificial selection. Natural selection

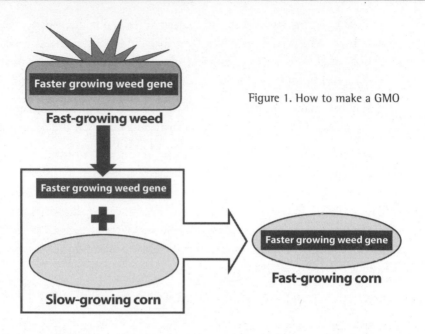

Figure 1. How to make a GMO

is the process designed by God that preserves the genetic makeup of a created kind. (Regrettably, many people incorrectly think that natural selection is equivalent to molecules-to-man evolution. Natural selection and evolution are not the same thing; they are very different.[8]) Artificial selection is the process humans use to choose certain desirable features within created kinds. Natural selection helps explain the diversity of Darwin's finches in the Galápagos, while artificial selection explains diversity among dog breeds. We have Great Danes, Doberman pinschers, dachshunds, and (yes) poodles as a result of artificial selection by humans from the original dog kind on Noah's ark. Whether talking about the artificial selection of dogs or plants, it is best to understand artificial selection as simply selective breeding. Ultimately, GMOs are a really sophisticated form of selective breeding. GMOs are slightly different from traditional selective breeding because we artificially introduce the desirable features from another organism in a single generation using technology. Even though certain features have moved between organisms, we are still involved in the selection process (i.e., this is still artificial selection). So the scientific methods of making GMOs does not violate biblical principles, but are GMOs safe for the environment and for human consumption?

---

8. See also *The New Answers Book 1*, question #22 "Is Natural Selection the Same Thing as Evolution?" (Green Forest, AR: Master Books, 2006).

If Nothing Is Wrong with GMOs Scripturally or Scientifically, Then What Is Holding Us Back?

The immediate benefits of GMOs include "increased pest and disease resistance, drought tolerance, and increased food supply."[9] Even with all those potential benefits, many countries have already banned the production and sale of GMOs. The Non-GMO Project is staunchly against GMOs and quite politically active against them. According to the Non-GMO Project:

> Most developed nations do not consider GMOs to be safe. In nearly 50 countries around the world, including Australia, Japan, and all of the countries in the European Union, there are significant restrictions or outright bans on the production and sale of GMOs. In the U.S., the government has approved GMOs based on studies conducted by the same corporations that created them and profit from their sale. Increasingly, Americans are taking matters into their own hands and choosing to opt out of the GMO experiment.[10]

Many people within the Non-GMO Project and its supporters want to educate the public and raise awareness about GMOs, and I couldn't agree more that education is important. So what does the actual research show about GMOs? All indications suggest that GMOs released in the United States are approved by the FDA, meeting significant scrutiny by multiple rounds of testing. Contrary to the claims that GMOs are unhealthy, the number of actual scientific reports in the scientific literature is very small that say GMOs cause cancer or other disease. The study titled "Long Term Toxicity of a Roundup Herbicide and a Roundup-tolerant Genetically Modified Maize"[11] has significant flaws and should not be considered authoritative. The flaws of the research include facts like the rodents fed increasing amounts of GMOs had better survival rates than those fed a smaller amount of GMOs. Additionally, their research mice that were fed non-GMO foods died at an alarming rate. According to the non-GMO lobby, the rodents fed non-GMO food should not have died under

---

9. http://www.webmd.com/food-recipes/features/are-biotech-foods-safe-to-eat, accessed 3-27-13.
10. http://www.nongmoproject.org/learn-more/ accessed 03-27-13.
11. Gilles-Eric Séralinia, Emilie Claira, Robin Mesnagea, Steeve Gressa, Nicolas Defargea, Manuela Malatestab, Didier Hennequinc, Joël Spiroux de Vendômoisa, "Long term Toxicity of a Roundup Herbicide and a Roundup-tolerant Genetically Modified Maize," *Food and Chemical Toxicology*, Volume 50, Issue 11, November 2012, Pages 4221–4231, http://www.sciencedirect.com/science/article/pii/S0278691512005637.

the same conditions as the rodents fed the GMOs; however, the non-GMO lobby's hypothesis was not supported by their own data and the mice fed non-GMO food also died. All this goes without mention that their sample size was extremely small and unrealistic to represent the 7 billion people of the world.

"Over three trillion servings of foods with [GMO] ingredients have been consumed, and in almost 20 years of experience with [GMO] crops, there has not been a single confirmed instance of harm to human health or disruption of an ecosystem."[12] There are no obvious warning signs that we should neither mass produce nor completely ban GMOs, contrary to the extreme positions of Monsanto supporters or the Non-GMO Project, respectively. More experimentation must happen to determine long-term consequences of GMOs in nature before we prematurely conclude that all GMOs are either greatly beneficial or extremely harmful in our food supply. We must remember that the science developing GMOs is the same science behind modern medical marvels such as antibiotics, vaccines, chemotherapy, pain relievers, antiseptics, blood transfusions, and many more. Those arguing wholeheartedly against GMOs must consider their logic and take care that they are not arguing against all forms of modern medicine at the same time.

Along those same lines, many accuse GMOs of being unhealthy foods that should not be sold without warning labels. Often, these accusations are unfounded. In reality, the real problem is not usually the GMO itself, but the actual food product. For instance, the high fructose corn syrup previously mentioned is unhealthy for you regardless of whether it comes from a natural/organic source or a GMO.[13] For every other food that includes a GMO, there are no legitimate reports of the GMOs damaging human health. Americans consume too much of everything and need to cut back on everything in general. We were never made to worship the material creation (i.e., our food) like an idol and overindulge.

As different world powers discuss GMOs, well-respected individuals are on both sides of this debate for a variety of legitimate reasons. All the biblical

---

12. http://www.genengnews.com/gen-articles/anti-ge-activism-will-it-ever-end/4825, accessed 04-22-13.

13. http://www.mayoclinic.com/health/high-fructose-corn-syrup/AN01588 is a site that demonstrates how having too many empty calories, like those found in high fructose corn syrup, increases the risk for obesity. http://www.webmd.com/food-recipes/features/are-biotech-foods-safe-to-eat emphasizes again that the current GMOs are 100% safe (even when entertaining all the supposed risks). When looking at the traditional soda pop with 39 g of sugar, that is equivalent to approximately 10 sugar cubes added to 12 ounces of liquid. I don't know anyone that adds 10 sugar cubes to a cup of coffee (let alone water) and maintains a healthy body mass index.

creationists are not on one side or the other; neither are the evolutionists. Creationists and evolutionists are on both sides of the argument, which is expected when some recently developed GMOs (like corn, soy, and rice) have not clearly violated either Scripture or secular principles. Ironically, the famed atheist Richard Dawkins offers advice based on biblical principles about GMOs. Dawkins says,

> I am undecided about the politics of GM foods, torn between the potential benefits to agriculture on the one hand and precautionary instincts on the other. But one argument I haven't heard before is worth a brief mention. The American grey squirrel was introduced to Britain by a former Duke of Bedford: a frivolous whim that we now see as disastrously irresponsible. It is interesting to wonder whether taxonomists of the future may regret the way our generation messed around with genomes. . . . The whole point of the precautionary principle, after all, is to avoid future repercussions of choices and actions that may not be obviously dangerous now.[14]

While Dawkins is a vehement atheist, his point about GMOs ultimately makes sense because he is unknowingly using biblical principles. The paraphrase of Proverbs 25:8 in *The Message* captures what to do with situations where there is no clear biblical direction: "Don't jump to conclusions — there may be a perfectly good explanation for what you just saw." Dawkins' argument is essentially what Solomon wrote thousands of years ago. In this instance, Dawkins acknowledges that we do not fully understand potential problems with GMOs in nature. He knows of no problem with GMOs in the lab. So he suggests some precautionary actions taken to not jump to a *hasty* decision. Public perception of GMOs is much worse than they deserve. It would be prudent to occasionally experiment with GMOs, collect the data, and then decide what to legislate before losing what we have on a global scale. GMOs are not problematic scientifically; the potential problem with GMOs is whether they harm God's creation in a way that cannot be fixed. If anyone should conclusively demonstrate a problem with a GMO, then that GMO should not be given to the public. Until potential harmful effects of GMOs are clearly documented scientifically, they should be used within reason and tested accordingly.

---

14. Richard Dawkins, *The Greatest Show on Earth* (New York: Simon and Schuster, 2009), p. 304.

Conclusions

Modified Organisms

	Instance	Result
1	Jacob and the flocks (e.g., Genesis 30)	Separating out the DNA
2	Grafting branches (e.g., Romans 11)	Mixing DNA
3	Hybridizing crops	Bringing DNA together
4	Artificial selection and breeds (e.g., Deuteronomy 32:14 with ram breeds)	Separating out DNA[a]
5	Natural variation	Separating out DNA
6	GMOs	Separating, mixing, bringing together DNA at a genomic level instead of an organismal level

a. In some cases, there could be a bringing together to form certain breeds as well. This would be the same for natural variations.

The question for this chapter remains: are GMOs wrong? I cannot give a biblical or scientific reason to wholeheartedly support or completely reject GMOs. Imaginary problems with GMOs arise when people take extreme positions on GMOs without using a biblical worldview. Too many Christians get too involved with picking sides on this debate when there is no clear violation of Scripture. Please stop the name-calling, develop a biblical worldview, and let's do good science to figure out the long-term effects of GMOs before picking an extreme (unbiblical) position.

In the meantime, if big business monopolizes the common farmer, then let the political process rectify the plight of the common farmer. If people are hungry because countries ban the sale of GMOs, then let the political process rectify the plight of the hungry people. Christians should obey the law of the land, work hard within their local church to help people, and be involved in the political process by making an informed vote. Ultimately, the Lord will rectify all injustice (Revelation 14:7) and redeem His creation (Revelation 21:1). In the meantime, the world will watch how America handles GMOs . . . and so should Christians.

We should do more research on GMOs to fully see their strengths or weaknesses. The intent of this chapter is to honestly examine our current knowledge of GMOs. At the end of the day, some people are opposed to eating GMOs and others are fine with GMOs. Regardless of whether we eat GMOs, we must keep a Christian attitude among the brethren and recall what Paul wrote while waiting for the research to finish: "So let no one judge you in food or in drink, or regarding a festival or a new moon or sabbaths, which are a shadow of things to come, but the substance is of Christ" (Colossians 2:16–17).

CHAPTER 29

What about Design Arguments Like "Irreducible Complexity"?

DR. STUART BURGESS

What Is the Design Argument?

The design argument says that design reveals a designer and the attributes of the designer. In the same way that the intricate design of an aircraft shows the skill and care of a human designer, so the intricate design of creation shows the skill and care of the divine Designer.

There are many verses in the Bible that contain the design argument. The most famous verse is Romans 1:20 which says, "For since the creation of the world His invisible attributes are clearly seen, being understood by the things that are made, even His eternal power and Godhead, so that they are without excuse." This verse teaches that God's handiwork in creation is clear for everyone to see and no one has an excuse not to believe in a Creator.

Another example of the design argument can be found in Hebrews 3:4 where we read, "For every house is built by someone, but He who built all things is God." In the same way that a house requires intricate design to make it suitable for humans to live in, so the earth requires intricate design to make it fit for human habitation. In fact, Isaiah 45:18 says that God deliberately designed the earth to be inhabited.

The Book of Job contains many verses on the wonder of creation, including the design of fish, birds, animals, dinosaurs, rain, snow, clouds, and the stars. The Book of Job speaks of how creation is so wonderfully designed that it is beyond human comprehension (Job 9:10 and 37:5). The Psalms also give glory to God for His creation. Psalm 139:14 speaks of the wonder of the design of the human body and how God deserves our praise for His workmanship.

Christians have used the design argument in preaching and writing down through the ages. The Apostle Paul used the design argument when he preached to the Athenians in Acts 17. In 1692, the Puritan preacher Thomas Watson used the following design argument in his writing:

> If one should go into a far country and see stately edifices he would never imagine that they could build themselves, but that there had been an artificer to raise such goodly structures; so this great fabric of the world could not create itself, it must have some builder or maker, and that is God.[1]

In 1802, William Paley wrote a famous book called *Natural Theology* in which he argued that in the same way that a mechanical watch must have a human designer, so the natural world must have a divine Designer. In recent times, creationists have written many books and articles on how creation is wonderfully designed. Creationists have explained how there are specific hallmarks of design such as irreducible complexity, common design, over-design and added beauty, which defy evolution. The following sections give a brief introduction to these arguments for design.

Irreducible Complexity

Irreducible complexity is an evidence for design that represents a key scientific test for evolution. Irreducible complexity is the term applied to a structure or mechanism that requires several precise parts to be assembled simultaneously for there to be a useful function for that structure or mechanism. Irreducible complexity cannot be produced by evolution because evolution is restricted to step-by-step change where every change must give a survival advantage. Evolution has no ability to bring about the many precise design changes that are necessary to make the leap from one design concept to another. If there are examples of irreducible complexity in nature, then the theory of evolution absolutely breaks down.

1. Thomas Watson, *The Creation* (London: Banner of Truth, 1965), ch. 13, "A Body of Divinity," p. 114.

Charles Darwin himself knew full well that irreducible complexity was a key test for evolution. Even though Darwin did not use the term "irreducible complexity," he said:

> If it could be demonstrated that any complex organ existed, which could not possibly have been formed by numerous, successive, slight modifications, my theory would absolutely break down. But I can find out no such case.[2]

Creation scientists have shown that creation actually does contain many cases of irreducible complexity. In microbiology there are many irreducible structures like the living cell and bacterial flagellum and there are irreducible processes like blood clotting.[3] Other examples of irreducible complexity are the eye,[4] human knee joint,[5] and the upright stature of humans.[6] Creationists have also shown how design requires information to be specified and that information must come from an intelligent source.[7] It would be fascinating to know if Charles Darwin would still believe his theory of evolution if he were here today and able to see the many case studies of irreducible complexity!

The Irreducible Human Arched Foot

Human feet represent a clear example of irreducible complexity.[8] Human feet have a unique arch structure that is completely different from the flat feet of apes. Arched feet are very important for the upright stature of humans because they allow fine control of the position of the body over the feet. When standing upright, a person can maintain balance by adjusting the relative pressures on the heels and balls of the feet.

Human feet have an arch between the heel and the ball of the foot, as shown in figure 1. The equivalent engineering arch is also shown in figure 1.

---

2. Charles Darwin, *The Origin of Species: A Facsimile of the First Edition* (Cambridge, MA: Harvard University Press, 1964), p. 189.

3. M.J. Behe, *Darwin's Black Box: The Biochemical Challenge to Evolution* (New York, NY: The Free Press, 1996), p. 46.

4. J. Sarfati, "Stumbling Over the Impossible: Refutation of Climbing Mt. Improbable," *Journal of Creation* 12(1) (1998): p. 29–34.

5. S.C. Burgess, "Critical Characteristics and the Irreducible Knee Joint," vol. 13, no. 2 of the *Creation Ex Nihilo Technical Journal*, 1999.

6. S.C. Burgess, "Irreducible Design and Overdesign: Man's Upright Stature and Mobility," *Origins, Journal of the Biblical Creation Society*, vol. 57 (2013): p 10–13.

7. A.C. McIntosh, *Genesis for Today: Showing the Relevance of the Creation/Evolution Debate for Today's Society* (Leominster, United Kingdom: Day One Publications, 1997).

8. Burgess, "Irreducible Design and Overdesign," p. 10–13.

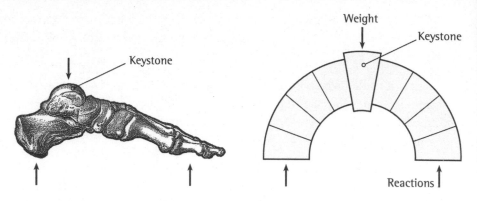

Figure 1. The irreducible human arched foot and equivalent man-made arch

The human foot has 26 precisely shaped bones, together with many ligaments, tendons, and muscles. Several of the bones are wedge-shaped so that a strong arch is formed. There are several parts in the foot that must be in place and correctly designed before the foot can function properly. In other words, the human foot cannot evolve step by step from a non-arched structure like a hand.

It is well known in engineering that an arched structure is an irreducible structure. An arch needs the right components, like a keystone and wedge-shaped blocks, to be in place to work, as shown in figure 1. Since the human foot has parts equivalent to a keystone and wedge-shaped blocks, the human foot must be an irreducible structure. Only an intelligent designer has the ability to think ahead and plan all the features needed to make an arch like the foot.

The arched structure of the human foot is a perfect design for giving humans upright mobility. In contrast to humans, apes have very flexible feet that are effectively a second pair of hands for gripping branches. In consequence, apes have very limited abilities for two-legged standing, walking, and running.

The Fossil Record Confirms Irreducible Complexity

The fossil record confirms the biblical truth that organisms have not gradually evolved step by step. One of the reasons we know that humans have not evolved from a type of ape-like creature is that there has never been a fossil of a foot that is a transitional form between the flat ape foot and the human arched foot. All fossils of so-called ape-men have either fully ape feet or fully human feet, showing that they are either fully ape or fully human, respectively.

The prominent evolutionist Stephen J. Gould has admitted that fossil evidence supports the creation worldview:

The absence of fossil evidence for intermediary stages between major transitions in organic design, indeed our inability, even in our imagination, to construct functional intermediates in many cases, has been a persistent and nagging problem for gradualistic accounts of evolution.[9]

The human foot, is a clear example of a structure where evolutionists cannot imagine what intermediate forms would look like. The reason for this is that there are no physically plausible intermediate structures due to the need for the foot to be assembled simultaneously.

Common Design

Common design is another important evidence for design that is a challenge for evolution. Common design is where the same design solution is used in different situations by a common designer. Human designers often carry out common design because it represents good design practice. For example, a designer will select nuts and bolts as a method for joining parts together in different products such as bicycles, cars, and spacecraft because this is the best design solution in each case. In the case of the common design of nuts and bolts, this is not an evidence of evolution but evidence of the careful work of a designer.[10]

The eye is a good example of common design by the common Designer in creation. The eye is seen in very different types of creatures like mammals, birds, fish, amphibians, and reptiles. In each case, there are specialized light-sensitive cells, nerve pathways for conveying the signals to the brain, and a part of the brain for processing the signals. In addition, there is usually some form of lens for directing the light onto the light-sensing cells. When you consider the great differences between different classes of creatures, it is remarkable how the eye for each creature is so similar in design. The similarity in design is just what would be expected from the common Designer, because He would know it is the best solution in each case. Interestingly, the Bible tells us in Proverbs 20:12 that the Lord "made the seeing eye."

The similarity of the eye in different classes of creature is not what would be expected from evolution, because evolution has no ability to coordinate designs in different applications. The evolutionist has to believe that the eye

---

9. Stephen Jay Gould, "Is a New and General Theory of Evolution Emerging?" *Paleobiology*, vol. 6(1) (January 1980): p. 127.
10. S.C. Burgess, *Hallmarks of Design*, 2nd Ed (Leomimster, UK: Day One Publications, 2008).

Figure 2. The eye is an example of common design by the common Designer.

evolved independently around 30 times.[11] It takes a lot of faith to believe that the same basic layout of eye evolved independently so many times. Some evolutionists argue that a common ancestor would help explain why structures like the eye appear in different creatures. However, the eye is found in such diverse creatures and has such similar design that common ancestry is not a credible explanation for the common design of the eye, even within the evolutionary worldview.

There is also a remarkable pattern in the design of the face across the whole animal kingdom with the easily recognizable features of two eyes, a nose, and a mouth. Such a common pattern is just what would be expected from the Creator who wanted to create an ordered and beautiful creation. A recognizable face also helps people to enjoy the company of animals like dogs, cats, and horses.

The principle of common design shows that it is wrong for secular biology books to use commonality of features in organisms as an evidence for evolution (sometimes referred to as homology). At the very least, biology books should mention that common design can be seen as evidence for the Creator *or* evidence for evolution. But the most accurate statement is that common design is more an evidence for creation than evolution.

Over-design

Over-design is another hallmark of design and a big challenge to evolution. Over-design involves design features that are above and beyond what is needed for survival. Human designers often carry out over-design, especially in luxury products like expensive cars where the aim is to greatly exceed the basic requirements.[12] Over-design should not be produced by evolution because, with evolution, every aspect of design must be capable of being explained in terms of what is needed to survive.

---

11. Sarfati, "Stumbling Over the Impossible: Refutation of Climbing Mt. Improbable," p. 29–34.
12. Ibid.

One area where we clearly see over-design in creation is in the design of the human being.[13] Humans are over-designed with skills and creativity that are far beyond what is needed to survive. The survival abilities of apes include the ability to find food and water, climb trees, build a den, defend territory, find a mate, and reproduce. The fact that humans have abilities that are vastly beyond these basic survival tasks provides great evidence that humans have not evolved from an ape-like creature but have been specially created to be beings of great skill and intelligence.

Over-design of Man

One aspect of over-design in humans is the ability to make facial expressions. Humans have around 25 unique facial muscles, as shown in figure 3. These muscles are dedicated to making expressions like smiling, grinning, and frowning, as shown in figure 4. Such expressions convey emotions such as happiness, pleasure, concern, anger, worry, and surprise. Researchers have found that humans have the amazing ability to make up to 10,000 different facial expressions![14] Facial expressions are very important in human communication even though we are often unaware that we are making expressions and responding to expressions. Smiling is one of the first things a baby does in its first few weeks of life, and one of the first things a baby can recognize.

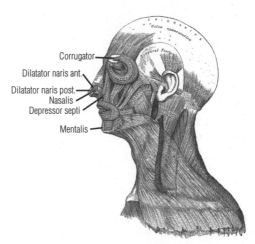

Figure 3. Muscles used for facial expressions

According to evolution, facial muscles and facial expressions came about because there was a survival advantage. But evolution cannot adequately explain what survival advantage comes from smiling or frowning. However, such

---

13. S.C. Burgess, The *Design and Origin of Man: Evidence for Special Creation and Over-design*, 2nd ed. (Leominster, UK: Day One Publications, 2013).

14. Paul Ekman and Wallace Friesen, Facial Action Coding System (Human Interaction Laboratory, Department of Psychiatry, University of California Medical Centre, San Francisco, Psychologist Consulting Press Inc., 577 College Avenue, Palo Alto, CA 94306, 1978.)

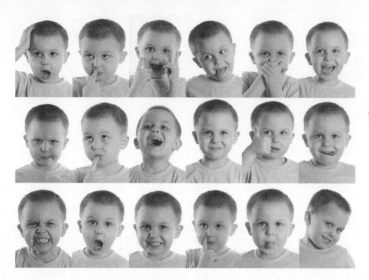

Figure 4.
Examples of facial
expressions in a
young boy.

expressions are just what would be expected since God has created humans to be emotional beings made in the image of God.

Skillful hands are another example of over-design in humans. According to evolution, human hands have evolved to perform survival tasks such as throwing spears, building dens, and making simple clothes. However, human hands are capable of so much more than these basic tasks. Humans have potential for immense skill in areas like playing music, carpentry, medicine, engineering, and craftwork. Evolution has no credible explanation for why humans are able to hold a pen and other instruments in a perfect tripod grip with thumb, index finger, and middle finger. In contrast, the dexterity of human hands is just what would be expected since man is made in the image of God as a creative being.

There are several other areas where over-design can be seen in human beings. For example, humans have the ability to think and communicate complex thoughts through intricate languages due to the specialized design of the throat, tongue, and brain. However, there is no credible reason why such ability was ever essential for survival. Also, humans have a uniquely fine skin that helps them enjoy the sense of touch. However, the ability to enjoy the sense of touch does not help survival. Perhaps the greatest example of over-design is in the human brain that is so much more powerful than is needed for a person to simply survive.

The over-design of man is just what would be expected since God had created humans to be creative beings, able to appreciate beauty, develop technology, create works of art, play sports, and be stewards of creation. As spiritual and creative beings, God had to equip humans with special skills and intelligence that are far beyond what is needed to *survive*. One of the reasons why humans are fearfully and wonderfully made (Psalm 139:14) is that they are over-designed.

Added Beauty

Added beauty is another powerful evidence for design. Human designers often add beauty solely for beauty's sake in architecture and engineering in order to create pleasing aesthetics. An example of added beauty is the embellishments in classical architecture. The intricate patterns on pillars and walls in classical architecture represent compelling evidence for design because there is no physical purpose for the intricate design. Of course, beauty is subjective and cannot be quantified. However, there are real and clearly recognizable features that produce beauty such as patterns, borders, embellishments, surface textures, colors, and variety. To produce intricate beauty requires not just creativity but also design information, and that design information has to come from somewhere.

Evolution cannot produce added beauty because, as with over-design, evolution can only produce what is needed for survival. Many evolutionists realize that beauty is a big problem for evolution. One leading evolutionist, Dr. John Maynard Smith, said:

> No topic in evolutionary biology has presented greater difficulties for theorists [than beauty]. [15]

Figure 5. The peacock tail feather

Some of the clearest examples of added beauty in creation are the brightly colored feathers of birds like peacocks, as shown in figure 5. There are several intricate design features in the peacock tail feather, such as the multi-layered segments that reflect light to produce bright and iridescent colors. These segments are so precisely designed and co-ordinated that amazing digital patterns are produced. There are also subtle features like multiple borders and a lack of stem in the eye pattern.

The peacock tail feather is a big problem for evolution because the only function of the feather is to create a beautiful display. The feather does not help the bird in any physical way. In fact, the feather makes flying harder and it

---

15. John Maynard Smith, "Theories of Sexual Selection," *Trends Ecol. Evol.*, 6 (1991): p. 146–151.

even makes the bird easier for predators to see. Evolutionists say that birds like peacocks need display feathers to attract a mate, but that does not explain the need for beauty. Most animals make very basic calls to attract a mate, showing that intricate beauty is not required. The fact that peacocks display their tails to attract mates is just what would be expected form the Creator who wanted the beauty of peacocks to be visible to humans.

Darwin was well aware that there was beauty for beauty's sake in creation. He said:

> A great number of male animals have been rendered beautiful for beauty's sake.[16]

Since the beauty of bird feathers contradicted Darwin's theory of evolution, he created another theory called the theory of sexual selection. However, that theory has been shown to be totally inadequate for giving a naturalistic explanation of the origin of beauty.[17]

There are many other areas of creation where we see added beauty such as birdsong, flowers, tropical fish, and the human being. Even though we live in a fallen world with death and decay, we still see glimpses of outstanding beauty that point to the Creator. We can also look forward to heaven, which is the perfection of beauty (Psalm 50).

The Effect of the Fall

Genesis 3 teaches that God cursed creation as a result of Adam's sin and rebellion. As a consequence, creation was changed very significantly, including the design of plants and animals. Thorns and hard-to-control plants appeared, and these made farming and gardening much more difficult. Evolutionists argue that thorns evolved as a way of protecting plants. However, the fact that many plants come with and without thorns, like blackberries, raspberries, and palm trees, shows that thorns are not necessary for survival.

Some creatures became carnivores, and this introduced violence and suffering into creation. Predators like cats and dogs were vegetarian before the Fall but became meat-eaters after the Fall. Predators may have had new design features for killing introduced at the time of the Fall, or they may have developed features through natural selection (or a combination of both). In

16. H. Cronin, *The Ant and the Peacock* (Cambridge, UK; New York: Cambridge University Press, 1991), p. 183.
17. S.C. Burgess, "The Beauty of the Peacock Tail and Problems with the Theory of Sexual Selection," *Journal of Creation* 15 (2) (August 2001): p. 94–102.

other cases, the designs may have been used for a different purpose such as vegetarianism.

There is no doubt that everything was beautiful in the Garden of Eden, because the Bible tells us that God made everything beautiful in its time (Ecclesiastes 3:11). The Curse that followed the Fall had the effect of tarnishing the beauty of creation. Some plants and creatures became marred with sin and reflected an "ugliness" where the predator-prey relationship meant many animals had to be camouflaged, thus reducing the number of brightly colored creatures in creation. Violence and suffering has also reduced the beauty of creation.

The negative effects of the Fall will not last forever. The Book of Isaiah teaches that in heaven, predators will be changed back to being harmless and pleasant creatures. Isaiah 11:16 says that predators like wolves, leopards, and lions will live peacefully with gentle animals like lambs and goats. In heaven, the full beauty of creation will be restored, because heaven is the perfection of beauty (Psalm 50:2).

What Is the Intelligent Design Movement?

The Intelligent Design (ID) movement argues the case for intelligent design without any reference to the identity of the Creator and without any reference to the Bible. The ID movement is helpful in some ways because it publicizes examples of design arguments like irreducible complexity and shows the weaknesses of evolution. However, there are limitations to the ID movement.[18]

One limitation is that it does not give an explanation for the origin of death and suffering in nature. This can be a problem because people always want to know why a Designer would design some creatures to kill. When people do not know the biblical origin of suffering, a result of man's sin, they may find it hard to believe there is a creator, or they may have an incorrect view of the Creator. Only with the right biblical understanding of the Fall can people understand that God is a loving Creator who cares deeply for His creation, including mankind.

A second limitation of the ID movement is that it does not promote a biblical worldview. Instead it attempts to be neutral, with no doctrinal agenda. However, it is impossible to be completely neutral, and everyone has a worldview that is ultimately biblical or non-biblical.

---

18. An important limitation is that it takes the glory due Jesus Christ as the Creator (Hebrews 1:1–4; Colossians 1:13–18) and gives that glory to some vague idea of an intelligent creator that could fit in with Islam, Hinduism, deism, and many forms of theism.

Conclusion

According to evolution, creation should contain designs that are inferior to the designs of humans because of the limitations of step-by-step evolution compared to intelligent design. However, the reality is clearly different; creation contains vastly superior designs to human designs showing that God must exist.

Creation reveals the Designer who is powerful (Romans 1:20), caring (Matthew 6:30), and perfect in knowledge (Job 37:16). I have personally worked with some of the best engineering designers in the world in America, Japan, and Europe, but it is clear that all of them are limited in their knowledge. This is why so many engineers today are keen to copy solutions from creation to make better airplanes, materials, and other products in order to utilize the brilliant designs that God has placed before us.

There has been a sad change of worldview in the majority of the scientific community. In past ages, most scientists acknowledged God and gave glory to God for His creation. That is no longer the case. However, there are still many scientists who are prepared to face criticism and even demotion by giving glory to the Creator. In addition, there are many believers today who have the joy of knowing, personally, the one true Creator God.

It is not possible to scientifically prove the truth about origins, as science is vastly limited in this area. Only God was there at the foundation of the world (Job 38:4), and so we rely on the testimony of His written Word to find out how the world was made. We also need faith to believe God's Word. This is why the Bible says, "By faith we understand that the worlds were framed by the Word of God" (Hebrews 11:3).

Keep in mind that it is important to realize that the faith of the Christian is not blind faith. God has left His fingerprints and hallmarks on His creation so that His existence and attributes are clear for all to see. However, faith is important, because without faith it is impossible to please God (Hebrews 11:5). The origins debate is ultimately about faith versus faith. The atheist has great faith in chance, and the Christian has faith in a great God who has given us eternal life through His Son, Jesus Christ.

CHAPTER 30

What about the Origin of the Solar System and the Planets?

DR. DANNY R. FAULKNER

Genesis 1 tells us that God created the earth "in the beginning." It is not until three days later on day 4 that God made the sun, moon, and stars. The Hebrew word for stars includes the planets,[1] their satellites, comets, and asteroids, so we can infer that the rest of the solar system was made after the earth was. This is very different from the evolutionary view of the origin of the solar system. Most scientists today think that the earth formed about the same time as the sun and everything else in the solar system — about 4.6 billion years ago. The solar system supposedly formed gradually from the collapse of a cloud of gas and dust. Obviously, this idea is at odds with the biblical creation narrative.

We can trace the origin of the modern theory of solar system formation to Emmanuel Swedenborg in 1734, but it was Emmanuel Kant who developed the idea in 1755. Pierre-Simon Laplace proposed a similar model in 1796. This nebular hypothesis was that the solar system began as a contracting and cooling proto-solar nebula. As the nebula contracted, it flattened into a disk, and most of the material fell to the center. The material in the center formed the sun, and the material in the disk eventually coalesced to form the planets. Any remaining material formed the satellites of the planets, asteroids, and comets. The nebular hypothesis enjoyed wide support throughout the 19th century, but eventually

---

1. Our English word *planet* comes from *asters planetai*, ancient Greek for "wandering stars." Ancient languages defined a star as any luminous object in the sky other than the sun and the moon.

astronomers realized there was an angular momentum problem. While the sun has more than 99 percent of the mass in the solar system, the planets possess more than 99 percent of the angular momentum. If the solar system formed via the nebular hypothesis, the distribution of angular momentum ought to be proportional to the distribution of mass. Because of this problem, astronomers abandoned the nebular hypothesis in the early 20th century.

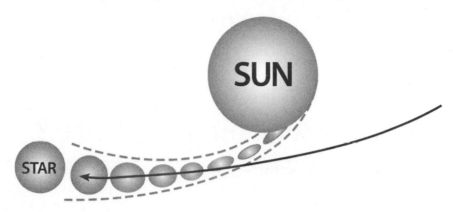

The first replacement theory was the tidal hypothesis of Thomas Chamberlin and Forest Ray Moulton in 1905. They suggested that shortly after the sun formed, another star passed very close to the sun, raising tidal bulges on the solar surface. The tidal bulges combined with solar prominences to eject material from the sun that produced two spiral-like arms. Much of the material in the spiral arms fell back onto the sun, but some coalesced into planets. As before, leftover matter formed the satellites, asteroids, and planets.

With both the nebular and tidal hypotheses, astronomers looked for confirmation elsewhere, and they thought that they found it in photographs of "spiral nebulae." The word *nebula* comes from the Latin word for cloud. A nebula is a cloudy, indistinct, luminous object in the night sky. A few were known to the ancients, but many more were discovered after the invention of the telescope. The telescope also revealed that many nebulae actually were star clusters in which the individual stars are too faint to be seen with the eye alone. Many other nebulae remained indistinct, from which astronomers concluded that they truly were clouds of gas in space. Today, we reserve the use of the word *nebula* to refer to one of these, and the true nebulae probably inspired Kant and Laplace in their ideas. Many of the "nebulae" appeared flattened with bulges in their centers, and many sported spiral arms. This appearance certainly inspired Kant and Laplace, but also Chamberlin and Moulton. In fact, a century ago first drawings and later photographs of the "spiral nebulae" often were used as proof of these naturalistic theories of the solar system's origin. I keep putting "spiral nebulae" in quotes because in 1924 Edwin Hubble showed that these were not nebulae at all, but instead were galaxies, vast collections of many billions of stars that are millions of light years away from us. Being so far away, the stars in other galaxies appear very faint to us. Astronomers up to that time had failed to recognize that the "spiral nebulae" were distant galaxies similar to our Milky Way galaxy, because their telescopes were not large enough to reveal any individual stars in them. However, in 1924, Hubble, using what was then the largest telescope in the world, was able to photograph a few of the brightest individual stars in a couple of these "nebulae." Since 1924, it has not been proper to refer to these objects as "spiral nebulae," though that term continued being used for decades afterward. It is important to note that for years astronomers used these objects as proof of the evolutionary view of the formation of the solar system, though astronomers eventually were forced to abandon this proof.

There were variations on the tidal interaction theme suggested by Chamberlin and Moulton. For instance, in 1918 Sir James Jeans and Sir Harold Jeffreys suggested that solar prominences were not involved and that a near miss by a passing star raised a single filament of material from the sun from which the planets and other bodies in the solar system formed. The tidal theory enjoyed broad support for much of the first half of the 20th century, but by 1940 problems had developed. One problem was that any column drawn out of the sun would dissipate rather than condense. Another problem was that material drawn out with sufficient speed to account for the angular momentum of the planets (especially Jupiter) would have left the solar system entirely, so the angular momentum problem remained. Consequently, during the middle of the 20th century there was no agreed-upon theory for the formation of the solar system.[2]

In the 1960s, astronomers began to revive a form of the old nebular hypothesis; though, I suppose in an attempt to dissociate it from the original, that name is not used to describe the modern version. As before, the solar system supposedly formed from the collapse of a gas cloud that flattened and concentrated in its center, with the sun forming from the central condensation and the planets forming from material in the disk. The modern theory borrows a term

---

2. Though it was far out of date, this theory was in science texts used in my elementary school in the mid 1960s. Those books were not very old, but this theory was probably included because there was no other alternative.

coined by Chamberlin, *planetesimal* (from the words "planet" and "infinitesimal"). A planetesimal is a small body amalgamated from microscopic particles. Planetesimals supposedly grew within the proto-planetary disk to form bodies large enough to begin gravitationally attracting other planetesimals to form the planets. As before, leftover planetesimals formed planetary satellites, asteroids, and comets. And, as before, the angular momentum problem remained. The most common explanation for that problem now is that magnetic effects removed angular momentum from the inner part of the nebula and transferred it to the outer portions of the nebula in the form of spiral arms or through jets extending fore and aft out of the disks.

The modern nebular hypothesis has other problems as well. What causes the microscopic bits of matter to coalesce into planetesimals? Gravity will work only when planetesimals have grown to kilometer size. Various mechanisms have been proposed to get the planetesimals up to that size. One mechanism is that static electricity attracted particles together. Another is that sticky, organic goo coated microscopic dust particles so that they stuck together when they happened to touch. Another idea is that gaseous molecules in space froze onto solid particles. Of course, none of this is actually observed, but astronomers generally assume that it must have happened somehow, or else how did those planets get here? Another problem is what caused the gas cloud to contract to begin with. This is the long-standing problem of star formation in general. One might answer that gravity drove the process. Gas clouds do have gravity, but they also possess gas pressure, and that pressure very effectively counteracts gravity. Early in the 20th century, Jeans showed that if a gas cloud is contracted down to a certain size, gravity can take over to complete the process. The problem is that all gas clouds that we see are far larger than Jean's length. Compression or cooling is needed to further contract the gas cloud so that gravity could complete the process. Some astronomers have suggested cooling from dust particles, but astronomers do not think that dust is primordial. Where did dust come from? This theory requires that several generations of stars must first create dust before stars could form by this mechanism. One might suppose that a gas cloud could get a sort of jump-start by an outside agent that compresses the cloud. For instance, a shock front from the explosion of a nearby supernova or associations of hot stars with strong UV radiation and stellar winds might do this, but this does not tell us where stars ultimately came from, because it requires that at least one star first exist. All theories of pre-stellar collapse of gas clouds suffer from this chicken-and-egg problem — stars must first exist to produce stars.

The modern theory of solar system formation has been refined with the addition of magnetic fields. If a gas cloud contained any magnetic field initially, the magnetic field would intensify as the cloud contracted. And as the cloud contracted it would have heated and ionized some of the gas. This produces plasma. In the swirling environment of the contracting cloud, models suggest that electromagnetic effects propel material outward in the two directions along the axis perpendicular to the plane of the disk. Astronomers call this bi-polar flow, a phenomenon found in some stars and in many galaxies and quasars. In more recent years, astronomers have created computer simulations supposedly to show how the solar system might have formed. One might question if the success of the simulation merely proves that the programmer was especially good at writing a program to produce the intended outcome.

In addition to improved models, since the early 1970s astronomers have made much progress in the development of technology, such as in the infrared (IR) part of the spectrum and the superb clarity of telescopes in space. These have resulted in observations of objects that astronomers generally think are stars and solar systems in the process of forming. For instance, in 1995 the Hubble Space Telescope took the stunning "Pillars of Creation" photograph of a dark dust and gas region in the Eagle Nebula that astronomers think is the site of active star formation. Orion is a region where astronomers think new stars are forming or recently formed. In this region, astronomers have used IR telescopes to detect star-like sources embedded in clouds of dust and gas, which are regions where they think stars likely form. Astronomers have observed bi-polar flows from stars or star-like objects in environments supposedly conducive for star formation, suggesting that these are stars that have nearly formed or very recently formed. Some stars have IR excess that suggest that they are surrounded by dust. The star β Pictoris was the first star discovered to have what appears to be a disk of dust surrounding it. This was interpreted as a proto-planetary disk that may yet condense into planets. More recently, astronomers have found disks of material around other stars that astronomers think are very young. All of these sorts of things have been put forth as proof of the prevailing theory of solar system formation.

But is this proof? The process of solar system formation is supposedly a very slow one, progressing far too slowly for us to witness any real change even in many human lifetimes. So these data all amount to sorts of snapshots of various stars and other astronomical bodies supposedly in various stages of the process of stellar and planetary formation but with no real evidence that these objects are actually undergoing the alleged processes. Rather, these snapshots are interpreted in terms of the ruling paradigm of solar system formation, and then they are offered up as proof of that paradigm. This amounts to circular reasoning, which is no proof at all. Remember that a century ago astronomers used the photographs of "spiral nebulae" as proof of the then-prevailing ideas of solar system formation. At the time, nearly everyone was convinced of the correctness of this view, but later observations proved otherwise. The supposedly iron-clad proof of solar system formation today could be interpreted very differently in just a few years. In fact, the history of science strongly suggests that the current paradigm of solar system formation eventually will be discarded.

Do stars form today? Biblically, we do not have a clear answer. Some recent creationists think that since Genesis 1 records that God made the stars on day 4, no more stars are being made. But Genesis 1 also tells us that God made horses on day 6, but new horses are born every day. While on one has never observed the formation of new stars, there is no reason why stars could not form today (e.g., it would not be inconsistent with a biblical worldview). The question is whether the star formation rate today is nearly great enough as required by the evolutionary paradigm.

In the 1990s, astronomers first discovered planets orbiting other stars. Since then the number of extra-solar planets has grown tremendously. This has shown that planets must be common in the universe, and hence planetary system formation must be common in the universe today. However, this conclusion stems entirely from an evolutionary worldview. That is, the assumption is made that planetary systems can arise only through natural means apart from a Creator. Therefore, if planetary systems are common, then all of them must have come about through evolutionary processes. Since planetary systems are common, planetary formation must be simple and straightforward, which proves that our solar system must have formed through such a process. Therefore, the solar system formed pretty much the way astronomers think that it did. Of course, this is circular reasoning, and no such inference of naturalism legitimately can be drawn. A creationist could just as easily state that since all things were made by God, then anything that exists was made by Him. Since so many other planetary systems exist, then God must have made them all, just as He made our solar system. Therefore, this proves creation. Of course, evolutionists would violently disagree with this conclusion, for it disagrees with their starting premise of naturalism. This illustrates that the data alone do not allow for a definite conclusion about the ultimate origin of planetary systems, including our own.

The purpose of looking for extra-solar planets is to show how common planets are and how typical our solar system is. But is our solar system common?

The evidence thus far suggests otherwise. In our solar system, the large gas giant planets are far from the sun and the small rocky planets are close to the sun. Planetary scientists have developed models of how this might have happened, and those theories indicate that the large gas giant planets ought to be far from the sun, as is the case in the solar system. But extra-solar planets tend to be very large and very close to their parent stars,[3] the opposite of the situation in the solar system, and contrary to the prevailing theories of planetary formation. Scientists have concocted multiple encounters of planets (again using computer simulations) to show how extra-solar planets might have formed far from their stars but then migrated inward. Evolutionists must devise these explanations because the observations defy their theories.

Evolutionary ideas of planetary formation are fraught with problems. Man's ideas about the origin of the solar system have changed, and they will continue to change. However, the Word of God does not change. While the Bible does not tell us much about how the solar system came into being, it does give us some information about when the earth and the rest of the solar system came into existence. The Christian has confidence that what God has revealed to us is true, so we ought to compare man's ideas to the revealed truth. The current thinking of solar system formation disagrees with the Genesis creation account, so we know that it is not correct.

3. With time, this situation might change. Observational bias is in favor of finding massive planets close to their host stars. With improvements in technology, we may eventually find smaller and more distant planets more easily.

CHAPTER 31

Did Noah Need Oxygen Tanks on the Ark?

BODIE HODGE

Why would someone ask this question? Let's back up and look at this from a big picture. Consider what the Bible says about the voyage of the ark:

> The water prevailed more and more upon the earth, so that all the high mountains everywhere under the heavens were covered. The water prevailed fifteen cubits higher, and the mountains were covered (Genesis 7:19–20).[1]

People look at the earth *today* and note that the highest mountain is Mt. Everest, which stands just over 29,000 feet above sea level. Then they put two and two together and say that Noah's ark floated at least 15 cubits above Mt. Everest — and at such high altitude, people need oxygen![2]

It sounds like a straightforward argument, doesn't it? But did you notice that I emphasized the word *today*? In light of this, the solution is quite simple: the Flood did not happen on today's earth, but rather on the earth of nearly 4,300 years ago (according to Ussher).

---

1. Scripture is taken from the *New American Standard Bible* for this chapter.
2. For cubit studies and lengths see (for laymen) Bodie Hodge, "How Long Was the Original Cubit? *Answers magazine*, March 19, 2007, http://www.answersingenesis.org/articles/am/v2/n2/original-cubit , and (semi-technical); T. Lovett, "A More Likely Cubit for Noah's Ark?" WorldwideFlood.com website, June 2005, http://www.worldwideflood.com/ark/noahs_cubit/cubit_paper.htm.

The world today is not the same as it was before the Flood, or even during the Flood. For instance, if the mountains, continents, and oceans basins of today's earth were more leveled out (as would be expected in a global Flood), the planet's surface water alone would cover the earth an estimated 1.66 miles deep — about 8,000 feet. Yet when I visited Cusco, Peru, which is around 11,000 feet above sea level, I didn't need an oxygen tank.

Furthermore, atmospheric air pressure is relative to sea level. So as rising sea levels pushed the air column higher, the air pressure at sea level would stay the same.

Psalm 104:6–9: Creation or the Flood?

Beginning on day 150 of the Flood, mountains began overtaking the water again, as the mountain-building phase had begun (Genesis 8:2–4). Poetic Psalm 104 gives further hints of this mountain building as the valley basins sank down:

> You covered it with the deep as with a garment; the waters were standing above the mountains. At Your rebuke they fled, at the sound of Your thunder they hurried away. The mountains rose; the valleys sank down to the place which You established for them. You set a boundary that they may not pass over, so that they will not return to cover the earth (Psalm 104:6–9).

This section of the Psalm is obviously speaking of the Flood, as water would no longer return to cover the earth — if this passage were speaking of creation week (as some commentators have stated), then God would have erred when the waters covered the whole earth during the Flood.

Consider this overview, as the entire Psalm continues down through history:

Psalm 104:1–5	Creation Week
Psalm 104:6–9	Flood
Psalm 104:10–35	Post-Flood

It makes sense that, because the Psalm is referring to the earth and what is in it, it begins with earth history (creation week). But mentions of donkeys (verse 11) and goats (verse 18) show variation within the created kind, which shows this would have taken place after the Flood. Also, a post-Flood geographic location is named (Lebanon, verse 16) as well as ships (verse 26) that indicate this Psalm was not entirely a look at creation week.

Lost in Translation?

While everyone agrees that Psalm 104:1–5 is referring to creation week, what of the argument — made by many commentators from the 1600s onward — that attributes Psalm 104:6–9 to creation week? One could suggest that much of this is due to the translation being viewed. Two basic variants of the translation of the Hebrew in Psalm 104:8 read:

1. "They went up over the mountains and went down into the valleys."
2. "Mountains rose and the valleys sank down."

In fact, a variety of translations yield some variant of one of these two possibilities.

Table 1. Translations of Psalm 104:8a[3]

Translation	Agrees with: "They went up over the mountains and went down into the valleys"	Agrees with: "Mountains rose and the valleys sank down"
New American Standard		X
New International Version	X	
King James Version	X	
New King James Version	X	
English Standard Version		X
Holman Christian Standard		X
English translation of the Septuagint	X	
Revised Version (UK)	X	
Amplified Bible		X
Good News Bible	X	
New English Bible	X	
Revised Berkley		X
J.N. Darby's		X

---

3. Data was taken from two sources: (1) Charles Taylor, "Did Mountains Really Rise According to Psalm 104:8?" *TJ* 12(3) (1998): p. 312–313; and (2) looked up individually on Online Bible, Larry Pierce, February 2009, or looked up separately.

Living Bible		X
New Living Translation		X
Jerusalem Bible	X	
R.G. Moulton	X	
Knox Version		X
The Holy Scriptures according to the Masoretic Text (a new translation by the Jewish Publication Society)		X
Revised Standard Version		X
Young's Literal Translation	X	
King James 21st Century Version	X	
Geneva Bible		X
New Revised Standard Version	X	
Webster's Bible	X	
New International Children's Version		X
Interlinear Bible		X

Obviously, there is no consensus on translation among these English versions. Looking at other languages, we see how the Hebrew was translated.

Table 2. Some Foreign Translations of Psalm 104:8[4]

Foreign translation	Agrees with: "They went up over the mountains and went down into the valleys"	Agrees with: "Mountains rose and the valleys sank down"
Luther's German		X
Menge's German		X
French Protestant Bible (Version Synondale)		X
Italian Edizione Paoline		X
Swedish Protestant		X

---

4. Ibid.

Spanish Reina Valera		X
Latin Vulgate (by Jerome)		X
La Bible Louis Segond 1910 (French)		X
Septuagint (Koine Greek)		X

Notice that there doesn't seem to be a discrepancy. Of course, there are many translations, so one cannot be dogmatic, but the point is that many foreign translations agree with "mountains rising and valleys sinking down."

Hebrew

In Hebrew, which reads right to left, the phrase in 104:8a is literally four words. Translated into English, the phrase in question is:

biq'ah	yarad	har	alah
valleys	down go/sink	mountains	up go/rise/Ascend

Take note that there are no prepositions like "over" or "into." It is literally "up go mountains, down go valleys." It makes sense why many translations, including non-English translations, use the phrase "mountains rose and the valleys sank down" — this is what it should be.

Why Would Commentators Miss This?

Commentaries could easily misinterpret this passage if they were based on translations that agree with "they went up over the mountains and went down into the valleys." For example, the most popular English translation for several hundred years, the King James Version, reads this way.

Furthermore, from a logical perspective, water doesn't flow uphill over mountains, but rather the opposite. Given language like this, commentators likely attributed this to a miraculous event during creation week, when many miracles were taking place anyway; also, creation week was referenced earlier in the chapter. Of course, the problems came when reading the rest of the context. One excellent commentator, John Gill, regarding verse 9 and the waters not returning to cover the earth, stated:

> That they turn not again to cover the earth; as they did when it was first made, #Ps 104:6 that is, not without the divine leave and power;

for they did turn again and cover the earth, at the time of the flood; but never shall more.[5]

Gill was forced to conclude that the waters *did* return to cover the earth, and he justified their return on "divine leave and power"! Yet this would mean that God breaks promises. Because we know that God does not break promises, this must be referring to the end of the Flood.

That said, we should understand the difficulty in commenting on the passage: it is a psalm of praise to God, and thus it is not as straightforward as literal history. It is difficult to determine where the shift from creation to the Flood occurs and where the shift from Flood to post-Flood occurs. However, there are a few more hints in the text.

A Few More Comments

We should use clear passages in Scripture to help interpret unclear passages. Consider that God's "rebuke" would not exist in a perfect world, where nothing would need rebuking or correcting. (Remember, a perfect God created a perfect world — Genesis 1:31, Deuteronomy 32:4.) One should expect nothing less of such a God.[6]

Therefore, during creation week when everything was good, there would be no need for any rebuking. If Psalm 104:6–9 were referring to creation week (specifically day 3), then why the rebuke in Psalm 104:7? This implies an imperfect, *not* very good creation. But if Psalm 104:6–9 is referring to the Flood, then of course a rebuke would exist in a fallen world where the judgment of water had overtaken the earth.

Additionally, note that Psalm 104:9 is clearly referencing Genesis 9:8–16 in saying that the waters would not return to cover the earth. (Some have asked how mountains and valleys could move up and down when the foundations are identified as immovable in Psalm 104:5. Keep in mind that mountains and valleys are not the foundation, but like the seas, they all sit above the foundation.)

Lastly, note that when the land appeared in Genesis 1 on day 3, the land that was being separated from the water was *dry*, not wet. The text in Genesis says that the waters were gathered into one place *and then* the dry land appeared. It says nothing of water flowing over the land to make it wet; otherwise, wet

---

5. J. Gill, Commentary notes, Psalm 104:9.
6. It was due to man's sin that the world is now imperfect and fallen.

land would have appeared and then *become* dry.[7] But during the Flood, the land was indeed overtaken by water that eventually stood above the land.

Conclusion

The Hebrew phrase in Psalm 104:8a is the basis for the correct translation of mountains rising and valleys sinking. This shows that mountains and valleys during the Flood were not the same height as they are today. Even today, mountains and valleys are changing their height; volcanic mountains, for instance, can grow very quickly, such as Surtsey or Paricutin (a volcanic mountain in Mexico that formed in 1943).

Therefore, with mountains and continents leveled out and ocean basins nowhere near the depth they are today, it makes perfect sense that Noah was not at the height of modern-day Mt. Everest. Instead, the ark would have been at sea level, where oxygen would have been nearly the same as today at sea level. Noah and those aboard the ark would not have required oxygen.

7. I understand some scientific models are built on this principle that the land and water separated and then the land *became* dry. But the text of Scripture, I suggest, leans in the direction of dry land appearing as a more supernatural occurrence, as opposed to naturalistic; especially considering the context of a supernatural creation week.

CHAPTER 32

The Image of God

DR. COREY ABNEY

You are special. Perhaps you've heard this from a parent, teacher, or member of your family. You received numerous compliments as the result of a special talent or accomplishment. Someone encouraged you because of your education and expertise. You were honored for a significant contribution. Or you grew up in a family where your grandmother reminded you of your "special" status every time you spent the night at her home (I can relate to this one)! Based on your background, personality, and life experience, you have a concept of what it means to be significant, and if you're like many people, you base how special you are on talent, education, or accomplishment. In other words, you look to yourself and to others. You play the comparison game. You try to measure up.

Unfortunately, many people aren't measuring up. The self-help industry is a multi-billion dollar industry with thousands of books published each year. Suicide is one of the leading causes of death among teenagers and young adults. Euthanasia is legal in the Netherlands, Belgium, and Luxembourg, with assisted suicide now legalized in Switzerland and in the U.S. states of Washington, Oregon, Vermont, and Montana. Humanism is weaving its way into the fabric of culture and institutions of higher learning. Many scholars believe and teach that human beings are no different than animals or plants. On this basis, human life is viewed in some circles as disposable, insignificant, or meaningless. Consider the teaching of Julian Huxley, a famous humanist, who writes,

> I use the word "humanist" to mean someone who believes that man is just as much a natural phenomenon as an animal or a plant;

that his body, mind, and soul were not supernaturally created, but are products of evolution, and that he is not under the control or guidance of any supernatural being or beings, but has to rely on himself and his own power.[1]

Joseph Krutch, an American author, critic, and naturalist, says, "There is no reason to suppose that man's own life has any more meaning than the life of the humblest insect that crawls from one annihilation to another."[2]

Even the former Chief Justice of the United States Supreme Court, Oliver Wendell Holmes, states, "I see no reason for attributing to man a significance different in kind from that which belongs to a baboon or a grain of sand."[3]

No wonder so many people struggle with identity and significance. If humans are no different than animals, plants, or grains of sand, one could argue that we aren't so special after all.

The Image of God Established

Thankfully, the Bible presents a very different picture of humanity. You are special, but not primarily as the result of your talents, accomplishments, education, or upbringing. Your significance is not tied to how you measure yourself, how you compare with others, or how others view you; rather, your significance is tied to how your *Creator* views you. And here's the good news: your Creator views you as special . . . significant . . . unique. Human beings are special in the eyes of God because we are unique in the order of creation. You see, when God created the heavens and the earth, He also created every creature after its own kind (Genesis 1:20–25). He created sea creatures, crawling creatures, birds, livestock, and wildlife, pronouncing that such animals were "good" (Genesis 1:25). But when God created mankind, He said,

> "Let Us make man in Our image, according to Our likeness; let them have dominion over the fish of the sea, over the birds of the air, and over the cattle, over all the earth and over every creeping thing that creeps on the earth." So God created man in His own image; in the image of God He created him; male and female He created them (Genesis 1:26–27).

---

1   Julian Huxley, *The Humanist Frame* (New York: Harper & Brothers, 1961).
2   Joseph Wood Krutch, *The Modern Temper* (New York: Harcourt Brace, 1929).
3   Richard Posner, *The Essential Holmes: Selections from the Letters, Speeches, Judicial Opinions, and other Writings of Oliver Wendell Holmes* (Chicago, IL: Chicago University Press, 1992).

God created human beings in His *image* and *likeness*. These words are used interchangeably in the Book of Genesis, but only when referring to mankind (Genesis 1:26, 5:1, 9:26). No animal or plant is made in God's image or likeness. For this reason, human beings should be viewed as the crowning jewel of God's creative activity. After God made man, He looked over His creation and declared everything "very good" (Genesis 1:31).

A Unique Dignity

According to Genesis 1:26–30, mankind has a unique dignity. Moreover, Genesis 5:1 states, "In the day that God created man, He made him in the likeness of God." Human beings have a special dignity because men and women are God's image-bearers. This does not mean we reflect the physical appearance of God, because God is spirit and not represented in a human form (John 4:24).

Rather, bearing God's likeness points to the *spiritual*, not the physical. To be created in the divine image includes having an interpersonal relationship with God. Anthony Hoekema says,

> In this way human beings reflect God, who exists not as a solitary being but as a being in fellowship — a fellowship that is described at a later stage of divine revelation as that between the Father, the Son, and the Holy Spirit.[4]

People can know God, love God, and worship God. We can also think, reason, and choose between right and wrong. We have the capacity to look at the world and deduce that everything has a Creator (Romans 1:19–20). The image of God is the defining mark of humanity that sets us apart from animals, plants, and grains of sand. You can teach an animal tricks, but only man can learn truth. You can make an animal work, but it is man who can worship. Animals can see the sun, but man can glorify God for the beauty of a sunset. Mankind has a unique dignity that is seen primarily in the spiritual ability to fellowship with God and others. Both animals and man were created material and immaterial,[5] but only man was created with a spiritual component as well.[6]

---

4 Anthony Hoekema, *Created in God's Image* (Grand Rapids, MI: Eerdmans, 1994).

5 Many animals were created with *nephesh* in Hebrew. This is often translated as living *creature* or living *soul*. Man is also described as *nephesh*, but unlike animals, our spiritual component is made in God's image.

6. Editorial note: There are three views of the nature of the human being but this paper is not the place to discuss this theological topic. For the astute reader, the three positions are (1) *dichotomous* [body and soul/spirit; where soul and spirit are merely interchangeable words of the same substance], (2) *trichotomous* [body, soul, and spirit; where each are

Human beings are special because we have a unique dignity that enables us to have a relationship with God.

A Unique Dominion

Not only does mankind have a special dignity; we also have a unique dominion. God created human beings to rule over the fish, birds, cattle, and everything that creeps on the earth (Genesis 1:26). Moreover, God commanded the first man and woman to exercise dominion over every living creature on the planet:

> Then God blessed them, and God said to them, "Be fruitful and multiply; fill the earth and subdue it; have dominion over the fish of the sea, over the birds of the air, and over every living thing that moves on the earth." And God said, "See, I have given you every herb that yields seed which is on the face of all the earth, and every tree whose fruit yields seed; to you it shall be for food. Also, to every beast of the earth, to every bird of the air, and to everything that creeps on the earth, in which there is life, I have given every green herb for food"; and it was so (Genesis 1:28–30).

Mankind is the lord of creation who represents the ultimate Lord in a formal sense. He is God's caretaker on the earth and is expected to maintain order and unity. God provides fruit and vegetation for both man and animals to eat, but man alone is charged with the responsibility to "subdue" and "have dominion over" the created order.[7] Human beings are commanded to rule the earth for God and to develop a culture that glorifies the Creator. Many years after our first parents were created and commanded to exercise this unique dominion, King David reflected upon mankind's role in the world. He wrote,

> When I consider Your heavens, the work of Your fingers, the moon and the stars, which You have ordained, what is man that You are mindful of him, and the son of man that You visit him? For You have made him a little lower than the angels, and You have crowned

---

truly separate and unique (1 Thessalonians 5:23)], or (3) *modified* [the spirit would be a modified *aspect* of the soul, like a flip side of the same coin. There is one coin, but two unique sides to it. In other words, our soul is specially fashioned with a spiritual aspect, like duality. So soul and spirit could almost be used interchangeably (being two parts to the same "coin"), which we find in Scripture (Luke 1:36–47). Yet soul and spirit could be seen as unique (two sides of the "coin"), which we also find in Scripture (1 Thessalonians 5:23; Hebrews 4:12)].

7. Plants are not seen as living creatures in the Bible, unlike animals and humans, so they could not die in a biblical sense.

him with glory and honor. You have made him to have dominion over the works of Your hands; You have put all things under his feet, all sheep and oxen — even the beasts of the field, the birds of the air, and the fish of the sea that pass through the paths of the seas (Psalm 8:3–8).

David is overwhelmed by God's grace and kindness toward humanity. As he surveys the mysteries of the heavens, the moon and the stars, and the existence of angels, he is amazed that God created man with glory and charged him with the responsibility of caring for the created order. David understood that human beings possess a unique dignity and dominion that set us apart from all other created beings.

The Image of God Tarnished

The image of God in mankind enables us to fellowship with our Creator and to exercise dominion over the earth. Sounds like a solid game plan, doesn't it? When you read the second chapter of Genesis, everything is certainly going according to plan. Initially, our first parents experienced unbroken communion with God and a peaceful relationship with each other (Genesis 2:21–25). Death was not a part of the world. The first man and woman did not experience distrust or disappointment. The question is, what happened?

Sin happened. The first man and woman (Adam and Eve) disobeyed God and rebelled against His will for their lives. God told them to eat from any tree on the earth with the exception of the tree of the knowledge of good and evil. Genesis 2:16–17 says, "And the LORD God commanded the man, saying, 'Of every tree of the garden you may freely eat; but of the tree of the knowledge of good and evil you shall not eat, for in the day that you eat of it you shall surely die.' "

Satan, a fallen angel who rejected God and His sovereign reign over the universe (Isaiah 14:12–14; Ezekiel 28:12–18; Luke 10:18), tempted the woman through the use of a serpent.[8] Adam and Eve yielded to the temptation and sinned by eating, and forever changed the course of human history:

> Then the serpent said to the woman, "You will not surely die. For God knows that in the day you eat of it your eyes will be opened, and you will be like God, knowing good and evil." So when the woman saw that the tree was good for food, that it was pleasant to the eyes, and a tree desirable to make one wise, she took of its fruit and ate. She also gave to her husband with her, and he ate (Genesis 3:4–6).

---

8. Bodie Hodge, *The Fall of Satan* (Green Forest, AR: Master Books, 2011), p. 43–45.

The rebellion of Adam and Eve plunged humanity into a sinful state where death, pain, and suffering entered the world. Moreover, the image of God in man was tarnished and broken from that point forward. Human beings now search for significance in themselves and their accomplishments instead of finding significance in the Creator whose image we bear. We remain rational, spiritual beings, but our rationality and spirituality no longer impart a true knowledge of God.

We are still relational people who possess the capacity to fellowship with God and others, but the outworking of our relationships no longer reflects the relationship between Father, Son, and Holy Spirit. In other words, mankind continues to reflect a unique dignity as God's image-bearers that no other creature enjoys, but the dignity is damaged significantly by the consequences of sin. Similarly, human beings continue to exercise dominion over the earth, but in many ways are selfish dictators who rule over nature for selfish gain, working against the will of God in the world.

The Image of God Restored

The image of God in man was tarnished, but not beyond repair. God the Father, in His infinite mercy and grace, reached out to Adam and Eve in the midst of their rejection and rebellion. Adam and Eve experienced consequences for their sin, but God also issued a promise of hope and restoration:

> So the Lord God said to the serpent: "Because you have done this, you are cursed more than all cattle, and more than every beast of the field; on your belly you shall go, and you shall eat dust all the days of your life. And I will put enmity between you and the woman, and between your seed and her Seed; He shall bruise your head, and you shall bruise His heel" (Genesis 3:14–15).

God promised to send a man who will conquer Satan and put an end to the reign of sin and death. According to this first of many prophetic statements in Genesis 3, God will send a deliverer who will save His people from their sins; He will send a healer who is able to restore the image of God in mankind.

Christ the Image of God

The New Testament makes it clear that Jesus Christ is the Son of God and the promised seed of the woman who dealt a fatal blow to death through His crucifixion and Resurrection. Satan bruised Jesus on the Cross, but Jesus crushed Satan's head when He rose from the dead (Genesis 3:15; Colossians

2:13–15). As a result, salvation from sin and death is found in Christ alone through faith alone (Ephesians 2:8–9). Moreover, the image of God is redefined in terms of Christ Himself as the true image. For example, Christ is called the *image* of God in three New Testament passages:

> But even if our gospel is veiled, it is veiled to those who are perishing, whose minds the god of this age has blinded, who do not believe, lest the light of the gospel of the glory of Christ, *who is the image of God*, should shine on them (2 Corinthians 4:3–4, emphasis added).

> He is *the image of the invisible God*, the firstborn over all creation. For by Him all things were created that are in heaven and that are on earth, visible and invisible, whether thrones or dominions or principalities or powers. All things were created through Him and for Him (Colossians 1:15–16, emphasis added).

> God, who at various times and in various ways spoke in time past to the fathers by the prophets, has in these last days spoken to us by His Son, whom He has appointed heir of all things, through whom also He made the worlds; who being the brightness of His glory and *the express image of His person*, and upholding all things by the word of His power, when He had by Himself purged our sins, sat down at the right hand of the Majesty on high (Hebrews 1:1–3, emphasis added).

Jesus is the true image of God. He is equally God and not a mere copy of the original. He *is* the original image. The Apostle Paul says, "For it pleased the Father that in Him all the fullness should dwell" (Colossians 1:19). Jesus shows us the glory of God (John 1:14), and when He comes again in His glorified humanity, He will be manifested directly as the true image of God. The Apostle John states, "Beloved, now we are children of God; and it has not yet been revealed what we shall be, but we know that when He is revealed, we shall be like Him, for we shall see Him as He is" (1 John 3:2).

The Image of Christ Restored in Us

The image of God in man needs restoration and renewal. In order for the image of God to be restored, however, we must look to Christ for salvation and sanctification. The Apostle Paul says, "Do not lie to one another, since you have put off the old man with his deeds, and have put on the new man who is renewed in knowledge according to the image of Him who created him" (Colossians 3:9-10). He also writes, "For whom He foreknew, He also predestined to be conformed to the image of His Son, that He might be the firstborn among many brethren" (Romans 8:29). We must pursue Christ and His image, knowing that we will be like Him in the new creation:

> And as we have borne the image of the man of dust, we shall also bear the image of the heavenly Man (1 Corinthians 15:49).

> But we all, with unveiled face, beholding as in a mirror the glory of the Lord, are being transformed into the same image from glory to glory, just as by the Spirit of the Lord (2 Corinthians 3:18).

Jesus Christ is our only hope for restoration. Without saving faith in the life, death, Resurrection, and return of Jesus, the image of God in us will remain tarnished by our sin and rebellion. We will continue to search for significance in ourselves, but we will never find it there, because our significance is ultimately tied to the image of God within us.

Conclusion

So, you really are special — not because of what you do, but because of who God created you to be. You are more than a plant, an animal, or a grain of sand. God created you in His image! Furthermore, despite your sin and rebellion that leads to the tarnishing of His image, God sent His Son to die for your sin, in your place, as a righteous substitute who satisfied the demands of the holy Judge. Three days later, God raised His Son from the dead, ensuring salvation and eternal life for all who believe in Him. Jesus Christ is the true image of God; therefore, when you submit your life to Jesus, God works through the power of His Holy Spirit to restore His broken image in you. And I can't think of anything more special than that.

CHAPTER 33

Dear Atheists . . . Are You Tired of It All?

BODIE HODGE

Are you tired of all the evil associated with the philosophy of atheism — Stalin, Hitler, Pol Pot, and so on?[1] After all, most murderers, tyrants, and rapists are not biblical Christians, and most have rejected the God of the Bible. Even if they claim to believe in the God of the Bible, they are not really living like a true Christ follower (who strives to follow God's Word), are they?

Do you feel conflicted about the fact that atheism has no basis in morality (i.e., no absolute right and wrong; no good, no bad)? If someone stabs you in the back, treats you like nothing, steals from you, or lies to you, it doesn't ultimately matter in an atheistic worldview, where everything and everyone are just chemical reactions doing what chemicals do. And further, knowing that you are essentially no different from a cockroach in an atheistic worldview (since people are just animals) must be disheartening.

Are you tired of the fact that atheism (which is based in materialism,[2] a popular worldview today) has no basis for logic and reasoning? Is it tough trying to get up every day thinking that truth, which is immaterial, really doesn't exist? Are you bothered by the fact that atheism cannot account for uniformity in nature[3]

---

1. B. Hodge, "The Results of Evolution," Answers in Genesis, July 13, 2009, http://www.answersingenesis.org/articles/2009/07/13/results-evolution-bloodiest-religion-ever.

2. J. Lisle, "Atheism: An Irrational Worldview," Answers in Genesis, October 10, 2007, http://www.answersingenesis.org/articles/aid/v2/n1/atheism-irrational.

3. J. Lisle, "Evolution: The Anti-science," Answers in Genesis, February 13, 2008, http://www.answersingenesis.org/articles/aid/v3/n1/evolution-anti-science.

(the basis by which we can do real science)? Why would everything explode from nothing and, by pure chance, form beautiful laws like E=MC^2 or F=MA?[4]

Do you feel like you need a weekend to recoup, even though a weekend is really meaningless in an atheistic worldview — since animals, like bees, don't take a day of rest or have a weekend? So why should atheists? Why borrow a workweek and weekend that comes from the pages of Scriptures, which are despised by atheists? Weeks and weekends come from God creating in six literal days and resting for a literal day; and then the Lord Jesus resurrected on the first day of the week (Sunday). And why look forward to time off for a holiday (i.e., holy day), when nothing is holy in an atheistic worldview?

For professing atheists, these questions can be overwhelming to make sense of within their worldview. And further, within an atheistic worldview, atheists must view themselves as God. Essentially, atheists are claiming to be God. Instead of saying there *may not* be a God, they say there is *no* God. To make such a statement, they must claim to be omniscient (which is an essential attribute of the God of the Bible) among other attributes of God as well.[5] So by saying there is no God, the atheist refutes his own position by addressing the question as though he or she were God!

Do you feel conflicted about proselytizing the faith of atheism, since if atheism were true then who cares about proselytizing? Let's face it, life seems tough enough as an atheist without having to deal with other major concerns like not having a basis to wear clothes, or no basis for marriage, no consistent reason to be clean (snails don't wake up in the morning and clean themselves or follow other cleanliness guidelines based on Levitical laws), and no objective reason to believe in love.

Are you weary of looking for evidence that contradicts the Bible's account of creation and finding none?[6] Do the assumptions and inconsistencies of dating methods weigh on your conscience when they are misrepresented as fact?[7] Where

---

4. K. Ham, Gen. Ed., *New Answers Book 1*, J. Lisle, J., "Don't Creationists Deny the Laws of Nature? (Green Forest, AR: Master Books, 2006), p. 39–46; http://www.answersingenesis.org/articles/nab/creationists-deny-laws-of-nature.
5. If one claims that God may exist or that there may be a spiritual realm, then that person is not an atheist, but an agnostic, at best. The agnostic says that one cannot know whether God exists, but how can they know that for certain apart from being omniscient themselves? Additionally, the Bible says in 1 John 5:13 that we can *know* for certain that we have eternal life. So an agnostic — who claims we cannot know — does not hold a neutral position regarding the biblical God.
6. K. Ham, "Missing? or Misinterpreted?" Answers in Genesis, March 1, 2004, http://www.answersingenesis.org/articles/cm/v26/n2/missing.
7. K. Ham, *New Answers Book 1*, M. Riddle, "Does Radiometric Dating Prove the Earth Is

do you suppose those missing links have gone into hiding? Surely the atheist sees the folly and hopelessness of believing that everything came from nothing.

In fact, why would an atheist care to live one moment longer in a broken universe where one is merely rearranged pond scum and all you have to look forward to is . . . death, which can be around any corner? And in 467 trillion years, no one will care one iota about what you did or who you were or how and when you died — because death is the ultimate "hero" in an atheistic, evolutionary worldview. Of course, as a Christian I disagree, and I have a basis to see you as having value.

Invitation

I invite you to reconsider that the false religion of atheism is simply that. I'm here to tell you that atheism is a lie (Romans 1:25).[8] As a Christian, I understand that truth exists because God exists, who is the Truth (John 14:6),[9] and we are made in His image.[10] Unlike an atheist, whose worldview doesn't allow him to believe in truth or lies, the Bible-believer has a foundation that enables him to speak about truth and lies. This is because believers in God and His Word have an authority, the ultimate authority on the subject, to base statements upon.

There is a God, and you are also made in His image (Genesis 1:26; 9:6).[11] This means you have value. Whereas consistent atheists teach that you have no value, I see you differently. I see you as a relative (Acts 17:26)[12] and one who — unlike animals, plants, and fallen angels — has the possibility of salvation from death, which is the result of sin (i.e., disobedience to God; see Romans 6:23).[13]

Old? (Green Forest, AR: Master Books, 2006), p. 113–134; http://www.answersingenesis.org/articles/nab/does-radiometric-dating-prove.

8. "Who exchanged the truth of God for the lie, and worshiped and served the creature rather than the Creator, who is blessed forever. Amen" (Romans 1:25)
9. "Jesus said to him, 'I am the way, the truth, and the life. No one comes to the Father except through Me' " (John 14:6).
10. Keep in mind that Christians, including me, do fall short due to sin and the Curse, but God never fails.
11. "Then God said, 'Let Us make man in Our image, according to Our likeness; let them have dominion over the fish of the sea, over the birds of the air, and over the cattle, over all the earth and over every creeping thing that creeps on the earth' " (Genesis 1:26); "Whoever sheds man's blood, by man his blood shall be shed; for in the image of God He made man" (Genesis 9:6).
12. "And He has made from one blood every nation of men to dwell on all the face of the earth, and has determined their preappointed times and the boundaries of their dwellings" (Acts 17:26).
13. "For the wages of sin is death, but the gift of God is eternal life in Christ Jesus our Lord" (Romans 6:23).

We have all fallen short of God's holy standard of perfect obedience thanks to our mutual grandfather, Adam (Romans 5:12).[14] And God sees you differently, too (John 3:16).[15] While you were *still* a sinner, God stepped into history to become a man to die in your place (Romans 5:8)[16] and offer the free gift of salvation (Ephesians 2:8–9).[17]

Atheists have no consistent reason to proselytize their faith, but Christians like me do have a reason — Jesus Christ, who is the Truth, commands us to (Matthew 28:19).[18] We want to see people repent of their evil deeds and be saved from death (Acts 8:22, 17:30).[19] What a wonderful joy (Luke 15:10).[20]

Where atheists have no basis for logic and reason (or even for truth, since truth is immaterial), Bible believers can understand that mankind is made in the image of a logical and reasoning God who is the truth. Hence, Christians can make sense of things because in Christ are "hidden all the treasures of wisdom and knowledge" (Colossians 2:3).[21] Christians also have a basis to explain why people sometimes don't think logically due to the Fall of mankind in Genesis 3. The most logical response is to give up atheism and receive Jesus Christ as Lord and Savior to rescue you from sin and death (Romans 10:13).[22] Instead of death, God promises believers eternal life (1 John 2:25; John 10:28)[23] and in 467 trillion years, you will still have value in contrast to the secular view of nothingness.

Christians do have a basis to wear clothes (to cover shame due to sin; see Genesis 2:25, 3:7),[24] a reason to uphold marriage (God made a man and a

---

14. "Therefore, just as through one man sin entered the world, and death through sin, and thus death spread to all men, because all sinned" (Romans 5:12).
15. "For God so loved the world that He gave His only begotten Son, that whoever believes in Him should not perish but have everlasting life" (John 3:16).
16. "But God demonstrates His own love toward us, in that while we were still sinners, Christ died for us" (Romans 5:8).
17. "For by grace you have been saved through faith, and that not of yourselves; it is the gift of God, not of works, lest anyone should boast" (Ephesians 2:8–9).
18. "Go therefore and make disciples of all the nations, baptizing them in the name of the Father and of the Son and of the Holy Spirit" (Matthew 28:19).
19. "Repent therefore of this your wickedness, and pray God if perhaps the thought of your heart may be forgiven you" (Acts 8:22); "Truly, these times of ignorance God overlooked, but now commands all men everywhere to repent" (Acts 17:30).
20. "Likewise, I say to you, there is joy in the presence of the angels of God over one sinner who repents" (Luke 15:10).
21. "In whom are hidden all the treasures of wisdom and knowledge" (Colossians 2:3).
22. "For 'whoever calls on the name of the Lord shall be saved' " (Romans 10:13).
23. "And this is the promise that He has promised us — eternal life" (1 John 2:25); "And I give them eternal life, and they shall never perish; neither shall anyone snatch them out of My hand" (John 10:28).
24. "And they were both naked, the man and his wife, and were not ashamed" (Genesis 2:25);

woman; see Genesis 1:27; Matthew 19:4–6),[25] a reason to be clean (Leviticus contains many provisions to counter diseases in a sin-cursed world), and a source of real love (since God made us in His loving image; see 1 John 4:8).[26] As Christians, we have a solid foundation for saying things like back-stabbing, theft, and lies are wrong (see the Ten Commandments in Exodus 20).

I invite you to leave the false religion of atheism and its various forms and return to the one true God who came to rescue you (John 17:3).[27] Jesus Christ, who is God the Son, loved you enough to come down and die in our place so we can experience God's goodness for all eternity instead of the wrath of God for all eternity in hell (Matthew 25:46).[28] And we all have sentenced ourselves to judgment because of our disobedience to God and rejection of Him (John 3:17–18).[29]

The day is coming when we all will give an account before God for our actions and thoughts (Romans 14:12).[30] Will you repent and receive Christ as your Lord and Savior today so that you will join Christ in the resurrection from the dead (John 11:25; Romans 6:5)?[31] I invite you personally to become an ex-atheist, join the ranks of the saved through Jesus Christ, and become a new creation (2 Corinthians 5:17)[32] as we continue to advance with the gospel in peace that only God can provide (Romans 5:1).[33]

"Then the eyes of both of them were opened, and they knew that they were naked; and they sewed fig leaves together and made themselves coverings" (Genesis 3:7).

25. "So God created man in His own image; in the image of God He created him; male and female He created them" (Genesis 1:27); "And He answered and said to them, 'Have you not read that He who made them at the beginning "made them male and female," and said, "for this reason a man shall leave his father and mother and be joined to his wife, and the two shall become one flesh"? So then, they are no longer two but one flesh. Therefore what God has joined together, let not man separate' " (Matthew 19:4–6).

26. "He who does not love does not know God, for God is love" (1 John 4:8).

27. "And this is eternal life, that they may know You, the only true God, and Jesus Christ whom You have sent" (John 17:3).

28. "And these will go away into everlasting punishment, but the righteous into eternal life" (Matthew 25:46).

29. "For God did not send His Son into the world to condemn the world, but that the world through Him might be saved. He who believes in Him is not condemned; but he who does not believe is condemned already, because he has not believed in the name of the only begotten Son of God" (John 3:17–18).

30. "So then each of us shall give account of himself to God" (Romans 14:12).

31. "Jesus said to her, 'I am the resurrection and the life. He who believes in Me, though he may die, he shall live' " (John 11:25); "For if we have been united together in the likeness of His death, certainly we also shall be in the likeness of His resurrection" (Romans 6:5).

32. "Therefore, if anyone is in Christ, he is a new creation; old things have passed away; behold, all things have become new" (2 Corinthians 5:17).

33. "Therefore, having been justified by faith, we have peace with God through our Lord Jesus Christ" (Romans 5:1).

Contributors

Ken Ham is the president and CEO of Answers in Genesis (USA). He has authored several books, including the best-seller *The Lie: Evolution*. He is one of the most in-demand speakers in the U.S. and has a daily radio program called *Answers...with Ken Ham*, which is heard on over 850 stations in the US and over 1,000 worldwide. Ken has a BS in applied science (with an emphasis in environmental biology) from Queensland Institute of Technology in Australia. He also holds a diploma of education from the University of Queensland (a graduate qualification for science teachers in the public schools in Australia). Ken has been awarded two honorary doctorates: a Doctor of Divinity (1997) from Temple Baptist College in Cincinnati, Ohio, and a Doctor of Literature (2004) from Liberty University in Lynchburg, Virginia.

Dr. Corey Abney earned a BA from Cedarville University, and a MDiv and PhD from Southern Baptist Theological Seminary in Louisville, KY. Dr. Abney has served the Kentucky Baptist Convention as both a member of the executive board and as a past president of the Pastors' Conference. He is also involved in the Southern Baptist Convention as a trustee of Golden Gate Baptist Theological Seminary located in Mill Valley, CA. Currently, he is the senior pastor at Florence Baptist Church in Florence, KY.

Dr. E. Calvin Beisner, PhD, is founder and national spokesman of the Cornwall Alliance for the Stewardship of Creation, author of several books on biblical economics and environmental ethics, and a former Christian college and seminary professor. He has testified as an expert witness on climate policy before committees of the U.S. Senate and House of Representatives and lectured on the subject at the Vatican, for International Conferences on Climate Change, and for colleges, seminaries, and churches.

Dr. Joel R. Beeke is president and professor of systematic theology and homiletics at Puritan Reformed Theological Seminary, a pastor of the Heritage Netherlands Reformed Congregation in Grand Rapids, Michigan, editor of *Banner of Sovereign Grace Truth*, editorial director of Reformation Heritage Books, president of Inheritance Publishers, and vice-president of the Dutch Reformed Translation Society. He has written, co-authored, or edited 70 books.

Dr. Stuart Burgess is professor of design and nature in the department of mechanical engineering at Bristol University-UK. He is author of three books:

Hallmarks of Design, He Made the Stars Also, and *The Origin of Man*, all published by Day One Publications (www.dayone.co.uk).

Dr. Andrew Fabich earned a BS from Ohio State University and PhD from the University of Oklahoma. He began his teaching career at Tennessee Temple University. Dr. Fabich is currently an assistant professor of microbiology at Liberty University. Dr. Fabich did his dissertation on understanding how good and bad *E. coli* colonize the mammalian intestine to cause disease. He continues working on gastrointestinal research using molecular techniques in animal models. His professional memberships include American Society of Microbiology and Virginia Academy of Sciences.

Dr. Danny R. Faulkner has a BS (math), MS (physics), MA and Ph.D. (astronomy, Indiana University). He is full professor at the University of South Carolina–Lancaster, where he teaches physics and astronomy. He has published about two dozen papers in various astronomy and astrophysics journals.

Bodie Hodge earned a BS and MS in mechanical engineering at Southern Illinois University at Carbondale in 1996 and 1998, respectively. His specialty was in materials science working with advanced ceramic powder processing. He developed a new method of production of submicron titanium diboride. Bodie accepted a teaching position as visiting instructor at Southern Illinois in 1998 and taught for two years. After this, he took a job working as a test engineer at Caterpillar's Peoria Proving Ground. Bodie currently works at Answers in Genesis (USA) as a speaker, writer, and researcher after working for three years in the Answers Correspondence Department.

Troy Lacey earned his bachelor of natural sciences (biology/geology) degree from the University of Cincinnati. Troy is the correspondence representative and chaplain services coordinator for Answers in Genesis–USA.

Don Landis is pastor of Community Bible Church in Jackson, Wyoming. He is founder and president of Jackson Hole Bible College (www.jhbc.edu), a one-year program with special emphasis on creation for young adults. Don is also the founding chairman of the board for Answers in Genesis-USA.

Tim Lovett earned his degree in mechanical engineering from Sydney University (Australia) and was an instructor for 12 years in technical college engineering courses. Tim has studied the Flood and the ark for 15 years and is widely recognized for his cutting-edge research on the design and structure of Noah's ark. He is author of the book *Noah's Ark: Thinking Outside the Box*.

Dr. David Menton was an associate professor of anatomy at Washington University School of Medicine from 1966 to 2000 and has since become Associate Professor Emeritus. He was a consulting editor in histology for *Stedman's Medical Dictionary*, a standard medical reference work. David earned his PhD from Brown University in cell biology. He is a popular speaker and lecturer with Answers in Genesis (USA), showing complex design in anatomy with popular DVDs such as *The Hearing Ear and Seeing Eye* and *Fearfully and Wonderfully Made*. He also has an interest in the famous Scopes Trial, which was a big turning point in the creation/evolution controversy in the USA in 1925.

Dr. Elizabeth Mitchell earned her MD from Vanderbilt University School of Medicine and practiced medicine for seven years until she retired to be a stay-at-home mom. Her interest in ancient history strengthened when she began to homeschool her daughters. She desires to make history come alive and to correlate it with biblical history.

Dr. Tommy Mitchell graduated with a BA with highest honors from the University of Tennessee–Knoxville in 1980 with a major in cell biology and a minor in biochemistry. He subsequently attended Vanderbilt University School of Medicine in Nashville, where he was granted an MD degree in 1984. Dr. Mitchell's residency was completed at Vanderbilt University Affiliated Hospitals in 1987. He was board certified in internal medicine, with a medical practice in Gallatin, Tennessee (the city of his birth). In 1991, he was elected to the Fellowship in the American College of Physicians (F.A.C.P.). Tommy became a full-time speaker, researcher, and writer with Answers in Genesis (USA) in 2006.

Dr. Gary Parker is a biologist who was with Answers in Genesis as a senior lecturer since AiG's first year (1994, and remained full-time until 1999). Dr. Parker was also the head of the science department at Clearwater Christian College (CCC) in Florida. For 12 years, he served on the science faculty of the Institute for Creation Research (ICR) in the San Diego area. En route to his BA in biology/chemistry, MS in biology/physiology, and EdD in biology/geology from Ball State, Dr. Parker earned several academic awards, including admission to Phi Beta Kappa (the national scholastic honorary), election to the American Society of Zoologists (for his research on tadpoles), and a 15-month fellowship award from the National Science Foundation. He has published five programmed textbooks in biology and six books in creation science (the latter translated into a total of eight languages), has appeared in numerous films and television programs, and has lectured worldwide on creation.

Roger Patterson earned his BS Ed degree in biology from Montana State University. Before coming to work at Answers in Genesis, he taught for eight years in Wyoming's public school system and assisted the Wyoming Department of Education in developing assessments and standards for children in public schools. Roger now serves on the Educational Resources team at Answers in Genesis–USA.

Dr. Georgia Purdom received her PhD in molecular genetics from Ohio State University in 2000. As an associate professor of biology, she completed five years of teaching and research at Mt. Vernon Nazarene University in Ohio before joining the staff at Answers in Genesis (USA). Dr. Purdom has published papers in the *Journal of Neuroscience,* the *Journal of Bone and Mineral Research*, and the *Journal of Leukocyte Biology*. She is also a member of the Creation Research Society, American Society for Microbiology, and American Society for Cell Biology. She is a peer-reviewer for *Creation Research Society Quarterly*. Georgia has a keen interest and keeps a close eye on the Intelligent Design movement.

Dr. Benjamin Shaw has earned a MDiv from Pittsburgh Theological Seminary and a ThM from Princeton Theological Seminary. He went on to earn a Ph.D. from Bob Jones University. Currently, Dr. Shaw is an associate professor in Hebrew and Old Testament and academic dean at Greenville Presbyterian Theological Seminary. He is a regular author and blogger.

Dr. Andrew A. Snelling is currently Director of Research with Answers in Genesis (US). He received a BS in applied geology with first-class honors at the University of New South Wales in Sydney, and earned his PhD in geology at the University of Sydney for his thesis entitled "A Geochemical Study of the Koongarra Uranium Deposit, Northern Territory, Australia." Between studies and since, Andrew worked for six years in the exploration and mining industries in Tasmania, New South Wales, Victoria, Western Australia, and the Northern Territory as a field, mine, and research geologist. Andrew was also a principal investigator in the RATE (Radioisotopes and the Age of The Earth) project hosted by the Institute for Creation Research and the Creation Research Society.

Dr. Michael Todhunter, who earned his doctorate in forest genetics from Purdue University, has spent 14 years in forest genetic research, industrial tree-breeding research, and project management. Dr. Todhunter has also published numerous works in his field of expertise.

John UpChurch serves as the editor for Jesus.org and is a contributor to the Answers in Genesis website. He graduated summa cum laude from the University of Tennessee with a BA in English.

Dr. Alan White earned his BS in chemistry from the University of Tennessee and his PhD in organic chemistry from Harvard University in 1981. He worked for 30 years at Eastman Chemical Company and reached the rank of Research Fellow. Alan spent his career at Eastman working in research and development in the fields of organic and polymer chemistry. Among his achievements are the discovery of a commercial biodegradable polymer and the improvement of many commercial polymer processes, including the new Integrex™ technology for producing PET, the soft drink bottle polymer. Alan has been granted 41 U.S. patents and is an author on 18 scientific publications. He has recently retired to spend more time in research, writing, and speaking in the area of creation science.

Dr. John Whitmore received a BS in geology from Kent State University, an MS in geology from the Institute for Creation Research, and a PhD in biology with paleontology emphasis from Loma Linda University. Currently an associate professor of geology, he is active in teaching and research at Cedarville University. Dr. Whitmore serves on the board of Creation Research Science Education Foundation located in Columbus, Ohio, and he is also a member of the Creation Research Society and the Geological Society of America.

Index

A Library of Answers for Families and Churches

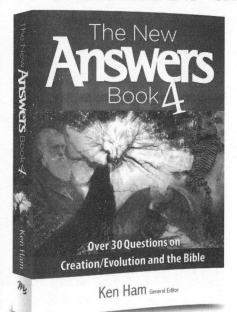

$14.99
978-0-89051-788-8

Over **120 Faith-Affirming Answers** to some of the Most Questioned Topics About Faith, Science & The Bible.

To help you find the answers, **Ken Ham** and the team of apologetic experts at Answers in Genesis authored *New Answers Book 1, 2, 3 and 4*.

Prepare yourself, your family, and your church to answer the questions of friends, and skeptics, and defend against the prevalent secular humanist culture that is invading our schools, government, and even the Christian community.

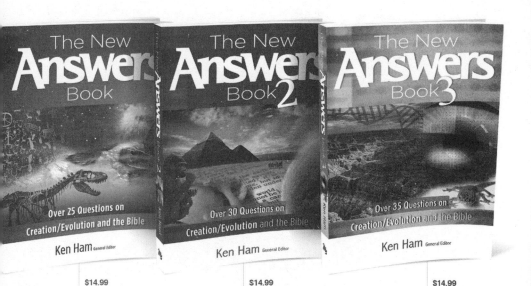

$14.99
978-0-89051-674-3

$14.99
978-0-89051-537-2

$14.99
978-0-89051-579-2

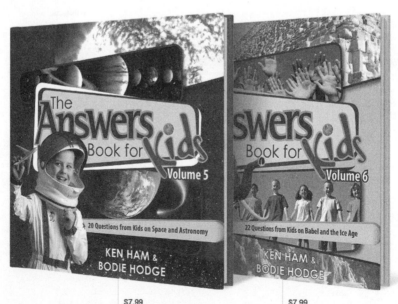